AGAINST THE AMERICAN GRAIN

AGAINST THE AMERICAN GRAIN

Dwight Macdonald

NEW INTRODUCTION BY
JOHN SIMON

A DA CAPO PAPERBACK

Letters from James Agee to Dwight Macdonald are used with permission of The James Agee Trust © copyright, 1962, by The James Agee Trust

Of the material in this book, the following articles originally appeared in:
  The New Yorker—"Mark Twain" (April 9, 1960), "James Joyce" (December 12, 1959), "James Agee" (November 16, 1957) "Inside *The Outsider*" (October 13, 1956), "The Book-of-the-Millennium Club" (November 29, 1952), "Updating the Bible" (November 14, 1953), "Howtoism" (May 22, 1954), "The String Untuned" (March 10, 1962);
  Partisan Review—"Masscult and Midcult" (Spring, 1960);
  Anchor Review—"The Triumph of the Fact (1957);
  Commentary—"By Cozzens Possessed" (January, 1958);
  Encounter—"Ernest Hemingway" (January, 1962), "Amateur Journalism" (November, 1956), "Looking Backward" (June, 1961);
  The Observer—"The Camford Bible" (March 26, 1961);
  Life International—"The Decline and Fall of English (April 9, 1962).

Library of Congress Cataloging in Publication Data

Macdonald, Dwight.
   Against the American grain.

   (A Da Capo paperback)
   1. United States—Popular culture—Addresses, essays, lectures. I. Title.
E169.1.M195 1983   306.4'0973   83-7665
ISBN 0-306-80205-9 (pbk.)

This Da Capo Press paperback edition of *Against the American Grain* is an unabridged republication of the first edition published in New York in 1962, here supplemented with a new introduction by John Simon. It is reprinted by arrangement with the author's estate.

Published by Da Capo Press, Inc.
A Subsidiary of Plenum Publishing Corporation
233 Spring Street, New York, N.Y. 10013

Grateful acknowledgment is due to the following for permission to quote material which appears in this book:

BRANDT AND BRANDT, for quotations from *John Brown's Body* by Stephen Vincent Benét. Published by Holt, Rinehart & Winston. Copyright 1927, 1928 by Stephen Vincent Benét. Copyright renewed, 1955, 1956, by Rosemary Carr Benét.

GROSSET & DUNLOP, INC. for quotation reprinted from James Agee's *A Death in the Family*, copyright © 1957 by the James Agee Trust.

HARCOURT BRACE JOVANOVICH, INC, for excerpts from *By Love Possessed* © 1957 by James Gould Cozzens, reprinted by permission of Harcourt Brace Jovanovich, Inc.

HARPER & ROW, for quotations from *Our Town* by Thornton Wilder, copyright 1938, 1957 by Thornton Wilder; for quotations from "Preface" to *Three Plays* by Thornton Wilder, copyright © 1957 by Thornton Wilder; for quotations from *Mark Twain's Autobiography* edited by Albert Bigelow Paine, 1924; for quotations from *The Autobiography of Mark Twain* edited by Charles Neider, 1959.

HOUGHTON MIFFLIN COMPANY, PETER OWEN LTD., and VICTOR GOLLANCZ LTD. for quotations from *Let Us Now Praise Famous Men* by James Agee and Walker Evans, copyright 1939 and 1940 by James Agee, copyright 1941 by James Agee and Walker Evans, copyright © renewed 1969 by Mia Fritsch Agee, reprinted by permission of Houghton Mifflin Company; for quotations from *The Outsider* by Colin Wilson, copyright © 1956, 1967 by Colin Wilson, reprinted by permission of Houghton Mifflin Company.

ALFRED KAZIN, for quotation from "The President and Other Intellectuals" in *Contemporaries*, copyright © 1961 by Alfred Kazin.

THE NEW YORK TIMES, for quotations from *New York Times* editorials.

OXFORD UNIVERSITY PRESS, for quotation from *The Present Age* by Soren Kierkegaard.

PARTISAN REVIEW, for quotation from "Art, Popular Art, and the Illusion of the Folk" by André Malraux.

GEORGE PLIMPTON, for the Appendix in this volume entitled "Dissenting Opinion."

CHARLES SCRIBNER'S SONS, for quotations from *In Another Country* by Ernest Hemingway. Copyright 1927 Charles Scribner's Sons; renewal copyright © 1955; for quotations from *The Undefeated* by Ernest Hemingway. Copyright 1927 Charles Scribner's Sons; renewal copyright © 1955 Ernest Hemingway; and for quotations from *A Farewell to Arms* by Ernest Hemingway. Copyright 1929 Charles Scribner's Sons; renewal copyright © 1957 Ernest Hemingway.

TIME, INC., for quotation from "Scotch Mist," *Time*, November 6, 1939; and for quotation from "Cash in on Culture," *Time*, April 20, 1962.

UNIVERSITY OF TEXAS PRESS, for quotation from "Mark Twain's Images of Hannibal" by Henry Nash Smith from *Studies in English, 1958*.

An edited version of John Simon's introduction appeared in the Spring 1983 issue of *Partisan Review*.

for my dear father

Dwight Macdonald

(1876-1926)

Introduction*

THAT Dwight Macdonald should die in the third week of December strikes me as a plot to overthrow Christmas. For anyone whose secular faith is in the trinity of truth, beauty, and decency, in culture as in life, Dwight was an authentic, tangible Santa Claus. Such mundane reasons as his white hair and goatee and his chortling merriment may have contributed something to this impression, but much more relevant was that, in writing as in conversation, he always came bearing gifts for the discerning and deserving: the gift of intelligence, the gift of wit, the gift of taste. He was, like Bernard Shaw in England or André Gide in France, a man whose opinion on any issue we waited for—whether that issue was political, social, cultural, artistic, or moral. His may not always have been the voice of ultimate, incontrovertible reason—whose voice is?—but it was consistently that of genuine, idiosyncratic, penetrant insight, salted with humor and peppered with pugnacity. Whether or not it provided ultimate answers—and often enough it did—it unfailingly set us thinking along the right track.

If what I am about to say is rather personal, that should be appropriate for a man whose criticism distinguished itself by the intense personalness—or personality—it so artfully and artlessly conveyed. It is his uncompromising yet utterly accessible, jargon-free, lavishly bequeathed individu-

*This essay was originally read as a eulogy at the memorial service for Dwight Macdonald in New York City on December 23rd, 1982.

ality that made Dwight the universal critic he was. And critic he was of everything he touched or was touched by. Because for him criticism meant explaining to himself— and, therefore, to others—the meaning and value, or use- lessness and harm, of whatever his curious and capacious mind engaged in a wrestling bout. He would search, sift, weigh, and savor in the most spontaneous and unpreten- tious, yet also intransigent, manner, in order to distinguish between what was real and what was sham, between what enhanced life and what merely encumbered or wasted it, between what was food for the soul and what was only its bubble gum or potato chips.

Dwight was an elitist, but not of the lazy sort who con- tent themselves with basking in the highness of their brows as reflected in a pier glass or the eyes of their peers. Rather, he was a hard-working elitist, one who tried to share his appetite for the best with anyone else in whom he could instill that holy hunger. Erich Heller told me once about talking with Dwight at a party and being suddenly ac- costed by a silly woman who proceeded to expound some ridiculous notion. Heller, who is a patient man, neverthe- less gave up arguing, he said, fairly quickly. But there was the celebratedly irascible Dwight Macdonald painstak- ingly laboring to enlighten the woman, with a dedication Heller said he admired and envied. An elitist, then, who would eagerly help others join the club, who would gladly have abandoned his badge of superiority for the sake of a world full of coequal elitists.

So great, I repeat, was Dwight's dedication to critical truth that, when he wrote an introduction to my first book, he did something, I dare say, no introducer had ever done to a living author (and seldom enough to a dead one) : He proceeded, in mid-introduction, to castigate me for my "weakness . . . for stylistic bravura, and especially for puns," Though he then generously added, "I know because I have the same weakness." And, again, in his last letter to me, thanking me for an introduction I wrote for the reissue of his book, *On Movies,* he immediately proceeded to make a couple of suggestions about how to improve that introduction. For example, he wanted me to omit the word "juicily" from a description of his style that included the phrase "juicily alive in its human presence." As it happens, it was too late for such editorial changes, and the offending adverb remained. Did Dwight consider "juicily" too prodigal praise or too purple prose—or would he have merely preferred some other term, say, "pungently" or "succulently"?

I never did find out, yet juicily alive is what the man and his writing were, as when, for instance, he answered a reader's letter that deemed a Dwightian attack on Norman Cousins unconstructive: "I've always specialized in negative criticism—literary, political, cinematic, cultural—because I've found so few contemporary products about which I could be 'constructive' without hating myself in the morning." Uncozened by Cousinses and Cozzenses alike, Dwight spoke up in critical reproof even when introducing a protégé, even in a thank-you note. For he understood, instinctively as well as intellectually, that a critic, like a doctor, had to be on call 24 hours a day—and, unlike today's doctors, Dwight was willing even to make house calls.

In a sense, Dwight's living presence was so dazzling that it tended to eclipse his works, which, for a man of his ample and diverse talents, were rather too few and scattered. But now, surely, his uncollected pieces will be collected, even as his conversation and personality are beginning to be recollected in other people's memoirs and biographies. In due time there will be biographies and appreciations of Dwight Macdonald, until Mallarmé's great verse, written, as it happens, about that Edgar Allan Poe whose poetry Dwight edited, will apply equally to Dwight himself: "Tel qu'en lui-même enfin l'éternité le change"—such as into himself at last eternity transforms him. I think we can draw some comfort today from the knowledge that we, and others yet to come, will get to know him better still now that he has gone into that eternal morning where, should he look back at his work, he would have spectacularly little cause for hating himself.

—JOHN SIMON
New York City
December 1982

Preface

WHEN I CAME to assemble these essays, written over the last ten years, I was hardly surprised to find they have a common theme: the influence of mass culture on high culture. As an earlier settler in the wilderness of masscult who cleared his first tract thirty years ago (with an article for *The Symposium* on Hollywood directors), I have come to feel like the aging Daniel Boone when the plowed fields began to surround him in Kentucky. The plowing of this particular field has been intense but, except for H. L. Mencken and Edmund Wilson, most writers on the subject have treated it in a sociological rather than a literary way. My interest in mass culture, however, puts the emphasis on "culture" rather than on "mass." My subject is not the dead sea of masscult but rather the life of the tide line where higher and lower organisms compete for survival.

In the last two centuries, our traditional culture has been under increasing pressure from mass culture, a conflict which has reached its greatest intensity in this country. The market for cultural products has steadily broadened until by now practically everybody is a customer. This is something new in history and it has had novel effects. As the masses have become more and more educated, prosperous and politically influential, the cultural question has moved into the foreground. Up to about 1750, art and thought were pretty much the exclusive province of an educated minority. Now that the masses—that is, everybody —are getting into the act and making the scene, the prob-

lem of vulgarization has become acute. I see only two
logical solutions: (a) an attempt to integrate the masses
into high culture; or (b) a contrary attempt to define two
cultures, one for the masses and the other for the classes. I
am for the latter.*

Let it be admitted at once, as Dr. Edward Shils and other
Panglosses of the sociological approach keep insisting, that
mediocrity has always been the norm even in the greatest
periods. This fact of life is obscured by another: when we
look at the past, we see only the best works because they
alone have survived. But the rise of masscult has introduced several new and confusing factors. Up to about 1800,
the important artists, writers, thinkers, etc., were usually
recognized as such during their lifetimes since their audience was limited to an upper-class elite that had some
expertise. There were, of course, misjudgments: Abraham
Cowley was, well into the eighteenth century, considered
the equal of Milton and the superior of Donne; but at least
Milton was also held in high esteem by his contemporaries
—and Shakespeare, for all his genius, was admired almost
as much as Ben Jonson. By the nineteenth century, however, contemporary responses had begun to become erratic.
Scott and Moore were famous, Blake and Stendhal obscure,
and so it went, through Cézanne and Rimbaud, right up to
the New York Armory Show which, as late as 1913, scandal-
ized the critics and the public by presenting Matisse and
Picasso as serious artists, right up to the first issue of *Time*
in 1925, which devoted its lead review in "Books" to a
respectful celebration of Gertrude Atherton's *Black Oxen*

* By "classes" I don't mean a social or economic upper-class but rather
an intellectual elite. In the original version of "Masscult and Midcult,"
published in my magazine, *Politics,* in 1944 under the title, "A Theory of
Popular Culture," I favored (a); by the 1953 version, published in *Diogenes,*
I had lost confidence in (a) and was edging toward (b); today, for reasons given in this book *passim,* I have come to think (b) is the only practical solution. A capsule history which demonstrates, depending on the
demonstrator's point of view, either hardening of the arteries or belated
maturity—I was almost forty, after all, when I wrote the first version.

and, as a jocular afterthought, dismissed a new poem called *The Wasteland* as an obvious leg-pull comparable to an earlier spoof entitled *Ulysses.*

There is today, if anything, a too ready acceptance of the avant-garde by a public, as respectful as it is undiscriminating, that has learned perhaps too much from the sad experiences of the past. The late vogue of the New York School of abstract expressionism is a case in point—for years it was as much as one's critical life was worth to express a reservation about those enormous globs and gloobs. Another instance is the recent change of line by Mr. Bosley Crowther, the film critic of the *New York Times.* He could once have been counted on to denounce as willfully obscure, perverse, etc., any film of originality, but he has now begun to praise just the kind of thing he used to find absurd before the little-cinema audience grew to its present impressive size—I am thinking of his reviews of Antonioni's *La Notte* and of Resnais' *Last Year at Marienbad.* These are interesting and admirable films and Mr. Crowther's conversion is welcome, but one suspects it has more to do with fashion than with criticism.

If serious and ambitious works of quality are now less likely to be overlooked, serious and ambitious works of no quality are more likely to be praised. The initial chorus of acclaim for such duds as *The Outsider* and *By Love Possessed* (see under "Pretenders" in this book) is usually followed by a reaction that has all the dreadful qualities of a hangover. But how could the critical establishment have gone on its bender in the first place? I think such miscalculations were less frequent before 1750.*

The section entitled "Traitors" is about what Julien

---

* It is too early, as of spring 1962, to be sure, but the air seems to be hissing out of the reputation of C. P. Snow. Kathleen Nott first pricked the balloon in a fine article in the February *Encounter* which explained to me why I had found his Two-Cultures line banal and his novels unreadable (apart, that is, from the style—I had decided about that on my own). She quotes an epigram of Sir Charles, "Satire is cheek," to

xii PREFACE

Benda once called "*le trahison des clercs.*" This is usually translated "the treason of the intellectuals," but the medieval term, *clercs,* is more what I mean; "academics" is the closest modern English can come. The three instances examined are the Hutchins-Adler fifty-volume set of "Great Books of the Western World," complete with a two-volume Syntopicon, or Handy Key to Kulture; the rebuilding of the King James Version of the Bible in contemporary ranch-house style; and the new edition of the Merriam-Webster unabridged dictionary which combines Science and Democracy to debase the language. Such misguided enterprises, conceived and executed on the grandest scale, were undertaken by those very *clercs* whose professional function, one might think, is to defend rather than undermine our cultural traditions. These traitorous *clercs* are also bunglers: they manage to have the worst of both the old and the new world. If they lack that respect for tradition that remote ages instinctively felt, they also lack that historical sense that was introduced in the Renaissance, that feeling for the special quality of each moment of historical time which, from Vico to Spengler, has enabled us to appreciate the past on its own terms. Here we have, as in the Stalin period in Russia, a simple obliteration of what has gone before, as a teacher erases from a blackboard the chalk marks of his predecessor. The trouble is not only that the predecessors had something to teach us but also that a people which loses contact with its past becomes culturally psychotic.

---

which she adds a definition of satire by Lady Snow, also known as Pamela Hansford-Johnson, which Sir Charles has quoted with approval: "the revenge of those who cannot really comprehend the world or cope with it." This is just the reverse of Dickens' view of reality, or Tolstoy's, or Stendhal's. For such writers, legal and bureaucratic procedures and power-struggles are absurd and unreal, while for Sir Charles they are the true reality, that is, the insider's reality. Sir Charles is a great insider. A few weeks after Miss Nott's article, F. R. Leavis swung into action in the *Spectator* with less acumen but more effect owing to his higher rank in the critical hierarchy—an irony the Snows must have appreciated.

To conclude on a more cheerful note: there seems to be an underground, far more widespread than one might think from observing only what appears in print (mostly the establishment view), which responds favorably to subversive questioning of the pretenders and the *clercs*. When in *Commentary*, I reviewed the reviewers of *By Love Possessed*, I received an extraordinary mail. So, too, with my reviews, in the *New Yorker*, of the new Bible, the new dictionary and the Great Books set. As any editor knows, people usually write in when they disagree, but here the opposite was the case; almost no letters came in defending the objects of my criticism. Indeed, and here is perhaps a gloomy note, the objects themselves, except for Mr. James Gould Cozzens who did write a jocularly abusive letter, have not felt it necessary to reply. Either they found my points unanswerable, which is unlikely, or they felt in a strong enough position to ignore criticism. And it is, unhappily, a fact that the new Bibles both here and in England have been best sellers, that the new dictionary has so far survived and that the Great Books are at this writing, ten years after publication, still being successfully peddled from door to door by a locust-horde of salesmen.

But there is still that underground.

Dwight Macdonald

New York City, April 1962

postscript: I am grateful to Miss Berenice Hoffman of Random House for suggesting the title of this book and for her scrupulous editorial work on it, and to Mr. William Shawn for giving me so much space and such latitude of expression in the *New Yorker* over the past ten years.

Contents

PART I

Masscult & Midcult

Masscult & Midcult

FOR ABOUT two centuries Western culture has in fact been two cultures: the traditional kind—let us call it High Culture—that is chronicled in the textbooks, and a novel kind that is manufactured for the market. This latter may be called Mass Culture, or better Masscult, since it really isn't culture at all. Masscult is a parody of High Culture. In the older forms, its artisans have long been at work. In the novel, the line stretches from the eighteenth-century "servant-girl romances" to Edna Ferber, Fannie Hurst and such current ephemera as Burdick, Drury, Michener, Ruark and Uris; in music, from Hearts and Flowers to Rock 'n Roll; in art, from the chromo to Norman Rockwell; in architecture, from Victorian Gothic to ranch-house moderne; in thought, from Martin Tupper's *Proverbial Philosophy* ("Marry not without means, for so shouldst thou tempt Providence;/But wait not for more than enough, for marriage is the DUTY of most men.") to Norman Vincent Peale. (Thinkers like H. G. Wells, Stuart Chase, and Max Lerner come under the head of Midcult rather than Masscult.) And the enormous output of such new media as the radio, television and the movies is almost entirely Masscult.

I

This is something new in history. It is not that so much bad art is being produced. Most High Culture has been undistinguished, since talent is always rare—one has only to walk through any great art museum or try to read some of the forgotten books from past centuries. Since only the best works still have currency, one thinks of the past in their terms, but they were really just a few plums in a pudding of mediocrity.

Masscult is bad in a new way: it doesn't even have the theoretical possibility of being good. Up to the eighteenth century, bad art was of the same nature as good art, produced for the same audience, accepting the same standards. The difference was simply one of individual talent. But Masscult is something else. It is not just unsucessful art. It is non-art. It is even anti-art.

There is a novel of the masses but no Stendhal of the masses; a music for the masses but no Bach or Beethoven, whatever people say . . . [André Malraux observes in "Art, Popular Art and the Illusion of the Folk"—(*Partisan Review*, September-October, 1951).] It is odd that no word . . . designates the common character of what we call, separately, bad painting, bad architecture, bad music, etc. The word "painting" only designates a domain in which art is possible. . . . Perhaps we have only one word because bad painting has not existed for very long. There is no bad Gothic painting. Not that all Gothic painting is good. But the difference that separates Giotto from the most mediocre of his imitators is not of the same kind as that which separates Renoir from the caricaturists of *La Vie Parisienne*. . . . Giotto and the Gaddi are separated by talent, Degas and Bonnat by a schism, Renoir and "suggestive" painting by what? By the fact that this last, totally subjected to the spectator, is a form of advertising which aims at selling itself. If there exists only one word . . . it is because there was a time when the distinction between them had no point. Instruments played real music then, for there was no other.

But now we have pianos playing Rock 'n Roll and *les sanglots longs des violons* accompanying torch singers.

Masscult offers its customers neither an emotional catharsis nor an aesthetic experience, for these demand effort. The production line grinds out a uniform product whose humble aim is not even entertainment, for this too implies life and hence effort, but merely distraction. It may be stimulating or narcotic, but it must be easy to assimilate. It asks nothing of its audience, for it is "totally subjected to the spectator." And it gives nothing.*

Some of its producers are able enough. Norman Rockwell is technically skilled, as was Meissonier—though Degas was right when he summed up the cavalry charge in *Friedland, 1806:* "Everything is steel except the breastplates." O. Henry could tell a story better than many contributors to our Little Magazines. But a work of High Culture, however inept, is an expression of feelings, ideas, tastes, visions that are idiosyncratic and the audience similarly responds to them as individuals. Furthermore, both creator and audience accept certain standards. These may be more or less traditional; sometimes they are so much less so as to be revolutionary, though Picasso, Joyce and Stravinsky knew and respected past achievements more than did their academic contemporaries; their works may be seen as a heroic breakthrough to earlier, sounder foundations that had been obscured by the fashionable gimcrackery of the academies. But Masscult is indifferent to standards. Nor is there any communication between individuals. Those who consume Masscult might as well be eating ice-cream sodas, while those who fabricate it are no more expressing themselves than are the "stylists" who design the latest atrocity from Detroit.

The difference appears if we compare two famous writers of detective stories, Mr. Erle Stanley Gardner and Mr.

* "Distraction is bound to the present mode of production, to the rationalized and mechanized process of labor to which . . . the masses are subject. . . . People want to have fun. A fully concentrated and conscious experience of art is possible only to those whose lives do not put such a strain on them that in their spare time they want relief from both boredom and effort simultaneously. The whole sphere of cheap commercial entertainment reflects this dual desire."—T. W. Adorno: *On Popular Music.*

Edgar Allan Poe. It is impossible to find any personal note in Mr. Gardner's enormous output—he has just celebrated his centenary, the hundredth novel under his own name (he also has knocked off several dozen under pseudonyms). His prose style varies between the incompetent and the nonexistent; for the most part, there is just no style, either good or bad. His books seem to have been manufactured rather than composed; they are assembled with the minimum expenditure of effort from identical parts that are shifted about just enough to allow the title to be changed from *The Case of the Curious Bride* to *The Case of the Fugitive Nurse*. Mr. Gardner obviously has the production problem licked—he has rated his "native abilities" as Very Good as a lawyer, Good as a business analyst, and Zero as a writer, the last realistic estimate being the clue to his production-line fertility—and his popularity indicates he has the problem of distribution well in hand. He is marketing a standard product, like Kleenex, that precisely because it is not related to any individual needs on the part of either the producer or the consumer appeals to the widest possible audience. The obsession of our fact-minded culture with the processes of the law is probably the lowest common denominator that has made Mr. Gardner's unromantic romances such dependable commodities.

Like Mr. Gardner, Mr. Poe was a money-writer. (That he didn't make any is irrelevant.) The difference, aside from the fact that he was a good writer, is that, even when he was turning out hack work, he had an extraordinary ability to use the journalistic forms of his day to express his own peculiar personality, and indeed, as Marie Bonaparte has shown in her fascinating study, to relieve his neurotic anxieties. (It is simply impossible to imagine Mr. Gardner afflicted with anything as individual as a neurosis.) The book review, the macabre-romantic tale, the magazine poem, all served his purposes, and he even invented a new one, the detective story, which satisfied the two chief and oddly disparate drives in his psychology—fascination with horror (*The Murders in the Rue Morgue*) and obsession with logical reasoning or, as he called it, "ratiocination" (*The Purloined Letter*). So that while his works are sometimes absurd, they are rarely dull.

It is important to understand that the difference between Mr. Poe and Mr. Gardner, or between High Culture and Masscult, is not mere popularity. From *Tom Jones* to the films of Chaplin, some very good things have been popular; *The Education of Henry Adams* was the top nonfiction best seller of 1919. Nor is it that Poe's detective stories are harder to read than Gardner's, though I suppose they are for most people. The difference lies in the qualities of Masscult already noted: its impersonality and its lack of standards, and "total subjection to the spectator." The same writer, indeed the same book or even the same chapter, may contain elements of both Masscult and High Culture. In Balzac, for instance, the most acute psychological analysis and social observation is bewilderingly interlarded with the cheapest, flimsiest kind of melodrama. In Dickens, superb comedy alternates with bathetic sentimentality, great descriptive prose with the most vulgar kind of theatricality. All these elements were bound between the same covers, sold to the same mass audience, and, it may well be, considered equally good by their authors—at least I know of no evidence that either Dickens or Balzac was aware of when he was writing down and when he was writing up. Masscult is a subtler problem than is sometimes recognized.

"What is a poet?" asked Wordsworth. "He is a man speaking to men . . . a man pleased with his own passions and volitions, and one who rejoices more than other men in the spirit of life that is in him." It is this human dialogue that Masscult interrupts, this spirit of life that it exterminates. Evelyn Waugh commented on Hollywood, after a brief experience there: "Each book purchased for motion pictures has some individual quality, good or bad, that has made it remarkable. It is the work of a great array of highly paid and incompatible writers to distinguish this quality, separate it and obliterate it." This process is called "licking the book"—i.e., licking it into shape, as mother bears were once thought to lick their amorphous cubs into real bears; though here the process is reversed and the book is licked not into but out of shape. The other meaning of "licked" also applies; before a proper Hollywood film can be made, the work of art has to be defeated.

II

The question of Masscult is part of the larger question of the masses. The tendency of modern industrial society, whether in the USA or the USSR, is to transform the individual into the mass man. For the masses are in historical time what a crowd is in space: a large quantity of people unable to express their human qualities because they are related to each other neither as individuals nor as members of a community. In fact, they are not related *to each other* at all but only to some impersonal, abstract, crystallizing factor. In the case of crowds, this can be a football game, a bargain sale, a lynching; in the case of the masses, it can be a political party, a television program, a system of industrial production. The mass man is a solitary atom, uniform with the millions of other atoms that go to make up "the lonely crowd," as David Riesman well calls our society. A community, on the contrary, is a group of individuals linked to each other by concrete interests. Something like a family, each of whose members has his or her special place and function while at the same time sharing the group's economic aims (family budget), traditions (family history), sentiments (family quarrels, family jokes), and values ("That's the way we do it in *this* family!"). The scale must be small enough so that it "makes a difference" what each person does—this is the first condition for human, as against mass, existence. Paradoxically, the individual in a community is both more closely integrated into the group than is the mass man and at the same time is freer to develop his own special personality. Indeed, an individual can only be defined in relation to a community. A single person in nature is not an individual but an animal; Robinson Crusoe was saved by Friday. The totalitarian regimes, which have consciously tried to create the mass man, have systematically broken every communal link—family, church, trade union, local and regional loyalties, even down to ski and chess clubs—and have reforged them so as to bind each atomized individual directly to the center of power.

The past cultures I admire—Periclean Greece, the city-states of the Italian Renaissance, Elizabethan England, are examples—have mostly been produced by communities, and remarkably small ones at that. Also remarkably heterogeneous ones, riven by faction, stormy with passionate antagonisms. But this diversity, fatal to that achievement of power over other countries that is the great aim of modern statecraft, seems to have been stimulating to talent. (What could be more deadly than the usual post-Marx vision of socialism as equality and agreement? Fourier was far more perceptive when he based his Utopia on cabals, rivalry, and every kind of difference including what he called "innocent mania.") A mass society, like a crowd, is inchoate and uncreative. Its atoms cohere not according to individual liking or traditions or even interests but in a purely mechanical way, as iron filings of different shapes and sizes are pulled toward a magnet working on the one quality they have in common. Its morality sinks to the level of the most primitive members—a crowd will commit atrocities that very few of its members would commit as individuals—and its taste to that of the least sensitive and the most ignorant.

Yet this collective monstrosity, "the masses," "the public," is taken as a human norm by the technicians of

Masscult. They at once degrade the public by treating it as an object, to be handled with the lack of ceremony of medical students dissecting a corpse, and at the same time flatter it and pander to its taste and ideas by taking them as the criterion of reality (in the case of the questionnaire-sociologists) or of art (in the case of the Lords of Masscult). When one hears a questionnaire-sociologist talk about "setting up" an investigation, one realizes that he regards people as mere congeries of conditioned reflexes, his concern being which reflex will be stimulated by which question. At the same time, of necessity, he sees the statistical majority as the great Reality, the secret of life he is trying to unriddle. Like a Lord of Masscult, he is—professionally —without values, willing to take seriously any idiocy if it is held by many people (though, of course, *personally* . . .). The aristocrat's approach to the masses is less degrading to them, as it is less degrading to a man to be shouted at than to be treated as nonexistent. But the *plebs* have their dialectical revenge: indifference to their human quality means prostration before their statistical quantity, so that a movie magnate who cynically "gives the public what it wants"—i.e., assumes it wants trash—sweats with anxiety if the box-office returns drop 5 per cent.

Whenever a Lord of Masscult is reproached for the low quality of his products, he automatically ripostes, "But that's what the public wants, what can I do?" A simple and conclusive defense, at first glance. But a second look reveals that (1) to the extent the public "wants" it, the public has been conditioned to some extent by his products, and (2) his efforts have taken this direction because (a) he himself also "wants" it—never underestimate the ignorance and vulgarity of publishers, movie producers, network executives and other architects of Masscult —and (b) the technology of producing mass "entertainment" (again, the quotes are advised) imposes a simplistic, repetitious pattern so that it is easier to say the public wants this than to say the truth which is that the public gets this and so wants it. The March Hare explained to Alice that "I like what I get" is not the same thing as "I get what I like," but March Hares have never been welcome on Madison Avenue.

For some reason, objections to the giving-to-the-public-what-it-wants line are often attacked as undemocratic and snobbish. Yet it is precisely because I do believe in the potentialities of ordinary people that I criticize Masscult. For the masses are not people, they are not The Man in the Street or The Average Man, they are not even that figment of liberal condescension, The Common Man. The masses are, rather, man as non-man, that is man in a special relationship to other men that makes it impossible for him to function as man (one of the human functions being the creation and enjoyment of works of art). "Mass man," as I use the term, is a theoretical construction, an extreme toward which we are being pushed but which we shall never reach. For to become wholly a mass man would mean to have no private life, no personal desires, hobbies, aspirations, or aversions that are not shared by everybody else. One's behavior would be entirely predictable, like a piece of coal, and the sociologists could at last make up their tables confidently. It is still some time to 1984 but it looks unlikely that Orwell's anti-Utopia will have materialized by then, or that it will ever materialize. Nazism and Soviet Communism, however, show us how far things can go in politics, as Masscult does in art. And let us not be too smug in this American temperate zone, unravaged by war and ideology. "It seems to me that nearly the whole Anglo-Saxon race, especially of course in America, have lost the power to be individuals. They have become social insects like bees and ants." So Roger Fry wrote years ago, and who will say that we have become less apian?

III

Like the early capitalism Marx and Engels described in *The Communist Manifesto,* Masscult is a dynamic, revolutionary force, breaking down the old barriers of class, tradition, and taste, dissolving all cultural distinctions. It mixes, scrambles everything together, producing what might be called homogenized culture, after another American achievement, the homogenization process that distributes the globules of cream evenly throughout the milk instead of allowing them to float separately on top. The interesting difference is that whereas the cream is still in the homogenized milk, somehow it disappears from homogenized culture. For the process destroys all values, since value-judgments require discrimination, an ugly word in liberal-democratic America. Masscult is very, very democratic; it refuses to discriminate against or between anything or anybody. All is grist to its mill and all comes out finely ground indeed.

Life is a typical homogenized magazine, appearing on the mahogany library tables of the rich, the glass cocktail tables of the middle class, and the oilcloth kitchen tables of the poor. Its contents are as thoroughly homogenized as its circulation. The same issue will present a serious exposition of atomic energy followed by a disquisition on Rita Hayworth's love life; photos of starving children picking garbage in Calcutta and of sleek models wearing adhesive brassières; an editorial hailing Bertrand Russell's eightieth birthday (A GREAT MIND IS STILL ANNOYING AND ADORNING OUR AGE) across from a full-page photo of a matron arguing with a baseball umpire (MOM GETS THUMB); nine color pages of Renoir paintings followed by a picture of a roller-skating horse; a cover announcing in the same size type two features: A NEW FOREIGN POLICY, BY JOHN FOSTER DULLES and KERIMA: HER MARATHON KISS IS A MOVIE SENSATION.*

---

* The advertisements provide even more scope for the editors' homogenizing talents, as when a full-page photo of a ragged Bolivian peon grinningly drunk on cocoa leaves (which Mr. Luce's conscientious reporters tell us he chews to narcotize his chronic hunger pains) appears opposite an ad of a pretty, smiling, well-dressed American mother with her two pretty, smiling, well-dressed children (a boy and a girl, of course—children are

Somehow these scramblings together seem to work all one way, degrading the serious rather than elevating the frivolous. Defenders of our Masscult society like Professor Edward Shils of the University of Chicago—he is, of course, a sociologist—see phenomena like *Life* as inspiriting attempts at popular education—just think, nine pages of Renoirs! But that roller-skating horse comes along, and the final impression is that both Renoir and the horse were talented.

IV

The historical reasons for the rise of Masscult are well known. There could obviously be no mass culture until there were masses, in our modern sense. The industrial revolution produced the masses. It uprooted people from their agrarian communities and packed them into factory cities. It produced goods in such unprecedented abundance that the population of the Western world has increased more in the last two centuries than in the preceding two millennia—poor Malthus, never has a brilliantly original theorist been so speedily refuted by history! And it subjected them to a uniform discipline whose only precedent was the "slave socialism" of Egypt. But the Egypt of the Pharaohs produced no Masscult any more than did the great Oriental empires or the late Rome of the proletarian rabble, because the masses were passive, inert, submerged far below the level of political or cultural power. It was not until the end of the eighteenth century in Europe that the majority of people began to play an active part in either history or culture.

Up to then, there was only High Culture and Folk Art.

---

always homogenized in our ads) looking raptly at a clown on a TV set, the whole captioned in type big enough to announce the Second Coming: RCA VICTOR BRINGS YOU A NEW KIND OF TELEVISION—SUPER SETS WITH "PICTURE POWER." The peon would doubtless find the juxtaposition piquant if he could afford a copy of *Life*, which, luckily for the Good Neighbor Policy, he cannot.

To some extent, Masscult is a continuation of Folk Art, but the differences are more striking than the similarities. Folk Art grew mainly from below, an autochthonous product shaped by the people to fit their own needs, even though it often took its cue from High Culture. Masscult comes from above. It is fabricated by technicians hired by businessmen. They try this and try that and if something clicks at the box office, they try to cash in with similar products, like consumer-researchers with a new cereal, or like a Pavlovian biologist who has hit on a reflex he thinks can be conditioned. It is one thing to satisfy popular tastes, as Robert Burns's poetry did, and quite another to exploit them, as Hollywood does. Folk Art was the people's own institution, their private little kitchen-garden walled off from the great formal park of their masters.* But Masscult breaks down the wall, integrating the masses into a debased form of High Culture and thus becoming an instrument of domination. If one had no other data to go on, Masscult would expose capitalism as a class society rather than the harmonious commonwealth that, in election years, both parties tell us it is.

The same goes even more strongly for the Soviet Union. Its Masscult is both worse and more pervasive than ours, a fact which is often not recognized because in form Soviet Masscult is just the opposite, aiming at propaganda and pedagogy rather than distraction. But like ours, it is imposed from above and it exploits rather than satisfies the

---

* And if it was often influenced by High Culture, it did change the forms and themes into its own style. The only major form of Folk Art that still persists in this country is jazz, and the difference between Folk Art and Masscult may be most readily perceived by comparing the kind of thing heard at the annual Newport Jazz Festivals to Rock 'n Roll. The former is musically interesting and emotionally real; the latter is—not. The amazing survival of jazz despite the exploitative onslaughts of half a century of commercial entrepreneurs, is in my opinion, due to its folk quality. And as the noble and the peasant understood each other better than either understood the bourgeois, so it seems significant that jazz is the only art form that appeals to both the intelligentsia and the common people. As for the others, let them listen to *South Pacific*.

needs of the masses—though, of course, for political rather than commercial reasons. Its quality is even lower. Our Supreme Court building is tasteless and pompous but not to the lunatic degree of most Soviet architecture; post-1930 Soviet films, with a few exceptions, are far duller and cruder than our own; the primitive level of *serious* Soviet periodicals devoted to matters of art or philosophy has to be read to be believed, and as for the popular press, it is as if Hearst or Colonel McCormick ran every periodical in America. Furthermore, while here individuals can simply turn their back on Masscult and do their own work, there no such escape is possible; the official cultural bodies control all outlets and a *Doctor Zhivago* must be smuggled out for foreign publication.

v

Masscult first made its appearance in eighteenth-century England, where also, significantly, the industrial revolution was just beginning. The important change was the replacement of the individual patron by the market. The process had begun in Elizabethan times, when journalists like Nashe and Greene made a hard living from the popular sale of their pamphlets and when the theatre depended partly on subsidies from noble patrons and partly on paid admissions. But Masscult's first sizable body of professionals were the hacks of Grub Street, ready to turn their hand to ballads, novels, history, encyclopedias, philosophy, reportage or anything else the publishers thought might go. Dr. Johnson was one of them in his impoverished youth, and his letter to Lord Chesterfield (who had neglected Johnson while the dictionary was being compiled and who, when it was finished, tried to wangle a dedication) was the consummate expression of the change.

Seven years, my Lord, have now passed since I waited in your outward rooms or was repulsed from your door; during which time I have been pushing on my work through difficulties, of which it is useless to complain, and have brought it at last to the verge of publication, without one act of assistance, one word of encouragement, or one smile of favor. Such treatment I did not expect, for I never had a patron before. . . .

Is not a patron, my Lord, one who looks with unconcern on a man struggling for life in the water, and when he has reached ground encumbers him with help? The notice which you have been pleased to take of my labors, had it been early had been kind. But it has been delayed till I am indifferent, and cannot enjoy it; till I am solitary, and cannot impart it; till I am known, and do not want it.

I hope it is no very cynical asperity not to confess obligations where no benefit has been received, or to be unwilling that the public should consider me as owing that to a patron which Providence has enabled me to do for myself. . . . For I have long been wakened from that dream of hope in which I once boasted myself with such exultation, my lord—

Your lordship's most humble, most obedient servant.

SAM. JOHNSON

This Declaration of Independence, written eleven years before our own, made a similar point: Sam. Johnson found the noble lord as superfluous to his existence as the American colonists did His Britannic Majesty.

It must be added that, however defective as a patron, Lord Chesterfield reacted in the grand manner. Far from crushing him, the muted thunders of Johnson's letter seem to have delighted him as a connoisseur. When the bookseller Dodsley called on him soon afterward, he found the letter open on a table for his lordship's visitors to enjoy. "He read it to me," Dodsley writes, "said 'this man has great power,' pointed out the severest passages, and observed how well they were expressed." Boswell thought Chesterfield's reaction "glossy duplicity," but there was more to it than that. The old order went out on a high note of aristocratic taste, very different from the new cultural forces that were superseding it.

For the eighteenth century in British letters began with optimism and ended with doubt and even despair; and both were reactions to the same phenomenon: the enormous increase in the audience. "From 1700 to 1800 the reading public expanded from one which had included mainly the aristocracy, clerics and scholars to one which also included clerks, artisans, laborers and farmers. . . . The annual publication of new books quadrupled."* At first almost every one, with the notable exceptions of Pope and Swift, assumed this growth was simply A Good Thing —the Victorians made the same mistake about popular education. The new readers would be elevated by contact with good literature and the result would be a larger but not a qualitatively different public. The initial success of Addison's and Steele's *Spectator* was encouraging. Published as a daily in 1711-1712, it quickly reached 3,000 circulation, about what some of our most respected Little Magazines have achieved in a population many times larger. (A real circulation-manager type, Addison estimated that with multiple readership in the coffee houses, the total coverage was close to 60,000).

But by the middle of the century, a similar magazine, Johnson's *Rambler,* never got above 500 and was abandoned as a failure. The new public, it would seem, had read the *Spectator* because there was nothing worse to read. The Grub Street publishers hastened to fill the gap,

* For this quote and for most of the material in this and the next paragraph, I am indebted to one of Leo Lowenthal's several interesting studies in Masscult, "The Debate over Art and Popular Culture in Eighteenth-Century England" (written in collaboration with Marjorie Fiske), which appears in a volume unpromisingly titled *Common Frontiers of the Social Sciences* (Free Press, 1951). Q. D. Leavis, in her *Fiction and the Reading Public* (Chatto & Windus, 1932), still the best book on the deterioration of standards as a result of the rise of the mass public, puts the turning point about a century later. The precise dating of a great historical change like this is, of course, a matter of opinion. I think Mrs. Leavis' book exaggerates the solid merits of the pre-1830 popular novels and journalism. But we can all agree on the main point—the effects of the mass market on literature.

Gresham's Law began to work, and the bad drove the good out of circulation (though for the opposite reason from the law's original application, for in currency people circulate the bad because they prefer the good and therefore hang on to it, while in books they circulate the bad because they like it better than the good). By 1790, a bookseller named Lackington was lyrical about the change:

The poorer sort of farmers, and even the poor country people in general, who before that period spent their winter evenings in relating stories of witches, ghosts, hobgoblins, etc., now shorten the winter nights by hearing their sons and daughters read tales, romances, etc., and on entering their houses you may see *Tom Jones, Roderick Random* and other entertaining books stuck up in their bacon racks. . . . In short all ranks and degrees now READ.

Lyrical, charming, democratically heartening, but few of the books in the bacon racks were on the level of *Tom Jones* and perhaps the farmers should have stuck to their witches and hobgoblins. Certainly the effect on literary taste was alarming. By the end of the century, even such successful writers for the new public as Johnson, Goldsmith and Fielding were showing concern as the flood of trash steadily rose.

The mass audience was taking shape and a corresponding shift in literary criticism was beginning, away from objective standards and toward a new subjective approach in which the question was not how good the work is but how popular it will be. Not that the creator is ever independent of his time and place; the demands of the audience have always largely determined his work. But before 1750, these demands were themselves disciplined by certain standards of excellence which were accepted by both the limited public of informed amateurs and the artists who performed for them. Today, in the United States, the demands of the audience, which has changed from a small body of connoisseurs into a large body of ignoramuses, have become the chief criteria of success. Only the Little

Magazines worry about standards. The commercial press, including the *Saturday Review* and the *New York Times Book Review*, consider books as commodities, rating them according to audience-response. The newspaper movie columns are extreme examples. There, the humble effort of the "critic"—and indeed one would have to put even "reviewer" in quotes—is merely to tell his readers which films they will probably like. His own tastes are suppressed as irrelevant.

With the prescience of a snob of genius, Alexander Pope wrote *The Dunciad* a half-century before the tide of vulgarization had begun to gather full force. Grub Street (read: Madison Avenue or perhaps Sunset Boulevard) was its target and its anti-heroes were Theobald and Cibber, the former a lawyer who pretended to scholarship and the latter an actor whose vanity led him to write serious books. These dunces, who were getting away with their impostures, symbolized the confusion in the world of letters that the expansion of the audience had introduced. Two centuries later, when the goddess of Dullness has so extended her realm that one takes it for granted that most current productions will be of her kingdom, one is startled by Pope's vindictive passion, as in the ending:

> *She comes! She comes! the sable throne behold*
> *Of Night primeval and of Chaos old!*
> *Before her, Fancy's gilded clouds decay,*
> *And all its varying rainbows die away.*
> *Wit shoots in vain its momentary fires,*
> *The meteor drops and in a flash expires.*
> . . . . .
> *Thus at her felt approach and secret might,*
> *Art after art goes out, and all is night.*
> . . . . .
> *Lo! thy dread empire, Chaos! is restored;*
> *Light dies before thy uncreating word;*
> *Thy hand, great Anarch! lets the curtain fall,*
> *And universal darkness buries all.*

This is magnificent but exaggerated. With the best will in the world, we have not been able to ring down the curtain; the darkness is still far from universal. Man's nature is tough and full of unexpected quirks, and there are still many pockets of resistance. But in some ways history has surpassed Pope's worst imaginings. With the French Revolution, the masses for the first time made their entrance onto the political stage, and it was not long before they also began to occupy a central position in culture. Grub Street was no longer peripheral and the traditional kind of authorship became more and more literally eccentric— out of the center—until by the end of the nineteenth century the movement from which most of the enduring work of our time has come had separated itself from the market and was in systematic opposition to it.

This movement, was, of course, the "avant-garde" whose precursors were Stendhal and Baudelaire and the impressionist painters, whose pioneers included Rimbaud, Whitman, Ibsen, Cézanne, Wagner, and whose classic masters were figures like Stravinsky, Picasso, Joyce, Eliot, and Frank Lloyd Wright. Perhaps "movement" is too precise a term; the avant-gardists were linked by no aesthetic doctrine, not even by a consciousness that they *were* avant-garde. What they had in common was that they preferred to work for a small audience that sympathized with their experiments because it was sophisticated enough to understand them. By an act of will dictated by necessity (the necessity of survival as a creator, rather than a technician) each of them rejected the historical drift of post-1800 Western culture and recreated the old, traditional situation in which the artist communicated with his peers rather than talked down to his inferiors. Later on, they became famous and those who survived even got rich—the avant-garde is one of the great success-stories of this century— but their creative work was done in a very different atmosphere.

VI

The two great early best sellers in Grub Street's triumph were Lord Byron and Sir Walter Scott. Both exploited romanticism, a new creed whose emphasis on subjective feeling as against traditional form was suitable to the democratization of taste that was taking place. But they differed interestingly. Each represented an aspect of Masscult, Scott the production line, Byron the emphasis on the artist himself. Antithetical but also complementary: the more literature became a branch of industry, the more the craving for the other extreme—individuality. Or rather, a somewhat coarser commodity, Personality.

It is hard for us to understand the effect of Scott's novels on his contemporaries. They were commonly compared to Shakespeare, for their variety and their broad human sympathy. "A great mind unequalled anywhere who naturally produces the most extraordinary effects upon the whole world of readers," was Goethe's judgment. But Croce, in his *European Literature in the Nineteenth Century,* places his finger on the radical, the fatal defect of the Waverley novels: "There are too many of them." He has much also to say about the monotony of Scott's style and the "mechanical method" with which he constructed his characters. But quantity is the point. "[He was] an industrial producer, intent upon supplying the market with objects for which the demand was as keen as the want was legitimate. . . . Is it not healthy to demand images of virtue, of courage, of generous feelings, and . . . to seek also to obtain instruction as to historical customs and events? Scott had the genius to carry out the commercial enterprise which supplied this want. . . . One has the impression, when reading his biography, that one is reading about a hero of industry." And indeed the chief interest is his enormous productivity, his big earnings, his baronial style of life, his heroic struggle to pay off his creditors after bankruptcy. "Nothing is said as to his inner life, his loves, his religion, his ideas; less than nothing about his spiritual struggles and development," Croce continues. Any more than such topics would occur to the biographers of Ford, Carnegie, Rockefeller or the present head of the U.S. Steel Corp.

For one has the impression, in reading even the greatest of the nineteenth-century popular novelists, that the demands of the market pushed them too hard. So Dickens, so Balzac, so Mark Twain. Today the pressure for production comes under the head of physics rather than of aesthetics. In the 1955-1956 season, a long-forgotten TV program called "Matinée" put on five original one-hour plays a week every week, or 260 a year; it took 100 writers, 20 directors and 4,000 actors to keep these Molochian fires stoked. The rate at which TV uses up comic talent was described by Fred Allen, a notable victim; one has merely to see a TV comedy show to realize how tragically right he was. A big publishing house like Doubleday must have hundreds of titles a year to keep its presses busy; the overhead goes on, the more books produced the cheaper to produce each one, and the fear that wakes publishers in the night is that the presses may for a moment stop. When birth control is exercised it is usually at the expense of original and distinguished manuscripts. Anything that is sufficiently banal is sure of a kinder hearing, on the assumption that a bad book *may* sell whereas a good one definitely *won't*. The vast amount of unprofitable junk the publishers issue every year might be expected to cause some misgivings about this notion—if mere banality were a guarantee of success, every Hollywood movie would make money—but somehow the lesson is never learned. Perhaps one should investigate the publishers' own tastes.*

---

* Another possibility is that every editor and publisher is daily buried under such an avalanche of nonsense that he loses his bearings. As any one who has ever taught a course in "creative writing" knows, it is a democratic right of every freeborn American to be a "writer." The obliteration

Byron was as romantic and almost as industrious as Scott but otherwise there were few similarities. His life was as disorderly as Scott's was respectable, his personality as rebellious as Scott's was conventional. It was this personality that won him his mass following: he was the first bohemian, the first avant-gardist, the first beatnik. If Scott was the artist as entrepreneur, Byron was the artist as rebel, and there was less difference between these extremes, from the standpoint of Masscult, than one might have thought. For Byron was a formidable competitor. Scott began as a romantic poet, but when Byron began to publish, Scott made a strategic retreat to prose and began to write the Waverley novels. It was a shrewd decision. *Marmion* and *The Lady of the Lake,* while accomplished exercises in the romantic-historical genre, quite lacked the personal note; readers could hardly "identify with" Roderick Dhu, while Childe Harold and Manfred were not only identifiable but also seemed to express their author's even more identifiable personality.

Byron's reputation was different from that of Chaucer, Spenser, Shakespeare, Milton, Dryden and Pope because it was based on the man—or what the public conceived to be the man—rather than on his work. His poems were taken not as artistic objects in themselves but as expressions of their creator's personality. Similarly, Clark Gable acted himself rather than any specific role; his opposite number is Laurence Olivier, who can actually impersonate, with style and passion, all kinds of other people, from Henry V to the seedy song-and-dance man of *The Entertainer.* Of course it wasn't really Byron himself but a contrived *persona* which fitted into the contemporary public's idea of a poet. Goethe was as obtuse on Byron as he was

of standards in the Masscult world is nowhere shown more clearly than in this innocent conviction. In the year 1956, for example, the *Ladies Home Journal* received 21,822 unsolicited manuscripts, of which it accepted sixteen. And even the sixteen lucky hits might not be considered worth the ink and paper by some critics.

on Scott; he praised him as a great poet but added the well-known proviso: "When he thinks, he is a child." The reverse was the truth: as a "great poet" Byron was banal—who reads his "serious" poetry now?—but when he thought, he was not at all childish; that is, when he (one senses with some relief) dropped the pretense of romantic passion and let his realistic eighteenth-century temperament play around, as in his diaries and letters and in *Beppo* and *Don Juan*. There were two Byrons, the public swashbuckler of *The Corsair* and *Childe Harold's Pilgrimage* and the private mocker of the same romantic attitudes, and this split between the two was to become characteristic. One thinks of Mark Twain, with his public pose as the genial homespun philosopher and his private hell of nihilist despair.

VII

Or of John Barrymore, whose profile and sexual-romantic prowess were as famous as Byron's and whose Masscult *persona* bound him to the wheel of endless portrayals of The Great Lover and repressed his real talents, which were a beautiful diction and a distinguished stage presence (as in his *Hamlet*), sensitivity as an actor (as in the movie of *A Bill of Divorcement*), and a gift for light comedy (curiously analogous to Byron's flair for burlesque) which glittered in a few scenes of sardonic, graceful mugging in such movie farces as *The Man From Blankley's* and *Twentieth Century*.

Since in a mass society people are related not to each other but to some abstract organizing principle, they are often in a state of exhaustion, for this lack of contact is unnatural. So Masscult attempts to provide distraction for the tired businessman—or the tired proletarian. This kind of art is necessarily at a distance from the individual since it is specifically designed to affect not what differentiates him from everybody else—that is what is of liveliest interest to *him*—but rather to work on the reflexes he shares with everybody else. So he is at a distance.

But people feel a need to be related to other people. The simplest way of bridging this distance, or rather of pretending to bridge it, is by emphasizing the personality of the artist; the individual buried in the mass audience can relate himself to the individual in the artist, since they are, after all, both persons. So while Masscult is in one sense extremely impersonal, in another it is extremely personal. The artist is thus charismatic and his works become the expression of this charisma rather than, as in the past, objective creations.

In his alcoholic last years, John Barrymore gave an extreme illustration of this principle.

Six months ago [ran a story in *Time* of November 6, 1939] a ham show opened in Chicago. Last week it was still running there. It had become a civic institution. It had played to 150,000 people and grossed over $250,000. The theater was sold out three weeks in advance. . . .

The answer was . . . that the leading man [was] the great John Barrymore—sometimes ill, sometimes tight, but always a trouper. . . . "Yep," says the doorman, "he arrives every night, dead or alive." . . . He says anything that comes into his head. When he is well wound up, *My Dear Children* may bumble on till after midnight. Once a fire engine sounded in the street. Sang out Barrymore: "I hope they get to the fire in time." Once he saw Ned Sparks in the audience. Walking to the footlights, Barrymore shouted: "There's that old bastard Ned Sparks." Once he couldn't hear the prompter in the wings, yelled: "Give those cues louder!" [etc.] Once, unable to stand up, he played the whole show sitting down. Another time, when he couldn't even issue from the dressing room to stage, he said: "Get me a wheel chair—I'll play Lionel."

Audiences eat it up. They complain to the box office only on those rare occasions when Barrymore plays his part straight.

Barrymore was not, by this time, exploiting his romantic personality; he was not even burlesquing it, since the *ad libs*—except for the crack about Lionel—were not funny. He was living on his capital, selling his gilt-edge bonds (his romantic reputation) and when he had liquidated them all (when the public began to think of him not as "the great John Barrymore" of the past but as the drunken cut-up of the present) he would have been bankrupt. Luckily, he died before that happened.

For their part, the mass public liked him in this final stage of disintegration precisely because it showed them he was no better than they were, in fact he was a good deal worse. In the "genius" act of the Masscult period, there is a strange ambivalence. The masses put an absurdly high value on the personal genius, the charisma, of the performer, but they also demand a secret rebate: he must play the game—*their* game—must distort his personality to suit their taste. Bryon did it when he wore an open collar and made sure that his hyacinthine locks were properly disordered. Robert Frost did it when he called a press conference, not so long ago, on moving into his office at the Library of Congress as Consultant on Poetry, and told the assembled reporters that his job might be called "Poet in Waiting" and further confided that he wanted some good paintings to hang in his office: "I want to get the place out of the small-potatoes class." Even the staid *New York Times* was stimulated to headline its story: POET IN WAITING BIDS FOR A RATING. That Frost is a fine poet isn't relevant here; he is also a natural showman, and the relevant question is why our most distinguished poet feels it desirable to indulge this minor talent, clowning around like another Carl Sandburg. Bernard Shaw is the most interesting case of all, combining arrogance and subservience in the most dazzling way, as in the postcards he wrote to his admirers explaining why he couldn't possibly be bothered to reply.

In Masscult (and in its bastard, Midcult) everything becomes a commodity, to be mined for $$$$, used for something it is not, from Davy Crockett to Picasso. Once a writer becomes a Name, that is, once he writes a book that for good or bad reasons catches on, the Masscult (or Midcult) mechanism begins to "build him up," to package him into something that can be sold in identical units in quantity. He can coast along the rest of his life on momentum; publishers will pay him big advances just to get his Name on their list; his charisma becomes such that people will pay him $250 and up to address them (really just to *see* him); editors will reward him handsomely for articles on subjects he knows nothing about. Artists and writers have always had a tendency to repeat themselves, but Masscult (and Midcult) make it highly profitable to do so and in fact penalize those who don't. Some years ago, I'm told, a leading abstract artist complained to a friend that he was tired of the genre that had made him famous and wanted to try something else; but his gallery insisted such a shift would be commercially disastrous and, since he had children to send through college, he felt obliged to comply. Or compare the careers of James T. Farrell and Norman Mailer. The former made a reputation with the *Studs Lonigan* trilogy in the early 'thirties and his many books since then have gone on repeating the mixture as before; although his later books have won small critical esteem, he is still considered a major American writer and still gathers all the perquisites and emoluments thereof; Farrell is a standard and marketable commodity, like Jello. Although Mailer is still a Name, with plenty of p. and e., he has crossed up his public and his publishers by refusing to repeat himself. His reputation was made with his first novel, *The Naked and the Dead,* in 1948, but he has insisted on developing, or at least changing, since then, and his three subsequent books have little in common, in either style or content, with his first great success. From the Masscult (or Midcult) point of view, he has jeopardized a sound investment in order to gratify his personal interests. "When a writer gets hold of a sure thing," Somerset Maugham, who should know, once observed, "you may expect him to hang on to it for a lifetime, like a dog worrying a bone." This is not at all to imply that James T. Farrell is deliberately hanging on to his bone for profit or prestige, or that Norman Mailer changes his bones for idealistic reasons. The truth probably is that the former really enjoys mumbling the same old bone while the latter, perhaps because he is more volatile and talented, has wanted to try something new. But the result is that Farrell has got a lot of mileage out of very little gas, while Mailer is still a real problem to his publishers.

VIII

Let us, finally, consider Masscult first from the standpoint of consumption and then from that of production.

As a marketable commodity, Masscult has two great advantages over High Culture. One has already been considered: the post-1750 public, lacking the taste and knowledge of the old patron class, is not only satisfied with shoddy mass-produced goods but in general feels more at home with them (though on unpredictable occasions, they will respond to the real thing, as with Dickens' novels and the movies of Chaplin and Griffith). This is because such goods are standardized and so are easier to consume since one knows what's coming next—imagine a Western in which the hero loses the climactic gun fight or an office romance in which the mousy stenographer loses out to the predatory blonde. But standardization has a subtler aspect, which might be called The Built-In Reaction. As Clement Greenberg noted in "Avant-garde and *Kitsch*" many years ago in *Partisan Review,* the special aesthetic quality of *Kitsch*—a term which includes both Masscult and Midcult

—is that it "predigests art for the spectator and spares him effort, provides him with a shortcut to the pleasures of art that detours what is necessarily difficult in the genuine art" because it includes the spectator's reactions in the work itself instead of forcing him to make his own responses. That standby of provincial weddings, "I Love You Truly," is far more "romantic" than the most beautiful of Schubert's songs because its wallowing, yearning tremolos and glissandos make it clear to the most unmusical listener that something very tender indeed is going on. It does his feeling for him; or, as T. W. Adorno has observed of popular music, "The composition hears for the listener." Thus Liberace is a much more "musical" pianist than Serkin, whose piano is not adorned with antique candelabra and whose stance at it is as business-like as Liberace's is "artistic." So, too, our Collegiate Gothic, which may be seen in its most resolutely picturesque (and expensive) phase at Yale, is more relentlessly Gothic than Chartres, whose builders didn't even know they *were* Gothic and so missed many chances for quaint effects.* And so, too, Boca Raton, the millionaires' suburb that Addison Mizener designed in Palm Beach during the Great Bull Market of the 'twenties, is so aggressively Spanish Mission that a former American ambassador to Spain is said to have murmured in awe, "It's more Spanish than anything I ever saw in Madrid." The same Law of the Built-In Reaction also insures that a smoothly air-brushed pin-up girl by Petty is more "sexy" than a real naked

---

* When I lived in Harkness Memorial Quadrangle some thirty years ago, I noticed a number of cracks in the tiny-paned windows of my room that had been patched with picturesquely wavy strips of lead. Since the place had just been built, I thought this peculiar. Later I found that after the windows had been installed, a special gang of artisans had visited them; one craftsman had delicately cracked every tenth or twentieth pane with a little hammer and another had then repaired the cracks. In a few days, the windows of Harkness had gone through an evolution that in backward places like Oxford had taken centuries. I wonder what they do in Harkness when a window is broken by accident.

woman, the emphasis of breasts and thighs corresponding to the pornographically exaggerated Gothic details of Harkness. More *sexy* but not more *sexual,* the relation between the terms being similar to that of *sentimentality* to *sentiment* or *modernistic* to *modern,* or *arty* to *art.*

The production of Masscult is a subtler business than one might think. We have already seen in the case of Poe that a serious writer will produce art even when he is trying to function as a hack, simply because he cannot help putting himself into his work. The unhappy hero of James's story, "The Next Time," tried again and again to prostitute his talents and write a best seller to support his family, but each time he created another unprofitable masterpiece; with the best will in the world, he was simply unable to achieve a low enough standard. The reverse is also true: a hack will turn out hack stuff even when he tries to be serious. Most of these examples will come later under Midcult, but Masscult also has its little tragedies. When I was in Hollywood recently, I was told by one of the most intelligent younger directors, Stanley Kubrick: "The reason movies are often so bad out here isn't because the people who make them are cynical money hacks. Most of them are doing the very best they can; they really want to make good movies. The trouble is with their heads, not their hearts." This was borne out by the film I was there to write about, a mawkish travesty of Nathanael West's *Miss Lonelyhearts* that was written and produced by Dore Schary with the noblest intentions.

There seem to be two main conditions for the successful production of *Kitsch.* One is that the producer must believe in what he is doing. A good example is Norman Rockwell, who since 1916 has painted over three hundred covers for the *Saturday Evening Post.* When a fellow illustrator remarked that their craft was just a way to make a living—"You do your job, you get your check, and nobody thinks it's art"—Rockwell was horrified. "Oh no no no. How can you say that? No man with a conscience can just bat out illustrations. He's got to put all of his talent, all of his feelings into them." Having just seen a most interesting exhibition of Rockwell's techniques at a local bank, I think he was telling the truth. He makes dozens of careful, highly competent pencil sketches, plus oil renderings of details, for just one *Post* cover; if genius were really "an infinite capacity for taking pains," Norman Rockwell would be a genius. The trouble is that the final result of all this painstaking craftsmanship is just —a *Post* cover, as slick and cliché in execution as in content. "There's this magazine cover," says the comedian Mort Sahl, "and it shows this kid getting his first haircut you know and a dog is licking his hand and his mother is crying and it's Saturday night in the old home town and people are dancing outside in the streets and the Liberty Bell is ringing and, uh, did I miss anything?" But Rockwell is sincere, so much so that he constantly wonders whether he is living up to his talents. In the 'twenties, according to a profile in the *Post*, he went through a crisis as comic as it was pathetic:

Professional friends, dabbling in modernism, told him he ought to learn something about dynamic symmetry, and their arguments worried him. . . . Rockwell packed up and went to Paris. He attended lectures and bought Picassos to hang in his studio for inspiration. On his return he set about applying what he had learned to *Post* covers. When editor George Horace Lorimer examined the first new Rockwell offerings, he laid them aside and gave the artist a paternal lecture on the value of being one's self, pointing out in passing that it was conceivably better to have one's work displayed on the *Post's* covers than embalmed in art museums. Chastened, Rockwell agreed and went back to being himself. He now refers to his temporary aberration as "my James-Joyce-Gertrude-Stein period."

Lorimer's missionary work was completed by a Stanford girl Rockwell married a few years later, a nice, sensible young bride who in good American fashion "helped get him back on the beam and keep him there." In this not exactly Herculean task, she appears to have succeeded. He was positively defiant some years ago when he was being interviewed for a *New Yorker* profile:

My creed is that painting pictures of any kind is a definite form of expression and that illustration is the principal pictorial form of conveying ideas and telling funny stories. The critics say that any proper picture should be primarily a series of technical problems of light, shadow, proportion, color and voids. I say that if you can tell a story in a picture and if a reasonable number of people like your work, it is art. Maybe it isn't the highest form of art, but it's art nevertheless and it's what I love to do. I feel that I am doing something when I paint a picture that appeals to most people. This is a democracy, isn't it?

To which last the reply is, in terms of Rockwell's covers, "Yep, sure is." Yet, despite this credo, which every popular artist should have printed in red and black and hung over his drawing board alongside Kipling's "If," Rockwell still keeps worrying. He had another crisis a couple of years ago, at sixty-five, when he again wondered what he might have done "if I hadn't gone commercial" and again began to talk of Picasso as "the greatest"; he took a year off to do some Serious painting (except for a mere six *Post* covers), with results unknown to me. He also wrote his autobiography. It is being serialized in the *Post*.

The other condition for success in Masscult is that the writer, artist, editor, director or entertainer must have a good deal of the mass man in himself, as was the case with Zane Grey, Howard Chandler Christy, Mr. Lorimer of the *Post*, Cecil B. DeMille, and Elvis Presley. This is closely related to sincerity—how can he take his work seriously if he doesn't have this instinctive, this built-in vulgar touch? Like Rockwell, he may know that art is good and honorable and worthy of respect, and he may pay tribute to it. But knowing it is one thing and feeling it is another. A journalistic entrepreneur like Henry Luce—by no means the worst—has the same kind of idle curiosity about the Facts and the same kind of gee-whiz excitement about rather elementary ideas (see *Life* editorials passim) as his millions of readers have. When I worked for him on *Fortune* in the early 'thirties, I was struck by three qualities he had as an editor: his shrewdness as to what was and what was not "a story," his high dedication to his task, and his limited cultural background despite, or perhaps because of, his having attended Yale College. All three are closely interrelated in his success: a more sophisticated editor would have gotten out of step with his millions of readers, a less idealistic one would have lacked the moral oomph to attract them, and he knew a "story" when he saw one because what interested them interested him.*

* An episode in my six years at *Fortune* is to the point here. In 1931-1932 I was active on a literary magazine (along with two friends who in 1938 were to become, with me, editors of *Partisan Review:* F. W. Dupee and George L. K. Morris) which had a circulation of about 600. Thinking Luce would be pleased, and interested, by this evidence of cultural enterprise on the part of one of his writers, I sent him up an issue of *The Miscellany,* as it was dismally called. His reaction was that I had betrayed Time, Inc. "But Henry," I said—in those days, long before *Sports Illustrated* or even *Life,* manners were still pastorally simple at Time, Inc., and Luce was merely *primus inter pares*—"But Henry, you can't expect *Fortune* to be my only interest. I give it a good day's work from nine to five, that's what you pay me for, and it's my business what I do in my spare time." This argument affected Luce much as his cynical colleague's did Norman Rockwell. With his usual earnestness—he was and I'm sure is a decent and honorable man, not at all the ogre the liberal press portrays—Luce expounded quite a different philosophy: *Fortune* was not just a job, it was a vocation worthy of a man's whole effort, and pay and time schedules weren't the point at all. "Why, the very name *Fortune* was thought up by so-and-so [one of my fellow editors] late one night on the West Side subway between the Seventy-second and the Seventy-ninth street stations [Luce was a *Time* man always]. This is a twenty-four-hour profession, you never know when you may get an idea for us, and if you're all the time thinking about some damn little magazine . . ." "But Henry . . ." It was an impasse, since I looked on *Fortune* as a means and he as an end, nor had it been resolved when I left the magazine four years later.

IX

As I have already noted in this essay, the separation of Folk Art and High Culture in fairly watertight compartments corresponded to the sharp line once drawn between the common people and the aristocracy. The blurring of this line, however desirable politically, has had unfortunate results culturally. Folk Art had its own authentic quality, but Masscult is at best a vulgarized reflection of High Culture and at worst a cultural nightmare, a *Kulturkatzenjammer*. And while High Culture could formerly address itself only to the *cognoscenti,* now it must take the *ignoscenti* into account even when it turns its back on them. For Masscult is not merely a parallel formation to High Culture, as Folk Art was; it is a competitor. The problem is especially acute in this country because class lines are especially weak here. If there were a clearly defined cultural elite here, then the masses could have their *Kitsch* and the classes could have their High Culture, with everybody happy. But a significant part of our population is chronically confronted with a choice between looking at TV or old masters, between reading Tolstoy or a detective story; i.e., the pattern of their cultural lives is "open" to the point of being porous. For a lucky few, this openness of choice is stimulating. But for most, it is confusing and leads at best to that middlebrow compromise called Midcult.

The turning point in our culture was the Civil War, whose aftermath destroyed the New England tradition almost as completely as the October Revolution broke the continuity of Russian culture. (Certain disturbing similarities between present-day American and Soviet Russian culture and society may be partly due to these seismic breaks, much more drastic than anything in European history, including the French Revolution.) The New England culture was simply pushed aside by history, dwindling to provincial gentility, and there was no other to take its place; it was smothered by the growth of mass industry, by westward expansion, and above all by the massive immigration from non-English-speaking countries. The great metaphor of the period was the melting pot; the tragedy was that it melted so thoroughly. A pluralistic culture might have developed, enriched by the contributions of Poles, Italians, Serbs, Greeks, Jews, Finns, Croats, Germans, Swedes, Hungarians, and all the other peoples that came here from 1870 to 1910. It is with mixed feelings one reads Emma Lazarus' curiously condescending inscription on the Statue of Liberty:

> *Give me your tired, your poor,*
> *Your huddled masses yearning to breathe free,*
> *The wretched refuse of your teeming shore,*
> *Send these, the homeless, tempest-tossed, to me:*
> *I lift my lamp beside the golden door.*

For indeed these *were* the poor and tempest-tossed, the bottom-dogs of Europe, and for just this reason they were all too eager to give up their old-world languages and customs, which they regarded as marks of inferiority. Uprooted from their own traditions, offered the dirtiest jobs at the lowest pay, the masses from Europe were made to feel that their only hope of rising was to become "Americanized," which meant being assimilated at the lowest cultural (as well as economic) level. They were ready-made consumers of *Kitsch*. A half-century ago, when the issue was still in the balance, Randolph Bourne wrote:

What we emphatically do not want is that these distinctive qualities should be washed out into a tasteless, colorless fluid of uniformity. Already we have far too much of this insipidity —masses of people who are half-breeds. . . . Our cities are filled with these half-breeds who retain their foreign names but have lost the foreign savor. This does not mean that . . . they have been really Americanized. It means that, letting slip from them whatever native culture they had, they have substituted for it only the most rudimentary American—the American culture of the cheap newspaper, the movies, the popular song, the ubiquitous automobile. . . .

Just so surely as we tend to disintegrate these nuclei of nationalistic culture do we tend to create hordes of men and women without a spiritual country, cultural outlaws without taste, without standards but those of the mob. We sentence them to live on the most rudimentary planes of American life.*

Bourne's fears were realized. The very nature of mass industry and of its offshoot, Masscult, made a pluralistic culture impossible. The melting pot produced merely "the tasteless, colorless fluid of uniformity." This much can be said for the dominant Anglo-Saxon Americans: they didn't ask the immigrants to accept anything they themselves were unwilling to accept. One recalls Matthew Josephson's vignette of Henry Clay Frick sitting on a Renaissance chair under a Rembrandt reading the *Saturday Evening Post*. They were preoccupied with building railroads, settling the West, expanding industry, perfecting monopolies and other practical affairs. Pioneers, O Pioneers! And the tired pioneer preferred Harold Bell Wright to Henry James.

x

We are now in a more sophisticated period. The West has been won, the immigrants melted down, the factories and railroads built to such effect that since 1929 the problem has been consumption rather than production. The

---

* From "Trans-National America." Of course the immigrants were not all "huddled masses." Many, especially the Jews, were quite aware of the inferior quality of American cultural life. In *The Spirit of the Ghetto* (1902), Hutchins Hapgood quotes a Jewish immigrant: "In Russia, a few men, really cultivated and intellectual, give the tone and everybody follows them. But in America the public gives the tone and the literary man simply expresses the public. So that really intellectual Americans do not express as good ideas as less intellectual Russians. The Russians all imitate the best. The Americans imitate what the mass of the people want." A succinct definition of Masscult.

work week has shrunk, real wages have risen, and never in history have so many people attained such a high standard of living as in this country since 1945. College enrollment is now well over four million, three times what it was in 1929. Money, leisure and knowledge, the prerequisites for culture, are more plentiful and more evenly distributed than ever before.

In these more advanced times, the danger to High Culture is not so much from Masscult as from a peculiar hybrid bred from the latter's unnatural intercourse with the former. A whole middle culture has come into existence and it threatens to absorb both its parents. This intermediate form—let us call it Midcult—has the essential qualities of Masscult—the formula, the built-in reaction, the lack of any standard except popularity—but it decently covers them with a cultural figleaf. In Masscult the trick is plain—to please the crowd by any means. But Midcult has it both ways: it pretends to respect the standards of High Culture while in fact it waters them down and vulgarizes them.*

The enemy outside the walls is easy to distinguish. It is its ambiguity that makes Midcult alarming. For it presents itself as part of High Culture. Not that coterie stuff, not those snobbish inbred so-called intellectuals who are only talking to themselves. Rather the great vital mainstream, wide and clear though perhaps not so deep. You, too, can wade in it for a mere $16.70 pay nothing now just fill in the coupon and receive a full year six hard-cover lavishly illustrated issues of *Horizon: A Magazine of the Arts*, "probably the most beautiful magazine in the world . . .

---

* It's not done, of course, as consciously as this suggests. The editors of the *Saturday Review* or *Harper's* or the *Atlantic* would be honestly indignant at this description of their activities, as would John Steinbeck, J. P. Marquand, Pearl Buck, Irwin Shaw, Herman Wouk, John Hersey and others of that remarkably large group of Midcult novelists we have developed. One of the nice things about Zane Grey was that it seems never to have occurred to him that his books had anything to do with literature.

seeks to serve as guide to the long cultural advance of modern man, to explore the many mansions of the philosopher, the painter, the historian, the architect, the sculptor, the satirist, the poet . . . to build bridges between the world of scholars and the world of intelligent readers. It's a good buy. Use the coupon *now*." *Horizon* has some 160,000 subscribers, which is more than the combined circulations, after many years of effort, of *Kenyon, Hudson, Sewanee, Partisan, Art News, Arts, American Scholar, Dissent, Commentary,* and half a dozen of our other leading cultural-critical magazines.

Midcult is not, as might appear at first, a raising of the level of Masscult. It is rather a corruption of High Culture which has the enormous advantage over Masscult that while also in fact "totally subjected to the spectator," in Malraux's phrase, it is able to pass itself off as the real thing. Midcult is the Revised Standard Version of the Bible, put out several years ago under the aegis of the Yale Divinity School, that destroys our greatest monument of English prose, the King James Version, in order to make the text "clear and meaningful to people today," which is like taking apart Westminister Abbey to make Disneyland out of the fragments. Midcult is the Museum of Modern Art's film department paying tribute to Samuel Goldwyn because his movies are alleged to be (slightly) better than those of other Hollywood producers—though why they are called "producers" when their function is to prevent the production of art (cf., the fate in Hollywood of Griffith, Chaplin, von Stroheim, Eisenstein and Orson Welles) is a semantic puzzle. Midcult is the venerable and once venerated *Atlantic*— which in the last century printed Emerson, Lowell, Howells, James, and Mark Twain—putting on the cover of a recent issue a huge photograph of Dore Schary, who has lately transferred his high-minded sentimentality from Hollywood to Broadway and who is represented in the issue by a homily, "To A Young Actor," which synthesizes Jefferson, Polonius and Dr. Norman Vincent Peale, concluding: "Behave as citizens not only of your profession but of the full world in which you live. Be indignant with injustice, be gracious with success, be courageous with failure, be patient with opportunity, and be resolute with faith and honor." Midcult is the Book-of-the-Month Club, which since 1926 has been supplying its members with reading matter of which the best that can be said is that it could be worse, i.e., they get John Hersey instead of Gene Stratton Porter. Midcult is the transition from Rodgers and Hart to Rodgers and Hammerstein, from the gay tough lyrics of *Pal Joey*, a spontaneous expression of a real place called Broadway, to the folk-fakery of *Oklahoma!* and the orotund sentimentalities of *South Pacific*.* Midcult is or was, "Omnibus," subsidized by a great foundation to raise the level of television, which began its labors by announcing it would "be aimed straight at the average American audience, neither highbrow nor lowbrow, the audience that made the *Reader's Digest, Life,* the *Ladies' Home Journal,* the audience which is the solid backbone of any

* An interesting Midcult document is the editorial the *New York Times* ran August 24, 1960, the day after the death of Oscar Hammerstein 2nd:
. . . The theatre has lost a man who stood for all that is decent in life. . . . The concern for racial respect in *South Pacific,* the sympathy and respect for a difficult though aspiring monarch in *The King and I,* the indomitable faith that runs through *Carousel* were not clever bits of showmanship. They represented Mr. Hammerstein's faith in human beings and their destiny. . . .
Since he was at heart a serious man, his lyrics were rarely clever. Instead of turning facetious phrases he made a studious attempt to write idiomatically in the popular tradition of the musical theatre, for he was a dedicated craftsman. But the style that was apparently so artless has brought glimpses of glory into our lives. "There's a bright, golden haze on the meadow," sings Curly in *Oklahoma!* and the gritty streets of a slatternly city look fresher. "June is bustin' out all over," sing Carrie and Nettie in *Carousel* and the harshness of our winter vanishes. . . . To us it is gratifying that he had the character to use his genius with faith and scruple.
The contrast of faith (good) with cleverness (bad) is typical of Midcult, as is the acceptance of liberalistic moralizing as a satisfactory substitute for talent. Indeed, talent makes the midbrow uneasy: "Since he was a serious man, his lyrics were rarely clever." The death of Mr. Hart did not stimulate the *Times* to editorial elegy.

business as it is of America itself" and which then proved its good faith by programming Gertrude Stein and Jack Benny, Chekhov and football strategy, Beethoven and champion ice skaters. "Omnibus" failed. The level of television, however, was not raised, for some reason.

XI

But perhaps the best way to define Midcult is to analyze certain typical products. The four I have chosen are Ernest Hemingway's *The Old Man and the Sea*, Thornton Wilder's *Our Town*, Archibald MacLeish's *J.B.* and Stephen Vincent Benét's *John Brown's Body*. They have all been Midcult successes: each has won the Pulitzer Prize, has been praised by critics who should know better, and has been popular not so much with the masses as with the educated classes. Technically, they are advanced enough to impress the midbrows without worrying them. In content, they are "central" and "universal," in that line of hollowly portentous art which the French call *pompier* after the glittering, golden beplumed helmets of their firemen. Mr. Wilder, the cleverest of the four, has actually managed to be at once ultra-simple and grandiose. "Now there are some things we all know, but we don't take 'm out and look at 'm very often," says his stage manager, sucking ruminatively on his pipe. "We all know that *something* is eternal. And it ain't houses and it ain't names, and it ain't earth, and it ain't even the stars. . . . Everybody knows in their bones that *something* is eternal, and that something has to do with human beings. All the greatest people ever lived have been telling us for five thousand years and yet you'd be surprised how people are always losing hold of it. There's something way down deep that's eternal about every human being." The last sentence is an eleven-word summary, in form and content, of Midcult. I agree with everything Mr. Wilder says but I will fight to the death against his right to say it in this way.

The Old Man and the Sea was (appropriately) first published in *Life* in 1952. It won the Pulitzer Prize in 1953 and it helped Hemingway win the Nobel Prize in 1954 (the judges cited its "style-forming mastery of the art of modern narration"). It is written in that fake-biblical prose Pearl Buck used in *The Good Earth*, a style which seems to have a malign fascination for the midbrows—Miss Buck also got a Nobel Prize out of it. There are only two characters, who are not individualized because that would take away from the Universal Significance. In fact they are not even named, they are simply "the old man" and "the boy"—I think it was a slip to identify the fish as a marlin though, to be fair, it is usually referred to as "the great fish." The dialogue is at once quaint (democracy) and dignified (literature). "Sleep well, old man," quothes The Boy; or, alternatively, "Wake up, old man." It is also very poetic, as The Boy's speech: "I can remember the tail slapping and banging . . . and the noise of you clubbing him like chopping a tree down and the sweet blood smell all over me." (Even the Old Man is startled by this cadenza. "Can you really remember that?" he asks.) In the celebrated baseball dialogues we have a fusion of Literature & Democracy:

"The great DiMaggio is himself again. I think of Dick Sisler and those great drives in the old park. . . . The Yankees cannot lose."
"But I fear the Indians of Cleveland."
"Have faith in the Yankees, my son. Think of the great DiMaggio."

And this by the man who practically invented realistic dialogue.

It is depressing to compare this story with "The Undefeated," a bullfighting story Hemingway wrote in the 'twenties when, as he would say, he was knocking them out of the park. Both have the same theme: an old-timer, scorned as a has-been, gets one last chance; he loses (the fish is eaten by sharks, the bullfighter is gored) but his defeat is a moral victory, for he has shown that his will and courage are still intact. The contrast begins with the opening paragraphs:

> Manuel Garcia climbed the stairs to Don Miguel Retana's office. He set down his suitcase and knocked on the door. There was no answer. Manuel, standing in the hallway, felt there was some one in the room. He felt it through the door.

> He was an old man who fished alone in a skiff in the Gulf Stream and he had gone eighty-four days now without taking a fish. In the first forty days a boy had been with him. But after forty days without a fish the boy's parents had told him that the old man was now definitely and finally *salao*, which is the worst form of unlucky, and the boy had gone at their orders in another boat which caught three good fish the first week. It made the boy sad to see the old man come in each day with his skiff empty and he always went down to help him carry either the coiled lines or the gaff and the harpoon and the sail that was furled around the mast. The sail was patched with flour sacks and, furled, it looked like the flag of permanent defeat.

The contrast continues—disciplined, businesslike understatement v. the drone of the pastiche parable, wordy and sentimental ("the flag of permanent defeat" fairly nudges us to sympathize). And all those "ands."

"Undefeated" is 57 pages long, as against *Old Man's* 140, but not only does much more happen in it but also one feels that more has happened than is expressed, so to speak, while *Old Man* gives the opposite impression. "Undefeated" has four people in it, each with a name and each defined through his words and actions; *Old Man* has no people, just two Eternal, Universal types. Indeed, for three-fourths it has one only one, since The Boy doesn't go along on the fishing trip. Perhaps a Kafka could have made something out of it, but in Hemingway's realistic manner it is

monotonous. "Then he began to pity the great fish"—
that sort of thing. At times the author, rather desperate
one imagines, has him talk to the fish and to the birds. He
also talks to his hand: "How does it go, hand?" In "Undefeated," the emotion arises naturally out of the dialogue
and action, but in *Old Man,* since there's little of either,
the author has to spell it out. Sometimes he reports the
fisherman's improbable musings: "He is a great fish and
I must convince him, he thought. . . . Thank God, they
are not as intelligent as we who kill them, although they
are more noble and more able." Sometimes the author tips
us off: "He was too simple to wonder when he had attained
humility. But he knew he had attained it." (A humble
man who knows he has attained humility seems to me a
contradiction in terms.) This constant editorializing—an
elementary sin against which I used to warn my Creative
Writing class at Northwestern University—contrasts oddly
with the stripped, no-comment method that made the
young Hemingway famous. "I am a strange old man," the
hero tells The Boy. Prove it, old man, don't say it.

OUR TOWN is an extraordinarily skillful bit of craftsmanship. I think it is practically actor-proof, which is why
it is so often given by local dramatic societies. With that
literary sensibility which has enabled him to fabricate each
of his books in a different mode, a miracle of imitative versatility, Mr. Wilder has here made the final statement of
the midbrows' nostalgia for small-town life, as Norman
Rockwell has done it for the lowbrows in his *Post* covers.
Our Town's combination of quaintness, earthiness, humor,
pathos and sublimity (all mild) is precisely Rockwell's, and
the situations are curiously alike: puppy lovers at the soda
fountain, wives gossipping over the back fence, decent little
funerals under the pines, country editor, family doctor,
high-school baseball hero, all running in their well-worn
grooves. What gives the play class, raising it into Midcult,

are the imaginary props and sets and the interlocutory stage manager, devices Mr. Wilder got from the Chinese theater (he always gets them from somewhere). Brecht used similar devices to get his "alienation effect," to keep the audience from being hypnotized by the stage illusion—an original and hence shocking idea. But Mr. Wilder has nothing artistically subversive in mind; on the contrary, *Our Town* is as hypnotic, in the usual theatrical sense, as *East Lynne*. The stage manager is its heart, and he is such a nice, pipe-puffing, cracker-barrel philosopher—pungent yet broad-minded—that only a highbrow can resist his spell (or, of course, a lowbrow). He comments on the local cemetery:

This is certainly an important part of Grover's Corners. It's on a hilltop—a windy hilltop—lots of sky, lots of clouds— often lots of sun and moon and stars. . . . Yes, beautiful spot up here. Mountain laurel and li-lacks. . . . Over there are the old stones—1670, 1680. Strong-minded people that come a long way to be independent. Summer people walk around there laughing at the funny words on the tombstones. It don't do any harm. . . . Over there are some Civil War veterans. Iron flags on their graves. New Hampshire boys . . . had a notion that the Union ought to be kept together, though they'd never seen more than fifty miles of it. All they knew was the name, folks—the United States of America. And they went and died about it. . . . Yes, an awful lot of sorrow has sort of quieted down up here.

Guess there just hasn't been anybody around for years as plumb mellow nor as straight-thinking neither, as Mr. Wilder's stage manager. Nope. 'Cept mebbe for Eddie Guest out Detroit way.

J.B. resembles *Our Town* in its staging—no sets, symbolic action accompanied by commentary—but in little else. Its language is high-falutin' where the other's is home-spun, the comment is delivered by no village sage but by God and Satan in person, and its theme is nothing less than the relationship of man to God. It is Profound and Soul-Searching, it deals with the Agony of Modern Man, and it has been widely discussed, often by the author, in the Midcult magazines.* Mr. MacLeish mixes advanced staging with advanced poetry ("Death is a bone that stammers.") with family stuff ("J.B., forking wishbone on Rebecca's plate: 'That's my girl!' ") with tough stuff ("Four kids in a car. They're dead. / Two were yours.") with melodrama ("No! Don't touch me!") with a Message of the grandest inconclusiveness. The question of God and man is chivvied about for two hours, no decision, and is then dropped in the last scene and a new toy is offered the audience, one they are familiar with from other Broadway plays, namely Love:

> Blow on the coal of the heart.
> The candles in the churches are out.
> The lights have gone out in the sky.
> Blow on the coal of the heart
> And we'll see by and by. . . .

Robert Brustein in *The New Republic* and Gore Vidal in *Partisan Review* have lately had some good things to say about the tendency of our playwrights to bring in love as a *deus ex machina* to magically resolve the problems raised by the preceding two hours of conspicuously loveless dramaturgy, so I merely note the fact here. The Boylston Pro-

---

* The Midcult mind aspires toward Universality above all. A good example was that "Family of Man" show of photographs Edward Steichen put on several years ago at the Museum of Modern Art to great applause. (The following summer it was the hit of the American exhibition in Moscow, showing that a touch of Midcult makes the whole world kin.) The title was typical—actually, it should have been called Photorama. There were many excellent photographs, but they were arranged under the most pretentious and idiotic titles—each section had a wall caption from Whitman, Emerson, Carl Sandburg or some other sage—and the whole effect was of a specially pompous issue of *Life* ("*Life* on Life"). The editorializing was insistent—the Midcult audience always wants to be Told—and the photographs were marshaled to demonstrate that although there are real Problems (death, for instance), it's a pretty good old world after all.

fessor of Rhetoric at Harvard made many mistakes in *J.B.*, but one was fatal—intermingling with his own versification some actual passages from the Book of Job. It is true that Elia Kazan, who directed the play with appropriate vulgarity, reduced the effects of these passages considerably by having them delivered over a loudspeaker in an orotund voice reminiscent of the fruitiest manner of Westbrook Van Voorhees on the March of Time. Even so, the contrast was painful between the somber and passionate elevation of the Book of Job and Mr. MacLeish's forcible-feeble style. It's really too much to go from:

> *Hast thou given the horse strength?*
> *Hast thou clothed his neck with thunder!*
> *He saith among the trumpets, Ha, Ha!*

to:

> *Job won't take it! Job won't touch it!*
> *Job will fling it in God's face*
> *With half his guts to make it spatter!*

The clever author of *Our Town* would never have made such a gaffe.

FINALLY, Mr. Benét's 377-page orgy of Americana, much admired in its day and still widely used in the schools as combining History and Literature. The opening Invocation strikes at once the right note, patriotic yet sophisticated:

> *American muse, whose strong and diverse heart*
> *So many men have tried to understand*
> *But only made it smaller with their art . . .*
> *And I have seen and heard you in the dry*
> *Close-huddled furnace of the city street*
> *Where the parched moon was planted in the sky*
> *And the limp air hung dead against the heat.*

Eliot echoes in the last four lines as Homer does in the section on Pickett's charge:

> *So they came on in strength, light-footed, stepping like*
> *   deer,*
> *So they died or were taken. So the iron entered their flesh*

Even Kipling's ballad manner:

> *Thirteen sisters beside the sea*
> *Builded a house called Liberty*
> *And locked the doors with a stately key.*
> *None should enter it but the free.*
> *(Have a care, my son.)*

Nor are humbler poetic models spurned:

> *She was the white heart of the birch . . .*
> *Her sharp clear breasts*
> *Were two young victories in the hollow darkness*
> *And when she stretched her hands above her head*
> *And let the spun fleece ripple to her loins,*
> *Her body glowed like deep springs under the sun.*

Mr. Benét is a master of the built-in reaction; it is impossible not to identify the emotion he wants to arouse. Sometimes solemn, sometimes gay, always straining to put it across, like a night-club violinist. Play, gypsy, play! One is never puzzled by the unexpected. The Wingates are Southern aristocrats and they are proud and generous and they live in a big white house with pillars. Abe Lincoln is gaunt, sad, kindly and "tough as a hickory rail." John Brown is strong, simple, fanatical—and "he knew how to die." Robert E. Lee does present a problem since no national cliché has been evolved for him. Mr. Benét begins cautiously: "He was a man, and as a man he knew / Love, separation, sorrow, joy and death." Safe enough. But he still hasn't found his footing by the end: "He wanted something. That must be enough. / Now he rides Traveller back into the west." A puzzling figure.

The final judgment on the United States is ambiguous: "the monster and the sleeping queen." For Mr. Benét on the one hand doesn't want to sell America short but on the other he doesn't want to make a fool of himself—the Midcult writer is always worried about those superior, sneering intellectuals, however he pretends to despise them. The ambivalence becomes a little frantic in the closing lines: "So when the crowd gives tongue / And prophets old and young / Bawl out their strange despair / Or fall in worship there, / Let them applaud the image or condemn, / But keep your distance and your soul from them. . . . / If you at last must have a word to say, / Say neither, in their way, / 'It is a deadly magic and accursed' / Nor 'It is blest' but only 'It is here.' " The American fear of ideas (bawling prophets) and in fact of consciousness (If you *must* have a word to say) has seldom been more naïvely expressed. Or the American device for evading these terrors: Let's stick to the *facts;* or, Say only "It is here." For ideas might lead to conclusions.

XII

The Enemy is clear. J.B.'s three comforters are men of ideas—Freudian, Marxist, theological—and each is presented as a repulsive bigot. (In the 'thirties, Mr. MacLeish would have given the Marxist better lines.) Mr. Wilder does it more suavely:

Belligerent man at back of auditorium: Is there no one in town aware of social injustice and industrial inequality?

Mr. Webb (editor of the Grover's Corners Sentinel): Oh yes, everybody is—somethin' terrible. Seems like they spend most of their time talking about who's rich and who's poor.

Belligerent man: Then why don't they do something about it?

Mr. Webb: Well, I dunno. I guess we're all hunting like everybody else for a way the diligent and sensible can rise to the top and the lazy and quarrelsome can sink to the bottom. But it ain't easy to find. . . . Are there any other questions?

Lady in a box: Oh, Mr. Webb? Mr. Webb, is there any culture or love of beauty in Grover's Corners?

Mr. Webb: Well, ma'am, there ain't much—not in the sense you mean. . . . But maybe this is the place to tell you that we've got a lot of pleasures of a kind here: we like the sun comin' up over the mountain in the morning, and we all notice a good deal about the birds. [etc.] But those other things, you're right, ma'am, there ain't much. *Robinson Crusoe* and the Bible; and Handel's *Largo,* we all know that; and Whistler's *Mother*—those are just about as far as we go.

And this is just about as far as the play goes. Those who question the values of Grover's Corners, New Hampshire, 1901, are presented as grotesques while Editor Webb is presented as the norm. This might be justified as historical realism—although small-town editors fifty years ago were often crusaders and idealists—but of course Mr. Wilder is not interested in the actual 1901 Grover's Corners. "*Our Town* is not offered as a picture of life in a New Hampshire Village," he wrote in the preface to the 1957 edition, "or as a speculation about the conditions of life after death (that element I merely took from Dante's *Purgatory*). [The "merely" is a master touch.—D. M.] It is an attempt to find a value above all price for the smallest events in our daily life." This is a half truth, which means it is mostly false. Not that Mr. Wilder is in any way insincere. Had he been, he could no more have written a Midcult masterpiece like *Our Town* than Norman Rockwell could have painted all those *Post* covers. But if one compares with *Our Town* a similar attempt to find a value "for the smallest events in our everyday lives," namely Sherwood Anderson's *Winesburg, Ohio,* one sees the difference between a work of art and a sincere bit of *Kitsch*. What Mr. Wilder is really doing is nothing either so personal or so universal as he thinks it is. He is constructing a social myth, a picture of a golden age that is a paradigm for today. He has the best of both tenses—the past is veiled by the nostalgic feelings of the present, while the present is softened by being conveyed in terms of a safely remote past. But what a myth and what a golden age! Here one does get a little impatient with the talented Mr. Wilder.

The stage manager is its demiurge. He is the perfect American pragmatist, folksy and relaxed because that's jest the way things are and if anybuddy hankers to change 'em that's their right only (pause, business of drawing reflectively on pipe) chances are 't won't make a sight of difference (pipe business again) things don't change much in Grover's Corners. There is no issue too trivial for him not to take a stand on. "That's the end of the first act, friends," he tells the audience. "You can go smoke now"—adding with a touch of genius, "those that smoke." Don't do any harm, really, one way or t'other.

XIII

The special threat of Midcult is that it exploits the discoveries of the avant-garde. This is something new. Midcult's historical predecessor, Academicism, resembled it in being *Kitsch* for the elite, outwardly High Culture but really as much a manufactured article as the cheaper cultural goods produced for the masses. The difference is that Academicism was intransigently opposed to the avant-garde. It included painters like Bouguereau, Alma-Tadema, and Rosa Bonheur; critics like Edmund Gosse and Edmund Clarence Stedman; composers like Sir Edward Elgar; poets like Alfred Austin and Stephen Phillips; writers like Rostand, Stevenson, Cabell, and Joseph Hergesheimer.* Academicism in its own dreary way was at least resisting Masscult. It had standards, the old ones, and it educated

* A typical Academic victory over the avant-garde was that by the "Beaux Arts" school of architecture, led by McKim, Mead & White, over the Chicago school, led by Louis Sullivan and including Frank Lloyd Wright, at the turn of the century. A stroll down Park Avenue illustrates the three styles. Academic: The Italian loggia of the Racquet & Tennis Club, the Corinthian extravagances of Whitney Warren's Grand Central Building. Avant-garde: the Seagram Building, by Mies van der Rohe and Philip Johnson, and the Lever Building, by Skidmore, Owings & Merrill. Midcult: the glass boxes—imitating as cheaply as possible the Lever and Seagram buildings—that are going up as fast as the old Academic-Renaissance apartment houses can be pulled down. One can hardly regret the destruction of the latter on either aesthetic or antiquarian grounds, but they did have a mild kind of "character" which their Midcult successors lack.

the *nouveaux riches,* some of whom became so well educated that they graduated to an appreciation of the avant-garde, realizing that it was carrying on the spirit of the tradition which the Academics were killing. It is possible to see Academicism as the growing pains of High Culture, the restrictive chrysalis from which something new might emerge. That it was always destroyed after a few decades carries out the simile—who looks at Alma-Tadema today, who reads Hergesheimer?

Midcult is a more dangerous opponent of High Culture because it incorporates so much of the avant-garde. The four works noticed above were more advanced and sophisticated, for their time, than were the novels of John Galsworthy. They are, so to speak, the products of lapsed avant-gardists who know how to use the modern idiom in the service of the banal. Their authors were all expatriates in the 'twenties—even Mr. Benét, who dates his Americanesque epic "Neuilly-sur-Seine, 1928." That they are not conscious of any shifting of gears, that they still think of themselves as avant-gardists is just what makes their later works so attractive in a Midcult sense. "Toward the end of the 'twenties I began to lose pleasure in going to the theater," Mr. Wilder begins the preface to the 1957 edition of *Three Plays.* He explains that, while Joyce, Proust and Mann still compelled his belief, the theater didn't, and he continues: "I began to feel that the theater was not only inadequate, it was evasive; it did not wish to draw on its deeper potentialities. . . . It aimed to be *soothing.* The tragic had no heat; the comic had no bite; the social criticism failed to indict us with responsibility. I began to search for the point where the theater had run off the track, where it had . . . become a minor art and an inconsequential diversion." That point, he found, was "the box-set stage," with its realistic sets and props and its proscenium dividing the actors from the audience. He fixed that, all right, but the plays he mounted on his advanced stage were evasive, soothing, without tragic heat or comic bite and spectacularly without social criticism. *The Skin of Our Teeth,* for instance, is as vast in theme as *Our Town* is modest, dealing with the whole history of the human race, but its spirit and its dialogue are equally folksy, and its point, hammered home by the maid, Sabina, is identical: life goes on and, to lapse into the idiom of Sabina's opposite number in *Our Town,* there ain't a thing you can do about it. "This is where you came in," she says at the final curtain. "We have to go on for ages and ages yet. You go home. The end of this play isn't written yet. Mr. and Mrs. Antrobus! Their heads are full of plans and they're as confident as the first day they began." A soft impeachment —but Midcult specializes in soft impeachments. Its cakes are forever eaten, forever intact.

The Skin of Our Teeth was first produced in 1942, at the low point of the war; its message—the adaptability and tenacity of the human race through the most catastrophic events—was a welcome one and was well received. "I think it mostly comes alive under conditions of crisis," writes the author. "It has often been charged with being a bookish fantasia about history, full of rather bloodless schoolmasterish jokes. But to have seen it in Germany soon after the war, in the shattered churches and beerhalls that were serving as theaters, with audiences whose price of admission meant the loss of a meal . . . it was an experience that was not so cool. I am very proud that this year [1957] it has received a first and overwhelming reception in Warsaw. The play is deeply indebted to James Joyce's *Finnegans Wake.*" Personally, its bookish quality is one of the things I like about the play, and its jokes are often good; in fact, as entertainment *The Skin of Our Teeth* is excellent, full of charm and ingenuity; its only defect is that whenever it tries to be serious, which is quite often, it is pretentious and embarrassing. I quite believe the author's statement about its reception in postwar Germany—he enjoys a much greater reputation abroad than here—and I agree that the audiences responded to it because it seemed to speak to them of the historical cataclysm they had just been through. I find this fact, while not unexpected, depressing. The bow to *Finnegans Wake* is a graceful retrieve of a foul ball batted up in the *Saturday Review* fifteen years earlier by Messrs. Campbell and Robinson, the authors of *A Skeleton Key to Finnegans Wake*. They hinted at plagiarism, but I think one should rather admire the author's ability to transmute into Midcult such an impenetrably avant-garde work. There seems to be no limit to this kind of alchemy in reverse, given a certain amount of brass.

XIV

Since 1900 American culture has moved, culturally, in a direction that on the whole appears to be up. Ella Wheeler Wilcox yields to Stephen Vincent Benét. Maxfield Parrish's *Day Dreams* is replaced on the living-room wall by Van Gogh's *Sunflowers,* or even a Picasso print. Billy Sunday's Bible-shouting acrobatics are toned down to Billy Graham's more civilized approach, though with what gain to religious feeling has yet to be seen. In literary criticism, the artless enthusiasm of a William Lyon Phelps has modulated into the more restrained yea-saying of a Clifton Fadiman or a Granville Hicks. The late Arthur Brisbane used to speculate in short, punchy paragraphs separated by asterisks (they have been compared to the pauses a barroom philosopher makes to spit reflectively into the sawdust) on such topics as whether a gorilla could beat up a heavyweight champion in fair fight; but he would hardly go over as a columnist today, not even in that Hearst press whose circulation he swelled fifty years ago. He has been superseded by types like Dr. Max Lerner of the New York *Post,* who can bring Freudian theory to bear on the sex life of Elizabeth Taylor and Eddie Fisher. Dr. Lerner was once managing editor of the Encyclopaedia of Social Sciences; more recently he compiled a Midcult classic titled *America as a Civilization* in which he amassed 1,036 pages of data and interpretations without offending any religious, racial, political or social group. It is a solemn thought what he would do with Brisbane's man v. gorilla problem; as I recall, Brisbane finally concluded the gorilla would win; Dr. Lerner would probably take a more rounded viewpoint; his humanistic frame of reference would incline him to favor the heavyweight, but he would be careful to explain that no intrinsic inferiority was involved; just a matter of social environment. Gorillas are people too.

A tepid ooze of Midcult is spreading everywhere. Psychoanalysis is expounded sympathetically and superficially in popular magazines. Institutions like the Museum of Modern Art and the American Civil Liberties Union, once avant-garde and tiny, are now flourishing and respectable; but something seems to have been mislaid in the process, perhaps their *raison d'être*. Hollywood movies aren't as terrible as they once were, but they aren't as good either; the general level of taste and craftsmanship has risen but there are no more great exceptions like Griffith, von Stroheim, Chaplin, Keaton; Orson Welles was the last, and *Citizen Kane* is twenty years old. An enterprising journalist, Vance Packard, has manufactured two best sellers by summarizing the more sensational findings of the academic sociologists, garnishing the results with solemn moralizings, and serving it up under catchy titles: *The Hidden Persuaders, The Status Seekers*. Bauhaus modernism has seeped down, in a vulgarized form, into the design of our vacuum cleaners, pop-up toasters, supermarkets and cafeterias.

The question, of course, is whether all this is merely growing pains—or, in more formal language, an expression of social mobility. Don't rising social classes always go through a *nouveau riche* phase in which they imitate the forms of culture without understanding its essence? And won't these classes in time be assimilated into High Culture? It is true that this has usually happened in the past. But I think there is a difference now. Before the last century, the standards were generally agreed on and the rising new classes tried to conform to them. By now, however, because of the disintegrative effects of Masscult I described in the first part of this essay, the standards are by no means generally accepted. The danger is that the values of Midcult, instead of being transitional—"the price of progress" —may now themselves become a debased, permanent standard.

I see no reason Midcult may not be stabilized as the norm of our culture. Why struggle with real poetry when the Boylston Professor of Rhetoric can give you its effects in capsule form—works twice as fast and has a "Blow on the coal of the heart" ending? Why read the sociologists when Mr. Packard gives you their gist painlessly?

XV

This whole line of argument may be objected to as undemocratic. But such an objection is beside the point. As T. S. Eliot writes in *Notes Toward the Definition of Culture:*

Here are what I believe to be essential conditions for the growth and for the survival of culture. If they conflict with any passionate faith of the reader—if, for instance, he finds it shocking that culture and equalitarianism should conflict, if it seems monstrous to him that anyone should have "advantages of birth"—I do not ask him to change his faith. I merely ask him to stop paying lip-service to culture. If the reader says: "The state of affairs which I wish to bring about is *right* (or is *just*, or is *inevitable*); and if this must lead to further deterioration of culture, we must accept that deterioration"—then I can have no quarrel with him. I might even, in some circumstances, feel obliged to support him. The effect of such a wave of honesty would be that the word *culture* would cease to be absurd.

That the word now *is* absurd—priggish, unctuous, worn slick with abuse—shows how mass-ified we have become. The great cultures of the past have all been elite affairs, centering in small upper-class communities which had certain standards in common and which both encouraged creativity by (informed) enthusiasm and disciplined it by (informed) criticism.

The old avant-garde of 1870-1930, from Rimbaud to Picasso, demonstrated this with special clarity because it was based not on wealth or birth but on common tastes. "Common" didn't mean uniform—there were the liveliest, most painful clashes—but rather a shared respect for certain standards and an agreement that living art often runs counter to generally accepted ideas. The attitude of the old avant-garde, in short, was a peculiar mixture of conservatism and revolutionism that had nothing in common with the tepid agreeableness of Masscult. It was an elite community, a rather snobbish one, but anyone could join who cared enough about such odd things. Its significance was that it simply refused to compete in the established cultural marketplaces. It made a desperate effort to fence off some area within which the serious artist could still function, to erect again the barriers between the *cognoscenti* and the *ignoscenti* that had been breached by the rise of Masscult. The attempt was against the whole movement of history; and our cultural sociologists, had they been anachronistically consulted by Yeats or Stravinsky, could have proved to them with irrefutable tables and research studies that it could not possibly come to anything. For it was, sociologically speaking, absurd. Nevertheless, the attempt did in fact succeed, perhaps because artists, writers and musicians are not very good at statistics—and to it we owe most of the major creations of the last seventy years.

The old avant-garde has passed and left no successors. We continue to live off its capital but the community has broken up and the standards are no longer respected. The crisis in America is especially severe. Our creators are too isolated or too integrated. Most of them merge gracefully into Midcult, feeling they must be part of "the life of our time," whatever that means (I should think it would be ambitious enough to try to be part of one's own life), and fearful of being accused of snobbishness, cliqueism, negativism or, worst of all, practicing "art for art's sake" (though for what better sake?). Some revolt, but their work tends toward eccentricity since it lacks contact with the past and doesn't get support from a broad enough intelligentsia in the present. The two currently most prominent groups, the "action painters" and the beatnik academy of letters, differ from the old avant-garde in two interesting ways. They are cut off from tradition: the works of Joyce and Picasso, for instance, show an extraordinary knowledge of (and feeling for) the achievements of the past, while those of the beats and the actionists, for instance, do not. And they have had too much publicity too soon; the more they try to shock the Midcult's audience, the more they are written up in the Lucepapers; they are "different," that potent advertising word whose charm reveals how monotonous the landscape of Midcult has become.

The beatnik's pad is the modern equivalent of the poet's garret in every way except the creation of poetry. Our well-oiled machinery of cultural exploitation provides those who are Different with lecture dates, interviews, fellowships, write-ups, and fans of both sexes (the word's derivation from "fanatics" is clearer in these circles than among the more restrained enthusiasts of baseball, possibly because the latter have a technical knowledge rarely found among the former). The machinery tempts them to extremes since the more fantastic their efforts, the more delighted are their Midcult admirers. *"Pour épater les bourgeois"* was the defiant slogan of the nineteenth-century avant-gardists but now the bourgeoisie have developed a passion for being shocked. "If possible," Kerouac advises young authors, "write without 'consciousness' in a semi-trance," while a prominent advanced composer has written a piece for Twelve Radios that is performed by turning each to a different station, a sculptor has exhibited a dozen large beach pebbles dumped loosely on a board, a painter has displayed an all-black canvas only to be topped by another who showed simply—a canvas. At last, one hears the respectful murmurs, The Real Thing! The avant-garde of the heroic period generally drew the line between experiment and absurdity—Gertrude Stein was the chief exception. Efforts like the above were limited to the Dadaists, who used them to satirize the respectable Academic culture of their day. But the spoofs of Dada have now become the serious offerings of what one might call the lumpen-avant-garde.

XVI

At this point, a question may be asked, and in fact should be asked, about the remarkable cultural change that has taken place since 1945. Statistically, a very good case can be made out that in the last fifteen years or so there has been a more widely diffused interest in High Culture than ever before in our history. The cause is the same as that for the development of Midcult, namely, the accelerating increase in wealth, leisure and college education. All three have been growing at an extraordinary rate since 1945, especially the last. Although the population between eighteen and twenty-one has increased only 2 per cent in the last ten years, college enrollment has almost doubled. There are now as many postgraduate students as there were undergraduates when I went to college in the late 'twenties. This enormous college population—one must add in several hundred thousand teachers—is the most important fact about our cultural situation today. It is far bigger, absolutely and relatively, than that of any other country. Some of its potentialities are being realized, but the most important—the creation and support of a living culture on a high level—is as yet hardly embryonic and perhaps never will come to birth. For this would mean drawing that line between Masscult and High Culture which the rise of Midcult has blurred. And there is something damnably American about Midcult.

Let us begin with the positive statistics. Since 1945 we have seen the following. The rise of the "quality" paperback, retailing at 95¢ up and presenting, at a third or less the cost of the original hard-cover edition, everything from Greek myths to the best contemporary scholars, critics and creative writers. The sales of classical records, now about a fourth of total record sales and actually equal in dollar volume to Rock 'n Roll. The proliferation throughout the country of symphony orchestras (there are now 1,100, double the 1949 number, and every city of 50,000 has one), local art museums (2,500 as against 600 in 1930), and opera-producing groups (there are now 500, a seven-fold increase since 1940). The extraordinary success of Noah Greenberg's Pro Musica Antiqua group, which specializes in medieval and Early Renaissance music, is a case in point. The increase in "art" movie theaters, from 12 in 1945 to over 600 in 1962. The existence today of some 5,000 community theatres and the development, in the last ten years, of a vigorous off-Broadway theatre. Finally, the beginnings, only recently, of what might be called an off-Hollywood cinema—low-budget serious films made and financed outside the industry, such as *Shadows, Pull My Daisy, Jazz on a Summer's Day, The Savage Eye,* and the film version of *The Connection.*

This is all very well and indeed extremely well. For this is not Midcult but for the most part the unadulterated article.* The books are the complete texts, the music is

* Although the two are often confused, it is one thing to bring High Culture to a wider audience without change; and another to "popularize" it by sales talk in the manner of Clifton Fadiman or Mortimer J. Adler, or by pastiches like *J.B.* and *John Brown's Body,* or by hoking it up as in

uncut and well performed, the art works the best going, the movies usually interesting (though there is an admixture of Brigitte Bardot, you gotta live), the off-Broadway plays usually serious and the community-theatre ones often so.

Nor is this all that can be said. It is probably no easier today to make a living in the marketplace by serious writing or painting or composing than it ever was, but since 1945 there have come into existence a whole new category of what the trade unionist calls "fringe benefits." Institutional support of the poet, writer, artist, composer now goes far beyond teaching jobs to (1) foundation grants, (2) prizes and awards by all kinds of arts-and-letters groups, (3) lecture fees (one wonders how some people ever get any work done at all), (4) luxury junkets to East-West, North-South, Up-Down cultural gatherings all over the world, (5) Fulbright and other fellowships, (6) fees for advising literary aspirants at what are misnamed "writers' conferences." As Wallace Markfield put it in the *New Leader* of March 18, 1957: "No other generation . . . has pursued the Good Job quite so wisely and so well. This is not to say that they have consigned themselves to the gas chambers of Madison Avenue or Luceland. Far from it: their desks are more likely to be littered with *Kenyon Review* than with *Printer's Ink*. To their lot fall the foundation plums, the berths with the better magazines and book-houses, the research sinecures. They are almost never unemployed; they are only between grants." Similarly, Greenwich Village bohemians now make a comfortable living selling leather sandals and silver jewelry to the tourists, just like the Indians in New Mexico. Nowadays everybody lives on the reservation.

Stokowski's lifelong struggle to assimilate Bach to Tchaikowsky or those Stratford, Connecticut, productions of Shakespeare, which surpass those of Stratford, England in showmanship as much as they fall short of them in style and intelligence.

So much for the positive side of our current boom in culture. The chief negative aspect is that so far our Renaissance, unlike the original one, has been passive, a matter of consuming rather than creating, a catching up on our reading on a continental scale. The quality paperbacks sell mostly the Big Names already established in hard covers. The records and the 1,100 orchestras play Mozart and Stravinsky rather than Elliott Carter. The art museums show mostly old masters or new masters like Matisse, with a Jackson Pollock if they are very daring. The new theatres present almost entirely old plays: off-Broadway has done well by Chekhov, Shaw, Ibsen, O'Neill, Brecht, Beckett, and Shakespeare, but except for some examples of the Theatre of the Absurd, it has had almost nothing of significance by hitherto-unknown playwrights. We have, in short, become skilled at consuming High Culture when it has been stamped PRIME QUALITY by the proper authorities, but we lack the kind of sophisticated audience that supported the achievements of the classic avant-garde, an audience that can appreciate and discriminate on its own.

For this more difficult enterprise, we shall need what we very well may not get for all our four million college population: a cultural community. The term is pompous but I can think of no more accurate one. It is strange how many brain-workers we have and how few intellectuals, how many specialists whose knowledge and interest are confined to their own "field" and how few generalists whose interests are broad and nonprofessional. A century ago Lord Melbourne, himself a strikingly nonspecialized and indeed rather ignorant intellectual, observed: "A man may be master of the ancient and modern languages and yet his manners shall not be in the least degree softened or harmonized. The elegance, grace and feeling which he is continually contemplating cannot mix with his thoughts or insinuate themselves into their expression—he remains as coarse, as rude and awkward, and often more so, than the illiterate and the ill-instructed." One of Melbourne's favorite quotations was Jaques's remark, in *As You Like It,* when the rustic clown quotes Ovid: "O knowledge ill-inhabited—worse than Jove in a thatched house!" One might also cite Ortega y Gasset's observation, apropos of "the barbarization of specialization": "Today, when there are more scientists than ever, there are fewer cultured men than, for example, in 1750." A comparison of Diderot's Encyclopaedia with the post-1920 American editions of the Britannica would be interesting—although, of course, Gasset's contention can never be proved (or disproved) if only because "a cultured man" is not a scientific category. Like all the important categories.

XVII

In England, cultural lines are still drawn with some clarity. The B.B.C., for instance, offers three distinct programs: the Light (Masscult), the Home (Midcult) and the tactfully named Third (High Culture). It is true that the daily papers are divided about like ours: three good ones (*Times, Guardian, Telegraph*) with relatively small circulations and many bad ones with big circulations. The popular papers are not only much bigger than ours—the *Mirror* and the *Express* have about five million each, twice the circulation of the New York *Daily News,* our biggest—but also much worse. One must go to London to see how trivial and mindless the popular press can become. But if the masses have their dailies, the classes have a type of periodical for which there is no American analogue, and I think the vulgarity of the mass press and the high quality of the class press are both the result of the sharper definition of cultural lines there.

This is a magazine-reading country. When one comes back from abroad, the two displays of American abundance that dazzle one are the supermarkets and the newsstands. There are no British equivalents of our Midcult magazines like the *Atlantic* and the *Saturday Review,* or of our mass magazines like *Life* and the *Saturday Evening Post* and *Look,* or of our betwixt-&-between magazines like *Esquire* and the *New Yorker* (which also encroach on the Little Magazine area). There are, however, several big-circulation women's magazines, I suppose because the women's magazine is such an ancient and essential form of journalism that even the English dig it.

The one kind of magazine we haven't had over here since the liberal weeklies stubbed their toes on the Moscow Trials is the serious, widely read weekly. The English have at least seven: the *Spectator,* the *New Statesman,* the *Economist,* the *Times Literary Supplement,* the *Listener,* the *Observer* and the *Sunday Times.* The first four have circulations between 40,000 and 90,000. The *Listener* has, I believe, over 200,000; it is published by the B.B.C. and is made up almost wholly of broadcast material—how long would it take to accumulate a similar issue from our own radio and television? Months? Years? The *Observer* and the *Sunday Times* (no connection with the daily *Times,* which doesn't come out on Sunday) are really Sunday magazines in a newspaper format; their special articles and their extensive review sections are on the level of the other weeklies; and they have circulations of over 700,000 and 1,000,000 respectively. (They are postwar phenomena, analogous to our boom in quality paperbacks.) These British weeklies have large enough circulations to be self-supporting and to pay their contributors a living wage. Their nearest parallels here, in quality, are our Little Magazines, which come out either quarterly or bimonthly, have small circulations (5,000 is par, 15,000 prodigious), run at a chronic deficit and pay contributors and editors meagerly.

What must be done here marginally, with help from "angels" either personal or institutional, can be done there as a normal part of journalism. Although a much smaller percentage of the English population goes to college, they have a larger and more cohesive cultural community than we do. The sale of a serious nonfiction book by a writer who is not a Name, for instance, is often larger there than here despite our three or four times larger population. Here a book tends to be either a best seller or nothing, as a writer is either a Success or a Failure; there is no middle ground because there is no intellectual class. This may also be the reason more titles are published there; in 1958 it was 16,700 there, 11,000 here; it is the difference between handicraft and mass production, between a number of articulated publics and one great amorphous mass market.

England still has something of a functioning class system, culturally speaking. The angry young men are angry about it. I can't think why. An American living in London is delighted by the wide interest in art and letters, the liveliness of the intellectual atmosphere, the sense he gets constantly from the press and from conversations of a general interest in what he is interested in. It is, of course, general only to perhaps 5 per cent of the population, but in America it isn't even this much general; it is something shared only with friends and professional acquaintances. But in London one meets stockbrokers who go to concerts, politicians who have read Proust.*

---

* Actually, I *can* think why the young men are angry. The Enemy looks very different from there than from here. From there, it is too little democracy; from here, too much. They see cultural lines as relics of a snobbish past, I see them as dikes against the corruption of Masscult and Midcult. They see standards as inhibiting. I see them as defining. They see tradition as deadening, I see it as nourishing. It may be that, as an American, I idealize the British situation. But I hope not as absurdly as they idealize ours. In 1959 I gave a talk on mass culture at a *Universities & Left Review* forum in London. I expected the audience, which was much younger than I, to object to my lack of enthusiasm for socialism, though it was distressing to find them still talking about capitalism and the working class in the simplistic terms I hadn't heard since I left the Trotskyists; the problems we thought about in the 'thirties seem to be just coming up now in England; the illusions we were forced to abandon seem still current there. But what I was not prepared for was the reaction to my attacks on our mass culture. These were resented in the name of democracy. Hollywood to me was an instance of the exploitation rather than the satisfying of popular tastes. But to some of those who took the floor after my talk,

The English amateur scholar—"just a hobby, really"—is a species little known over here. Most educated Englishmen seem to take an interest in cultural matters as a matter of course, and many of them have a personal, nonprofessional knowledge of one or two fields—a disinterested interest, so to speak—which is quite impressive. Our college graduates are not apt to "keep up" with such things unless they teach them. Their hobbies are less likely to be Jacobean madrigals than home workshops equipped with the latest in power tools and their equivalent of the British weekly is likely to be *Time* or *Newsweek*. In only one field do we match their amateur scholarship. The sports pages are our equivalent of the *Times Literary Supplement*; in each case, experts write for a sizable audience that is assumed to understand the fine points. Perhaps our closest approach to a living tradition is in sports. The recent centenaries of Poe and Melville passed without undue excitement in the press, but *Sports Illustrated* devoted four pages to the fiftieth anniversary of Fred ("Bonehead") Merkle's failure to touch second base in a World Series game.

XVIII

It is indicative of the disorganized quality of our intellectual life that, for all the remarkable increase in the consumption of High Culture since 1945, not one new intellectual weekly has been produced. There have been a number of new "little" magazines, such as *New World Writing*, the *Evergreen Review*, *Contact*, the *Second Coming*, the *Dial* and the *Noble Savage*—they should perhaps be called big-little magazines since they aspire to the broader circulation of the quality paperback—but, like the

---

Hollywood was a genuine expression of the masses. They seemed to think it snobbish of me to criticize our movies and television from a serious viewpoint. Since I had been criticizing Hollywood for some thirty years, and always with the good conscience one has when one is attacking from the Left, this proletarian defense of our peculiar institution left me rather dazed.

old ones, they are essentially anthologies. They print the best current fiction, poetry, essays and criticism—or at least what the editors think is the best—but, if only because they are quarterlies, they cannot form a center of consciousness as the English weeklies do, since this requires (1) at least monthly topical comment, and preferably weekly; and (2) a regular interchange between writers and editors and readers such as is provided in the correspondence columns of the English weeklies. (The extraordinary development of the latter is one more evidence of a cultural community; the most recondite topic may set off a spate of letters from clubs and manses, bars and offices that is finally dammed only by the editor's ritual *This correspondence must now cease.*) The nearest approach to a "center of consciousness" in our magazines is in the Midcult ones like *Harper's*, the *Atlantic*, the *Reporter* and the *Saturday Review*, and the trouble with these is that the editors consistently—one might almost say on principle—underestimate the intelligence of the readers.

A great abstract force governing our present journalism is a conceptualized picture of the reader. [Mary McCarthy wrote several years ago in a prospectus for a monthly of political, social and cultural comment which never materialized because we couldn't get enough backing.] The reader, in this view, is a person stupider than the editor whom the editor both fears and patronizes. He plays the same role the child plays in the American home and school, the role of an inferior being who must nevertheless be propitiated. *What our readers will take* is the watchword. . . . When an article today is adulterated, this is not done out of respect for the editor's prejudices (which might at least give us an individualistic and eccentric journalism) but in deference to the reader's averageness and supposed stupidity. The fear of giving offense to some hypothetical dolt and the fear of creating a misunderstanding have replaced the fear of advertisers' reprisals.

The new magazine's editors do not accept this picture of the reader; they make no distinction between the reader and themselves. And in fact they insist on this as a cardinal democratic premise; the only premise on which free communication between human beings can be carried on. They do not look upon *Critic* as a permanent philanthropic enterprise. They believe there are 100,000 people in a country of 150,000,000 who will buy it regularly, once they have been made aware of its existence.

As I say, the money was not raised and *Critic* did not appear. But I don't think Mary McCarthy's estimate of the possible circulation was unrealistic; a masochistic underestimation of the audience for good work in every field, even the movies, even television, is typical of the American cultural entrepreneur. Some good movies have made money, after all, and many bad ones, though concocted according to the most reliable formulae, have failed to. Nobody really knows and it seems to me more democratic, as Miss McCarthy observes, to assume that one's audience is on one's own level than that they are the "hypothetical dolts" which both the businessmen of Hollywood and the revolutionaries of the *Universities & Left Review* [now *New Left Review*] assume they are.

Recently a friend had a manuscript rejected by a prominent Midcult magazine. "It's full of speculative *aperçus*," wrote the editor, "but it's just not a 'journalistic' piece of the kind we need. What I mean is, it is *too* speculative. *I* find the speculations fascinating [they always do] but they simply go beyond the pragmatics of the problems, which are necessarily crucial to us." This attitude, of course, is neither new nor limited to this country. One recalls the report that Edward Garnett wrote in 1916 for the London firm of Duckworth, which was considering a manuscript by an obscure Irish writer:

[It] wants going through carefully from start to finish. There are many 'longueurs.' Passages which, though the publisher's reader may find them entertaining, will be tedious to the ordinary man among the reading public. That public will call the book, as it stands at present, realistic, unprepossessing, unattractive. We call it ably written. The picture is 'curious,' it arouses interest and attention. But the . . . point of view will be voted 'a little sordid.' . . . . Unless the author will use restraint and proportion, he will not gain readers.

The book was *A Portrait of the Artist as a Young Man,* Mr. Garnett was one of a celebrated English literary family, and the episode (see Richard Ellmann's *James Joyce,* 416-419) shows the limitations of my Anglophilia, if the point needs demonstrating. For the first edition of the *Portrait* was finally published by an American, B. W. Huebsch.

In some ways the closest parallel we have to the British weeklies is the *New Yorker,* which has always been edited with the assumption that the readers have the same tastes as the editors and so need not be in any way appeased or placated; the reader is the forgotten man around the *New Yorker,* whose editors insist on making their own mistakes, a formula that has worked for thirty years of successful publishing, perhaps because it has crystallized around the magazine a cultural community of its own. "The pragmatics of the problem" are not "crucial" to the *New Yorker,* a Midcult magazine but one with a difference. It, too, has its formula, monotonous and restrictive, but the formula reflects the tastes of the editors and not their fear of the readers. And, because it is more personally edited, there are more extra-formula happy accidents than one finds in its Midcult brethren.*

* This essay, in an abbreviated form, was originally written for the *Saturday Evening Post* as one of its "Adventures of the Mind" series. (The introduction of this series into the *Post* two years ago—it has included Randall Jarrell, C. P. Snow and Clement Greenberg—is an interesting symptom of the post-1945 renaissance. George Horace Lorimer never thought his magazine needed a highbrow look.) The last three sentences above about the *New Yorker,* which appear exactly as they did in the final version I submitted to the *Post,* were responsible for the article's rejection.

In the fall of 1958, the *Post* invited me to contribute an article to the series and since they offered $2,500 for 5,000 words and promised to let me say what I liked, I agreed. A year later—after a five-page summary had

XIX

What is to be done? Conservatives like Ortega y Gasset and T. S. Eliot argue that since "the revolt of the masses" has led to the horrors of totalitarianism and of California roadside architecture, the only hope is to rebuild the old class walls and bring the masses once more under aristocratic control. They think of the popular as synonomous with the cheap and vulgar. Marxian radicals and liberal sociologists, on the other hand, see the masses as intrinsically healthy but as the dupes and victims of cultural exploitation—something like Rousseau's "noble savage."

---

been agreed on—I sent in the piece. They had perhaps a dozen editorial objections, all but one of which I accepted as either trivial or justified. The one difficulty was their suggestion that the *New Yorker* was just another Midcult magazine and that I must therefore criticize it in the same terms as the others. Since I did not agree with this opinion—and had in fact evaluated the *New Yorker* quite differently, though not without criticism, in the November, 1956, *Encounter*—I resisted. As the correspondence developed, it became clear they thought I was "going easy" on the *New Yorker* because I worked for it, a not unreasonable assumption in a police court but one that I somehow resented. The sentences above were my final attempt to "place" the magazine. It was rejected and so was the article ("otherwise eminently acceptable" wrote the sub-editor I dealt with). I finally wrote to Mr. Ben Hibbs, the editor-in-chief (how perfect a name, one of Norman Rockwell's covers come to life!) complaining that I had been promised a free hand as to opinion and that the *Post* had reneged. He was not sympathetic. "We are dealing here with facts, not opinion," he replied, adding that unless I came clean on the *New Yorker*, the piece would be "open to suspicion of insincerity." Mr. Hibbs' notion of *fact* and *opinion* seemed to me mistaken and I wrote back citing my dictionary's definition of *fact* ("a truth known by actual experience or observation") and *opinion* ("a judgment or estimate of a person or thing with respect to character, merit, etc."). He replied suggesting the correspondence be closed. I replied agreeing but could not resist a few Parthian shots, namely: (1) in future the *Post* should employ some reliable detective agency—I suggested Pinkerton's—to make an advance assessment of the moral character of contributors to their Adventures of the Mind; (2) if I had accepted under pressure their opinion of the *New Yorker*, this should have shaken their confidence in the honesty of my other opinions; (3) the *Post* owed me $1,500—I had been foresighted enough to insist on $1,000 on delivery of the manuscript, although they seemed rather shocked at such commercialism—since they had gone back on their guarantee of freedom of expression. Like other Parthian shots, these may have been harassing to Pro-Consul Hibbs—he never replied—but, also as per history, the Romans won.

If only the masses were offered good stuff instead of *Kitsch*, how they would eat it up! How the level of Masscult would rise! Both these diagnoses seem to me fallacious because they assume that Masscult is (in the conservative view) or could be (in the liberal view) an expression of *people*, like Folk Art, whereas actually it is, as I tried to show earlier in this essay, an expression of *masses*, a very different thing.

The conservative proposal to save culture by restoring the old class lines has a more solid historical basis than the liberal-cum-Marxian hope for a new democratic, classless culture. Politically, however, it is without meaning in a world dominated by the two great mass nations, the USA and the USSR, and a world that is becoming more industrialized and mass-ified all the time. The only practical thing along those lines would be to revive the spirit of the old avant-garde, that is to re-create a cultural—as against a social, political or economic—elite as a countermovement to both Masscult and Midcult. It may be possible, in a more modest and limited sense than in the past—I shall return to this point later—but it will be especially difficult in this country where the blurring of class lines, the lack of a continuous tradition and the greater facilities for the manufacturing and distribution of *Kitsch*, whether Masscult or Midcult, all work in the other direction. Unless this country goes either fascist or communist, there will continue to be islands above the flood for those determined enough to reach them and live on them; as Faulkner has shown, a writer can use Hollywood instead of being used by it, if his purpose be firm enough. But islands are not continents.

The alternative proposal is to raise the level of our culture in general. Those who advocate this start off from the assumption that there has already been a great advance in the diffusion of culture in the last two centuries—Edward Shils is sure of this, Daniel Bell thinks it is probably the case—and that the main problem is how to carry this even further; they tend to regard such critics of Masscult as

Ernest van den Haag, Leo Lowenthal or myself as either disgruntled Left romantics or reactionary dreamers or both. Perhaps the most impressive—and certainly the longest—exposition of this point of view appears in Gilbert Seldes' *The Great Audience*. Mr. Seldes blames the present sad state of our Masscult on (1) the stupidity of the Lords of *Kitsch* (who underestimate the mental age of the public), (2) the arrogance of the intellectuals (who make the same mistake and so snobbishly refuse to try to raise the level of the mass media), and (3) the passivity of the public itself (which doesn't insist on better Masscult). This diagnosis seems to me superficial because it blames everything on subjective, moral factors: stupidity (the Lords of *Kitsch*), perversity (the intellectuals), or failure of will (the public). My own notion is that—as in the case of the "responsibility" of the German (or Russian) people for the horrors of Nazism (or of Soviet Communism)—it is unjust and unrealistic to blame large social groups for such catastrophes. Burke was right when he said you cannot indict a people. Individuals are caught up in the workings of a mechanism that forces them into its own pattern; only heroes can resist, and while one can hope that everybody will be a hero, one cannot demand it.

I see Masscult—and its recent offspring, Midcult—as a reciprocating engine, and who is to say, once it has been set in motion, whether the stroke or the counterstroke is responsible for its continued action? The Lords of *Kitsch* sell culture to the masses. It is a debased, trivial culture that avoids both the deep realities (sex, death, failure, tragedy) and also the simple, spontaneous pleasures, since the realities would be too real and the pleasures too lively to induce what Mr. Seldes calls "the mood of consent": a narcotized acceptance of Masscult-Midcult and of the commodities it sells as a substitute for the unsettling and unpredictable (hence unsalable) joy, tragedy, wit, change, originality and beauty of real life. The masses—and don't let's forget that this term includes the well-educated fans of *The Old Man and the Sea, Our Town, J.B.,* and *John Brown's Body*—who have been debauched by several generations of this sort of thing, in turn have come to demand such trivial and comfortable cultural products. Which came first, the chicken or the egg, the mass demand or its satisfaction (and further stimulation), is a question as academic as it is unanswerable. The engine is reciprocating and shows no signs of running down.

xx

"Our fundamental want today in the United States," Walt Whitman wrote in 1871, "is of a class and the clear idea of a class, of native authors, literatures, far different, far higher in grade than any yet known, sacerdotal, modern, fit to cope with our occasions, lands, permeating the whole mass of American mentality, taste, belief, breathing into it a new life, giving it decision, affecting politics far more than the popular superficial suffrage. . . . For know you not, dear, earnest reader, that the people of our land may all read and write, and may all possess the right to vote—and yet the main things may be entirely lacking? . . . The priest departs, the divine literatus comes."

The divine literatus is behind schedule. Masscult and Midcult have so pervaded the land that Whitman's hope for a democratic culture shaped by a sacerdotal class at once so sublime and so popular that they can swing elections— that this noble vision now seems absurd. But a more modest aspiration is still open, one adumbrated by Whitman's idea of a new cultural class and his warning that "the main things may be entirely lacking" even though everybody knows how to read, write and vote. This is to recognize that two cultures have developed in this country and that it is to the national interest to keep them separate. The conservatives are right when they say there has never been a broadly democratic culture on a high level. This is not because the ruling class forcibly excluded the masses—this is Marxist melodrama—but quite simply because the great majority of people at any given time (including most of the ruling class for the matter) have never cared enough about such things to make them an important part of their lives. So let the masses have their Masscult, let the few who care about good writing, painting, music, architecture, philosophy, etc., have their High Culture, and don't fuzz up the distinction with Midcult.

Whitman would have rejected this proposal as undemocratic, which it is. But his own career is a case in point: he tried to be a popular bard but the masses were not interested, and his first recognition, excepting Emerson's lonely voice, came from the English pre-Raphaelites, a decadent and precious group if ever there was one. If we would create a literature "fit to cope with our occasions," the only public the writer or artist or composer or philosopher or critic or architect should consider must be that of his peers. The informed, interested minority—what Stendhal called "We Happy Few." Let the majority eavesdrop if they like, but their tastes should be firmly ignored.

There is a compromise between the conservative and liberal proposals which I think is worth considering—neither an attempt to re-create the old avant-garde nor one to raise the general level of Masscult and Midcult. It is based on the recent discovery—since 1945—that there is not One Big Audience but rather a number of smaller, more specialized audiences that may still be commercially profitable. (I take it for granted that the less differentiated the audience, the less chance there is of something original and lively creeping in, since the principle of the lowest common denominator applies.) This discovery has in fact resulted in the sale of "quality" paperbacks and recordings and the growth of 'art" cinema houses, off-Broadway theatres, concert orchestras and art museums and galleries. The mass audience is divisible, we have discovered—and the more it is divided, the better. Even television, the most senseless and routinized expression of Masscult (except for the movie newsreels), might be improved by this approach. One possibility is pay-TV, whose modest concept is that only those who subscribe could get the program, like a magazine; but, also like a magazine, the editors would decide what goes in, not the advertisers; a small gain but a real one. The networks oppose this on philanthropic grounds—they don't see why the customer should pay for what he now gets free. But perhaps one would rather pay for bread than get stones for nothing.

As long as our society is "open" in Karl Popper's sense —that is unless or until it is closed by a mass revolution stimulated by the illusion of some "total solution" such as Russian-type Communism or Hitler-type Fascism, the name doesn't really matter—there will always be happy accidents because of the stubbornness of some isolated creator. But if we are to have more than this, it will be because our new public for High Culture becomes conscious of itself and begins to show some *esprit de corps,* insisting on higher standards and setting itself off—joyously, implacably—from most of its fellow citizens, not only from the Masscult depths but also from the agreeable ooze of the Midcult swamp.

IN "The Present Age," Kierkegaard writes as follows:

In order that everything should be reduced to the same level it is first of all necessary to procure a phantom, a monstrous abstraction, an all-embracing something which is nothing, a mirage—and that phantom is the public. . . .

The public is a concept which could not have occurred in antiquity because the people *en masse in corpore* took part in any situation which arose . . . and moreover the individual was personally present and had to submit at once to applause or disapproval for his decision. Only when the sense of association in society is no longer strong enough to give life to concrete realities is the Press able to create that abstraction, "the pubic," consisting of unreal individuals who never are and never can be united in an actual situation or organization—and yet are held together as a whole.

The public is a host, more numerous than all the peoples together, but it is a body which can never be reviewed; it cannot even be represented because it is an abstraction. Nevertheless, when the age is reflective [i.e., the individual sees himself only as he is reflected in a collective body] and passionless and destroys everything concrete, the public becomes everything and is supposed to include everything. And . . . the individual is thrown back upon himself. . . .

A public is neither a nation nor a generation nor a community nor a society nor these particular men, for all these are only what they are through the concrete. No single person who belongs to the public makes a real commitment; for some hours of the day, perhaps, he belongs to a real public— at moments when he is nothing else, since when he really is what he is, he does not form part of the public. Made up of such individuals, of individuals at the moment when they are nothing, a public is a kind of gigantic something, an abstract and deserted void which is everything and nothing. But on this basis, any one can arrogate to himself a public, and just as the Roman Church chimerically extended its frontiers by appointing bishops *in partibus infidelium,* so a public is something which every one can claim, and even a drunken sailor exhibiting a peep-show has dialectically the same right to a public as the greatest man. He has just as logical a right to put all those noughts *in front of* his single number.

This is the essence of what I have tried to say.

PART II

Heroes / Victims

Mark Twain

IN THE LAST THREE DECADES of his life, between 1880 and 1910, Mark Twain spent a lot of time writing (or, more usually dictating) a voluminous series of reminiscences that he called his autobiography. This has suffered the fate of another large edifice, the Colosseum—it has been used as a quarry for builders. In 1924, Albert Bigelow Paine, Twain's biographer, friend, and literary executor, hacked out two volumes from it. In 1940, the late Bernard DeVoto extracted from the unpublished remainder another volume, to which he gave the unfortunate title *Mark Twain in Eruption*. And in 1960, Charles Neider, a literary Jack-of-all-trades whose interests have ranged from Kafka to the diaries of Mrs. Robert Louis Stevenson, constructed still a third edifice, which he called *The Autobiography of Mark Twain*—the Paine volumes were called *Mark Twain's Autobiography*—and which, like its predecessors, was published by Harper. One's first reaction is: why? Four-fifths of the new book, according to Mr. Neider's introduction, have already appeared in the Paine and De-Voto volumes. If there is any need for a new edition, it is for a complete one, edited by a specialist in Mark Twain. A good deal of the manuscript is still unpublished, and such an edition would be useful at least to scholars. It would also be costly, however, and would certainly not sell as well as the present version, and publishing is a business.

Each of the three architects built in a different style. Paine followed the author's plan. Twain had the notion that he could assemble a book by free association, putting down whatever came into his head and printing the result in the order in which it was written: "The past and the present are constantly brought face to face, resulting in contrasts which newly fire up the interest all along like contact of flint with steel." He thought this would be not only livelier but more true-to-life than a more formal organization—or, rather, he thought he thought this; he was a notably self-indulgent writer, and he may have hoped that his vices might miraculously become virtues. The miracle didn't happen. The Paine volumes were simply a jumble, and it is not surprising that they fell flat with both public and critics. The most interesting feature is the index, which begins with "About a meeting in Carnegie Hall" and continues through such items as "Comment on a newspaper clipping," "Delight of Clemens's secretary in forceful language," and "Invitation from Augustin Daly" (a more pedestrian indexer might have put this under "D"). I imagine a maiden aunt of Mr. Paine's constructing it as a labor of love; she was a small-town librarian, myopic and gently insistent on doing things her own way, and I like to think she derived much quiet pleasure from putting "Little girl's letter about *Huckleberry Finn*" under "L."

Warned by his predecessor's fate, DeVoto arranged the manuscript according to subject, which worked out much better. Mr. Neider has thought up a third method. He has ordered the material according to the chronology of Twain's life, and he insists that the result is a narrative—in fact, an autobiography. It isn't. Nor is his criticism of DeVoto's arrangement justified. He writes, "His thematic order was an imposed one and could not accurately be called the tightest which can be given the Autobiography, the essence of whose internal order is time." If one grants there *is* any internal order to the manuscript, a concession I see no need to make, one would have to see it as Twain did, as the sequence of moments in which he was writing or dictating each item, and one would have to follow Paine's disastrous policy. Far from conceiving of the work as a narrative, Twain dipped up memories at random, saying as much as he felt like upon the occasion and then turning to something else.

"In my opinion," Mr. Neider begins his introduction, "Mark Twain's autobiography is a classic of American letters, to be ranked with the autobiographies of Benjamin Franklin and Henry Adams. I think that it will be regarded as such over the years. The final work of one of our country's most beloved authors, it is the product of one of those nineteenth-century giants whom we of this century are slow in replacing. It has the marks of greatness in it— style, scope, imagination, tragedy." Blurbs used to be written in the publisher's office, but now, as in television, the master of ceremonies modulates smoothly into the commercials.

Mark Twain's autobiography seems to me largely an embarrassment. Its style is relaxed to the point of garrulity, its scope is limited, its imagination goes no deeper than the top surface of the author's mind, and its few personal sections are pathetic rather than tragic. There are some good things, such as the chapter on Jim Gillis, the monologue about Grandfather's Old Ram, the chapter on American humorists, the corrosive portrait of Bret Harte (a kind of *ur*-beatnik), and the encounter between the Reverend Twichell and some innocently profane talkers at a village inn. But the rest is mild stuff. There are a great many long and trivial anecdotes—someone gets stung by wasps, someone overdoses himself against seasickness, Twain swears without realizing his wife is listening. There is a good deal of facetiously exaggerated rhetoric, which probably went down very well with Twain's lecture audiences: "He landed a stone on the side of my head which raised a bump there which felt like the Matterhorn." There are many pages on the stupidity, and worse, of people with whom

Twain had business relations that didn't turn out well. (It has been established by now that [a] Twain was a bad businessman, and [b] his accusations were largely unfounded.) And there is a vast amount of just plain after-dinner chat, which might have been entertaining when delivered by an accomplished talker like Twain but which as printed matter has a low voltage. It is significant that when DeVoto came to compile *The Portable Mark Twain*, he gave only fifteen of its 785 pages to the autobiography.

OUR national past is now very much in fashion. Not the past of our classical period, the early republic of Jefferson and Madison and Adams, and not the Gilded Age—to use a term coined by Mark Twain—of Grant and Rockefeller and McKinley. Either of these might be instructive, the first as a tradition, the second as a warning. But what is wanted is romance rather than instruction, a past to escape into, not a past to learn from. So the vogue is for the forty-niners, the Civil War, the frontier, the Wild West. The editors of *Life* have celebrated the Winning of the West in seven installments; some of the most popular television shows are Westerns, and a six-shooter is now as prosaic a utensil as an egg beater; all publishing is divided into three parts—fiction, nonfiction, and Civil War; Carl Sandburg, the good gray laureate of the hinterland, has intoned a Lincoln's Birthday address, full of piety and glucose, to a hushed session of Congress. Mr. Neider's edition of the Twain autobiography is conceived in this spirit. "It brings back the tone and flavor of an America which was young and optimistic," he writes in his introduction, "a home-spun, provincial America but an America with greatness in its heart. Thoreau's America may have contained many lives of quiet desperation. Mark Twain's decidedly did not." This is, of course, nonsense. One has only to read the grim material on Twain's boyhood town of Hannibal, Missouri, that scholars have turned up—indeed, Mr. Neider had only

to read some of the material in his own edition of the autobiography—to see how much desperation there was in
Mark Twain's America. Thoreau's Concord seems a placid,
cheerful place in comparison. But since we no longer feel
very young or optimistic or greathearted, we yearn for the
myth of the frontier.

Stagehands like Mr. Neider have long been at work on
the figure of Mark Twain, turning up the lights to get rid
of those frightening shadows—for without such adjust-
ments it is difficult not to see Twain's own life as one of
desperation, however unquiet. The strategy is to concentrate on the early Twain. Mr. Neider's edition is almost
half over before we have reached *The Innocents Abroad*
(1869). He reprints almost all the early material that
appears in the Paine and DeVoto editions, but he has no
space for any of the later comments on the Gilded Age—
the picture of Teddy Roosevelt ("Hard . . . coarse . . . the
worst president we have ever had"), the irreverent descriptions of Gould, Carnegie, and other plutocrats, the indignation at the butcheries of Filipino patriots by American
troops. A fourth of DeVoto's edition of the autobiography
is taken up with such material, and even the squeamish
Paine puts in a lot of it, including fourteen pages on a
massacre of Moro tribesmen—and tribeswomen—for
which President Roosevelt had congratulated General
Leonard Wood. But these earlier editions came out before
our national past was thoroughly mythologized; it was still
possible then to present Mark Twain not only as a picturesque old party but as a social critic. Writing in the
Soviet magazine *Literaturnaya Gazeta,* Y. Bereznitsky
charged that Mr. Neider's omission of such material betrayed a political bias. Mr. Neider replied that he had
merely omitted "dated, dull, trivial, and journalese sections" and that "for me, Mark Twain is essentially a great
fabulist and not a great maker of political utterances." For
once, I think the comrades have had the better of a literary

argument. Twain's attacks on the oligarchy were much less dated, dull, and trivial than a good deal of what Mr. Neider *has* included, and an autobiography that leaves out Twain's indignation at what was happening to America in the last two decades of his life does not give a true picture.

But the "fabulist" side of Twain is most certainly now the fashionable one, for reasons that Comrade Bereznitsky could analyze, I'm sure, far better than I could. In 1959, a young actor named Hal Holbrook got himself up into a remarkable facsimile of the picturesque old party—the program stated it took him three hours to apply the make-up—and for five months delivered Mark Twain's platform material to enthusiastic New York audiences. Granting all credit to the historical accuracy of Mr. Holbrook's imper-sonation, for which he studied phonograph records and even motion pictures of Twain, I was disturbed by its reception. It was a strange experience to sit in a house full of contemporary theatregoers who were roaring at wit-ticisms like "Heaven for climate, Hell for company" and arch confessions to such sins as smoking and profanity. It was the ghost of a ghost, a Williamsburgian reconstruction of the twinkling, drawling, cigar-puffing old sinner that even in 1895 was synthetic.

In fairness to Messrs. Holbrook and Neider it must be said that Twain himself, who, like all actors, was sensitive to the demands of his public, created the part. He stultified his best gifts by playing the provincial iconoclast. It was as if Lincoln had played Raymond Massey. There is a series of photographs in the Neider volume showing Twain lounging in a rocking chair, twiddling his eyebrows and cigar, and ruminating, in captions written in his own hand:

1. SHALL I learn to be good? . . . I will sit here and think it over.
2. There do seem to be so many diffi . . .
3. And yet if I should *really* try . . .
4. . . . and just put my whole *heart* into it . . .

5. But then I couldn't break the Sab . . .
6. . . . and there's so many other privileges that perhaps . . .
7. Oh, never mind, I reckon I'm good enough just as I am.

These were written in 1906, when Twain was seventy-one. But he still played Tom Sawyer, and the farthest reach of deviltry Twain could imagine—or, more accurately, his public image could imagine—was breaking the Sabbath. One of the reasons for Twain's enormous popularity in his lifetime and for his "availability" as a reassuring folk figure today is that he was, like Tom Sawyer, in form a bad boy but in content a good boy, tirelessly mocking a morality that was already, in 1890, decrepit—the morality of his small-town boyhood, before the Civil War—and so allowing his audience to feel broad-minded without disturbing any of their real prejudices. With beating of drums and rattle of musketry, he reduced fortresses that had long been abandoned.

IF this were all there was to Mark Twain, he would now be forgotten with Petroleum V. Nasby and Artemus Ward. There was, of course, a great deal more. He struck the pose his audience seemed to want, but it didn't satisfy him. The Mark Twain Problem has been copiously explored by two generations of critics; Arthur L. Scott's *Mark Twain: Selected Criticism* (Southern Methodist University Press, 1955) gives a fair sampling of the material, beginning in 1867, long before there *was* a Mark Twain Problem. The Problem is, essentially, the change that took place in the last twenty-five years of his life. Up to then, the line of development is straightforward enough: the boyhood in Hannibal, the young manhood as a Mississippi river pilot, the Western years, the leap into national fame with *Innocents Abroad,* the marriage to the respectable Olivia Langdon, the years of happy family life in respectable Hartford, and the production of most of his best work, culminating in *Huckleberry Finn,* in 1884. Then the complications begin. Twain kept on producing books, he became the beloved sage and humorist, the most eminent American author of his time. But the note of baffled despair sounds more and more even in his published work, while in his unpublished manuscripts it becomes dominant. The amount of this unpublished material is enormous; DeVoto estimates that in his last ten years Twain wrote fifteen thousand pages, almost all for uncompleted projects. He had lost his bearings as a craftsman, he had lost his faith in God and man, his mood was one of neurotic bitterness. It is true he had misfortunes—the failure of his publishing house, his own bankruptcy after spending a fortune on the unsuccessful Paige typesetting machine, the death of one daughter, the invalidism and death of his wife. But are these troubles enough to explain what happened?

A classic controversy arose between Van Wyck Brooks and Bernard DeVoto. It is important because it involves not only two theories about Twain but also two radically opposed interpretations of our culture. "There is no denying that for half a century the American writer as a type has gone down to defeat," Brooks wrote in 1921. He was referring to the desert between the Civil War and the First World War; he wrote at the beginning of the renaissance of the 'twenties, of which he was a herald. The year before, he had published *The Ordeal of Mark Twain*, presenting Twain as an artist *manqué*, a victim of the forces of Philistinism. The *Ordeal* is still by far the best study of Mark Twain. It is organized emotionally rather than intellectually; it uses much concrete data, but as a poet would—for color and mood. In some ways Brooks is much too serious; he insists that Twain's humor was merely an unnatural protective disguise, and he sometimes takes Twain's humorous self-denigration too literally, with disastrous results. But it is an eloquent, imaginative, thorough study, and it has the root of the matter in it—

that Twain's genius was perverted by the pressures of his time and place. Twelve years later, DeVoto, then the apostle of middlebrow heartiness and no-nonsense, reacted with *Mark Twain's America,* a ham-handed celebration of the myth of the frontier. Brooks had taken a dim view of Hannibal and the Wild West as milieus for a developing artist; DeVoto pictured them as just the right background, vital and full of beans, to produce an authentic American writer. Brooks saw Twain as frustrated; DeVoto saw him as fulfilled. They disagreed even on Twain's last, black decades, which Brooks felt confirmed his thesis and De-Voto felt were merely the result of Twain's personal disasters—"I cannot see in what is called his pessimism anything but the fruit of his experience."

The later history of the conflict is strange. DeVoto succeeded Paine as literary executor of the Mark Twain Estate. For the first time, he was able to go through the great mass of unpublished manuscripts; in 1942 he published *Mark Twain at Work,* an unsparing documentation of Twain's dark side. Some of the material seems close to madness, as, for that matter, does some of the published work of Twain's later years. There is, for example, a lengthy fantasia called "A Horse's Tale," which is a peculiar mixture of Kipling, *Black Beauty,* Laura Jean Libbey, and Krafft-Ebing. It makes uncomfortable reading, alternately sentimental and sadistic, tedious and grotesque. Twain thought well of it. "I did not tell the 'Horse's Tale,' " he writes in the autobiography. "The horse himself told it through me. . . . When a tale tells itself, there is no trouble about it . . . nothing to do but hold the pen and let the story talk through it." If it really was Twain's unconscious speaking, as he suggests, this bit of automatic writing is an alarming production. It may communicate to horses, since it was told by one, but it makes no contact with a human reader.

Although DeVoto never admitted it, and may never have

realized it, reading these manuscripts seems to have brought him around to Brooks's tragic view of Twain. The contrast between the bombastic swagger of *Mark Twain's America* and the sober mood of *Mark Twain at Work* is striking. On the other hand, Van Wyck Brooks, in the 'thirties and 'forties, changed from a critic into a nostalgic impressionist, as his five volumes of American literary history demonstrate. The antagonists neatly exchanged places, DeVoto becoming more precise and rigorous, Brooks becoming vague, euphoric, seeming to feel a personal need to be positive about the cultural past he had once seen largely in negative terms. Now Twain strikes him not as a crippled genius but as "an American legend," the authentic voice of "this old primitive Western world, its first pathfinder in letters, its historian and poet." Now the Gilded Age becomes solid gold. *Innocents Abroad* (of all books!) had "somehow struck the keynote of his epoch, the boisterous geniality and self-confidence of the triumphant nation, unified by the Civil War, aware of the resources it was rapidly exploiting, good-naturedly contemptuous of the Europe it had once revered. . . . In his large, loose easygoing way, he seemed to speak for the pioneer West. . . . Mark Twain was a symbol of the new America." Or of the new Van Wyck Brooks.

THE bulk of Mark Twain's work is no longer readable. No other major nineteenth-century author, not even Balzac, produced so much that was so markedly inferior to his best. One thinks of the coarse-grained journalese (*Innocents Abroad*), the all too fine respectablese (*Joan of Arc*), the painful burlesque (*A Connecticut Yankee* when it isn't moralistic melodrama), the simplistic philosophizing (*What Is Man?*), the grotesque extravaganzas ("The Stolen White Elephant," and half a dozen other stories collected in a Bantam paperback by the devoted Mr. Neider), and the extraordinary amount of just plain trivia. The miracle, and the puzzle, are that such a writer should have produced one great book and several books that are still fresh. For we are still left with *The Mysterious Stranger,* that oddly perfect late fruit of a tree that had seemed long past bearing, the first half of *Life on the Mississippi,* some excellent yarns in the vernacular, a little of *Pudd'nhead Wilson (pace* F. R. Leavis, who, it seems to me, reads it intellectually rather than aesthetically), more of *Tom Sawyer,* and almost all of *Huckleberry Finn.* A few miscellaneous items might be added—"Fenimore Cooper's Literary Offenses," some chapters from *Roughing It,* and several satirical pieces, like "The War Prayer" and "To the Person Sitting in Darkness." But, by and large, this is all that can still be read with pleasure.

Tom Sawyer is his "best-loved" book—for poor reasons, I think. Tom is the matrix from which such later stereotypes as Penrod, Andy Hardy, and Henry Aldrich were stamped—the kind of boy that adults like to imagine they once were and the kind of boy they like to deal with. He is swaggering, "full of mischief," but for all that he is basically "just a real boy" (alternatively, "all boy"), which is to say he is a Fifth Columnist in the juvenile world, his rebellion is phony, and when the chips are down he is amenable to adult control. Huck Finn has produced no stereotypes, partly because he is a real rebel, quite outside society, but chiefly because, while Tom is a sentimental abstraction, Huck is Huck.

Tom is the All-American Boy. He tries to avoid washing, he resists medicine, he plays hooky, he teases the cat, he patronizes the old (ole) swimming (swimmin') hole (hole), he squirms in church, he wriggles in school, he is ritualistically absurd in love, he is fertile in mischief. By page 2, Aunt Polly is saying, "I never did see the beat of that boy!" By page 3, "He's full of the Old Scratch!" The first chapters are fascinating, for here, as in the first glimpses of Sherlock Holmes in *A Study in Scarlet,* we can see a mass-culture hero taking form. The sureness with which Twain builds up the cliché is something to be admired (or deplored). One of Tom's most endearing (or irritating) qualities is his love of romantic mystification. He is a general, a Robin Hood, a pirate: "There comes a time in every rightly constructed boy's life when he has a raging desire to go somewhere and dig for hidden treasure. This desire came upon Tom one day. He sallied out. . . ." Tom can't even lose a tooth without adding to the cliché: "But all trials bring their compensations. As Tom wended to school after breakfast, he was the envy of every boy he met because the gap in his upper row of teeth enabled him to expectorate in a new and admirable way." There is a lot of "fine" writing in *Tom Sawyer*. Sometimes, as in "sallied out," "wended," and "expectorate," it is ironic; describing boyhood trivia in inflated language is, or was, a reliable comic device. More often, it is the kind of stylistic lapse one often finds in Whitman, another self-taught folk writer. The folk tradition had become feeble by the second half of the nineteenth century, and naïve geniuses were more open to corruption by the elegant rhetoric of their time than they would have been a century earlier. So one gets sentences like "The two boys flew on and on, toward the village, speechless with horror. . . . The barkings of the aroused watchdogs seemed to give wings to their feet."

But *Huckleberry Finn* is a masterpiece from its first sentence: "You don't know about me without you have read a book by the name of The Adventures of Tom Sawyer; but that ain't no matter." By speaking through Huck, Mark Twain solved the problem of style; he knew how Huck talked and so the tone is always right. He was able to raise the vernacular into a great style, no small feat if one recalls what even a Kipling perpetrated in *Soldiers Three*. It was an achievement comparable to Wordsworth's revival of common speech after the artificiality of eighteenth-century verse. I think this is what Hemingway had in mind when he made his famous statement that "All modern American literature comes from one book by Mark Twain called *Huckleberry Finn.*" Twain felt comfortable inside the skin of Huck, the outcast. The problem that James worried so much about and that Twain didn't but should have—namely, the point of view—was perfectly resolved by letting Huck tell the story. Even more important, all those worries about gentility that bothered poor Twain so much vanished once the speaker was a real bottom-dog. "Judge Driscoll could be a free-thinker and still hold his place in society," we read in *Pudd'nhead Wilson*, "because he was the person of most consequence in the community, and therefore could venture to go his own way and follow out his own notions. [Pudd'nhead Wilson], the other member of his pet organization [The Free-thinkers' Society], was allowed the like liberty because he was a cipher in the estimation of the public, and nobody attached any importance to what he thought or did. He was liked, he was welcome enough all around, but he simply didn't count for anything." So, too, with Huck—"I was so ignorant, and so kind of low-down and ornery." For the first and last time in his life, Twain had found a point of view from which he could speak with moral and artistic freedom. In *Tom Sawyer,* written in his own voice, he couldn't venture beyond local color and conventional humor; Jim is just a superstitious darky, Huck is a picturesque genre figure. They become people in *Huckleberry Finn.*

It is interesting that Twain originally tried to write *Tom Sawyer,* too, in the first person. In *Mark Twain at Work,* DeVoto prints a very early draft, twenty pages long, which he found among the Mark Twain papers. It is first-person and it makes dreary reading, "cute" and contrived; Twain just didn't feel at home inside a middle-class boy. He was quite right to do *Tom Sawyer* in the third person.

For Tom is too respectable, too close to what Twain had become after his literary success and his marriage to the daughter of the leading coal dealer of Elmira, New York. "Mark Twain was a man who . . . never became in all respects mature," T. S. Eliot writes. "We might even say that the adult side of [Twain] was boyish, and that only the boy in him, that was Huckleberry Finn, was adult. As Tom Sawyer grown up, he wanted success and applause. (Tom himself always needed an audience.) He wanted prosperity, a happy romantic life of a conventional kind, universal approval, and fame."

And yet even *Huckleberry Finn* is marred by its last hundred pages, in which the insufferable Tom Sawyer reappears to carry out one of his foolish and boring mystifications. Jim has been captured and is imprisoned in a flimsy hut until he can be returned to slavery. Tom and Huck could free him easily, but Tom insists on pretending he is a prisoner in the Bastille and on doing it all "in style," with rope ladders smuggled in pies, letters written in his blood, rats and spiders tamed by him—but one really cannot go on. Then, almost on the last page, Tom reveals that Jim has been free all the time, Miss Watson having emancipated him on her deathbed, so the masquerade is doubly pointless. Both Mr. Eliot and Lionel Trilling have taken a genial view of this ending, arguing that Twain was simply rounding off his tale by returning to the Tom Sawyerish mood of the opening chapters. But the point is precisely that the fake "adventures" initiated by Tom in the opening chapters yield to the real adventures of Huck and Jim, and a corresponding deepening of their characters. (Tom Sawyer is constitutionally incapable of experience, since he is a professional Small Boy.) To return to the mode of the opening is, in my opinion, to falsify and not to round out the artistic logic. The true novel begins when Old Man Finn suddenly comes back into Huck's life; he is a real villain, not a melodramatic one like Injun Joe in *Tom Sawyer,* and his appearance liberates Huck from his role of straight man for Tom. I agree with Leo Marx's "Mr. Eliot, Mr. Trilling, and 'Huckleberry Finn,'" in the Autumn, 1953, issue of the *American Scholar.* Mr. Marx points out that the farcical ending is out of key with what has gone before, and that it is not reasonable to suppose that Jim, who rebukes Huck for a minor practical joke during the trip down the Mississippi and who has become the moral hero of the book, would submit to being the passive butt of Tom, especially in anything so vital to him as his freedom. Or that Huck, who, just before the arrival of Tom, has reached his greatest moral development with his decision to try to free Jim even if it is a sinful act ("All right, then, I'll *go* to hell"), would become again an ally in the most tedious—and tasteless—of Tom's "tricks."

This dismaying change of key—as if Siegfried were to start singing falsetto—is characteristic. *Tom Sawyer* begins as a humorous idyll and ends as Victorian melodrama; *Life on the Mississippi* begins as a poem and ends as a travelogue; *Pudd'nhead Wilson* teeters crazily back and forth between realism, melodrama, and burlesque. And it could have been much worse with *Huckleberry Finn.* De-Voto quotes one of Twain's working notes: "Farmer has bought an elephant at auction. Gives him to Tom, Huck and Jim and they go about the country on him making no end of trouble." "That elephant," adds DeVoto, "might easily have wandered into *Huckleberry Finn.*" It might indeed. Arnold Bennett called Twain "the divine amateur." Becky Thatcher, of *Tom Sawyer,* becomes Bessie Thatcher when she reappears in *Huckleberry Finn* because Twain didn't bother to check back, and he thanked his literary mentor, William Dean Howells, for relieving him of "the dreary and hateful task of making final revision of *Tom Sawyer.*" He didn't even read all the final proofs of *Huckleberry Finn,* but just gave Howells carte blanche.

THE writing of books and magazine matter was always play, not work," Twain says in the autobiography. "I enjoyed it; it was merely billiards to me." There is bravado here, not to be taken at face value. But he may be telling us more than he intended, for in his unhappy last decades billiards was for him what drugs, liquor, and gambling are for others; he played for hours, often till dawn, walking around the table like a bear shuffling around his cage, always willing to postpone his re-entry into reality for "just one more game." The endless writing of his later years, most of it uncompleted and inchoate, had a similarly compulsive quality. But whether he used writing as a diversion or as an escape, the notion of literary effort was foreign to Mark Twain. In a way, he wasn't a writer at all. He was a speaker, an actor, who paid much more attention to the niceties of delivering a lecture than to literary technique. He says nothing on the craft of writing to match the subtle analysis, in the autobiography, of the timing of The Pause, as illustrated in his platform experiences with the "Grandfather's Old Ram" monologue and the Negro ghost story "The Golden Arm." He gave Browning readings at his home in Hartford. "It is very enjoyable work," he wrote a friend, "only it takes three days to prepare an hour's reading." There is no record of such effort being spent on anything he *wrote*. Twain's prose style has often been praised, perhaps too often. He wrote an easy, fluid, idiomatic English, but it is a spoken English that gets its effects the way a raconteur does. The texture is coarse—the ear accepts things the eye rejects—and the individual phrases are rarely memorable and often infected with cliché. But when he is going right, they fall together to convey the general sense. Most of the time he wasn't going quite right, and the result is watery and verbose; squads of adjectives and platoons of subordinate clauses could be mustered out without altering the line of march.

"As long as the book would write itself," he says in a

celebrated passage in the autobiography, "I was a faithful and interested amanuensis and my industry did not flag, but the minute that the book tried to shift to *my* head the labor of contriving its situations, inventing its adventures, and conducting its conversations, I put it away and dropped it out of my mind. Then I examined my unfinished properties to see if among them there might not be one whose interest in itself had revived through a couple of years' restful idleness and was ready to take me on again."

This happened to *Huckleberry Finn,* which he laid aside after the first dozen chapters, returning to it a year or two later, laying it aside again, and so on, so that it took him ten years to finish it. In that time, he also wrote a pleasant travel book, *A Tramp Abroad;* an insipid historical novel for boys, *The Prince and the Pauper;* and a number of stillborn tales, including "The Loves of Alonzo Fitz Clarence and Rosannah Ethelton," a spoof of majestic ineptitude about a courtship by long-distance telephone. And when he was finishing *Huckleberry Finn,* he was also working on a project that interested him much more— "1002," a lengthy burlesque of the Arabian Nights that DeVoto thinks "probably the dullest of all Mark's work . . . almost lethal." Fortunately, Howells didn't like "1002," and it was never completed. Of all his books, the two Mark Twain thought the most highly of were just the ones entirely lacking in his special qualities—*The Prince and the Pauper* and *Joan of Arc,* genteel excursions into pseudo-history that could have been written by dozens of hacks of the period. Looking back on his lifework at the age of seventy-three, he said, "I like *Joan of Arc* best of all my books; and it *is* the best; I know it perfectly well. And besides, it furnished me seven times the pleasure afforded me by any of the others: twelve years of preparation and two years of writing. The others needed no preparation, and got none." Perhaps it was just as well that he *was* so careless. Perhaps the divinity was inseparable from the amateurishness.

WRITERS are often poor judges of their own work, but Mark Twain's obtuseness reached the pathological. Not only did he share his present editor's illusions about the autobiography—he boasted it "would live a couple of thousand years without any effort and would then take a fresh start and live the rest of the time"—but he insisted it was precisely the kind of book it was not. He pictures all other autobiographers, with the possible exception of Cellini, as sitting at a window and commenting on the famous people who pass by. "This Autobiography of mine is a mirror and I am looking at myself in it all the time. . . . I rejoice when a king or a duke comes my way . . . but they are rare customers. . . . For real business I depend upon the common herd." The psychological phenomenon of easing one's conscience about one's failings by projecting them onto others has seldom been more neatly illustrated. Twain dearly loved a lord. The common herd is here represented by a few picturesque "characters," but eminent persons abound. He dwells in detail on his dinner with the Kaiser, his honorary degree from Oxford, his oratorical triumphs at great banquets, his contacts with authors like Kipling and Stevenson, generals like Grant and Sherman, capitalists like H. H. Rogers.

As for the mirror simile, it is safe to say that no autobiography is *less* inward-looking. The tone is that of the public performer; the mirror is used not for introspection but to put on the makeup. Twain's strategy for avoiding self-examination was the platform humorist's trick of accusing himself of vanity, ignorance, cowardice, and laziness, but always in stock situations that avoid the concrete personal note and seduce the sympathy of the audience by suggesting "I'm no better than you." Yet Twain was convinced that for the first time in human history a man was putting down his real thoughts and feelings. Only Paine was naïve enough to print his "Preface, as from the Grave":

In this Autobiography I shall keep in mind the fact that I am speaking as from the grave . . . because I shall be dead when the book issues from the press.

I speak from the grave rather than with my living tongue, for a good reason: I can speak thence freely. When a man is writing a book dealing with the privacies of his life—a book which is to be read while he is still alive—he shrinks from speaking his whole frank mind; all his attempts to do it fail, he recognizes that he is trying to do a thing which is wholly impossible to a human being.

But the promised record of a soul laid bare reads as impersonally as, and very much like, one of those after-dinner speeches Twain was so good at.

His accounts, for instance, of his mother and his wife, two strong-willed and proper ladies who there is reason to believe had even more influence on his development than mothers and wives usually do, are not revealing. One gathers he loved and admired them, but he hardly needed to hide in the grave to say that. Of his mother he writes, "I knew her well during the first twenty-five years of my life, but after that I saw her only at wide intervals, for we lived many days' journey apart. . . . She had a character, and it was of a fine and striking and lovable sort." Some anecdotes support this characterization, but it still seems undernourished. And one wonders *why* he saw his mother "only at wide intervals." The "many days' journey apart" isn't very convincing, for Twain was a great traveler. The mists are even thicker about his wife:

Under a grave and gentle exterior burned inextinguishable fires of sympathy, energy, devotion, enthuiasm, and absolutely limitless affection. . . . Perfect truth, perfect honesty, perfect candor were qualities of my wife's character. . . . Her judgments of people and things were sure and accurate. In her judgments of the characters and acts of both friends and strangers there was always room for charity, and this charity never failed. I have compared and contrasted her with hundreds of persons and my conviction remains that hers was the most perfect character I have ever met. And I may add that she was the most winningly dignified person I have ever known. Her character and disposition were of the sort that not only invite worship but command it. No servant ever left her service who deserved to remain in it.

One begins to detest poor Olivia Clemens, one even suspects that she fired at least one servant unjustly, because one knows she couldn't have been as good as all that. Twain was a devoted husband and father, but the quality of his devotion was false, like the loving pride of the mother who sees her darling as the brightest star in the seventh grade. In sexual love, this attitude can produce literature because there really is something mythological, something absolute, about Eros. But in the prose of family life it comes out wrong. The chapters written after the deaths of his wife and of his daughters Susy and Jean move one humanly but not imaginatively. On Christmas Eve, 1909, a few hours after the sudden death of Jean by epileptic seizure, he writes:

> I lost Susy thirteen years ago; I lost her mother—her incomparable mother!—five and a half years ago . . . and now I have lost Jean. How poor I am who was once so rich! . . . She lies there, and I sit here—writing, busying myself, to keep my heart from breaking. How dazzlingly the sunshine is flooding the hills around! It is like a mockery!
>
> Seventy-four years old, twenty-four days ago. Seventy-four years old yesterday. Who can estimate my age today?
>
> I have looked upon her again. . . . The sweet placidity of death! It is more beautiful than sleep.

This might have been written by any bereft father with a knack for the banal. Not that he is overstating his feelings —his own death a few months later may have been hastened by this unexpected blow. He simply lacks the vocabulary for this kind of writing. Even here, "as from the grave," he cannot drop the public mask, even here he conceals his grief beneath the standard jargon of bereavement.

THE tragedy of Mark Twain, I think, is this peculiar inability to speak in his own voice. "The frankest and freest and privatest product of the human mind and heart is a love letter," he writes in the autobiography. "The writer gets his limitless freedom of statement and expression from his sense that no stranger is going to see what he is writing. . . . It has seemed to me that I could be as frank and free and unembarrassed as a love letter if I knew that what I was writing would be exposed to no eye until I was dead, and unaware, and indifferent." This is interesting because of the hostility it assumes between the writer and his readers, who are thought of as Peeping Toms, with no right to share one's "private" thoughts. It is a notion that could not have existed before the end of the eighteenth century, when the rise of a mass market for culture introduced a novel division between creator and consumer. Up to then, the artist or writer had worked for his peers, a small upper-class group who were sophisticated enough to know what he was doing. He could "be himself"—to use a significant idiom—because they "spoke his language," to use another. But as the industrial revolution, democracy, and popular education brought ever larger masses of people into the cultural market, expanding and adulterating it, the writer was forced to choose between addressing this vast new public and speaking in his own voice. Some deliberately ignored the market (Stendhal), some deliberately wrote for it (Scott), some straddled the issue without being conscious of it, producing work that fluctuated between *Kitsch* and genius. The novels of

Balzac and Dickens are unstable compounds of originality and cliché.

Mark Twain was one of these two-level writers, and the least conscious of all. While he appeared never to know when he was being himself and when he was manufacturing for the market, he sensed that something was wrong. "Writers are manacled servants of the public," he admitted in *Life on the Mississippi*. "We write freely and fearlessly, but then we 'modify' before we print." Perhaps "admitted" is not the word. So deeply had he accepted the necessity, so unaware seems he to have been of any alternative, that he probably thought of his statement as a mere truism. In the autobiography, he records at length a talk in 1907 with Elinor Glyn, whose erotic best-seller *Three Weeks* was the *Lady Chatterley's Lover* of the period. The topic was "free love," and Twain apparently sympathized with Mrs. Glyn's advanced views, though, even writing from the grave, he found it inadvisable to state just what they were: "Take it all around, it was a very pleasant conversation and glaringly unprintable, particularly those considerable parts of it which I haven't had the courage to more than vaguely hint at in this account of our talk." Mrs. Glyn "implores" him to let her publish his endorsement of her views. "But I said, 'No, such a thing is unthinkable.' I said that if I, or any other wise, intelligent, and experienced person should suddenly throw down the walls that protect and conceal his *real* opinions on almost any subject under the sun, it would at once be perceived that he . . . ought to be sent to the asylum. I said I had been revealing to her my private sentiments, *not* my public ones; that I, like all other human beings, expose to the world only my trimmed and perfumed and carefully barbered public opinions and conceal carefully, cautiously, wisely my private ones."

But the most remarkable statement of this theme is another preludial note to the autobiography, which appears only in Paine:

What a wee little part of a person's life are his acts and his words! His real life is led in his head and is known to none but himself. All day long, and every day, the mill of his brain is grinding, and his *thoughts,* not those other things, are his history. His acts and his words . . . are so trifling a part of his bulk! a mere skin enveloping it. The mass of him is hidden— it and its volcanic fires that toss and boil, and never rest, night nor day. These are his life, and they are not written, and cannot be written.

What a curious conception of a writer—that his thoughts, which "cannot be written," are his real history and not "those other things" (i.e., his writings); that what is written is "a mere skin" over inarticulate volcanic depths. In short, that the writer is just like everybody else. He keeps himself *to* himself, and he is not such a fool as to chatter in public about what goes on in the privacy of his head. But the writer is not like everybody else, and his specialty is just to make his private thoughts public. Only a writer who felt profoundly alienated from his public would express himself in these terms.

MARK TWAIN'S was a peculiarly difficult period for a writer who wanted to strike his own note. The old New England tradition, already enfeebled, was submerged by the materialistic expansion, one might almost say explosion, that followed the Civil War, and it was not until the First World War that there were signs of a literary renaissance. The half-century between the wars, when Twain wrote, was a bad time for the arts. A provincial society of merchants and small farmers was changing into a cosmopolitan one of mass industry and finance capital. Great cities were arising (Chicago had three hundred thousand inhabitants in 1870 and a million seven hundred thousand thirty years later), the West was being settled, our imperialistic adventures were beginning overseas, and —possibly the most important change from a literary viewpoint—the needs of industry were attracting vast numbers of immigrants, most of whom didn't speak English. Standards, cultural as well as ethical, were simply swept away in the rush. Everybody was making money or dreaming of doing so. The common man was entering his kingdom; "America from about the middle of the last century," observes an English critic, A. C. Ward, "experienced the most extraordinary spate of professional funny men ever known in any country. The success of the dialect humorists depended chiefly upon the fact that their sayings and writings were a subtle if unconscious flattery of the great unlettered American public, which was tickled to death to find literary gentlemen speaking a language every one could understand and cracking jokes comprehensible to the most unassuming intelligence." Mark Twain was one of these funny men, and while he was above the crude dialect and grotesque misspellings the others relied on, his spirit was often theirs.

The Philistinism of *Innocents Abroad* was to remain with him all his life. Although he was an ardent traveler and lived abroad almost continuously from 1890 to 1900, remarkably little rubbed off on him. The forty-odd pages of the autobiography devoted to his years in Florence are almost all about the plumbing, heating, and other aspects of the domestic economy of his villas there. There is nothing on art, nothing on architecture, and the only passage on the city is a banal set piece that begins, "To see the sun sink down, drowned on his pink and purple and golden floods, and overwhelm Florence with tides of color that make all the sharp lines dim and faint and turn the solid city to a city of dreams, is a sight to stir the coldest nature and to make a sympathetic one drunk with ecstasy." This Burton Holmes Kodachrome, which misses the point that it is the sharp lines and the solidity that are the city's distinctive quality, is all we get about Florence, but there are five glowing pages on a parade in Vienna: "All the centuries

were passing by; passing by in glories of color and multi-
plicities of strange and quaint and curious and beautiful
costumes not to be seen in this world outside the opera
and the picture books. . . . I have been looking at proces-
sions for sixty years, and, curiously enough, all my really
wonderful ones have come in the last three years." Parades
were the one art form Twain responded to; he might have
written more about Florence had there been some really
good parades while he was there. One is reminded of Roger
Fry's comment on the elder J. P. Morgan's feeling for art:
"A crude historical imagination was the only flaw in his
otherwise perfect insensibility." One imagines that Morgan
would have relished Twain's historical romances.

Writing to Andrew Lang in 1889, Mark Twain formulated a literary credo:

The critic assumes every time that if a book doesn't meet
the cultivated-class standard, it isn't valuable. . . . The critic
has actually imposed upon the world the superstition that a
painting by Raphael is more valuable . . . than is a chromo . . .
and the Latin classics than Kipling's far-reaching bugle-note.
. . . If a critic should start a religion, it would not have any
object but to convert angels, and they wouldn't need it. It is
not that little minority who are already saved that are best
worth lifting up, I should think, but the mighty mass of the
uncultivated who are underneath! That mass will never see the
old masters—that sight is for the few; but the chromo-maker
can lift them all one step upward toward appreciation of
art. . . .
I have never tried . . . to help cultivate the cultivated classes.
I was not equipped for it either by native gifts or training.
And I never had any ambition in that direction but always
hunted for bigger game—the masses. . . . I have always catered
for the Belly and the Members but have been . . . criticised
from the culture-standard—to my sorrow and pain; because,
honestly, I never cared what became of the cultured classes;
they could go to the theatre and the opera; they had no use
for me and the melodeon. . . .

My audience is dumb; it has no voice in print, and so I cannot know whether I have won its approval or only got its censure.

Like most of Mark Twain's thinking, this is not substantial. If standards are a "superstition," what can the masses be "lifted up" *to?* And were chromos a step toward Raphael or a substitute for Raphael? It is also characteristically *ad hoc.* If consistency be the bugbear of little minds, Twain's intellect was of Goethian proportions. His actor's sensibility led him to play wildly different roles at different times. When he wrote to Lang, he was in his *Connecticut Yankee* phase, as the tribune of the American common man against the aristocratic privilege of the Old World—and, besides, Lang had not liked *Yankee.* But fifteen years earlier Twain had expressed himself in just the opposite way. When his friend Howells had told him reassuringly, as editor of the *Atlantic,* apropos of his first efforts for that awesome journal, "Don't write *at* any supposed *Atlantic* audience, but yarn it off as if into my sympathetic ear," Twain had replied, "It isn't the *Atlantic* audience that distresses me; for *it* is the only audience that I sit down before in perfect serenity (for the simple reason that it don't require a 'humorist' to paint himself striped & stand on his head every fifteen minutes)."

But the letter to Lang did express an important truth about Mark Twain—his feeling of identity with the masses rather than with the classes. He was, at his best, a folk writer. "Our one American example of the bardic type of artist and sayer," Ludwig Lewisohn calls him, adding, "He was not essentially divided from the folk for which he wrote . . . by any difference of *vision,* only by genius—like the tribal bards of old. . . . In his small and homespun way Mark Twain is related to Homer . . . A poor relation, a late descendant, but of the authentic lineage and blood." Yet despite the laughter of his lecture audiences, despite the sales figures on his books, Twain felt out of touch: "My audience is dumb; it has no voice in print, and so I cannot know whether I have won its approval." By his time, the folk audience had become as inflated and corrupted as the aristocratic audience. It was no longer a specific group with certain values and standards in common; it had been absorbed into the mass audience, an abstract, heterogeneous crowd whose tastes were those of everybody in general and nobody in particular. This was the audience before whom Twain postured as the frontier humorist and cracker-barrel philosopher, for whom he wrote his endless journalese. His genius led him to create a folk epic in *Huckleberry Finn,* but neither he nor his mass audience realized it. They preferred the mechanical jocosity of *Innocents Abroad*—as late as 1908 it was still outselling *Huckleberry Finn*—and he preferred the synthetic romance of *Joan of Arc.*

There was an alternative to the mass audience, and it had an even worse effect on Mark Twain's work. This was the genteel school that arose after the Civil War as a rearguard defense of the New England tradition against the vulgarity of the new-rich and the ignorance of the immigrants. Rear-guard actions can only delay the defeat, but this one failed to do even that. It was like a proper Bostonian spinster in charge of a class of slum kids. The cultural values became desiccated, and the kids didn't get educated, either. Twain was very much under the influence of such genteelists as Thomas Bailey Aldrich (whom he unrecognizably described as "always brilliant . . . a fire opal set round with rose diamonds"), Edmund Clarence Stedman (who complained that the word "sewer" appeared three times in *A Connecticut Yankee*), Richard Watson Gilder (who represented bohemian avant-gardism on the *Century* and who, when *Huckleberry Finn* was serialized in his magazine, deleted "I was in a sweat," "Dern your skin!," "We was always naked," and several dozen other low-class expressions), and the most sophisticated of them all, William Dean Howells (who wrote Twain that the description, in *Tom Sawyer,* of a dog who had sat down on a pinch bug sailing up the church aisle "with his tail shut down like a hasp" was "awfully good but a little too dirty;" the impropriety was deleted). But Twain himself was always prudish, and he did a lot of self-bowdlerizing. It really took considerable ingenuity to find anything to clean up.

What was more important was that Mark Twain's genteel tutors bowdlerized his talent, diverting it into flaccid historical pageants and away from American themes, where it could be dangerous. They also discouraged his natural tendency toward satire. The age of Grant and McKinley could have done with a Swift, but, except for a few flashes like that mordant bit of pacifist irony "The War Prayer," Twain prudently confined himself to making fun of the Sabbath. Had not Howells, for all his realistic doctrine and his Socialist sympathies, pronounced "the more smiling aspects of life . . . the large cheerful average of health and success and happy life" to be "the more American"?

In compensation, Mark Twain went far toward pessimism in anonymous works like *What Is Man?* and posthumous ones like the autobiography. In fact, much too far. It isn't that, as he fondly imagined, his ideas are particularly shocking. His surviving daughter still refuses to release five chapters of religious speculation from the autobiography. "Not to be exposed to any eye until the edition of A.D. 2406—S.L.C.," he solemnly scrawled at the head of two of them. However, judging by Mr. Neider's description of their content, they would cause no seismic upheavals if they were published five minutes instead of five hundred years hence. No, this is village-atheist stuff that goes too far emotionally and not far enough intellectually. In its frantic overstatement, denying any value to God, to man, to life itself, it is like a severely compressed spring that leaps back when it is released, reminding one of those

Twain curiosa like the skit about the court of Queen Elizabeth called "1601," in which repressed sex explodes into scatology. And just as "1601" was written specially for his pastor, so, one imagines, the schoolboy nihilism was directed at Howells, Aldrich, Stedman, and his other tutors. That Twain felt the need for such defiance was to his credit, yet if only he had realized that the most effective riposte would have been not cosmic rebuttal—for which he had no gift and which absurdly inflated the issue, since these opponents based their position on nothing more profound than provincial convention—but merely to write in his own natural vein! This would have been more difficult, and Twain was not a man to seek out difficulty. Also, he was never clearly aware that his genteel mentors *were* his opponents. Much easier to muffle his bitterness in slashing generalities not to be exposed to any eye until A.D. 2406.

MARK TWAIN'S difficulty was a peculiarly modern one—he was damaged by success, as, later on, Fitzgerald and Hemingway were to be. He was simply too popular for his own good, with both of the important publics of his time—the masses and the genteel school. He was overfed with praise and starved for understanding; the ponderous machinery of exploitation drew him in and he was processed. A generation earlier, Melville had failed in the old-fashioned way. His early books of exotic adventure (*Typee, Omoo, Mardi*) and straightforward reportage (*White Jacket, Redburn*) had been successful, but when he at last spoke out fully in his own voice, *Moby Dick* sold less than a thousand copies, and he entered on the obscurity that lasted till his death, forty years later. Twain's only important contemporaries, James and Whitman, also experienced the old-fashioned kind of failure. Like Melville, James was reasonably popular in his early decades, but he lost his audience when he began to extend his range and to reflect stylistically his maturing sense of the complexity of human relations. *The Bostonians,* published in 1886, the year after *Huckleberry Finn,* was the turning point. It was his best up to then, but it was too "difficult" for the general public—Twain, who as a reader was a part of that public, said he would rather be consigned to the Puritan heaven than read it—and it also managed to offend the genteel with its satire of New England provincialism. The same year, *The Princess Casamassima,* with its anarchistic background, hardly improved matters, and James slowly resigned himself to writing for a small audience and sometimes, he felt, for no audience at all. He gave up the hope of popularity with reluctance—the stillborn plays he wrote after these two failures were pathetic efforts to regain it—but he did give it up. He also gave up his country, living abroad and finally becoming a British citizen. Like Twain, he wanted popularity, but he was unwilling to pay the price. He paid a good deal for his isolation—the sometime eccentricity of his later style, for instance—but it was less than Twain paid for success.

Mark Twain had little in common with James—except, as F. W. Dupee has acutely noted, humor—but much with Whitman. Both were folk writers, identifying themselves with the people in their diction, their defiant innocence of higher education, and their personal "style"—Whitman's open-collared flannel shirt, prospector's beard, and slouch hat, Twain's Western drawl, unruly mop of hair, gambler's mustache and cigar. Both shared with their fellow Americans two deep and inconsistent faiths, in democracy and in the technological progress that was its executioner. Twain had the first private telephone and was the first literary man to use a typewriter; Whitman's apostrophes to Progress were a poor man's substitute for such equipment. But Whitman resembled James in being unwilling—or, rather, unable—to make important concessions for the sake of popularity. His shabby little house in Camden was as isolated from American life as James's country place in

Sussex. His poetry was more appreciated in England than here—the genteelists rightly thought it barbarically improper (though Emerson upheld the honor of the older New England tradition with his "I greet you at the beginning of a great career"), while the masses he addressed with unfaltering democratic faith paid no attention to him, finding Ella Wheeler Wilcox and James Whitcomb Riley more to their taste. Whitman thought he was a bard—"essentially not divided from the folk for which he wrote ... by any difference of *vision,* only by genius"—but he was in fact an avant-gardist. He yearned to be one with the common people, but his vision was incomprehensible—even worse, boring—to them. They couldn't see why he thought they were so exciting. Twain would have guffawed if anyone had called him a bard, which was one reason why, in that period, he was. That Whitman was poor and of simple tastes while Twain was rich and lived in princely style is beside the point; the one was hopelessly recherché, for all his bardic aspirations, while the other was a bard—at times—in spite of his keen sense of the literary marketplace.

In 1887, Twain attended a lecture by Whitman on, of all appropriate subjects, Lincoln. There is no record of his reactions, but, as a master of the platform, he must have been distressed by Whitman's inept performance. Not that Whitman was at all averse to appearances of this sort. On the contrary, he sought them out as assiduously as Twain came to avoid them. But he was as stiff and self-conscious as Twain was easy, his bardism being as theoretical as Twain's was spontaneous, and he got pitifully few invitations. Perhaps his major public appearance was in New York, at the fortieth National Industrial Exhibition, in 1871. Horace Greeley usually gave the opening address, but he was out of town that year and the committee offered Whitman a hundred dollars and expenses to write and recite an ode for the opening. He accepted with delight; the fee was, for him, munificent, and the poem would be published in the newspapers. Whitman wrote some verses celebrating industrial progress; he urged the Muse to emigrate to the United States and he ended with a spread-eagle salute to the flag. "It was more like an oration than a poem," writes Gay Wilson Allen in his biography. "It is difficult to understand how a poet who had recently written 'Passage to India' could have composed so bad a poem as 'After All, Not to Create Only.' Yet this is what the desire to be topical and *popular* could bring him to." Whitman, who promoted his works with a shame-lessness that would have appalled Twain, sent out fulsome press releases, but only two or three hundred people came to listen. Even these faithful few were frustrated, for by one of the ironies of literary history, Whitman's delivery, which was ineffectual to begin with, was drowned out by proletarian static—the hammering and sawing of workmen making last-minute installations. Although twelve of the seventeen daily papers the city then boasted (*eheu, fugaces*) printed the poem, their reaction was largely hostile. "The vacancy caused by Mr. Greeley was regarded with painful emotion," observed the *World,* while the *Tribune* printed a savage parody by Bayard Taylor, beginning:

> *Who was it sang of the procreant urge, recounted sextil-*
> *   lions of subjects?*
> *Who but myself, the Kosmos, yawping abroad, concerned*
> *   not at all about either the effect or the answer.*

Whitman tried to repair the damage by planting anony-mous articles (written by himself) in out-of-town papers. These gave a flattering account of the proceedings—the workmen laid down their tools, spellbound, to listen; the audience (multiplied by ten) interrupted with applause; most pathetic of all, his delivery was admired ("His gestures are few, but significant. . . . He was perfectly self-possessed. . . . The main impression was markedly serious, animated,

& earnest. . . . All the directors & officers of the Institute crowded around him & heartily thanked him"). This face-to-face meeting with the American common man—and with the press that spoke for him—was a traumatic experience for Whitman. "He made himself ridiculous with his poem and mannerisms," Mr. Allen says in concluding his account of the episode, "and the resulting travesties on him and his poetry left wounds that would continue to fester until the end of his life." The subtler wounds that Mark Twain suffered from his adoring public were more paralyzing to him as an artist. Perhaps Whitman had the better of it, after all. Acceptance can be worse for a writer than rejection.

TWO generations later, another American humorist had a similar career. Ring Lardner was another small-town boy who came East (from Niles, Michigan) and made good. He, too, was a master of the vernacular, second only to Twain himself. He, too, played the hillbilly ignoramus, wrote quantities of dreary funnyman stuff for the market (as well as a few extremely good things), even produced his own *Innocents Abroad*—namely, *The Other Side,* another journal of a provincial American wisecracker who isn't impressed by Europe. He, too, was a congenital improviser, unable—indeed, one feels, unwilling—to add a cubit to his stature by taking however little thought. The one area of literary technique in which Lardner showed any interest was the only one that Twain was sensitive to—the usage, and abusage, of words. One recalls Twain's burlesque of the German language, his "English As She Is Spoke," his analysis of Fenimore Cooper's prose. As for Lardner, almost every word he wrote was a commentary on usage. "Lardner's hypersensitivity to language," Delmore Schwartz has observed, "was a hypersensitivity to human suffering. . . . His acute sense of the disparity between the way people should behave and the way they do is very often expressed in his stories by a use of English that dramatizes the disparity between the way English ought to be used and the way it is used." The same could be said of Twain.

They were even alike in their prudery. There was Lardner's remarkable campaign, in the radio column he conducted for the *New Yorker* in the thirties, against the allegedly "dirty" lyrics of popular songs: He objected to lines like "Thrill me with a kiss that's vicious, with love delicious"; he detected smut in an opus entitled "Paradise" because it had a hummed refrain he found disturbing; and he sternly listed "suggestive" titles, including "Let's Put Out the Lights and Go to Sleep," which he rated as "just on the border," adding darkly, "They say that in the original lyric the last word was not 'sleep.' " (It was "bed.") One recalls Mark Twain's observations, in *A Tramp Abroad,* on Titian's "Venus," in the Uffizi: "the foulest, the vilest, the obscenest picture the world possesses. . . . It isn't that she is naked and stretched out on a bed—no, it is the attitude of one of her arms and hand. If I ventured to describe that attitude, there would be a fine howl." Except for Van Wyck Brooks's *The Ordeal of Mark Twain,* there is almost nothing in the copious literature on Twain about the relation of his attitude toward sex to his work. Yet, in both his and Lardner's case, this would seem to be a promising clue. A starting-off point might be Freud's description of wit as "the economic expenditure of suppressed libido."

The similarities go much farther. Like Twain, Lardner was one of our very few writers who have won both the affection of the masses and the admiration of the critics. Yet he, too, became increasingly bitter in spite of all the success and applause; he, too, entered a dark period at the end of his life, shorter than Twain's but even more desperate. "Of late a sharply acrid flavor has got into Lardner's buffoonery," H. L. Mencken wrote in 1926. "His baseball players and fifth-rate pugilists, beginning in his first stories as harmless jackasses, gradually convert themselves into loathsome scoundrels." The same acrid flavor crept into Twain's later writings. They were small-town boys lost in a big-town age, folk writers overwhelmed by mass culture. They were bored by the formulas that had made them famous and they came to despise the popular audience that was so easily pleased. Yet they didn't feel at home with the others, either, for they were both singularly lacking in intellectual curiosity. One feels that they were at a great distance from themselves. Their surroundings were so alien that they didn't dare remove the mask of the ironic hillbilly. Lardner's letters to his friends and his family, which appear in Donald Elder's fascinating biography (Doubleday, 1956), are even more inhibited than Twain's autobiography.

Above all, both felt the terrible American pressure to conform. When Maxim Gorki came to New York in 1905 to collect funds for the Russian revolutionists, Twain and Howells, as open enemies of czarist despotism, took the lead in organizing a great dinner for him. Then it was discovered that Gorki's traveling companion was not his wife; the press roared, Gorki and his companion were barred from every respectable hotel in the city—and Twain and Howells called off the dinner. The Russian revolution was forgotten once the sexual revolution was on the agenda. A few naïve spirits defended Gorki, but Twain, in a private memorandum, exposed their folly. He respected their efforts, he wrote, "but I think the ink was wasted. Custom is custom; it is built of brass, boiler-iron, granite; facts, reasonings, arguments have no more effect upon it than the idle winds have upon Gibraltar."

Ring Lardner, a simpler, or at least a more internally consistent, man, has left no such record of being split into public and private personalities. He would not have acted badly in the Gorki affair because he wouldn't have been around in the first place. "When the Sacco-Vanzetti case enlisted the passionate sympathy of almost all the writers in the country, many of them Ring's close friends," writes Mr. Elder, "he kept still. He did not think it was his place to take any public stand." The problem of public utterance v. private opinion, over which Twain agonized, had no reality for Lardner. Outward conformism had become so deeply a part of his nature that he seems not to have been conscious of it. His drinking jags were his only release. He was perhaps the most taciturn man of letters in history; he often sat for hours in company without saying a word; on one occasion he escaped conversation by pretending he didn't speak English. But there is a desperation in much of his writing that suggests a disgust with the world he lived in far deeper than Swift's (who, after all, lived in a more sensible age)—a disgust so profound that it shatters the satirical form. This appears most clearly in his mock autobiography, *The Story of a Wonder Man,* of which Mr. Elder writes:

There is one consistent note throughout the book—a note of utterly relentless burlesque carried to the point of exaspera-tion; and the exasperation is not so much the reader's as Ring's own. He was perpetrating a joke on himself, as a humorist, on the very idea of humor, and on the audience that thought it was funny. He seemed to be saying, "If this is what people think is funny, let them have it." He could give them all the old stale vaudeville routines, the tortured puns and Joe Millers without even trying. And so he parodied them all. . . . It is not that he let himself go, or that his flights of fancy got out of control. It is all perfectly deliberate. It shows not only strain but contempt for himself and for the audience at which this barrage of mixed comedy was hurled.

This contempt is also pronounced in Mark Twain, as is the note of desperate burlesque. But Lardner, arriving after the mold of American mass culture had hardened, exhibits the symptoms in a more advanced state. Both men had great satirical talents, which they ventured to

exercise only on the periphery of society—Lardner's spoof-
ing of ballplayers was analogous to Twain's defiance of the
Puritan Sabbath—but Twain was at least conscious of a
conformism he didn't dare break through. If Twain was
a village atheist, Lardner was a corn-fed nihilist. The difference was half a century of American history. Twain
wrote his autobiography straight; he tried to speak out and
failed. Lardner, who was born in 1885, just fifty years later
than Twain, could write only a burlesque autobiography;
he didn't even try to lift the mask.

A reporter asked Lardner, in 1917, about American
humorists:

LARDNER: Well, I wouldn't consider Mark Twain our greatest humorist. I guess that George Ade is. Certainly he appeals
to us more than Mark Twain does because he belongs to our
own time. He writes of the life we are living, and Mark Twain's
books deal with the life we know only by hearsay. I suppose
my forebears would say that Mark Twain was a much greater
humorist than George Ade. . . . You see, I didn't travel along
the Mississippi in Mark Twain's youth, so I don't know his
people. Harry Leon Wilson is a great humorist. . . .

REPORTER [rather desperately, one imagines]: But you admire
Huckleberry Finn, don't you?

LARDNER: Yes, but I like Booth Tarkington's *Penrod* stories
better. I've known Booth Tarkington's boys and I've not
known those of Mark Twain. Mark Twain's boys are tough
and poverty-stricken and they belong to a period very different
from that of our own boys. But we all know Penrod and His
friends.

The point is not that Lardner didn't respond to *Huckleberry Finn.* After all, Twain himself wasn't so enthusiastic.
"I have written four hundred pages on it—therefore it is
nearly half done," he wrote in 1876. "I like it only toler-
ably well, as far as I've got, and may possibly pigeonhole or
burn the MS when it is done." The point is rather that
Lardner senses a chasm between his own time and Twain's

("the life we know only by hearsay") and that he feels no imaginative bond with Twain's. One must believe that a master of the vernacular like Lardner had at least a craftsman's appreciation of what Twain had achieved in *Huckleberry Finn*, and yet he still prefers the smart-aleck slang of a George Ade, the tepid humor of *Penrod* and even the faded jocosities of the *Saturday Evening Post*'s Harry Leon Wilson, simply because they "belong to our own time." This is, of course, barbarous—Lardner was no more sophisticated a critic than Twain was. But the real problem is: How could the continuity of our tradition have been so completely broken in two generations?

THE question of Mark Twain is the question of America. Was the Hannibal of his boyhood idyllic or squalid? Was the West of his young manhood Mr. Brooks's vision of it (as of 1920) or Mr. DeVeto's (as of 1932)? Was the Gilded Age of his maturity a degeneration from the past or was it merely the growing pains of progress? And which Mark Twain are we to believe, the cocksure American jingo of *Innocents Abroad* or the disillusioned cynic of "Pudd'n-head Wilson's Calendar"?

Mark Twain's life spanned the Great Divide in our history, the Civil War. The period from which all his significant work came was his boyhood; he returned to it again and again, compulsively, in abortive gropings like *Tom Sawyer Abroad,* and *Tom Sawyer, Detective* and even in *The Mysterious Stranger,* like a dog returning to a bone he has buried too deeply. He was never at home in the postwar period. He felt that a money-grubbing age, conformist and corrupt, had replaced what he remembered as a larger, more innocent time. ("You feel mighty free and easy and comfortable on a raft," Huck says.) At the same time, he was an ardent believer in Progress. *A Connecticut Yankee* is a how-to-do-it book, demonstrating the superiority of advanced technology; the triumphs of Sir Boss over Merlin and other feudal reactionaries suggest our own Point Four program in their more benevolent aspects and, in their more severe, what the Chinese Communists did in Tibet. "All you men," orated Mark Twain to a dinner party of prosperous fellow-citizens who had assembled to celebrate his sixty-seventh birthday, "all you men have won your places not by heredities and not by family influence or extraneous help, but only by the natural gifts God gave you at your birth, made effective by your own energies. This is the country to live in." Some years earlier, in 1889, he had written, on behalf of a committee of literary men, a curious letter to Walt Whitman, for his seventieth birthday. It is curious because there is no reference to Whitman's poetry —which Twain very likely had never read—and because, instead of congratulating the age on Whitman, it congratulates Whitman on the age. It is also curious, and significant, as a full-blown expression of that religion of Progress in which both sender and recipient believed—or, more accurately, wanted to believe:

To Walt Whitman:

You have lived just the seventy years which are greatest in the world's history and richest in benefit and advancement to its peoples. These seventy years have done much more to widen the interval between man and the other animals than was accomplished by any of the five centuries which preceded them.

What great births you have witnessed! The steam press, the steamship, the steelship, the railroad etc. etc. . . . Yes, you have indeed seen much—but tarry for a while, for the greatest is yet to come. Wait thirty years, and *then* look out over the earth! You shall see marvels upon marvels! . . . man at almost his full stature at last! . . . Wait till you see that great figure appear, and catch the far glint of the sun upon his banner. Then you may depart satisfied, as knowing you have seen him for whom the earth was made, and that he will proclaim that human wheat is more than human tares, and proceed to organize human values on that basis.

Mark Twain

So one true believer reassured another, and it was perhaps merciful that both were dead before the thirty years ended with a war that destroyed the historical base for the doctrine of Progress.

Like Twain, Whitman had lived on both sides of the Great Divide; he, too, felt that the quality of American life had changed for the worse. But he was more optimistic than Twain—perhaps because his contacts with the great world were so much slighter—and, for all his misgivings, he died in the faith. It was the avant-garde poet who continued to believe in Progress and Democracy, while it was the popular entertainer who was profoundly disillusioned.

There is something heroic about those last black years of Mark Twain's life. His personal disasters coincided with his growing pessimism about America. "He had no philosophy, no values . . . with which to face [these problems]," Lewisohn observes. "Nor did he seek in books or converse any knowledge of the thoughts whereby men in the past have sought to wring from the stubborn universe a triumph for the spirit of man. He knew neither Plato nor Spinoza nor Kant; there is no evidence that he had ever read Emerson. He sat down to develop out of his own head, like an adolescent, like a child, a theory to fit the facts as he seemed to see them, and the only influence discernible in his theory is that of Robert Ingersoll!" (This is an extremely slight overstatement—Twain was also influenced by Lecky's *History of Morals*.) But he did insist on facing the bleak reality. He lacked the equipment to cope with the theme, but it was a great one, nothing less than the breakdown of the American dream, and he wouldn't settle for less. As Henry Nash Smith has demonstrated in "Mark Twain's Images of Hannibal" (University of Texas *Studies in English,* 1958), there is a significant change in Twain's concept of his boyhood town, so important throughout his creative life, from the idyllic St. Petersburg of *Tom Sawyer,* through the more realistic river towns of *Huckleberry Finn,* to the folly and cruelty of the Eseldorf ("Asses' Town") of *The Mysterious Stranger*. Professor Smith's conclusion is not overdrawn:

Mark Twain came nearer registering in fiction the death of nineteenth-century culture than did such contemporaries as Howells, whose remarkable gifts as a novelist could not in the end overcome his intellectual confusion, or James, who created the technique of the modern novel but paid the price for his single-minded devotion to art by failing to recognize the countenance of the twentieth century until the outbreak of the First World War. From the 1890's onward Mark Twain was struggling with his perception that democracy had been corrupted by money and that war was the normal behavior of modern as well as of ancient nations. When he tried to ignore these insights his work had no vitality, yet he could not devise a form to embody them. *The Mysterious Stranger,* his nearest approach to such a feat, was left unfinished at his death. He had bet too much on the doctrine of Progress and the belief in an orderly benign universe to be able to emulate the younger writers who in his old age were finding literary capital in the master image of the Waste Land and were beginning to produce a whole literature of alienation.

Unfinished *The Mysterious Stranger* may be, yet it is more of a piece than any other work of Mark Twain. It is not his highest flight, but it is the only sustained one; there are none of those changes of key, those unfortunate improvisations that mar Twain's other books. There is a miracle here, especially since the book was written in his final decade, when nothing seemed to come together, artistically, for him. It is as if Twain's personal griefs and his anxiety about America were compacted, as a diamond is formed under pressure, into this sad, hard little fable. The style is simple and muted, quite different from the unbuttoned journalese of his other late works. Of course he didn't dare have it published while he was alive, of course he stipulated that it be excluded from any collected edition of his works, and of course Harper brought it out as a boy's book, with illustrations by N. C. Wyeth in his most romantic vein.

One suspects that the juvenile format and the Wyeth illustrations would have tickled Mark Twain's sense of irony. *Gulliver's Travels* has been defused in the same way. *The Mysterious Stranger* is an even grimmer parable than *Gulliver*, whose satire was restricted to mankind. Twain's target is cosmic. Satan is the book's hero, and God, with his "moral sense," which always seems to produce even greater cruelties than uninstructed human nature could think up by itself, is the villain. There is no afterlife and there is considerable doubt even about this life. Satan, who manifests himself as Philip Traum (Philip Dream), tells the boy narrator at the end, "Life itself is only a vision. . . . Nothing exists save empty space—and you! . . . I myself have no existence; I am but a dream—your dream. . . ." Lewis Carroll's Alice is told she exists only because the Red King is dreaming her, a sufficiently disturbing idea. But little Theodore Fischer, of Eseldorf, is the solitary dreamer who has the nightmare responsibility of creating the Red King (or Satan) himself. In Philip Traum's world, the *summum bonum* is death, which is at least a release from the sordid agony of living. "He did not seem to know any way to do a person a kindness but by killing him," the boy Fischer wonderingly observes.*

---

* Mr. John Keliher, of Tacoma, Washington, has pointed out to me that "Philip Traum" is not Satan but Satan's nephew (with the same name) and also that, more important, he has remained faithful to God. I apologize for my careless misreading, which minimizes the bitter blasphemy of *The Mysterious Stranger*, since Satan-Traum, though an unfallen angel and therefore God's emissary, behaves about as one expects his uncle to. Worse, in fact, Twain implies in a passage when the boys first meet Satan-Traum:

"It is a good family, ours," said Satan; "there is not a better. He is the only member of it that has ever sinned." [Though what became of Beelzebub, Mammon and all the other host who fell with Satan, according to Milton?—D. M.] . . . "No, the Fall did not affect me or the rest of the relationship. It was only he that I was named for who ate of the fruit of the tree and then beguiled the man and the woman with it. We others are still ignorant of sin; we are not able to commit

As for Progress, that last refuge of the noblest spirits of his age, Mark Twain, speaking through Satan, is explicit:

You perceive that you have made continual progress. Cain did his murder with a club; the Hebrews did their murders with javelins and swords. . . . The Christian has added guns and gunpowder; a few centuries from now he will have so greatly improved . . . his weapons . . . that all men will confess that without Christian civilization war must have remained a poor and trifling thing. . . . In five or six thousand years five or six high civilizations have risen, flourished, commanded the wonder of the world, then faded out and disappeared; and not one of them except the latest invented any sweeping or adequate way to kill people. They all did their best—to kill being the chiefest ambition of the human race . . . but only the Christian civilization has scored a triumph to be proud of. Two or three centuries from now it will be recognized that all the competent killers are Christians; then the pagan world will go to school to the Christian.

When he wrote this, Mark Twain was thinking of such toys as the Gatling gun and the Maxim rifle. And his prediction that it would take "two or three centuries" for Christian civilization to perfect its mass-killing techniques was just ten times too optimistic. Before Twain had done with *The Mysterious Stranger*, Albert Einstein had pub-

---

it; we are without blemish and shall abide in that state always. We—" Two of the little workmen [Satan-Traum had created a miniature feudal estate for the boys' enjoyment] were quarrelling, and in buzzing little bumblebee voices they were cursing and swearing at each other. . . . Satan reached out his hand and crushed the life out of them with his fingers, threw them away, wiped the red from his fingers on his handkerchief, and went on talking where he had left off: "We cannot do wrong; neither have we any disposition to do it, for we do not know what it is."

Thus it is not God's, or his emissary Satan-Traum's, "moral sense" that is satirized—*peccavi*, again!—but rather their complete lack of it, although as the tale goes on it becomes an increasingly fine point as to which party commits the greater atrocities, the human beings who have been given the knowledge of good and evil by Uncle Satan, or the innocent, amoral Nephew Satan and the God he serves. I suspect that in his bleakly nihilistic old age, Mark Twain wanted to score off the whole pack of them—God, Satan, and humankind.

lished the equation from which the atomic bomb was to be created. It would be an interesting exercise in historical imagination to think of what he and Mark Twain might have had to say to each other if, by some odd chance, they had ever met—perhaps at a parade in Vienna. The mere notion is enough to discourage a satirist.

James Joyce

In the year 1904, an arrogant, penniless and to all appearances rather shiftless young Irishman arrived in Trieste to teach English in the Berlitz school there. He was accompanied by a semiliterate chambermaid to whom he was not married and with whom he lived the rest of his life. (The unmarriage was on principle; in 1931 he stretched a point and they were legally married.) He owed small sums all over Dublin, was adept at not paying rent, and was addicted to drink. When he died, thirty-seven years later, he had become the most famous and admired writer of his generation, in the circles that count. (And as for the circles that don't, he had been on the cover of *Time*.) It was a Horatio Alger success story—a triumph of Hard Work and Perseverance over Humble Beginnings and Bad Habits.

This is the admirable and contemptible man Richard Ellmann has given us, with none of the contradictions toned down, in *James Joyce*. The only other biography, Herbert Gorman's, is comparatively slight and was written in 1939, when the subject was still alive to censor it, which he did—heavily. Here is the definitive work, and I hope it will become a model for future scholarly biographies. We are familiar with the American Academic style in such enterprises, those great lumbering dinosaurs with brains the size of a teacup. We have endured their wooden writing, their congenital lack of ideas, their magpie heapings-up of Facts. Facts pasteurized, Facts tuberculin-tested, Facts indubitable, Facts Unlimited, Facts presented with so little sensibility (or simple common sense) that the subject never emerges from their scholarly welter. One recalls the ending of Roy Campbell's "On Some South African Novelists":

> They use the snaffle and curb all right,
> But where's the bloody horse?

Although Mr. Ellmann is a full Professor of English at Northwestern University, and although his book weighs slightly over two pounds and has a high density of Facts, the bloody horse is there, all right. In fact, everything is there—Joyce as man and as artist, his family life, his friends and enemies, his literary career, the biographical sources of his books (only Proust, among modern masters, drew more from his own life), everything but the kitchen stove and the meeting George L. K. Morris and I had with Joyce in 1932. I can't think how Mr. Ellmann overlooked it.

Morris and I, four years out of Yale, were in Paris that spring. After doing the Louvre and Notre Dame—it was my first trip abroad—we naturally went next to Shakespeare and Company's shop, on the Rue de l'Odéon. I bought a copy of *Ulysses,* whose light-blue-and-white cover was then an oriflamme for such as me, and we got into talk with Sylvia Beach, who presently startled us by asking if we would like to meet Mr. Joyce. We admitted we would, and a few days later she told us it was arranged. Nervous, overflowing with awe and questions, we presented ourselves at his door. He opened it himself—although he was wearing a gray dressing gown, I remember an impression of jaunty elegance—and led us down an interminable corridor to his study, where he sank exhaustedly into a chair. The next twenty minutes were hell. We thanked him for letting us come, we hoped we weren't disturbing him, we said we greatly admired his work. He said nothing. Every now and then he passed a limp hand over his face, a gesture that became more and more unnerving. We began to ask direct questions; he would answer yes or no, and then relapse into silence. Typical dialogues were:

G. L. K. M.: What do you think of Gertrude Stein, Mr. Joyce?
J. J.: Who?
G. L. K. M.: Gertrude Stein, the—writer. Do you know her work?
J. J.: No.

MYSELF *(brightly)*: You know, Mr. Joyce, I'm very much interested in the movies. *(Pause)* And I've always thought *Ulysses* would make a great movie. *(Pause)* [I learn from Mr. Ellmann's book that Joyce had considered several years earlier making *Ulysses* into a film.] Eisenstein ought to do it, really. *(Pause)* Do you know his films?
J. J.: Mmmmmmmmmmm.
MYSELF: Have you ever thought of *Ulysses* as a movie, Mr. Joyce?
J. J.: Mmmmmmmmmmm.

It was like trying to open a safe without the combination, and we were no Jimmy Valentines. At one point the subject of language came up—or, rather, we hauled it up—and I observed, desperately, that Mr. Joyce must know all there was to know about words, a gambit to which Morris assented with an enthusiastic giggle. The effect was frightening; a look of pain came over Joyce's face, and he slowly raised his hands, as if to ward off evil. We dropped the subject. There were, however, three lively—or not wholly unlively—moments. One came when either Morris or I, in a context I've forgotten, said something about people not knowing what to do with their lives. Joyce, his face flushed with animosity, gestured toward the window: "There are people who go walkin' up and down the street and they don't know what they want." We were impressed —his voice had an epic ring—but neither of us could think of anything more to say. The second moment came when Morris chanced to say he had an apartment in Paris. For the first time, Joyce took the initiative. "Where *is* your apartment, Mr. Morris?" he asked; he sounded almost interested. Later, as we were trying to get him to make a pronouncement on the Revolution of the Word his disciple Eugene Jolas had recently proclaimed, he broke in: "How many *rooms* are there in your apartment, Mr. Morris?" And still later: "Ah, Mr. Morris, how much do you *pay* for your apartment?" Presently one of us cleared his throat and said, nervously but resolutely, that we must be going. We all rose instantly. "Mr. Macdonald," said Joyce, addressing me for the first time, "I understand you are on *Fortune* magazine." "Yes." (It was nice to be in the monosyllabic position.) "An old school friend of mine is shortly going to New York. His name is Brian O'Leary [or some such] and he is a writer and he needs a job." At this point I must admit to a flash of suspicion about why Mr. Joyce had agreed to receive us. "I wonder if you could put in a word for him at *Fortune,* Mr. Macdonald?" he continued. I said, untruthfully, that I would be glad to. There was another long pause. Then we put on our coats, Joyce helping us cordially, and left. Outside the door, we turned to each other. "Well!" From Mr. Ellmann's biography, I gather this was a typical conversation with Joyce—parakeets was his sole topic with Le Corbusier, headaches and truffles with Proust. But we didn't know this in 1932.

As I say, this encounter has somehow escaped Mr. Ellmann's unsleeping vigilance. But there seem to be no other important lacunae in *James Joyce.* Miraculously, Mr. Ellmann combines industry and intelligence. He has ranged far beyond the library. A good part of his reference notes, which number 2,421 by my count, relates to interviews with people who knew Joyce and to letters from them. He has ordered this enormous mass of data in a clear narrative set down in good prose, perhaps a touch neutral in tone—

but the Recording Angel is probably using a colorless style, too. Nor has he shirked generalizations of his own, skillfully balancing truth and sympathy (in writing about Joyce, that is necessary). True, the academic stigmata are not wholly absent. Page 26 sounds an alarm that happily turns out to be a false one. The statement is made, with appropriate citations, that Joyce's mother had fair hair. This is foot-noted "It soon turned white," which is buttressed with a reference note. I thought the author might have ventured upon such descriptions on his own, and when I read, a few lines farther down, that Joyce's father had paid twenty-five pounds a year for him at Clongowes Wood school, a Fact that I was willing to accept without further argument but that nevertheless was footnoted "Reduced, because of Joyce's age, from forty-five guineas" and followed by "(it went up in 1890)," I fell to wondering what light this cast on the young Joyce, and I began to worry a little. How-ever, the pedantries turned out to be infrequent, and so did such academic circumlocutions as "He enjoyed some of the fleshly pleasures of Paris." (Or does this mean he relished *biftecks?*)

As a literary biographer, Mr. Ellmann has some unfair advantages over most of his academic colleagues. For one thing, he has a novelistic sense; he establishes the personal-ity of not only Joyce but the other main characters—his mother, his father, his brother Stanislaus, and his wife, Nora. The relations between the two brothers alone would make a good novel, which Joyce never wrote, perhaps be-cause it was too close to the bone. Stanislaus was all he was not and vice versa, he being imaginative, undependable, self-indulgent, and irresponsible (except in his writing), and his brother being critical, loyal, disciplined, and trust-worthy. Stanislaus was also perceptive and just about brother James. His *My Brother's Keeper* is an excellent picture of the young, or Dublin, Joyce, as Frank Budgen's *James Joyce and the Making of Ulysses* is of the middle, or

Zurich, Joyce. (As one might expect of so urban and international a writer, Joyce lived his life in four cities: Dublin
[1882-1904], where he was born and grew up to manhood;
Trieste [1905-1915], where he taught English at the Berlitz school, wrote *Dubliners* and *A Portrait of the Artist
as a Young Man,* and waited for fame—and, indeed, merely
for publication; Zurich [1915-1920], whither he went as a
refugee from Austrian Trieste at the beginning of the
First World War and where he wrote *Ulysses* and began
to be famous, published, and patronized; and Paris, which
he left in 1939, again a refugee, to return to Zurich for the
last two years of his life.) Secondly, Mr. Ellmann has a dry
wit and the kind of humor, sedate and insinuating, the
Scotch call "pawky." Apropos of the arrival of Stanislaus in
Trieste in the first year of Joyce's unmarriage, he writes,
"Stanislaus was able to help his brother and Nora over this
crisis, not so much, as he supposed, by the force of his ad-
monitions, as by supplying them with a common target of
complaint—himself." Apropos of Joyce's convivial drinking, which landed him in gutters all over Europe (the time
he spent in them shortened as his fame lengthened; after
Ulysses there was always some admirer around to pull him
out) but which never interfered with the next day's work:
"He engaged in excess with considerable prudence."
Thirdly, Mr. Ellmann has a good eye for *le mot juste.*
When someone asked Joyce what he had got out of his
Jesuit schooling, he gave a good definition of the aims of
education: "I have learnt to arrange things in such a way
that they become easy to survey and to judge." He made a
new calendar of weekdays, mocking his Irish tendency to
lugubrious complaint: "Moansday, Tearsday, Wailsday,
Thumpsday, Frightday, and Shatterday." When a young
enthusiast asked Joyce's permission to kiss "the hand that
wrote *Ulysses*," Joyce said, "No, it did a lot of other things,
too." There is also Jung's comment, after Joyce had objected to the diagnosis of schizoid tendencies in his daugh-

ter (Jung proved tragically right) and had asked why her verbal distortions were not similar to his own work: "You are both going to the bottom of the river, but she is falling and you are diving." Finally, Mr. Ellmann's style rises, ponderously but neatly, like Dr. Johnson's, to the high points of his narrative. There is the fine peroration that closes Chapter 32:

So, in spite of pain and sporadic blindness, Joyce moved irresistibly ahead with the grandest of all his conceptions. No ophthalmologists could seriously impede him. Through blear eyes he guessed at what he had written on paper, and with obstinate passion filled the margins and the space between the lines with fresh thoughts. His genius was a trap from which he did not desire to extricate himself.

One may wish, as I do, that he *had* extricated himself; one may find *Finnegans Wake* a crossword puzzle of genius, often funny or moving but in general a dead end. I once attended a session of a Finnegan Club at Northwestern University in which a dozen savants from various departments, including Mr. Ellmann, spent two hours on three or four pages; I was struck by the ingenuity of their hypotheses and also by the number of words they had to give up on. But whatever one's estimate of *Finnegans Wake,* one must regard Joyce's carrying it through as perhaps mistaken but certainly heroic—a literary Charge of the Light Brigade.

FOR, oddly, *James Joyce* gives an impression of heroism. Oddly because in most ways Joyce was decidedly unheroic. He was a coward, scared of dogs, panicked by thunderstorms. He refused to return to Ireland in 1931 to visit his dying father, whom he loved and whom he had not seen since 1920, because he thought it "not safe" (his wife, during "the trouble" many years earlier, had been briefly under fire). He was a sponger and deadbeat, deft at extracting small loans, shameless with landlords. Insolvency was his natural element. Even after 1919, when Miss Harriet

Weaver, as generous and understanding a patron as a literary man ever had, settled on him a comfortable yearly income, even after he began to make money from his writing—in 1928 two American publishers offered him an eleven-thousand-dollar advance on *Finnegans Wake,* for example—he whined about being hard up, which he always was, since he ate in the most expensive Paris restaurants and elsewhere indulged a notable talent for spending. All his life he had to be looked after by somebody—Stanislaus, Nora, Miss Weaver, Sylvia Beach, Eugene and Maria Jolas, his dedicated secretary Paul Léon. He was full of self-pity but shy on gratitude, better at taking than giving, as Miss Beach, among others, was to discover. He was vindictive— *vide* his lifelong hostility to Oliver St. John Gogarty, stemming from an episode most people would have forgotten in a few months. His most attractive trait was his strong feeling for his family and his friends; even so, Nora had to put up with a lot, brother Stanislaus was pretty much dropped after brother James became famous, and Léon was abruptly dismissed when he took the wrong side in a family quarrel.

The most unpleasant of such episodes was Joyce's break with Ottocaro Weiss, a close and loyal friend of the lean early years in Zurich. In 1918, Mrs. Edith Rockefeller Mc-Cormick, who was living there as patron and patient of Carl Jung, instructed her bankers to pay Joyce a thousand francs a month. The next year, being endowed, like others of her kind, with more money than sense, she decided that Joyce must be analyzed by Jung, at her expense. Joyce, who thought psychoanalysis a bore and a joke, predictably refused, and she cut off the subsidy. Because Weiss knew Jung and was acquainted with Mrs. McCormick, Joyce, who always suspected conspiracies, leaped to the false conclusion that Weiss was responsible and sent a special-delivery postcard demanding the instant repayment of fifty francs Weiss owed for wine they had drunk together. Weiss pawned his watch and sent the money—about ten dollars—to Joyce, who had been getting money not only from Mrs. McCormick but also from Miss Weaver, and had acquired an additional seven hundred dollars that summer, mostly from Scofield Thayer, the editor of the *Dial*. A few days later, the bewildered Weiss decided to make it up with his friend and sought him out in the café he frequented. Weiss was snubbed. Later he managed to find out what Joyce had against him, but his protestations of innocence were coolly received, and thenceforth Ottocaro Weiss drops out of James Joyce's biography.

From such evidence, provided in abundance by the admirably objective Mr. Ellmann, certain literary journalists who confuse biography and criticism might conclude that James Joyce was not a hero and not even, by some curious logic, much of a writer. They would be wrong. For all his failings, Joyce was a great man. The *locus classicus* on this topic is in Hegel's *Philosophy of History*:

They are great men because they willed and accomplished something great; not a mere fancy, a mere intention, but that which met the case and fell in with the needs of the age. This mode of considering them . . . excludes the so-called "psychological" view, which—serving mostly the purpose of envy —contrives . . . to bring [all actions] under such a subjective aspect that their authors appear to have done everything under the impulse of some passion, mean or grand, some morbid *craving*. . . .

These psychologists are particularly fond of contemplating those peculiarities of great historical figures which appertain to them as private persons. Man must eat and drink; he has relations with friends and acquaintances; he has passing impulses and ebullitions of temper.

"No man is a hero to his valet" is a well-known proverb. I have added—and Goethe repeated it ten years later: "But not because the former is no hero, rather because the latter is a valet." He takes off the hero's boots, assists him to bed, knows that he prefers champagne, etc. Historical personages waited upon . . . by such psychological valets come poorly off. They are brought down by these, their attendants, to a level with— or rather a few degrees below—the morality of such exquisite critics of the human spirit.

It is one of the merits of Mr. Ellmann's biography that he does not go in for valetlike moralizing. And, while he describes fully the dark side of the moon, he is equally informative on the bright side. This latter is Joyce's single-mindedness as a writer. He was a hero because he was courageous about the one great thing in his life. "Daring, noble, intrepid, determined" are some of the definitions of "heroic," and they apply to Joyce the writer as much as they don't to Joyce the man. He had, of course, enormous talent, but talent is more common than is generally believed. He also had character, which is less common than is generally believed. In his work, he was incapable of compromise or concession. He was objective about his own writing. "I may have oversystematized *Ulysses*," he once remarked casually and, I think, accurately. "The actual difficulties of my life are incredible," he wrote Nora in 1904, "but I despise them." It was not rhetoric. He had no job, no money, no reputation in Dublin except as a brilliant waster, and he was in violent opposition to the dominant "Irish Literary Renaissance." That same year, he showed his contempt for actual difficulties by emigrating with Nora to Trieste on less than nothing—he had to borrow train fare in Paris—and making do there for the next ten years on his meager earnings from teaching English (with chronic emergency supplements from Stanislaus) while his writing brought him in no money at all. But he knew he had to leave Ireland in order to survive as a writer. Just before he left, he wrote "The Holy Office," a broadside against his fellow Irish littérateurs that in metre and savagery reminds one of Swift: not the only resemblance; both were passionate rationalists, immoderately objective, burning cold in their contempt for sentimentality—just the opposite from the usual notion of the Irish temperament. After hitting off Yeats, Æ, Lady Gregory, Synge, Padraic Colum, and lesser leaders of the Irish Renaissance, he concludes:

> So distantly I turn to view
> The shamblings of that motley crew,
> Those souls that hate the strength that mine has
> Steeled in the school of old Aquinas.
> Where they have crouched and crawled and prayed
> I stand the self-doomed, unafraid,
> Unfellowed, friendless and alone,
> Indifferent as the herring-bone. . . .
> And though they spurn me from their door
> My soul shall spurn them evermore.

This is exaggerated. Far from spurning him from their door, Yeats and Æ had been generous in their encouragement, and far from spurning them evermore, Joyce a few months later was passing the hat among them (successfully) to pay for his trip. But it was essentially true. In what was important—writing—Joyce dared to defy them all; he recognized Yeats' poetic gift, but this just made him all the more angry. For a long time he did stand unfellowed and self-doomed, and if he was not entirely unafraid, that made it all the more heroic.

His first book—except for a slight volume of poems—was eight years getting printed. A London publisher, Grant Richards, accepted *Dubliners* in 1906, put it aside almost at once when his printer pointed out a number of "immoral" passages, and finally brought it out in 1914. (Of the 1,250 copies, only 379 had been sold a year later, and these included 120 that Joyce himself was obliged by the terms of the contract to buy.) Even this modest triumph was due, indirectly, to Ezra Pound, who "discovered" Joyce in 1914, a year after he had discovered Frost and the same year he discovered a young American poet, then studying philosophy at Oxford, named T. S. Eliot. (Pound was also, in that *annus mirabilis,* sharing a summer cottage in Sussex with Yeats, who was too famous to be discovered but whom Pound unsuccessfully tried to remake—and vice versa.) With his usual energy, Pound began to promote his find. He had just become literary editor of the *Egoist*—Harriet Weaver was business manager—and presently the *Egoist* began publishing chapters from Joyce's new work, *A Portrait of the Artist as a Young Man.* In December, 1916, this was brought out in America—after the cautious Grant Richards had refused it—by B. W. Huebsch, who combined acumen with boldness and who had published, a few weeks earlier, the first American edition of *Dubliners.* Two years later, Pound persuaded, with no difficulty, Margaret Anderson and Jane Heap of the *Little Review* to begin printing *Ulysses* in installments. "This is the most beautiful thing we'll ever have," exclaimed Miss Anderson when she read the first installment. "We'll print it if it's the last effort of our lives!" It nearly was. The early installments drew no official notice, but in 1919 and 1920 the Post Office confiscated four issues. Then the New York Society for the Prevention of Vice came to life, and in 1921 the editors were convicted of publishing obscenity. They got off with fifty-dollar fines, on condition that they stop printing *Ulysses.* This situation worried Huebsch, who had a contract to publish the book; he declined to go ahead unless Joyce would agree to changes, which he wouldn't. Joyce, who had met Sylvia Beach the year before ("Is this the great James Joyce?" she had asked; "James Joyce," he had noncommittally replied, holding out his hand), went around to see her. "My book will never come out now," he said, to which she replied impulsively, "Would you let Shakespeare and Company have the honor of bringing out your *Ulysses?*" He agreed, and so it was done, one of the advantages being that the French compositors didn't understand English. Among the initial subscribers was Winston Churchill, along with such predictable names as Yeats,

Gide, and Hemingway. Among them was not Bernard Shaw, who disliked his fellow-Irishman's works—the feeling was mutual—but pretended, after the usual Shavian fireworks, that the price was too high. It wasn't.

SUCCESS changed Joyce, but only superficially. (As Gatsby said contemptuously about Tom Buchanan's love for Daisy: "It was just personal.") Joyce knew exactly the work he was put on earth to do, and he did it, unaffected by affluence or poverty, fame or obscurity. Ibsen was his first love among writers and almost his last—his lack of interest in modern writers was extensive, including Proust, James, Mann, Eliot, Kafka, and Lawrence. He thought Ibsen a better dramatist than Shakespeare. It was Ibsen's realism that attracted him; the banal, the everyday, the actual always moved him more than the ideal (which, indeed, moved him not at all). But Joyce's realism was not in the reductive tradition of Zola. "The initial and determining act of judgment in his work," Mr. Ellmann writes, "is the justification of the commonplace. [Not the recording, note, but the justification; Sherwood Anderson's *Winesburg, Ohio* uses the same aesthetic.] Joyce's discovery, so humanistic that he would have been embarrassed to disclose it out of context, was that the ordinary is the extraordinary. . . . He denudes man of what we are accustomed to respect, then summons us to sympathize."

Even his choice of a wife was consistent with Joyce's literary creed. Nora Barnacle—"she'll never leave him," John Joyce, who like his son enjoyed plays on words, said when he heard her name—was a tall, handsome peasant girl from Galway, one of the most primitive parts of Ireland. She was a chambermaid when he met her, or, rather, picked her up. "To any other writer of the time," Mr. Ellmann observes, "Nora Barnacle would have seemed ordinary; Joyce, with his need to seek the remarkable in the commonplace, decided she was nothing of the sort." He proved to be right, if only because, although the sole quality of a family man Joyce had was the desire to be one, Nora bore him two children and stuck to him with the tenacity his father had predicted. The social gap, especially important in a provincial capital like Dublin, was the first difficulty. When he was courting her, he called her Nora and she called him Mr. Joyce. There is a touching passage in one of his letters to her: "Certain people who know that we are much together often insult me about you. I listen to them calmly, disdaining to answer them, but their least word tumbles my heart about like a bird in a storm." Touching, but a lover less sensitive to his feelings and more to hers might have suppressed this information. To the end, there was a wide intellectual gap. Nora never made any pretense of sharing her husband's literary life, perhaps wisely. She couldn't understand even *Dubliners,* she thought *Ulysses* was dirty, and her reaction to *Finnegans Wake* was "Why don't you write sensible books that people can understand?" After one quarrel, Nora sat down to write her mother that she was coming back to Galway for good. Said James, looking over her shoulder, "If you're going home, at least write 'I' with a capital letter." "What difference does it make?" said Nora. But she tore up the letter. She could never understand why her husband insisted on being a writer at all at all. "I've always told him he should give up writing and take up singing," she said to a family friend in 1924. "To think he was once on the same platform with John McCormack!" Almost the only recorded instance of her speaking of her husband's profession with approval occurred when a shopkeeper balked at exchanging a pair of shoes. "My husband is a writer," said Nora firmly, "and if you don't change them, I'll have it published in the paper." The shoes were changed.

Because he got drunk and frequented brothels, the young Joyce was considered immoral by respectable Dublin. But, as he remarked after seven years of unmarried married life with Nora, "I am more virtuous than all that lot—I, who am a real monogamist and have never loved but once in my life." It was true. "The most important thing that can happen to a man is the birth of a child," he said after his son was born. But Nora was for him far more than the mother of his children. He demanded, and she was willing and able to give, the whole range of feminine roles: the mother ("O that I could nestle in your womb like a child born of your flesh and blood, be fed by your blood, sleep in the warm secret gloom of your body!"), the divinity and the whore ("One moment I see you like a virgin or madonna, the next moment I see you shameless, insolent, half-naked, and obscene"), the cruel mistress of Sacher-Masoch ("I feel I would like to be flogged by you. I would like to see your eyes blazing with anger"), the romantic ideal ("But then I saw that the beauty of your soul outshone that of my verses. There was something in you higher than anything I had put into them"), the beauty to be spied on voyeuristically (he insisted on knowing, in detail, about her previous experiences with men, her "every thought . . . especially the most embarrassing"). He summed it up in an early letter: "You made a man of me."

Quite soon, the erotic seems to have ebbed from their marriage—the quotations above all date from the first five years, and Mr. Ellmann gives no further evidence—but she was still indispensable: "He depended upon Nora to hold his life together by her loyalty and by her contempt for his weaknesses." The contempt was real enough. "He's a weakling, Kathleen," she confided to her sister after twenty years of life with Joyce. "I wish I was married to a man like my father. Being married to a writer is a very hard life." But the loyalty was real, too, even if it was expressed most freely after his death. When a priest wanted to horn in on the funeral, Nora refused—"I couldn't do that to him." Later she complained, "Things are very dull now. There was always something doing when he was about." And when a journalist tried to get some reminiscences of André Gide out of her, she couldn't be bothered: "Sure, if you've been married to the greatest writer in the world, you don't remember all the little fellows."

And in his own way Joyce repaid her. Anniversaries fascinated him, as did all coincidences and other manifestations of the chance symmetry of life, including puns. He conceived so high a regard for James Stephens because they had the same birthday (February 2, 1882) and the same first name and because his last name was (almost) Dedalus' first that he suggested, in case he died before *Finnegan* was done, Stephens would be the ideal writer to complete it. Joyce's extreme rationality sought a compensation in fortuitous imitations of logic; it was his private entrance into the world of magic. So it is significant that the action of *Ulysses* takes place on June 16, 1904, the day he had his first date with Nora. And Finn's Hotel, where she was then working, may be memorialized—though Mr. Ellmann seems unaccountably to have overlooked the possibility— in *Finnegans Wake* and in the fact that H. C. Earwicker (Here Comes Everybody) is a descendant of the legendary Irish hero Finn MacCumhal. (Some think that Nora was the original of Molly Bloom, though she herself protested, "But she's much fatter than I am!") Toward the end of their life together, when they were sitting in a café with friends, Nora burst out, "I don't bother with him any more, he can do what he pleases. . . . I never get but three words out of him all day these days: in the morning, 'The papers!,' at lunch, 'What's that?,' and the third—Jim, what is the third, I can't remember it? Ah yes, about his bottle of water on the floor: 'Don't touch that!' " A bleak vignette of married life, in the true Joycean style— perhaps she had taken in more than she admitted—but it is worth noting that she felt free to appeal to him for the clinching detail.

JAMES JOYCE was a typical hero of our times in that he was a specialist. As Edison specialized in inventing and

Rockefeller in making money, so Joyce specialized in writing, and outside his specialty his interests were almost as
narrow as theirs. His years in Italy were confined to the
artistically barren city of Trieste, and not only because of
poverty. A bank job took him to Rome for seven months.
He hated the place—"Rome reminds me of a man who
lives by exhibiting to travellers his grandmother's corpse."
He sneered at Henry James's "tea-slop" about Rome. He
dismissed Renaissance painting: "I hate to think that
Italians ever did anything in the way of art. But I suppose
they did. What did they do but illustrate a page or two of
the New Testament!" In Zurich, the Alps bored him—
"those great lumps of sugar." Mr. Ellmann records nothing
of his reactions to Paris, one may assume because there were
none, not even when he first went there, at the age of
twenty. The only city he was ever interested in was Dublin,
on which he was the world's greatest expert. Almost the
only reference to modern art in the book is his complaint,
in 1927, that "My position is a farce. Picasso is not a higher
name than I have, I suppose, and he can get 20,000 to
30,000 francs for a few hours' work. I am not worth a
penny a line."

Politics was also subordinated to his speciality. He
thought of himself as a socialist partly because he hated the
Catholic Church, partly because "he thought . . . that a
political conscience would give his work distinction," and
partly because he believed a state subsidy would provide
artists like him with more freedom than they had under
capitalism, an illusion still possible in 1905. But, beyond
drinking in working-class bars, he never did anything about
socialism. In 1938 he refused to contribute to a German
refugee magazine because, a year before, Thomas Mann
had stated in it his anti-Nazi position, and therefore, concluded Joyce, it was "politically oriented"; he didn't want
Finnegans Wake banned in Germany. He was a Parnellite,
but Parnell was safely dead when he was only nine. As a

young writer in Dublin, he was unique in caring nothing one way or the other about Irish independence, and in later years he opposed it because he had a big literary investment in Ireland just as she was. "Tell me," he asked a friend, "why you think I ought to change the conditions that gave Ireland and me a shape and a destiny." Pacifism was the one creed he really believed in, though he did nothing about that, either. As a schoolboy, when he was assigned the topic "My Favorite Hero," he chose not the warlike Achilles but Ulysses, the man of many counsels, the intellectual, "the only man in Hellas against the war" (as he said later). It was a stroke of genius to make the modern Ulysses a Jewish bourgeois, reasonable and civilized, surviving by his wits in a savage Irish environment dominated by Achilles types like Blazes Boylan and Polyphemus types like The Citizen.

In *Finnegans Wake,* Joyce narrowed his specialty still further, from writing to words. "I have discovered I can do anything with language I want," he wrote late in his life. The pun is the ultimate in the manipulation of words, playing with their meaning the better to concentrate on them themselves—that is, on their sound—and *Finnegan,* essentially a collection of puns, is to other writing as abstract art is to other art. It was not liked by some of Joyce's most important supporters. T. S. Eliot, according to Virginia Woolf, had been more "rapt" and "enthusiastic" about *Ulysses* than she had ever seen him about any work before; he had reviewed it favorably in the *Dial*: "It has given me all the surprise, delight, and terror that I can require, and I will leave it at that," wrote young Mr. Eliot, magisterial even then. But Eliot never committed himself about *Finnegan.* Even Pound was hostile; even Miss Weaver, most tolerant and diffident of patrons, had to confess, "I am made in such a way that I do not care much for the output of your Wholesale Safety Pun Factory. . . . It seems to me you are wasting your genius. But I daresay I

am wrong." Joyce was so upset by this letter that he took
to his bed. (But he didn't give up *Finnegan*.) He had, of
course, some support. Archibald MacLeish was an early
convert. And in 1929 twelve writers contributed to his
defense a brief entitled *Our Exagmination Round His Factification for Incamination of Work in Progress*. Generally,
however, the auspices were never favorable; of the twelve
collaborators on the *Exagmination,* only William Carlos
Williams and Samuel Beckett are much remembered today.
But Joyce continued to work on *Finnegan* and to revise it,
right up to his death, in 1941. In the terrible summer of
1940, Joyce, a refugee in the provinces after the Germans
had taken Paris, devoted several hours a day to correcting
misprints in *Finnegan*. This is what is meant by "character," I think. Perhaps *Finnegan* was a blind alley, but it
was *his* blind alley.

Whatever claim James Joyce has to heroism is summed
up in a letter Ezra Pound wrote in 1920 to that most
percipient patron of the avant-garde, the American lawyer
and collector John Quinn: "Thank God, he has been
stubborn enough to know his job and stick to it." (I now
understand the contemptuous ring in Joyce's voice when
he told Morris and me, "There are people who go walkin'
up and down the street and they don't know what they
want.") It was also Pound who, in 1931, summed up Joyce
as a modern hero of specialization: "I respect Mr. Joyce's
integrity as an author in that he has not taken the easy
part. I never had any respect for his common sense or for
his intelligence, apart from his gifts as a writer." Joyce's
lack of common sense—almost as great as Pound's—appears in every chapter of this biography, and his intellectual
narrowness is apparent in Mr. Ellmann's collection, *The
Critical Writings of James Joyce*. But his gifts as a writer
were extreme and he carried them without compromise to
their extremity. "The most important expression which the
present age has found," the young Eliot called *Ulysses,*

adding, "It is a book to which we are all indebted, and from which none of us can escape." Singularly uninfluenced by either academic tradition or avant-garde fashion, Joyce worked out his solitary destiny as a writer, pushing through to completion each of his four major works in spite of enormous obstacles, not the least of which was his own nature.

They are great men because they willed and accomplished something great; not a mere fancy, a mere intention, but that which met the case and fell in with the needs of the age.

James Agee

THE LATE JAMES AGEE'S *A Death in the Family* is an odd book to be written by a serious writer in this country and century, for it is about death (not violence) and love (not sex). Death is conceived of in a most un-American way, not so much a catastrophe for the victim as a mystery, and at the same time an illumination, for the survivors. As for love, it is not sexual, not even romantic; it is domestic— between husband, wife, children, aunts, uncles, grand- parents. This love is described tenderly, not in the tough, now-it-can-be-told style dominant in our fiction since Dreiser. The negative aspects are not passed over—Agee is, after all, a serious writer—but what he dwells on, what he "celebrates," is the positive affection that Tolstoy presented in "Family Happiness" but that now is usually dealt with in the women's magazines. Very odd.

There are other original features. We are used to novels that describe the professional and regional background more fully than the human beings, but here there is no "local color," and we are not even told what the father's occupation is. We are used to novels about "plain people" that are garnished with humanitarian rhetoric and a conde- scending little-man-what-now? pathos, as in *The Grapes of Wrath* and such exercises in liberal right-mindedness. But Agee felt himself so deeply and simply part of the world of his characters—the fact that they were his own family by no means explains this empathy—that he wrote about them as naturally as Mark Twain wrote about the people of Hannibal. The 1915 Tennessee vernacular sounds just right, not overdone yet pungent: " 'Well,' he said, taking out his watch. 'Good Lord a mercy!' He showed her. Three-forty-one. 'I didn't think it was hardly three. . . . Well, no more dawdling. . . . All right, Mary. I hate to go, but— can't be avoided.' " The last sentence, in rhythm and word choice, seems to me perfect. We are used, finally, to novels of action, novels of analysis, and novels that combine the two, but not to a work that is static, sometimes lyrical and sometimes meditative but always drawn from sensibility rather than from intellection. It reminds me most of Sherwood Anderson, another sport in twentieth-century American letters—brooding, tender-minded, and a crafts-man of words.

James Agee died in 1955 at the age of forty-five. He died of a heart attack in a taxicab, and the platitudes about "shock" and "loss" suddenly became real. A friend I had for thirty years respected intellectually and sympathized with emotionally and disapproved of temperamentally and been stimulated by conversationally had vanished, abruptly and for good. I had always thought of Agee as the most broadly gifted writer of my generation, the one who, if anyone, might someday do major work. He didn't do it, or not much of it, but I am not the only one who expected he would. He really shouldn't have died, I kept thinking, and now this posthumous book makes me think it all the harder.

The book jacket is, for once, accurate when it describes Agee as "essentially a poet." For this is really not a novel but a long poem on themes from childhood and family life. The focal point is the death, in an automobile ac-cident, of Jay Follet, a young husband and father who lived in Knoxville around the time of the First World War. This is about all that "happens." There are other episodes grouped around the death, and they are often vividly rendered, in novelistic terms, but there is no plot, no suspense, no development, and thus no novel. The point of view is mostly that of Jay's six-year-old son, Rufus, who is in fact James Agee, who is writing about his actual childhood and about the actual death of his father. Even those parts that are not told directly in terms of Rufus-Agee's experience are affected by this viewpoint. The father and mother, although they are major figures, are barely individualized, since to a small child his parents are too close to be distinctly seen. The more distant and lesser figures, like Aunt Hannah, are more definite. Parents are big, vague archetypes to a child (Strength, Love, or—alas —Coldness, Failure), but aunts are people. In this child-centered structure, at least, *A Death in the Family* is in the American grain. (Why are our writers so much more at home with children than with adults?) Many of the best things are connected with Rufus: his delight over his new cap, his comic and appalling relations with his little sister, his nightmares ("and darkness, smiling, leaned ever more intimately inward upon him, laid open the huge, ragged mouth"), his innocent trust in the older boys, who tease and humiliate him with subtle cruelty. These parts of it can be recommended as an antidote to *Penrod*.

Agee was a very good writer. He had the poet's eye for detail. "Ahead, Asylum Avenue lay bleak beneath its lamps. ... In a closed drug store stood Venus de Milo, her golden body laced in elastic straps. The stained glass of the L & N depot smoldered like an exhausted butterfly ... an outcrop of limestone like a great bundle of dirty laundry. ... Deep in the valley, an engine coughed and browsed." He could get magic into his writing the hardest way, by precise description:

First an insane noise of violence in the nozzle, then the still irregular sound of adjustment, then the smoothing into steadiness and a pitch as accurately tuned to the size and style of stream as any violin ... the short still arch of the separate big drops, silent as a held breath, and the only noise the flattering noise on leaves and the slapped grass at the fall of each big drop. That, and the intense hiss with the intense stream; that, and that same intensity not growing less but growing more quiet and delicate with the turn of the nozzle, up to that extreme tender whisper when the water was just a wide bell of film.

I haven't watered a lawn in forty years, but I remember that was the way it was in Sea Girt, New Jersey. And this was the way trolley cars were:

A street car raising its iron moan; stopping, belling and starting; stertorous; rousing and raising again its iron increasing moan and swimming its gold windows and straw seats on past and past and past, the bleak spark crackling and cursing above it like a small malignant spirit set to dog its tracks; the iron whine rises on rising speed; still risen, faints; halts; the faint stinging bell; rises again, still fainter; fainting, lifting, lifts, faints forgone: forgotten.

These passages are from "Knoxville: Summer of 1915," which appeared in *Partisan Review* twenty years ago; the publishers have had the good idea of reprinting it as a prelude to *A Death in the Family*. "We are now talking of summer evenings in Knoxville, Tennessee, in the time I lived there so successfully disguised to myself as a child," he begins, and he concludes, "After a little I am taken in and put to bed. Sleep, soft smiling, draws me unto her: and those receive me, who quietly treat me, as one familiar and well-beloved in that home: but will not, oh, will not, not now, not ever; but will not ever tell me who I am." In between are five pages of reverie, lyrical and yet precise, about the after-dinner time when families sit around on porches and the fathers water the lawns. "Knoxville" is typical of Agee's prose: in the weighty authority with which words are selected and placed; in getting drama, as Dickens and Gogol did, out of description; in the cadenced, repetitive, sometimes Biblical rhythm; in the keyed-up emotion that teeters on the verge of sentimentality ("soft smiling" falls in, and "unto" comes too close for comfort); in the combination, usual only in writers of the first rank, of acute sensuousness with broad philosophical themes.

Although *A Death in the Family* is not a major work, Agee, I think, had the technical, the intellectual, and the moral equipment to do major writing. By "moral," which has a terribly old-fashioned ring, I mean that Agee believed in and—what is rarer—was interested in good and evil. Lots of writers are fascinated by evil and write copiously about it, but they are bored by virtue; this not only limits their scope but prevents a satisfactory account of evil, which can no more be comprehended apart from good than light can be comprehended apart from darkness. Jay Follet is a good husband and father, Mary is a good wife and mother, and their goodness is expressed in concrete action, as is the evil in the boys who humiliate their son or the lack of "character" Jay's brother, Ralph, shows in a family crisis. (Character is another old-fashioned quality that interested Agee.) The theme is the confrontation of love, which I take to be life carried to its highest possible reach, and death, as the negation of life and yet a necessary part of it.

Admittedly, the book has its *longueurs,* and very long *longueurs* they are sometimes, but for the most part it is wonderfully alive. For besides his technical skill, his originality and integrity of vision, Agee had a humorous eye for human behavior. The nuances of the husband-and-wife relationship come out in a series of everyday actions: Mary peppering the eggs to Jay's taste; Jay straightening up the covers of the bed ("She'll be glad of that, he thought, very well pleased with the looks of it"); Mary insisting on getting up at three in the morning to cook breakfast for her husband, and his mixed reaction: "He liked night lunchrooms and had not been in one since Rufus was born. He was very faintly disappointed. But still more, he was warmed by the simplicity with which she got up for him, thoroughly awake." The bondage and the binding of marriage are both there. This is realism, but of a higher order than we have become accustomed to, since it includes those positive aspects of human relations which are so difficult to describe today without appearing sentimental. The uneasiness the Victorians felt in the presence of the base we feel in the presence of the noble. It is to Agee's credit that he didn't feel uneasy.

This livelier, more novelistic side of Agee appears in such episodes as the scene in which Aunt Hannah takes Rufus shopping for his first cap (up to then he had been allowed only babyish *hats*):

He submitted so painfully conservative a choice, the first time, that she smelled the fear and hypocrisy behind it, and said carefully, "That is very nice, but suppose we look at some more, first." She saw the genteel dark serge, with the all but invisible visor, which she was sure would please Mary most, but she doubted whether she would speak of it; and once Rufus felt that she really meant not to interfere, his tastes surprised her. He tried still to be careful, more out of courtesy, she felt, then meeching, but it was clear to her that his heart was set on a thunderous fleecy check in jade green, canary yellow, black and white, which stuck out inches to either side above his ears and had a great scoop of a visor beneath which his face was all but lost. It was a cap, she reflected, which even a colored sport might think a little loud, and she was painfully tempted to interfere. Mary would have conniption fits. . . . But she was switched if she was going to boss him! "That's very nice," she said, as little drily as she could manage. "But think about it. Rufus. You'll be wearing it a long time, you know, with all sorts of clothes." But it was impossible for him to think about anything except the cap; he could even imagine how tough it was going to look after it had been kicked around a little. "You're very sure you like it," Aunt Hannah said.

"Oh, yes," said Rufus.

"Better than this one?" Hannah indicated the discreet serge.

"Oh, yes," said Rufus, scarcely hearing her.

"Or this one?" she said, holding up a sharp little checker-board.

"I think I like it best of all," Rufus said.

"Very well, you shall have it," said Aunt Hannah, turning to the cool clerk.

Agee was a very American writer, and this passage, in its humor, its sensitivity to boyhood, its directness of approach, and its use of the rhythms and idioms of everyday speech, seems to me in the peculiarly American tradition of Twain and Anderson.

A Death in the Family should be read slowly. It is easy to become impatient, for the movement is circular, rumina-tive, unhurried. He dwells on things, runs on and on and on. Perhaps one *should* be impatient. What Agee needed was a sympathetically severe editor who would prune him as Maxwell Perkins pruned Thomas Wolfe, whom Agee resembled in temperament, though I think he was superior artistically. A better comparison is with Whitman, who also runs on and on, hypnotizing himself with his material, losing all sense of proportion, losing all sense of anyone else reading him, and simply chanting, in bardic simplicity, to himself. Like Whitman and unlike Wolfe, Agee was able at last to come down hard on The Point and roll it up into a magically intense formulation; the weariest river of Ageean prose winds somewhere safe to sea. After pages of excessive, obsessive chewing-over of a funeral, including a morbid detailing of the corpse's appearance and several prayers in full, Agee comes down, hard and accurate, to earth and to art: "[Rufus] looked towards his father's face and, seeing the blue-dented chin thrust upward, and the way the flesh was sunken behind the bones of the jaw, first recognized in its specific weight the word, *dead*. He looked quickly away, and solemn wonder tolled in him like the shuddering of a prodigious bell." Should one be impatient? I suspect one should. Granted the preceding *longueurs* were necessary for the writer if he were to work up enough steam for this climax, it doesn't follow that they are necessary for the reader. Would not a more conscious, self-disciplined writer have written them and then, when he had reached the final effect, have gone back and removed the scaffolding? It would have been interesting to see if Agee would have done this had he lived to give final form to *A Death in the Family*.

Agee was seldom able to tell when he was hitting it and when he wasn't. That he should have hit it so often is a sign of his talent. There are many passages in *A Death in the Family* that can only be called great, much though the word is abused these days, great in the union of major emotion with good writing.

IN some literary circles, James Agee now excites the kind of emotion James Dean does in some nonliterary circles. There is already an Agee cult. This is partly because of the power of his writing and his lack of recognition—everyone likes to think he is on to a good thing the general public has not caught up with—but mainly because it is felt that Agee's life and personality, like Dean's, were at once a symbolic expression of our time and a tragic protest against it. It is felt that not their weakness but their vitality betrayed them. In their maimed careers and their wasteful deaths, the writer and the actor appeal to a resentment that intellectuals and teen-agers alike feel about life in America, so smoothly prosperous, so deeply frustrating.

James Agee was born in Knoxville in 1909. He went to St. Andrew's School there, then to Exeter and Harvard. In 1932, the year he graduated from Harvard, Agee got a job on *Fortune*. For fourteen years, like an elephant learning to deploy a parasol, Agee devoted his prodigious gifts to Lucean journalism. In 1939, he moved over to *Time*, where he wrote book reviews and then was put in charge of Cinema. In 1943, he began writing movie reviews for the *Nation*, too. He resigned from *Time* and the *Nation* in 1948, specifically to finish *A Death in the Family* but also because he realized that otherwise he would never get down to his own proper work. There was reason for his concern. Although he wrote constantly, in a small, shapely script that contrasted oddly with his oceanic personality, he finished very little; I remember grocery cartons full of manuscripts he had put aside. In 1948 he was thirty-nine, and he had published, aside from his journalism, only a book of poems, *Permit Me Voyage* (1934), and a long prose work, *Let Us Now Praise Famous Men* (1941).

In the seven years that were left to him, he did manage to bring *A Death in the Family* close to final form and to publish a novelette, *The Morning Watch* (1951), and a short story, "A Mother's Tale" (*Harper's Bazaar*). But again most of his energies were diverted. For before he settled down to work in his old farmhouse in Hillsdale, New York, with his third wife, Mia, he had to get out of the way two profitable articles for *Life*, which he planned to knock out in six weeks and which took him six months. One was on silent-movie comedians; the second was on the films of John Huston. Agee had already, in 1947, written the commentary for one movie, *The Quiet One*, a documentary about Harlem life that was a great *succès d'estime*, but he had never worked in Hollywood. Huston liked his article, and commissioned him to do a script for a film version of Stephen Crane's *The Blue Hotel*. Huston never made the film, but he was impressed by Agee's script (and by Agee) and asked him to do one for *The African Queen*. This is mostly just another movie, but it does have several Agee touches—the Anglican service with only shining black faces in the congregation, Bogart's stomach rumblings at the tea party, the peculiar horror of the leeches and the gnats. It was ironical, and typical, that Agee's work with Huston was limited to a conventional adventure-romance film. Before they met, Huston made *The Red Badge of Courage*, and later he wanted Agee to work on *Moby Dick*, but Agee had an interfering commitment. So two jobs that would have given scope for his powers were lost by luck, or was it destiny? Whichever it was, it was rarely on his side.

After *The African Queen,* Agee did a number of other scripts—for *The Night of the Hunter,* which is realistic and at times macabre in a most unHollywoodian way; for a delightful short comedy, *The Bride Comes to Yellow Sky,* taken from a story by Crane, in which he played the town drunk; for a film on the life of Gauguin (this, said to be his most remarkable script, was never used); for *Genghis Khan,* a Spanish-language Filipino film; for an "Omnibus" television series on the life of Lincoln; for a documentary about Williamsburg. Then he died.

ALTHOUGH he achieved much, it was a wasted, and wasteful, life. Even for a modern writer, he was extraordinarily self-destructive. He was always ready to sit up all night with anyone who happened to be around, or to go out at midnight looking for someone: talking passionately, brilliantly, but too much, drinking too much, smoking too much, reading aloud too much, making love too much, and in general cultivating the worst set of work habits in Greenwich Village. This is a large statement, but Agee's was a large personality. "I wish I knew how to work," he said to a friend. He wrote copiously, spending himself recklessly there, too, but there was too much else going on. He seemed to have almost no sense of self-preservation, allowing his versatility and creative energy to be exploited in a way that shrewder, cooler men of talent don't permit. His getting stuck for so long in the Luce organization is an instance; like Jacob, he drudged fourteen years in another man's fields, but there was no Rachel in view.

"Jim seemed to want to punish himself," another friend says. "He complicated his creative life so much that he was rarely able to come to simple fulfillment. He would

put off work until he got far enough behind to feel satisfactorily burdened with guilt. Somehow he managed to
turn even his virtues into weaknesses. Jim was bigger than
life, had enormous energy—my God, the man was inexhaustible! He reacted excessively to *everything*. The
trouble was he couldn't say No. He let people invade him,
all kinds, anyone who wanted to. He thought he had time
and energy enough for them all. But he didn't, quite. His
heart trouble began on Huston's ranch out West, when he
was working with him on the script of *The African Queen*.
Huston was in the habit of playing two or three sets of
singles before breakfast—*he* was a prodigal live-it-upper,
too; that was one reason they got on so well together—
and Agee, who hadn't played in years and was out of condition, went at it with him every morning, trying for
every shot, until he collapsed on the court with his first
heart attack. The doctors told Jim to take it easy, to drink,
smoke, and live moderately. But that was the one talent
he didn't have."

The waste one senses in Agee's career had other roots as
well. He was spectacularly born in the wrong time and
place. He was too versatile, for one thing. In art as in
industry, this is an age of specialization. There is a definite
if restricted "place" for poetry; there is even a Pulitzer
Prize for it, and poets of far less capacity than Agee have
made neat, firm little reputations. But his best poetry is
written in prose and is buried in his three books. Nor was
he solely dedicated to literature. Music was also important
to him, and the cinema, so closely related to music, was his
first love, and his last. I think he never gave up the dream
of becoming a director, of expressing himself directly with
images and rhythm instead of making do at one remove
with words. His best writing has a cinematic flow and im-
mediacy; his worst has a desperate, clotted quality, as
though he felt that nobody would "get" him and was
trying to break through, irritatedly, by brute exaggeration

and repetition. But he was typed as a writer, and the nearest he could come to making movies was to write scripts—scripts that go far beyond what is usual in the way of precise indications as to sequence of shots, camera angles, visual details (the raindrops on a leaf are described in one), and other matters normally decided by the director. They are the scripts of a frustrated director.

The times might have done better by Agee. They could exploit one or two of his gifts, but they couldn't use him *in toto*—there was too much there to fit into any one compartment. In another sense, American culture was not structured *enough* for Agee's special needs; it was overspecialized as to function but amorphous as to values. He needed definition, limitation, discipline, but he found no firm tradition, no community of artists and intellectuals that would canalize his energies. One thinks of D. H. Lawrence, similar to Agee in his rebellious irrationalism, who was forced to define his own values and his own special kind of writing precisely because of the hard, clear, well-developed cultural tradition he reacted so strongly against.

If his native land offered Agee no tradition to corset his sprawling talents, no cultural community to moderate his eccentricities, it did provide "movements," political and aesthetic. Unfortunately, he couldn't sympathize with any of them. He was always unfashionable, not at all the thing for the post-Eliot thirties. His verse was rather conventional and romantic. In the foreword to *Permit Me Voyage,* Archibald MacLeish, than whom few have been more sensitive to literary fashions, accurately predicted, "It will not excite the new-generationers, left wing or right. . . . Agee does not assume . . . a Position." Ideologically, it was even worse. In an age that was enthusiastic about social issues, Agee's whole style of being was individualistic and antiscientific. He was quite aware of this; oddly, considering the constellation of his traits, he had a strong bent toward ideas. Unlike, say, Thomas Wolfe, he was an intellectual; it was another aspect of his versatility. This awareness comes out clearly in a passage from that extraordinary grab bag *Let Us Now Praise Famous Men*:

"Description" is a word to suspect.

Words cannot embody; they can only describe. But a certain kind of artist, whom we will distinguish from others as a poet rather than a prose writer, despises this fact about words or his medium, and continually brings words as near as he can to an illusion of embodiment. [Here the frustrated movie-maker speaks, for if words cannot embody, pictures can, and without illusion—a picture is an artistic fact in itself, unlike a word.] In doing so he accepts a falsehood but makes, of a sort in any case, better art. It seems very possibly true that art's superiority over science and over all other forms of human activity, and its inferiority to them, reside in the identical fact that art accepts the most dangerous and impossible of bargains and makes the best of it, becoming, as a result, both nearer the truth and farther from it than those things which, like science and scientific art, merely describe, and those things which, like human beings and their creations and the entire state of nature, merely are, the truth.

As MacLeish observed, Agee appealed neither to the Left nor to the Right. "I am a Communist by sympathy and conviction," he wrote in the thirties, and at once went on to put a tactless finger right on the sore point:

But it does not appear (just for one thing) that Communists have recognized or in any case made anything serious of the sure fact that the persistence of what once was insufficiently described as Pride, a mortal sin, can quite as coldly and inevitably damage and wreck the human race as the most total power of "Greed" ever could: and that socially anyhow, the most dangerous form of pride is neither arrogance nor humility, but its mild, common denominator form, complacency. . . . Artists, for instance, should be capable of figuring the situation out to the degree that they would refuse the social eminence and the high pay they are given in Soviet

Russia. The setting up of an aristocracy of superior workers is no good sign, either.

The idiom ("the sure fact . . . figuring the situation out . . . no good sign, either") and the rhythm are in the American vernacular, and thus hopelessly out of key with the style in which everybody else wrote about these matters then. Nor was Agee any more congruous with the Right. Although he was deeply religious, he had his own kind of religion, one that included irreverence, blasphemy, obscenity, and even Communism (of his own kind). By the late forties, a religio-conservative revival was under way, but Agee felt as out of place as ever. "If my shapeless comments can be of any interest or use," he characteristically began his contribution to a *Partisan Review* symposium on Religion and the Intellectuals, "it will be because the amateur and the amphibian should be represented in such a discussion. By amphibian I mean that I have a religious background and am 'pro-religious'—though not on the whole delighted by this so-called revival—but doubt that I will return to religion." Amateurs don't flourish in an age of specialization, or amphibians in a time when educated armies clash by night.

THE incompatibility of Agee and his times came to a head in the sensational failure of Agee's masterpiece, *Let Us Now Praise Famous Men*. It is a miscellaneous book, as hard to classify as that earlier failure *Moby Dick*, which it resembles, being written in a "big" style, drawing poetry from journalistic description, and making the largest statements about the human condition. It is mostly a documentary account of three Southern tenant-farming families, illustrated with thirty-one magisterial photographs by Walker Evans, Agee's close friend, who is listed on the title page as co-author and whose influence was strong on the text. But it is many other things as well—philosophy, narrative, satire, cultural history, and autobiography. It is a

young man's book—exuberant, angry, tender, willful to the
point of perversity, with the most amazing variations in
quality; most of it is extremely good, some of it is as great
prose as we have had since Hawthorne, and some of it is
turgid, mawkish, overwritten. But the author gives himself
wholly to his theme and brings to bear all his powers; he
will go to any lengths to get it just right. From this emerges
a truth that includes and goes beyond the truth about
poverty and ignorance in sociological studies (and
"realistic" novels), the truth that such squalid lives, imaginatively observed, are also touched with the poetry, the
comedy, the drama of what is unexpected and unpredictable because it is living. It is illuminating to compare
Agee's book with one of those New Deal surveys of "the
sharecropping problem." It is also interesting to read a
professional work on grade-school education and then to
read Agee's twenty-seven pages of notes on the subject:

Adults writing to or teaching children: in nearly every
word within these textbooks, for instance [he has three devastating pages on one of them, which every writer for children
should read], there is a flagrant mistake of some kind. The
commonest is this: that they simplify their own ear, without
nearly enough skepticism as to the accuracy of the simpli-
fication, and with virtually no intuition for the child or children; then write or teach to satisfy that ear; discredit the child
who is not satisfied, and value the child who, by docile or innocent distortions of his intelligence, is.

The "esthetic" is made hateful and is hated beyond all other
kinds of "knowledge." It is false-beauty to begin with; it is
taught by sick women or sicker men; it becomes identified
with the worst kinds of femininity and effeminacy; it is made
incomprehensible and suffocating to anyone of much natural
honesty and vitality.

The book grew out of an assignment to Agee and Evans
from *Fortune* in 1936 to do a story on Southern share-

croppers. For two months they lived in the Alabama back country. *Fortune,* unsurprisingly, couldn't "use" the article. Harper then staked Agee to a year off the Luce payroll to write the book. When it was done, they couldn't use it, either; they wanted deletions in the interests of good taste, and Agee refused; since the higher-ups weren't enthusiastic anyway about this strange, difficult work, Harper stood firm. Finally, Houghton Mifflin bought it out in 1941. The critics disliked it—Selden Rodman, Lionel Trilling, and George Marion O'Donnell were honorable exceptions —and it sold less than six hundred copies the first year. *Moby Dick* sold five hundred, which was six times as good a showing, taking into account the increase of population.

The mischance that dogged Agee's career is evident in the timing of his death. Those who knew him best say that in the last few years of his life Agee changed greatly, became more mature, more aware of himself and of others, shrewder about his particular talents and problems. In the very last year, he had even begun to pay some attention to doctors' orders. He was by then getting such good fees for scripts that he was looking forward to doing only one a year and spending the rest of the time on his own writing. He might even have found out who he was. *A Death in the Family* contrasts significantly with *Let Us Now Praise Famous Men*. It rarely achieves the heights of the earlier book—I think Agee's literary reputation will be mostly based on about half of *Let Us Now Praise Famous Men*— but it is written in a more controlled and uniform style; it has more humor and none of the self-consciousness that often embarrasses one in the earlier work; its structure is classical, without Gothic excrescences; and, most significant of all, human beings are seen objectively, with the novelist's rather than the poet's eye. There is also the remarkable short story, "A Mother's Tale," he wrote three years before his death: a Kafka-like allegory, perfectly ordered and harmonious all through, of the human situation in this age of total war. I think only a thoroughly developed writer could have done it. Like Keats, Agee died just when he was beginning to mature as an artist. That Keats was twenty-five and Agee forty-five doesn't alter the point. Agee was an American, of a race that matures slowly, if ever.

"He was at his best just short of his excesses, and he tended in general to work out toward the dangerous edge. He was capable of realism . . . but essentially he was a poet. . . . He had an exorbitant appetite for violence, for cruelty, and for the Siamese twin of cruelty, a kind of obsessive tenderness which at its worst was all but nauseating. . . . In his no longer fashionable way, he remained capable, and inspired. He was merely unadaptable and unemployable, like an old, sore, ardent individualist among contemporary progressives. . . . He didn't have it in him to be amenable, even if he tried." So Agee wrote after D. W. Griffith died. He may have been describing the film director. He was certainly describing himself.

Appendix:

JIM AGEE, A MEMOIR

AUTHOR'S NOTE: *George Braziller has recently published* The Letters of James Agee to Father Flye. *These extraordinary letters were written over a period of thirty years, from his admission to Exeter in 1925 to his death in 1955. Father Flye is an Episcopalian priest who was Agee's teacher, before Exeter, at St. Andrews School in Tennessee and who became a substitute for the father he had lost at the age of six. (That Father Flye was normally addressed as "Dear Father" is a Freudian pun too deep for tears.) What follows is an article, considerably expanded, I wrote for the house organ of the Book Find Club.*

IN the 'twenties, James Agee and I both attended Phillips Exeter Academy, which then had an extraordinary English department: Myron Williams, E. S. W. Kerr, Hank Couse, Dr. Cushwa, James Plaisted ("Cokey Joe") Webber, to set down the names of those who taught us something about writing. Jim and I just missed each other at Exeter, I graduating in the spring of 1924 and he arriving there in the fall of 1925. I find I wrote an old Exeter friend, Dinsmore Wheeler, in 1929, apropos of a project for starting an intellectual community on his farm in Ohio: "Our generation is one of great power, I think. There's talent running around like loose quicksilver. A fellow named Jim Agee, onetime editor of the P.E.A. *Monthly*, has The Stuff. I've never met him but I've corresponded with him. He is all there when it comes to creative writing, or rather *will be* all there."

Agee was then at Harvard and I on *Fortune* and we kept on corresponding, mostly about movies, which interested us as a form of self-expression much more than writing did. "A fellow in my dormitory," he wrote me that year, "owns a movie camera (not the kind you set buzzing and jam into the diaphragm) and has done some interesting work with it. . . . It's possible we'll do two movies [a documentary on Boston and a film version of a short story he had written]. The idea is that I'll devise shots, angles, camera work, etc., and stories; he'll take care of the photography and lighting." (Like my own dream of an Ohio Brook Farm, neither of these projects seems to have come to anything.) We both admired the standard things—Griffith, Chaplin, Stroheim, the Russians, the Germans—despised the big American productions ("*Noah's Ark* is the worst and most pretentious movie ever made," he wrote) and looked desperately for signs of life in Hollywood: "Saw a movie today, *Hearts in Dixie* was its unfortunate title. The thing itself struck me as pretty swell [though] there was no camera work and very little else to recommend it from the real director's point of of view." His enthusiasm seems to have been based mostly on the fact it was less melodramatic than *Porgy*. Similarly, his "Ever noticed Dorothy Mackaill? Along the general lines of Esther Ralston" was intended as a compliment. We really were hopeful then.

"I'm going to spend the summer working in the wheat-fields, starting in Oklahoma in June," he wrote May 10, 1929. "The thing looks good in every way. I like to get drunk and will; I like to sing and learn dirty songs and hobo ones—and will; I like to be on my own—the farther from home the better—and will; and I like the heterogeneous gang that moves north on the job. . . . Also I like bumming. . . . Finally, I like saving money, and this promises from $5 to $7 a day." That summer I got a pencil-scrawled note dated "Oshkosh, Neb., maybe August 1" (the postmark is August 5):

DEAR DWIGHT—
If pen and ink and white paper gave you trouble, this should rival the Rosetta stone. To add insult to injury, it's written in a wagon-bed—about my only chance to write is between loads.

Am now working at hauling and scooping grain on a "combine" crew. . . . Kansas is the most utterly lousy state I've ever seen. Hot as hell and trees ten miles apart. I worked near a town which proudly bore the name "Glade" because of a clump of scrawny, dusty little trees it had somehow managed to assemble.

The first town across the Nebraska line was so different I declared a holiday, sat on a bench in the court-house park and wrote a story. I rather think I've stumbled onto the best possible surroundings and state of mind in which to write. I certainly was more at home with it than at Harvard, home or Exeter.

That night I saw a rather interesting movie, "The Leathernecks." . . . It seems to me Richard Arlen is capable of pretty big stuff. I wish some one would give Von Sternberg a story for him. . . . Have to tackle a load now.

Jim

An extract from another letter, written in 1936, may be of interest:

It seems to me, comrades, that *New Masses* readers should treat Dostoevsky kindly yet strictly. There are inexcusable gaps and deviations in his ideology and they must not be condoned; on the other hand, we must not on their account make an enemy of a man who has come far and who may turn out to be inestimably useful to the Movement. (signed) Granville Hicks. I think *The Brothers Karamazov* deserves the co-operation of all the finest talents in Hollywood and wd. richly repay all research & expenditure. A fullsized replica, complete down to the last tpmizznmst, of the Mad Tsar Pierre (Charles Laughton). Papa Karamazov (Lionel Barrymore). His comic servant Grigory (Wallace Berry). Grigory's wife (Zazu Pitts). Smerdyakov (Charles Laughton). Smerdyakov's Familiar, a cat named Tabitha (Elsa Lanchester, the bride of Frankenstein). Zossima (Henry B. Walthall). . . . Miusov (Malcolm Cowley). . . . in Alyosha's Dream: Alyosha (Fred Astaire). Puck (Wallace Beery). Titania (Ginger Rogers or James Cagney). . . . Routines by Albertina Rasch. Artificial snow by Jean Cocteau. . . . Entire production supervised by Hugh Walpole. . . . To be played on the world's first Globular Screen, opening at the Hippodrome the night before *Jumbo* closes. Mr. Dostoevsky will be unable to appear at the opening but Charles A. Lindbergh has agreed to be on hand (you may recognize him by the smoked glasses & unassuming manner) and a troupe of selected ushers will throw epileptic fits during the intermission (courtesy Max Jacobs). Margaret Anglin will sell signed copies of Countee Cullen's *Medea* in the lobby. President Roosevelt will plant a tree. The Italian Expeditionary Force will observe two minutes silence in honor of the birth of the little Christ child. Artificial foreskins will be handed out at the north end of the Wilhelmstrasse to anyone who is fool enough to call for them. The film will be preceded by *Glimpses of the New Russia,* photographed by M. Bourkeovitz [Margaret Bourke-White who, after her marriage to Erskine Caldwell, no foe of the Soviets, did do some such book of photographs, as I recall] . . . Suggested tie-ins for hinterland exhibitors: arrange to have your theatre picketted by your local chapters of the American Legion, the Catholic Church, the Parent-Teachers Association, the Sheet-metal Workers Union and the Youth for Peace Movement.

Set up Jungle Shrubbery and a Stuffed Gorilla in your lobby (your Police Station will be glad to furnish latter in return for a mention). If you are in the South, stage Negro Baptism (in white gowns) in front of your theatre. If in North, an Italian Saint's Day or a Jewish Funeral will do as well. Plug this feature hard. It will richly repay you.

Until I came to transcribe this, I had not realized how tasteless it is, calculated to offend the sensibilities of every right-thinking and wrong-thinking group in the country, minority or majority. It goes beyond buffoonery to express a nihilistic, destructive, irreverent, vulgar, alienated, un-American and generally lousy attitude. And why drag in the Sheetmetal Workers Union? And if the union, why the cops? There is something very old-fashioned about the whole thing, more like 1926 than 1936—and certainly not at all like 1962.

ONE of the unexpected things about Agee—and there were many, he was what used to be called "an original"— is that he was able to think in general terms without making a fool of himself, therein differing from most American creative writers of this century. This may have been because of his education or, more likely, because he had a gift that way. (He had so many gifts, including such odd ones, for intellectuals, as reverence and feeling.) Considering his hell-for-leather personality, Agee was a remarkably sophisticated, even circumspect, thinker. "Was just reading in *New Masses* Isidore Schneider welcoming Archie into the new pew," he wrote me in 1936.* "Still have my ways of believing in artforart and, more especially, of conviction

* The reference is to Archibald MacLeish, who had, under pressure from the *Zeitgeist*, temporarily edged over toward the Communists. Four years later the war had begun—no one ever had to ask Archie "Don't you know there's a war on?"—and MacLeish was attacking Dos Passos, Farrell, Hemingway and such as "The Irresponsibles" who had betrayed the American Dream. Shortly thereafter he was running Roosevelt's Office of Facts and Figures, as our wartime propaganda agency was at first quaintly called.

Marx—Marx plus Freud for that matter—isn't the answer
to everything." Then he adds, with his typical balance,
the last quality one would expect if one merely saw his
picturesque side: "But just because Copernicus didn't
settle all the problems of the universe is no reason at all to
go on insisting that the sun moves around the earth and
comes out a little southwest of purgatory." Jim was always
moderate in an immoderate way, he was always out of step,
and he had very little respect for the *Zeitgeist*. This was his
tragedy and his triumph.

In his last letter to Father Flye, written a day or two before he died, Agee sketches out a fantasy about elephants—
how they have been degraded by man from the most intelligent and the noblest of beasts to figures of fun. He felt
he was dying and this was his last, most extraordinary
insight. For wasn't this just what happened to him? Wasn't
he also a large, powerful being who was put to base uses?
The same note is struck in his fine parable, "A Mother's
Tale"—also written toward the end of his life—in which
a mother cow tells her children and nephews and nieces a
strange tale that has come down through the generations
about the ultimate fate of their kind. I venture that here
too Agee was thinking of himself when he wrote about the
slaughter of one species for the benefit of another. The
cattle have their own life and purpose, as he did, and they
are used by more powerful beings for a different purpose,
as he was. This, at least, is how I imagine he may have
thought, or rather felt (for it may not have been wholly
conscious), about it in his last years. It was emotionally
true for him, and was also true in general. But looking at
it more coldly, one must say something more. While Time,
Inc., has in common with the Chicago packing houses one
important thing—that its purpose is to convert something
living, namely talent, into a salable commodity—it is not
really an abattoir because those who, like Agee or myself,
took its paychecks did so, unlike the cattle, of our own

free will. The great question is, as Lenin once remarked of politics, who uses whom (I think he had a more pungent verb in the original Russian). It is possible to use instead of being used: Faulkner wrote Hollywood scripts for years. But Agee didn't have this kind of toughness and shrewdness. He was, in a way, too big and too variously talented.

There is something helpless about elephants precisely because of their combination of size and intelligence; it is a fact they can be tamed and trained as few wild animals can. It's not the fault of the tamers. Henry Luce was a decent fellow when Jim and I worked for him on *Fortune* and I'm sure Luce was, like me, charmed and impressed by Agee. But what a waste, what pathetic docility, what illusions!* As late as 1945, after thirteen years with Time, Inc., Agee can still write to Father Flye that he has now been offered a job of "free-lance writing through all parts of the magazine," and this not in despair but hopefully. As if for a writer to be given the run of *Time* were not like a collector of sculpture being offered his pick of wax figures from Madame Tussaud's Museum. He was always looking for a way out—in 1932, his first year on *Fortune*, he is

* On both sides. In *Fortune's* case, they never really knew just where to have this strange creature. When he first arrived on *Fortune*, Agee speedily became, largely because nobody could figure out any other way to use him, the staff specialist in rich, beautiful prose on such topics as Rare Wines, Famous Orchid Collections, and The World's Ten Most Precious Jewels. When this finally reached the attention of Henry Luce, he was indignant, for he had a theory that a good writer could write on anything—also *Fortune* was supposed to be about business. He thought it somehow immoral that a writer should do only what he was best at—there was a lot of the Puritan in Luce. So he assigned to Agee as occupational therapy an article on The Price of Steel Rails, and furthermore announced he, Luce, would personally edit it (as he often did in those days). It was a fascinating topic for any one with the slightest interest in economics, since the price of steel rails, which had been exactly the same for some fifty years, was the classic example of monopolistic price-fixing. But Agee, of course, had not even a slight interest in economics. He did his best and Luce did his best—"Now, Jim, don't you see . . . ?"—but finally Luce had to admit defeat and the article was assigned to some one else (me, I think) who did a workmanlike job. The trouble with Agee as a journalist was that he couldn't be just workmanlike, he had to give it everything he had, which was not good for him.

wondering whether he shouldn't try for a Guggenheim grant, two years later he is asking Father Flye about the chances for a teaching job at St. Andrews, etc.—but he also was always full of innocent, elephantine hope.

In his perceptive introduction to the letters, Robert Phelps states that Jim got his job on *Fortune* because they were impressed by "an ingenious parody of *Time*" he had put out when he was editing The *Harvard Advocate*. I wish this were the whole story, but I remember in 1932 recommending Jim, then looking for a post-graduation job, to Ralph Ingersoll, then managing editor of *Fortune*, where I'd been working since my graduation from Yale. And I've dug up a letter from Jim which is almost unbearable in dramatic irony, the audience knowing how it is going to turn out: "Noted contents of your letter with eyes rolling upward and stomach downward with joy, relief, gratitude and such things. I shall send a wire in the morning to beat this letter down. . . . I don't want to miss any chances of losing this chance (for which thank you, God, and Managing Editor Ingersoll). . . . Words fail me re. the job: besides the fairly fundamental fact that I don't want to starve, there are dozens of other reasons I want *uh* job and many more why I am delighted to get this one."

But I didn't do him a favor, really.

Ernest Hemingway

H<small>E WAS A BIG MAN</small> with a bushy beard and everybody knew him. The tourists knew him and the bartenders knew him and the critics knew him too. He enjoyed being recognized by the tourists and he liked the bartenders but he never liked the critics very much. He thought they had his number. Some of them did. The hell with them. He smiled a lot and it should have been a good smile, he was so big and bearded and famous, but it was not a good smile. It was a smile that was uneasy around the edges as if he was not sure he deserved to be quite as famous as he was famous.

He liked being a celebrity and he liked celebrities. At first it was Sherwood Anderson and Ezra Pound and Gertrude Stein. He was an athletic young man from Oak Park, Illinois, who wanted to write and he made friends with them. He was always good at making friends with celebrities. They taught him about style. Especially Gertrude Stein. The short words, the declarative sentences, the repetition, the beautiful absence of subordinate clauses. He always worked close to the bull in his writing. In more senses than one *señor*. It was a kind of inspired baby talk when he was going good.* When he was not going good, it was just

* "And what if she should die? She won't die. People don't die in childbirth nowadays. That was what all husbands thought. Yes, but what if she should die? She won't die. She's just having a bad time. The initial labor is usually protracted. She's only having a bad time. Afterwards we'd say what a bad time, and Catherine would say it wasn't really so bad. But what if she should die? She can't die. Yes, but what if she should die? She can't, I tell you. Don't be a fool. It's just a bad time. It's just nature giving baby talk.* Or so the critics said and the hell with them. Most of the tricks were good tricks and they worked fine for a while especially in the short stories. Ernest was stylish in the hundred-yard dash but he didn't have the wind for the long stuff. Later on the tricks did not look so good. They were the same tricks but they were not fresh any more and nothing is worse than a trick that has gone stale. He knew this but he couldn't invent any new tricks. It was a great pity and one of the many things in life that you can't do anything about. Maybe that was why his smile was not a good smile.

After 1930, he just didn't have it any more. His legs began to go and his syntax became boring and the critics began to ask why he didn't put in a few subordinate clauses just to make it look good. But the bartenders still liked him and the tourists liked him too. He got more and more famous and the big picture magazines photographed him shooting a lion and catching a tuna and interviewing a Spanish Republican militiaman and fraternizing with bullfighters and helping liberate Paris and always smiling bushily and his stuff got worse and worse. Mr. Hemingway the writer was running out of gas but no one noticed it

---

her hell. It's only the first labor, which is almost always protracted. Yes, but what if she should die? She can't die. Why should she die? What reason is there for her to die? . . . But what if she should die? She won't. She's all right. But what if she should die? She can't die. But what if she should die? Hey, what about that? What if she should die?"—*A Farewell to Arms.*

* I remember waking in the morning. Catherine was asleep and the sun was coming in through the window. The rain had stopped and I stepped out of bed and across the floor to the window. . . .

"How are you, darling?" she said. "Isn't it a lovely day?"

"How do you feel?"

"I feel very well. We had a lovely night."

"Do you want breakfast?"

She wanted breakfast. So did I and we had it in bed, the November sunlight coming in through the window, and the breakfast tray across my lap.

"Don't you want the paper? You always wanted the paper in the hospital."

"No," I said. "I don't want the paper now."—*A Farewell to Arms.*

because Mr. Hemingway the celebrity was such good copy. It was all very American and in 1954 they gave him the Nobel Prize and it wasn't just American any more. The judges were impressed by "the style-forming mastery of the art of modern narration" he had shown in *The Old Man and the Sea*, which he had published in *Life* two years earlier. *Life* is the very biggest of the big picture magazines and *Life* is exactly where *The Old Man and the Sea* belonged. Literary-prize judges are not always clever. This is something you know and if you don't know it you should know it. They gave him the prize and the King of Sweden wrote to him. Mr. Hemingway meet Mr. Bernadotte.

After 1930 his friends were not named Anderson or Pound or Stein. They were named Charles Ritz and Toots Shor and Leonard Lyons and Ava Gardner and Marlene Dietrich and Gary Cooper. He almost had a fight with Max Eastman because he thought Max Eastman had questioned his virility and he almost fought a duel with someone he thought might have insulted the honor of Ava Gardner but he didn't have the fight and he decided that Ava Gardner's honor had not been insulted after all. It is often difficult to tell about honor. It is something you feel in your *cojones*. Or somewhere. He liked Marlene Dietrich very much. They had good times together. He called her "The Kraut" and she called him "Papa." His wife called him "Papa" too. Many other people called him "Papa." He liked being called "Papa."

He wrote a novel called *Across the River and Into the Trees*. It was not a good novel. It was a bad novel. It was so bad that all the critics were against it. Even the ones who had liked everything else. The trouble with critics is that you can't depend on them in a tight place and this was a very tight place indeed. They scare easy because their brains are where their *cojones* should be and because they have no loyalty and because they have never stopped a charging lion with a Mannlicher double-action .34 or done any of the other important things. The hell with them. Jack Dempsey thought *Across the River* was OK. So did Joe Di Maggio. The Kraut thought it was terrific. So did Toots Shor. But it was not OK and he knew it and there was absolutely nothing he could do about it.

He was a big man and he was famous and he drank a great deal now and wrote very little. He lived in Havana and often went game fishing and *Life* photographed him doing it. Sometimes he went to Spain for the bullfights and he made friends with the famous bullfighters and wrote it up in three installments for *Life*. He had good times with his friends and his admirers and his wife and the tourists and the bartenders and everybody talked and drank and laughed and was gay but it all went away when he was alone. It was bad when he was alone. Nothing helped then. He knew he had been very good once, he knew he had been as good as they come at the special kind of thing he was good at, and he knew he had not been good for a long time. He talked big to interviewers: "I trained hard and I beat Mr. De Maupassant. I've fought two draws with Mr. Stendahl, but nobody is going to get me in any ring with Mr. Tolstoy unless I'm crazy or keep getting better." But he knew he was getting worse, and not better. He was a writer and his writing had gone soft a long time ago and he knew this no matter what the Nobel Prize judges and the editors of *Life* told him and he was a writer and nothing else interested him much. He took shock treatments for depression at the Mayo Clinic. He went twice and he stayed there a long time but they didn't work. He was overweight and his blood pressure was high and his doctor made him cut down on the eating and drinking. That spring his friend Gary Cooper died. He took it hard. The position is outflanked the lion can't be stopped the sword won't go into the bull's neck the great fish is breaking the line and it is the fifteenth round and the champion looks bad.

Now it is that morning in the house in Ketchum, Idaho. He takes his favorite gun down from the rack. It is a 12-gauge double-barreled shotgun and the stock is inlaid with silver. It is a very beautiful gun. He puts the end of the gun barrel into his mouth and he pulls both triggers.

That week his great shaggy head looks down from the covers of the picture magazines on the news stands and the graduate students smile thinly as they realize that a definitive study of the complete *œuvre* of Ernest Hemingway is now possible.

A PROFESSOR of English in North Carolina State College recently called Hemingway "essentially a philosophical writer." This seems to me a foolish statement even for a professor of literature. It is true that Hemingway originated a romantic attitude which was as seductive to a whole generation, and as widely imitated, as Byron's had been. (It is still attractive: Norman Mailer, for instance, is a belated Hemingway type, though his prose style is different.) But Hemingway was no more a philosopher than Byron was; in fact, he was considerably less of one. A feeling that loyalty and bravery are the cardinal virtues and that physical action is the basis of the good life—even when reinforced with the kind of nihilism most of us get over by the age of twenty—these don't add up to a philosophy. There is little evidence of thought in Hemingway's writing and much evidence of the reverse—the kind of indulgence in emotion and prejudice which the Nazis used to call "bloodthinking." For all the sureness of his instinct as a writer, he strikes one as not particularly intelligent. Byron wrote *Manfred* but he also wrote *Don Juan* and the letters and journals; underneath the romantic pose there was a tough, vigorous, and skeptical mind, a throwback to the eighteenth century and the Age of Reason. There were two Byrons but there was (alas) only one Hemingway. He was hopelessly sincere. His life, his writing, his public personality and his private thoughts were all of a piece. Unlike Byron, he believed his own propaganda. I hate to think what his letters and journals must be like. I suspect he kept no journals, since to do so implies reflection and self-aware-ness; also that one has a private life as apart from one's pro-fessional and public existence; I don't think Hemingway did—indeed I think it was this lack of private interests which caused him to kill himself when his professional career had lost its meaning.

We know what his conversation was like, in his later years at least, from Lillian Ross's minute account of two days spent with Hemingway and his entourage (*New Yorker*, May 13, 1950). The article presents a Hemingway who sounds as fatuous and as self-consciously he-man as his general in *Across the River*. At least that is how it sounds to me. But Miss Ross has a different ear. She insists, and I believe her, that (a) she simply reported what Hemingway said and did, and (b) that she liked and respected him (and what he said and did). She also states that she showed advance proofs to Hemingway and that he made no objec-tions to the article and in fact was pleased with it. One can only admire his objectivity and good nature. But perhaps his reaction was a little *too* objective. Perhaps it shows an alienation from himself that is neurotic—one should feel a certain amount of prejudice in favor of one's self, after all. Or perhaps, worse, it means that Hemingway by then had accepted the public personality that had been built up for him by the press—a well-trained lion, he jumped through all the hoops—and even gloried in the grotesque (but virile) Philistine Miss Ross had innocently depicted. This latter possibility is suggested by a letter from Heming-way which Miss Ross quoted in The *New Republic*, August 7, 1961, when she protested against Irving Howe's assump-tion that she had been out to "smear" Hemingway in her *New Yorker* piece. "The hell with them," Hemingway wrote her after the piece had been published, apropos of people who had found it "devastating" (as I must confess I still do). "Think one of the 'devastating' things was that I drink a little in it and that makes them think I am a rummy. But of course if they (the devastate people) drank what we drink in that piece they would die or something. Then (I should not say it) there is a lot of jealousy around and because I have fun a lot of the time and am not really spooky and so far always get up when they count over me some people are jealous. They can't understand you being a serious writer and not solemn." This seems to me, taken in conjunction with Miss Ross's reportage, to indicate the opposite of what the writer intended to indicate.

HEMINGWAY'S importance, I think, is almost entirely as a stylistic innovator. I have just reread *A Farewell to Arms* and *Men Without Women* and what strikes me most is their extreme mannerism. I don't know which is the more surprising, after twenty years, the virtuosity of the style or its lack of emotional resonance today. Consider the opening paragraphs of *In Another Country:*

In the fall the war was always there, but we did not go to it any more. It was cold in the fall in Milan and the dark came very early. Then the electric lights came on, and it was pleasant along the streets looking in the windows. There was much game hanging outside the shops, and the snow powdered in the fur of the foxes and the wind blew their tails. The deer hung stiff and heavy and empty, and small birds blew in the wind and the wind turned their feathers. It was a cold fall and the wind came down from the mountains.

We were all at the hospital every afternoon, and there were different ways of walking across the town through the dusk to the hospital. Two of the ways were alongside canals, but they were long. Always, though, you crossed a bridge across a canal to enter the hospital. There was a choice of three bridges. On one of them a woman sold roasted chestnuts. It was warm, standing in front of the charcoal fire, and the chestnuts were warm afterwards in your pocket. The hospital was very old and very beautiful, and you entered through a gate on the other side. There were usually funerals starting from the court-yard. Beyond the old hospital were the new brick pavilions, and there we met every afternoon and were all very polite and interested in what was the matter, and sat in the machines that were to make so much difference.

This is a most peculiar way to begin a story. Nothing "happens" until the last sentence of the second paragraph. Up to then everything is simply atmosphere but not atmosphere as it was generally known before Hemingway, except for the wonderful two sentences about the game hanging outside the shops. It is an original mixture of the abstract and the concrete, as in the first sentence, and the effect is to describe not a particular state of mind but rather a particular way of looking at experience, one which makes as sharp a break with previous literary methods as Jackson Pollock made with previous ways of painting. The primitive syntax is the equivalent of Pollock's "drip and dribble" technique and, like it, is a declaration of war against the genteel and academic style. There is also a parallel with the architecture of Mies van der Rohe, whose "Less is more" applies to Hemingway's style, which gets its effect from what it leaves out. (Maybe this is the characteristic twentieth century manner in the arts: I'm told that in the music of Webern and the jazz of Thelonious Monk one should listen not to the notes but to the silences between them.) Because Mies van der Rohe's buildings are simple in form and without ornamentation many people think they are functional, but in fact they are as aggressively unfunctional as the wildest baroque. The same goes for Hemingway's style which is direct and simple on the surface but is actually as complexly manneristic as the later James. "Prose is architecture, not interior decoration," Hemingway once said, "and the Baroque is over." But there is Baroque with curlicues and Baroque with straight lines, Baroque with ornamentation and Baroque with blank spaces, seventeenth-century Baroque and twentieth-century Baroque.

"Refinements in the use of subordinate clauses are a mark of maturity in style," writes Albert C. Baugh in *A History of the English Language*. "As the loose association of clauses (parataxis) gives way to more precise indications of logical relationship and subordination (hypotaxis), there is need for a greater variety of words effecting the union." Hemingway was a most paratactical writer. Not because he was primitive but because he was stylistically sophisticated to the point of decadence. Supremely uninterested in "precise indications of logical relationship," he needed very few words; his vocabularly must be one of the smallest in literary history.

I can see why, in the 'twenties, the two paragraphs quoted above were fresh and exciting, but today they seem as academically mannered as *Euphues* or *Marius the Epicurean*. This is, of course, partly because Hemingway's stylistic discoveries have become part of our natural way of writing, so that they are at once too familiar to cause any any excitement and at the same time, in the extreme form in which Hemingway used them, they now sound merely affected. This kind of writing is lost unless it can create a mood in the reader, since it deliberately gives up all the resources of logic and reason. But I was, in 1961, conscious of the tricks—and impatient with them. *Why* must we be told about the two ways of walking to the hospital and the three bridges and the chestnut seller? The aim is probably to create tension by lingering over the prosaic—writers of detective stories, a highly artificial literary form, have learned much from Hemingway—just as the purpose of stating that it is warm in front of a fire and that newly roasted chestnuts feel warm in one's pocket is to suggest the coldness of Milan that fall. But these effects didn't "carry" with me, I just felt impatient.

A Farewell to Arms is generally considered Hemingway's best novel. It has aged and shriveled from what I remembered. I found myself skipping yards of this sort of thing:

"We could walk or take a tram," Catherine said.
"One will be along," I said. "They go by here."
"Here comes one," she said.
The driver stopped his horse and lowered the metal sign on his meter. The top of the carriage was up and there were drops of water on the driver's coat. His varnished hat was shining in the wet. We sat back in the seat and the top of the carriage made it dark.
[Half a page omitted]
At the hotel I asked Catherine to wait in the carriage while I went in and spoke to the manager. There were plenty of rooms. Then I went out to the carriage, paid the driver, and Catherine and I walked in together. The small boy in buttons carried the package. The manager bowed us towards the elevator. There was much red plush and brass. The manager went up in the elevator with us.

There is a great deal of paying cab drivers and finding it dark at night inside a closed carriage.

I found both the military part and the love story tedious except at moments of ordeal or catastrophe. The wounding of the narrator, Lieutenant Henry, and his escape after Caporetto are exciting, and the chapters on the retreat from Caporetto are as good as I remembered, especially the four pages about the shooting of the officers by the battle police. As long as the lieutenant and Catherine Barkley are making love and having "a good time" together, one is bored and skeptical. To my surprise, I found that Catherine was like the heroines of *For Whom the Bell Tolls* and *Across the River and Into the Trees*, not a person but an adolescent daydream—utterly beautiful and utterly submissive and utterly in love with the dreamer: "You see I'm happy, darling, and we have a lovely time. . . . You are happy, aren't you? Is there anything I do you

don't like? Can I do anything to please you? Would you
like me to take down my hair? Do you want to play?" "Yes
and come to bed." "All right. I'll go and see the patients
first." The conversation of these lovers is even more protracted and boring than that of real lovers. (It is curious
how verbose Hemingway's laconic style can become.) But
at the end when Catherine dies in childbed, the feeling
comes right and one is moved—just as the preceding ordeal
of the escape to Switzerland by rowing all night is well
done. This deathbed scene is one of the few successful ones
in literary history; it is the stylistic antithesis to Dickens'
Death of Little Nell (of which Oscar Wilde remarked,
"One must have a heart of stone to read it without laughing").

The fact is Hemingway is a short-story writer and not
a novelist. He has little understanding of the subject matter of the novel: character, social setting, politics, money
matters, human relations, all the prose of life. Only the
climactic moments interest him, and of those only ordeal,
suffering, and death. (Except for a lyrical feeling about
hunting and fishing.) In a novel he gets lost, wandering
around aimlessly in a circle as lost people are said to do,
and the alive parts are really short stories, such as the lynching of the fascists and the blowing up of the bridge in *For
Whom the Bell Tolls*. In the short story he knows just
where he is going and his style, which becomes tedious in
a novel, achieves the intensity appropriate to the shorter
form. The difference may be seen in comparing the dialogue in *A Farewell to Arms* with that in the little short
story, "Hills like White Elephants," which is directed with
superb craftsmanship to the single bitter point the story
makes. Every line of this apparently random conversation
between a man and a girl waiting at a Spanish railway station—she is going to Madrid for an abortion he wants but
she doesn't—develops the theme and when toward the end
she asks, "Would you do something for me now?" and he

replies, "I'd do anything for you," and she says, "Would you please please please please please please please stop talking?"—then one feels that tightening of the scalp that tells one an artist has made his point.

"HEMINGWAY'S tragedy as an artist," Cyril Connolly writes in *Enemies of Promise*, "is that he has not had the versatility to run away fast enough from his imitators. . . . A Picasso would have done something different; Hemingway could only indulge in invective against his critics—and do it again." The list of Hemingwayesque writers includes James M. Cain, Erskine Caldwell, John O'Hara, and a school of detective fiction headed by Dashiel Hammett and Raymond Chandler. It also includes Hemingway. Connolly wrote before Hemingway had begun to parody himself in *The Old Man and the Sea*—which is simply his early story, "The Undefeated," perhaps the best thing he ever did, retold in terms of fishing instead of bullfighting and transposed from a spare style into a slack, fake-biblical style which retains the mannerisms and omits the virtues— and in *Across the River and Into the Trees*, an unconscious self-parody of almost unbelievable fatuity. The peculiar difficulty American creative writers have in maturing has often been commented on. Emotionally, Hemingway was adolescent all his life; intellectually, he was a Philistine on principle. His one talent was aesthetic—a feeling for style, in his writing and in his life, that was remarkably sure. But the limits of aestheticism unsupported by thought or feeling are severe. Hemingway made one big, original stylistic discovery—with the aid of Gertrude Stein—but when he had gotten everything there was to be gotten out of it (and a bit more) he was unable, as Connolly notes, to invent anything else. He was trapped in his style as a miner might be trapped underground; the oxygen is slowly used up without any new air coming in.

Hemingway's opposites are Stendhal and Tolstoy—interesting he should feel especially awed by them—who had no style at all, no effects. Stendhal wrote the way a police sergeant would write if police sergeants had imagination —a dry, matter-of-fact style. Tolstoy's writing is clear and colorless, interposing no barrier between the reader and the narrative, the kind of direct prose, businesslike and yet Olympian, that one imagines the Recording Angel uses for entries in *his* police blotter. There is no need for change or innovation with such styles. But the more striking and original a style is, the greater such necessity. Protean innovators like Joyce and Picasso invent, exploit, and abandon dozens of styles; Hemingway had only one. It was not enough. But he did write some beautiful short stories while it was working. Perhaps they are enough.

Appendix:

DISSENTING OPINION

AUTHOR'S NOTE: *George Plimpton, whose interview with Hemingway in* Paris Review *will be remembered, wrote me the following letter after my article appeared. Because he knew Hemingway (and I didn't) and because he provides some information which is a useful counterweight to my parody biography (which is a parody and therefore exaggerated) I think it only fair to print his views. In the April, 1962, Encounter, Harvey Breit, who also knew Hemingway, makes much the same points. The two rebuttals that seem to me important are that (a) Hemingway in his last years was working hard at his writing, and (b) that his public and private personalities were not "all of a piece" as I claim. On (a): I was wrong factually, since I was judging only by the little that he published; but the real question is whether what he wrote in that last decade was as good as his pre-1930 stuff; if so, then my whole view of his later years is askew; but we must wait until these writings are published before we can judge; I find it hard to believe that a writer like Hemingway would withhold from print his best things; but we shall see. On (b): the resolution must also wait until his journals, letters, etc., are published; such quotations as I have seen, especially in the Ross profile, seem to me congruent with my portrait, but perhaps there will be revealed, in posthumous documents, a quite different Hemingway; again, we shall see. I hope I am wrong on both (a) and (b).*

I have been told that, since I didn't know Hemingway, I shouldn't have talked about his personality; such critics, however, never object to my talking about Byron, whom I didn't know either.

WELL dammit, Dwight, let's start off with his smile. I don't think Hemingway smiled a smile that was "uneasy around the edges." It was a big smile, his shoulders shook when he laughed, and he showed his teeth. If he sometimes had a startled look on his face in the photos, that was because of the flashbulbs, which hurt his eyes and gave him fierce headaches.

He didn't dislike critics as much as you suppose. So much is made of his anti-intellectualism. Doubtless some critics annoyed him. I don't think *your* essay would have pleased him. But, after all, he carried on a long correspondence with Malcolm Cowley, Edmund Wilson, Harvey Breit, Carlos Baker, Archibald MacLeish, and any number of others, and while he was very sensitive to criticism, I doubt he thought collectively of critics as "having his number."*

* Mr. Plimpton has the floor and I shan't heckle him with footnotes. But this is rather too much. The June, 1958, issue of a magazine entitled (actually) *Wisdom* happens to be to hand and in it a Mr. John Atkins has an article on Hemingway in which he quotes him on critics as follows: "They are like those people who go to ball games and can't tell the players without a score card. I am not worried about what anybody I do not like might do. If they can do you harm, let them do it. . . . At present we have two good writers who cannot write because they have lost confidence through reading critics. . . . The critics have made them impotent. . . . Some critics are well-intentioned, most of them I believe. But some are not. When you ask understanding, they bring envy and jealousy. Sometimes they give off an odor you only smell in the armpits of the shirts of traitors after they have been hanged. But these are the rare ones. I believe

Another canard—that he cultivated celebrities. Besides, it's stretching a point, isn't it, to speak of Anderson, Stein and Pound as celebrities—at least in the contemporary sense? In the 'twenties Stein and Pound were relatively obscure and actually it was Hemingway who was responsible for getting Stein's first work published—*The Making of Americans*. He went to them to learn. One might say he cultivated the celebrated, but surely not that he ever cultivated celebrities. If that's what amused him in life he would hardly have holed up in such out-of-the-way places as San Francisco de Paula, Key West, or Ketchum, Idaho, or devoted himself to the safaris and the ferias. Actually his range of friends was enormous—generals, prize fighters, baseball players, jockeys, matadors, actresses, revolutionaries, writers, hunters, tycoons, and others he described as living their lives "all the way up." He liked these people and he sought out their experiences. But by no means were they all celebrities. A constant boarder in Cuba was a retired Spanish seaman. He was supposed to know an incredible number of sea chanties, but he drank and I never saw him in condition to get any of them out. The one friend Hemingway often talked about was Jean-Franco, the son of the family in whose home he convalesced following his wounding at Fossalta di Piave. Also Lanham, who commanded the Twenty-second Regiment of the Fourth Division. Maxwell Perkins of Scribner's was a friend whose death he never got over. Besides, what does this have to do with Hemingway's ability as a writer?*

You suggest that Hemingway's writing was going so badly that he took to the bottle. Absurd. He always drank

---

there is a segment of criticism which would be happier if there were no books written and if they could only write about each other and their own opinions. But perhaps nature, or God, will provide a bloody flux for which there will be no antidote and to which they only will be susceptible and it will do away with them." In short, the only good critic is a dead critic. Or one who is "understanding," i.e., encouraging.

* Nothing, absolutely nothing.—D.M.

and he liked it. You say he wrote "very little." Not so. I believe the only completely slack period in his writing was during the war years, when he wrote just enough articles for *Look* to qualify as a war correspondent—six, I believe. In San Francisco de Paula he wrote almost every day (see interview in *Paris Review* #18). Recently boxes full of unpublished manuscripts have turned up from his Key West days. In the last years he was working on the vast book of which *The Old Man and the Sea* is a small section, completing a series of Paris sketches and reminiscences, and revising and up-dating an edition of *Death in the Afternoon* (some of the material for this appeared in a different form in "The Dangerous Summer" in *Life*). What has been published of this is bad, of course, and Leland Heyward tells me that much of the big novel is bad too—at least the volume which he read, which is about submarine hunting off the coast of Cuba with your Yale classmate Winston Guest on the *Pilar*. Some of it he says is wonderful, but much of it tedious and worked and dull. On the other hand, I was fortunate enough to read some of the Paris-in-the-'twenties reminiscences, and the sections I read (on Stein and Ford Madox Ford) were very funny and fresh, and curiously detached considering they are told in the first person, which so often, as Edmund Wilson points out, causes Hemingway to lose his bearings, not merely as a critic of life, but even as a craftsman. But even if the quality of these pieces should prove questionable, certainly Hemingway can't be accused of neglecting his profession to wallow in praise and "good times," which is the portrait you give.

You suggest that Hemingway's lack of confidence, his inability to write, caused deep depressions which he tried to relieve with shock treatments at the Mayo Clinic. I don't think you or I can, or should, speculate on what caused those depressions. A whole complex of problems, physical and mental, may have been responsible. His closest friends believe the depressions were a natural consequence of his physical ills—which, I might add, were numerous and debilitating. He had kidney trouble. His liver was bad. You could see the bulge of it stand out from his body like a long, fat leech. His family had a history of high blood pressure and he, to his sorrow and considerable worry, was no exception. The bathroom wall at the finca was covered with penciled diastolic/systolic recordings. His letters invariably referred to his health, usually a postscript with his weight. When the doctors told him to lose weight as part of the therapy for the hypertension, he got his weight down from 215 to the 160's. That isn't good for any one's state of health or mind, and it's worth considering that the pills one takes for reducing weight and hypertension are depressants. Hemingway often had low periods, and you can find it in the writing as far back as *Big Two-Hearted River*.

I think your fundamental error is your assumption that Hemingway's writing, public personality and private thoughts were all of a piece. The man at home, at work, or with close friends bears little resemblance to the public personality of the columns and the magazines, sources prone to emphasizing the more picturesque aspects of his character. I was always amazed how shy he was. I think much of the boy-scout, Indian-talk character, the "code" made so much of in the Lillian Ross article, was put on, not only because he had fun with it but also as a protective device. You say that Hemingway was too "objective" about the Ross article and that perhaps he even "gloried" in the portrait she drew of him. The letter you quote is kinder than he felt—after all, he's trying to put her mind at ease about her critics, not about the accuracy of her portrait.

As for your conjecture that it was a "lack of private interests" which caused Hemingway to kill himself when his professional career had lost its meaning, I don't think any one who knew Hemingway, even from the news columns, could read that line and think you had the same man in mind. What stunned his friends about his death more than anything was that he had so *many* interests in life it seemed inconceivable he could end it.

PART III

Pretenders

By Cozzens Possessed

THE MOST ALARMING literary news in years is the enormous success of James Gould Cozzens' *By Love Possessed*. It sold 170,000 copies in the first six weeks of publication —more than all eleven of the author's previous novels put together. At this writing [December, 1957] it has been at the top of the best-seller lists for two months. Hollywood and the *Reader's Digest* have paid $100,000 apiece for the privilege of wreaking their wills upon it. And the *New Yorker* published a cartoon—one matron to another: "I was looking forward to a few weeks of just doing nothing after Labor Day when along came James Gould Cozzens."

There's nothing new in all this—after all, *something* has to be the No. 1 Best Seller at any given moment. What is new appears if one considers Grace Metalious' *Peyton Place*, which was at the top for a full year, before *By Love Possessed* displaced it. *Peyton Place* is a familiar kind of best seller, a pedestrian job, an artifact rather than a work of art (putting it mildly) that owes its popularity to nothing more subtle than a remarkably heavy charge of Sex. Perhaps its best-known predecessor is *Forever Amber*, fabricated a decade ago by another notably untalented lady. But Cozzens is not of the company of Kathleen Winsor, Edna Ferber, Daphne Du Maurier, Lloyd C. Douglas, and other such humble, though well-paid, artisans. Nor can he be "placed" at the middle level of best-sellerdom, that of writers like Herman Wouk, John Hersey, and Irwin Shaw, nor even (perhaps) on the empyrean heights occupied by

Marquand and Steinbeck. He is a "serious" writer, and never more serious than in this book. That so uncompromising a work, written in prose of an artificiality and complexity that approaches the impenetrable—indeed often achieves it—that this should have become what the publishers gloatingly call "a run-away best seller" is something new. How do those matrons cope with it, I wonder. Perhaps their very innocence in literary matters is a help—an Australian aboriginal would probably find *Riders of the Purple Sage* and *The Golden Bowl* equally hard to read.

The requirements of the mass market explain a good deal of bad writing today. But Cozzens here isn't writing down, he is obviously giving it the works: *By Love Possessed* is his bid for immortality. It is Literature or it is nothing. Unfortunately none of the reviewers has seriously considered the second alternative. The book is not only a best seller, it is a *succès d'estime*. Such reviews, such enthusiasm, such unanimity, such nonsense! The only really hostile review I have been able to find was by William Buckley, Jr., of all people, in his *National Review*. Granted that he was somewhat motivated by a nonliterary consideration—the book is lengthily anti-Catholic—still I thought his deflation skillful and just.

Looking through Alice Payne Hackett's *Sixty Years of Best Sellers*, I find among the top ten novels between 1935 and 1955 just seven that I would call in any way "serious," namely: Wolfe's *Of Time and the River* (1935), Huxley's *Eyeless in Gaza* (1936), Virginia Woolf's *The Years* (1937), Steinbeck's *The Grapes of Wrath* (1939), Hemingway's *For Whom the Bell Tolls* (1941), Norman Mailer's *The Naked and the Dead* (1948), and James Jones's *From Here to Eternity* (1951). About one every three years, with a significant falling off in the last decade. It is a slim harvest, in both quantity and quality, but the difference between the least of these and *By Love Possessed* is the difference between a work of art on some level and to some extent achieved, and one that falls below any reasonable literary criterion. Yet the reviewers almost to a man behaved as if they were possessed. This sincere enthusiasm for a mediocre work is more damaging to literary standards than any amount of cynical ballyhoo. One can guard against the Philistines outside the gates. It is when they get into the Ivory Tower that they are dangerous.

THERE seems little doubt that *By Love Possessed* has been selling on the strength of the reviews. (Word-of-mouth comment has probably worked the other way; I've found only two people who liked it, and the most common reply is: "I couldn't read it.") All the commercially important journals reviewed it prominently and enthusiastically. The Sunday *Times* and *Herald Tribune* book sections gave it front-page reviews, by Malcolm Cowley ("one of the country's truly distinguished novelists") and Jessamyn West ("Rich, Wise, Major Novel of Love"). *Time* put Cozzens on the cover—Herman Wouk was there a year or two ago—and pronounced *By Love Possessed* "the best American novel in years." Orville Prescott in the *Times* thought it "magnificent," Edwards Weeks in the *Atlantic* found it "wise and compassionate," and Whitney Balliet in the *Saturday Review* divined in it "the delicate and subtle tension between action and thought that is the essence of balanced fiction."

The most extraordinary performances were those of Brendan Gill in the *New Yorker* and John Fischer in *Harper's*. The former praised it in terms that might have been thought a trifle excessive if he had been writing about *War and Peace:* "a masterpiece . . . the author's masterpiece . . . almost anybody's masterpiece . . . supremely satisfying . . . an immense achievement . . . spellbinding . . . masterpiece." The mood is lyrical, stammering with heartfelt emotion and bad grammar: "No American novelist of the twentieth century has attempted more than Mr. Cozzens attempts in the course of this long and bold and delicate book, which, despite its length, one reads through at headlong speed and is then angry with oneself for having reached the end so precipitately."

Mr. Fischer was more coherent but equally emphatic. Speaking from "the Editor's Easy Chair," as *Harper's* quaintly styles it, he headed his piece: "NOMINATION FOR A NOBEL PRIZE," and he meant it. For one slip or another— sentimentality, neuroticism, subjectivism, sloppy plot construction, or habitual use of "characters who are in one way or another in revolt against society"—he faults all the other competitors (the habitual-use-of-deleterious-characters rap alone disposes of Faulkner, Hemingway, Steinbeck, Algren, Mailer, Capote, Bellow, Jones, Paul Bowles, and Tennessee Williams) until finally James Gould Cozzens stands out in superb isolation, a monument of normality, decency, and craftsmanship.*

The provincial reviewers followed their leaders: "COZZENS PENS ENDURING TALE" (Cleveland *News*), "ONE OF THE GREAT NOVELS OF THE PRESENT CENTURY" (San Francisco *Call-Bulletin*), "finest American novel I have read in many a year" (Bernardine Kielty in the *Ladies Home Journal*), "COZZENS WRITES ABSORBING STORY IN EXCELLENT AND PROFOUND NOVEL" (Alice Dixon Bond in the Boston *Herald;* her column is called "The Case for Books"—is there an adjacent feature, "The Case Against Books"?). Leslie Hanscom in the New York *World-Telegram*—there are pro-

---

* Actually, even according to Mr. Fischer's absurd standards, Cozzens doesn't deserve this eminence. He is not "a classic mind operating in a romantic period" nor does his novel run counter to "the Gothic extravagance of current fiction"; as I shall show, his mind lacks clarity, control, and form and his prose is as Gothic as Harkness Memorial Quadrangle (also as unaesthetic). As for the alleged normality of his characters—"ordinary people, living ordinary lives, in ordinary circumstances" with whom the reader "can identify himself as he never can with the characters of an Algren or a Mailer"—they are normal only on the surface; once this is broken through, they are as neurotic and fantastic in their behavior as other current fictional people. The chief difference is that their creator often doesn't realize it.

vincials in big cities, too—was impressed by Cozzens' "awesome scrupulosity as an artist." Mr. Hanscom's scrupulosity as a critic inspired little awe; "Hemingway and Faulkner, move over!" he summed up. The frankest of the provincials was Carl Victor Little in the Houston *Press:* "The *N.Y. Times, Saturday Review* and other publications have taken out of the ivory tower the most accomplished critics available to join in the hallelujahs. So about all I can do is ditto the dithyrambs."

The literary quarterlies have not yet been heard from, but the liberal weeklies have. They didn't exactly ditto the dithyrambs, except for Granville Hicks in the *New Leader:* ". . . a novel to which talk of greatness is not irrelevant." But they didn't exactly veto them, either. Howard Nemerov in the *Nation,* Sarel Eimerl in the *New Republic,* and Richard Ellmann in the *Reporter* were all critical but respectful.

PERHAPS we should now take a look at what Cozzens has to say in *By Love Possessed,* and how he says it. The normative hero is Arthur Winner, a reputable, middle-aged lawyer and family man who is exposed, during the two days and nights covered by the action, to a variety of unsettling experiences, which stimulate in him some even more unnerving memories. Winner is presented as a good man— kind, reasonable, sensitive, decent—and so he is taken by the reviewers: "The grandest moral vision in all Cozzens' work—a passionately good, passionately religious, yet wholly secular man, whose very failures are only bad dreams" (Balliett), "intelligent, successful, tolerant . . . the quintessence of our best qualities" (Gill). I'm unwilling to go farther than the Kansas City *Star:* "thoroughly honest, genteel, devoted to his work, and conscientious." Passion seems to me just what is most obviously missing in Arthur Winner; he's about as passionate as a bowl of oatmeal.

He is, in fact, a prig. His responses to the many appeals made to him in the course of the story—he's always on top, handing down advice and help, a great temptation to prig-gishness—while decent enough in form ("genteel") are in reality ungenerous and pompous and self-protective. To a Catholic lady who tries to justify her faith: " 'Where there are differences in religion, I think it generally wiser not to discuss them.' " To a seduced girl's father, who has flour-ished a gun: " 'Be very careful! Return the gun; and mean-while, show it to no one else. Don't take it out of your pocket; and don't consider pointing it. Pointing a weapon is a separate indictable offense, and would get you an addi-tional fine, and an additional jail term.' " To his teen-age daughter, who wants to go dancing: " 'A real gone band? I believe I grasp your meaning. Clearly a good place to know. Where is it?' 'Oh, it's called the Old Timbers Tavern. It's down toward Mechanicsville, not far.' 'Yes; I've heard of it. And I'm afraid, whatever the reputed quality of the band, I must ask you not to go there.' 'Oh, Father!' That he is right in each case, that the Catholic lady is addle-witted, that the father is a fool and a braggart, that the Old Timbers Tavern is in fact no place for a young girl to go—all this is beside the point. A prig is one who delights in demonstrating his superiority on small occasions, and it is precisely when he has a good case that he rises to the depths of prigocity.

Although Winner behaves like a prig, he is not meant to be one, if only because the main theme of the novel, the moral testing and education of a good man, would then collapse, and the philosophical tragedy that Cozzens has tried to write would have to be recast in a satiric if not a downright farcical mode. Here as elsewhere, the author is guilty of the unforgivable novelistic sin: he is unaware of the real nature of his characters, that is, the words and ac-tions he gives them lead the reader to other conclusions than those intended by the author.

His characters often speak brutally, for example, not because they are supposed to be brutes, but because their creator apparently thinks this is the way men talk. An elderly lawyer, civilly asked by a client to make some changes in the investing of her trust fund, replies: " 'You're getting senile, Maud. Try not to be more of a fool than you can help.' " A doctor, presented as a gentleman, meets the wife of a friend at a party, and, no dialogue or motivation given before, opens up: " 'What's your trouble, baby? Or can I guess? . . . Tell Pappy how many periods you've missed. . . . You know as well as I do you're one of those girls who only has to look at him to get herself knocked up.' " She leaves the room "indignantly" (the adverb implies she's a mite touchy) and he turns to Clarissa, Winner's wife:

"I knew it as soon as I looked at her. Sure. One night she thinks: Too much trouble to get up; the hell with it! You two ought to trade apparatus. Then everybody'd be happy."
    Clarissa said: "Reg, you're not being very funny—"
    "That's right. I don't feel very funny. Sometimes you get your bellyful of women—their goddam notions; their goddam talk-talk-talk; their goddam sacks of tripes!"

No reason is given for any of these onslaughts, aside from the fact that all three recipients are women; this seems to be Cozzens' idea of manly straight-from-the-shoulder talk. Curious. Curious, too, Winner's pooh-poohing attitude when he is appealed to by the feminine victims.
    For Winner, too, is something of a brute, without his creator suspecting it. There is, for example, that odd business on page 428 when Mrs. Pratt, after her silly, hysterical religiosity has beaten vainly for some thirty pages against the rock of Winner's Episcopalian rectitude (Mrs. Pratt is a Roman Catholic), is finally checkmated. She has to go to the bathroom. For reasons obscure to me, this is presented as the decisive proof of hypocrisy: "At fact's surely unkindest prank of all, Arthur Winner must protest, gener-

ously indignant." ("Meanly delighted" would be more accurate.) For a page, Winner ruminates on his antagonist's discomfiture, concluding: "But how in the world of fancy did you put delightfully the human circumstance whose undressed substance was that Celia, Celia, Celia shits—or even that Mrs. Pratt most urgently requires to piss?" Methinks the gentleman doth protest too much, and methinks that Swift's allusion to Celia's necessity was positively healthy compared to Cozzens-Winner's resort to scatology to win an argument.

THIS leads us, in a way, to sex. The crucial episode, the one that more than any other shakes Winner's faith in himself and in the uprightness of his life, is something that happened years before the action begins and that keeps coming back into his mind: his affair with Marjorie, the wife of his close friend and law partner, Julius Penrose. On the day after his first wife's death, Marjorie—another silly, hysterical woman—comes to the house and in a rush of emotion offers herself to him. He is about to take her, on his wife's bed, when the phone rings. That time he is literally saved by the bell, but later, one summer when Penrose is away, they do have a frantic affair. At no time is love or even lust involved: "Far from coveting his neighbor's wife, he rather disliked her, found her more unattractive than not." The only reason given for Winner's reaction to Marjorie is that she was there. Like that mountain climber. Or as Marjorie's remorselessly philosophical husband puts it in his pidgin (or shall we say turkey) English: "I venture to assert that when the gadfly's sting is fairly driven in, when this indefeasible urge of the flesh presses them, few men of normal potency prove able to refrain their feet from that path." But then (a) why hasn't Winner had dozens of such affairs instead of only this one—and for that matter, why was Marjorie able to seduce him only that one summer?; and (b) granted that some men do indeed so behave, why Winner? Does an Episcopalian lawyer, a rational, decent family man with no more and no different sexual urges than the normal ones, act like a dead-end kid? Cozzens insists that the best of us do so behave, but if we do, then we aren't the best. There might be some individual quirk in Winner to explain it, but it is not given; on the contrary, Cozzens' point is precisely Winner's lack of such quirks—"few men of normal potency prove able to refrain their feet from that path." This is neither realistic nor imaginative. It is the shocked revulsion of the adolescent who discovers that papa and mama do it.

The formula for a best seller now includes a minimum of "outspoken" descriptions of sexual activities, and *By Love Possessed* doesn't skimp here. Its inventory includes rape, seduction, marital and extramarital intercourse, with touches of sadism, lesbianism, onanism, and homosexuality. *By Sex Possessed* would be a more accurate title. There is very little love, which the author presents as at best a confusing and chancey business, to be patiently endured, like the weather. The provincials, for some reason, get the point here much better than their urban leaders did. The Chattanooga *Times* wonderfully summed up the theme as "the situation of rational man beset by passion," adding: "Cozzens regards each form of love as a threat to Arthur Winner's power to reason, to his ability to live life with meaning." It's too bad this acuteness in diagnosis was not accompanied by equal skill in evaluation; Cozzens' notion of love was accepted as valid; but it isn't, since love, even passion, is not an extraneous monkey wrench thrown into the machinery of life, but rather a prime mover which may burst everything apart but which must function if there is to be any motion at all. This is, at any rate, how the makers of our literature, from Homer to Tolstoy, Proust, and James, have treated the theme; Cozzens' efficiency-expert approach (Gumming Up the Works) is *echt*-American but creatively impoverishing.

"The readers didn't go much for Cozzens," observed the Detroit *Times,* "until he wrote something with some sex in it." This cynicism is not wholly justified. The literary prestige conferred by the reviewers was, I think, the chief factor. One of the consumer's goods to which every American feels he has a right in this age of plenty is Culture, and *By Love Possessed* on the living-room table is a symbol of the owner's exercise of this right. Granted that the reviews may have led many proprietors of living-room tables to think they could combine business with pleasure, so to speak, word must have gotten around fairly soon that the sexual passages were unrewarding.

For even the sex is meager—perhaps the real title should be *By Reason Possessed.* I have the impression that Cozzens is as suspicious of sex as of love. Most of the sexual encounters he conscientiously describes are either fatuous (Winner and his first bride), sordid (Ralph and Veronica), or disgusting (Winner and Marjorie). Far worse—from a sales viewpoint—they are written in his customary turgid and inexpressive style. Take for example the two pages (264-65) on Winner's love-making with his second wife, the most concrete description of the sexual act in the book and also the only place where sex is presented as one might say positively. This passage sounds partly like a tongue-tied Dr. Johnson: "the disposings of accustomed practice, the preparations of purpose and consent, the familiar mute motions of furtherance." But mostly like a *Fortune* description of an industrial process: "thrilling thuds of his heart . . . moist manipulative reception . . . the mutual heat of pumped bloods . . . the thoroughgoing, deepening, widening work of their connection; and his then no less than hers, the tempo slowed in concert to engineer a tremulous joint containment and continuance . ·. . the deep muscle groups, come to their vertex, were in a flash convulsed."*

* "The passages having to do with physical love have a surprising lyric power."—Jessamyn West in the New York *Herald Tribune.*

THE reviewers think of Cozzens, as he does himself, as a cool, logical, unsentimental, and implacably deep thinker. "Every character and event is bathed in the glow of a reflective intelligence," puffs *Time,* while Brendan Gill huffs: "The Cozzens intellect, which is of exceptional breadth and toughness, coolly directs the Cozzens heart." In reality, Cozzens is not so much cool as inhibited, not so much unsentimental as frightened by feeling; he is not logical at all, and his mind is shallow and muddy rather than clear and deep. I think Julius Penrose may fairly be taken as Cozzens' beau ideal of an intellectual, as Winner is his notion of a good man. If Penrose is meant to be taken ironically, if his pompous philosophizings are supposed to be burlesques, then the novel collapses at its center—leaving aside the fact they would be tedious as parodies—since it is Penrose who throughout the book guides Winner toward the solution of his problems. There's a Penrose in Homer, but he's not confused with Ulysses. His name is Nestor.

The reviewers, of course, were impressed by this club bore: "a dark, supernal intelligence" (Balliett), "one of the most compelling [what *does* that critical standby mean, I wonder] and memorable figures in recent writing" (Jessamyn West), "the scalded mind of the archskeptic . . . a corrosive nonstop monologuist with a tongue like a poisoned dart" (*Time*). The intellectual climax—more accurately, anticlimax—of the book is a thirty-page conversation between Penrose and Winner—at their club, appropriately enough—about life and love. It reminds me of two grunt-and-groan wrestlers heaving their ponderous bulks around without ever getting a grip on each other. " 'How could she like these things [sadistic acts by her first husband]?' " Penrose rhetorically asks at one point, immediately continuing in the strange patois of Cozzensville: " 'My considered answer: Marjorie, though all unknowing, could! She could see such a punishment as condign. She had to submit, because in an anguished way, she craved to have done to her what she was persuaded she deserved to have done to her.' " Having got off this bit of kindergarten Freudianism: "He gazed an instant at Arthur Winner. 'You find this far-fetched?' he said. 'Yes, we who are so normal are reluctant to entertain such ideas.' " Ideas are always entertained in Cozzensville, though they are not always entertaining. After fifteen more lines of elaboration, Penrose again fears he has outstripped his audience: "You consider this too complicated?" To which Winner, manfully: " 'Perhaps not. But I've often wondered how far anyone can see into what goes on in someone else. I've read somewhere that it would pose the acutest head to draw forth and discover what is lodged in the heart.' " Now where could he have read *that?*

It is interesting to note that Penrose and Winner, the two "point-of-view" characters, are lawyers, and that the processes of the law occupy a considerable amount of the book. The reviewers marvel that Cozzens has been able to master so much legal knowhow, but I think there is more to it than that. We Americans have always had a weakness for the law. Its objectivity reassures our skittish dread of emotion and its emphasis on The Facts suits our pragmatic temper. But above all the law is our substitute for philosophy, which makes us almost as nervous as emotion does. Its complicated, precise formulae have the external qualities of theoretical thinking, lacking only the most essential one—they don't illuminate reality, since what is "given" is not the conditions of life but merely a narrow convention. Dickens, Tolstoy, and other novelists have written law-court scenes showing that truth is too small a fish to be caught in the law's coarse meshes. But to Cozzens a trial is reality while emotional, disorderly life is the illusion. He delights in the tedious complications of lawyer's talk, the sort of thing one skips in reading the court record of even the most sensational trials. On page 344 a clergyman incautiously asks Winner about the property rights of churches in Pennsylvania. "The difference is technical," Winner begins with gusto, and three pages later is still expatiating.

This fascination with the law is perhaps a clue to Cozzens' defects as a novelist. It explains the peculiar aridity of his prose, its needless qualifications, its clumsiness, its defensive qualifications (a lawyer qualifies negatively—so he can't be caught out later; but a novelist qualifies positively —to make his meaning not safer but clearer). And his sensibility is lawyer-like in its lack of both form and feeling, its peculiar combination of a brutal domineering pragmatism ("Just stick to the facts, please!") with abstract fancywork, a kind of Victorian jigsaw decoration that hides more than it reveals. I, too, think the law is interesting, but as an intellectual discipline, like mathematics or crossword puzzles. I feel Cozzens uses it as a defense against emotion ("sentimentality"). Confusing it with philosophy, he makes it bear too heavy a load, so that reality is distorted and even the law's own qualities are destroyed, its logic and precision blurred, its technical elegance coarsened. There's too much emotion in his law and too much law in his emotion.

THE three earlier Cozzens novels I've read, *The Last Adam, The Just and the Unjust,* and *Guard of Honor,* were written in a straightforward if commonplace style. But here Cozzens has tried to write Literature, to develop a complicated individual style, to convey deeper meanings than he has up to now attempted. Slimly endowed as either thinker or stylist, he has succeeded only in fuzzing it up, inverting the syntax, dragging in Latin-root polysyllables. Stylistically, *By Love Possessed* is a neo-Victorian cakewalk.* A cakewalk by a singularly awkward contestant.

* "CAKEWALK—a form of entertainment among American Negroes in which a prize of a cake was given for the most accomplished steps and figures." —WEBSTER.

Confusing laboriousness with profundity, the reviewers have for the most part not detected the imposture.

There is some evidence, if one reads closely and also between the lines, that some of the reviewers had their doubts. But they adopted various strategies for muffling them. Messrs. Gill, Fischer, and Balliett, while applauding the style in general, refrained from quoting anything. The last-named, after praising the "compact, baked, fastidious sentences," went into a long, worried paragraph which implied the opposite. "The unbending intricacies of thought . . . seem to send his sentences into impossible log-jams," he wrote, which is like saying of a girl, "She doesn't seem pretty." Jessamyn West warned, "You may come away with a certain feeling of tiredness," and left it at that. Malcolm Cowley managed to imply the book is a masterpiece without actually saying so—the publishers couldn't extract a single quote. With that cooniness he used to deploy in the 'thirties when he was confronted with an important work that was on the right (that is, the "left") side but was pretty terrible, Cowley, here also confronted with a conflict between his taste and his sense of the *Zeitgeist,* managed to praise with faint damns. One magisterial sentence, in particular, may be recommended to all ambitious young book reviewers: "His style used to be as clear as a mountain brook; now it has become a little weed-grown and murky, like the brook when it wanders through a meadow." A meadowy brook is pretty *too*—it shows the mature Cozzens now feels, in Cowley's words, that "life is more complicated than he once believed."

A favorite reviewer's gambit was that Cozzens' prose may be involved but so is James's. "One drawback is the style," *Time* admitted, "which is frosted with parenthetical clauses, humpbacked syntax, Jamesian involutions, Faulknerian meanderings." I am myself no foe of the parenthesis, nor do I mind a little syntactical humping at times, but I feel this comparison is absurd. James's involutions are (a) necessary to precisely discriminate his meaning; (b) solid parts of the architecture of the sentence; and (c) controlled by a fine ear for euphony. Faulkner does meander, but there is emotional force, descriptive richness behind his wanderings. They both use words that are not only in the dictionary but also in the living language, and use them in conversational rhythms. Their style is complex because they are saying something complicated, not, as with Cozzens, because they cannot make words do what they want them to do.

BUT the main burden of the reviewers was not doubt but affirmation. In reading their praise of Cozzens' prose, I had an uneasy feeling that perhaps we were working with different texts.

"Every sentence has been hammered, filed and tested until it bears precisely the weight it was designed to carry, and does it with clarity and grace," wrote John Fischer. The sentences have been hammered all right:

Recollected with detachment, these self-contrived quandaries, these piffling dilemmas that young love could invent for itself were comic—too much ado about nothing much! Arthur Winner Junior was entangled laughably in his still-juvenile illogicalities and inconsistencies. Absurdly set on working contradictories and incompatibles, he showed how the world was indeed a comedy for those who think. By his unripe, all-or-nothing-at-all views, he was bound to be self-confounded. By the ridiculous impracticalness of his aspirations, he was inescapably that figure of fun whose lofty professions go with quite other performances. The high endeavor's very moments of true-predominance guaranteed the little joke-on-them to follow.

This is not a Horrible Example—we shall have some later —but a typical run-of-the-mill Cozzens paragraph, chosen at random. It seems to me about as bad as prose can get —what sensitive or even merely competent novelist would write a phrase like "the ridiculous impracticalness of his aspirations"?

"Mr. Cozzens is a master of dialogue," wrote Orville Prescott. On the contrary, he has no ear for speech at all. "You answer well, Arthur!" says one matron. "But, to my very point!" And another: "They're all, or almost all, down at the boathouse, swimming, Arthur." A practicing lawyer, not supposed to be either pompous or barmy, uses the following expressions during a chat: "I merit the reproof no doubt. . . . My unbecoming boasting you must lay to my sad disability. . . . I'm now in fettle fine. . . . Our colloquy was brief." In short, Cozzens' people tend to talk like Cozzens. They're out for that cake, too.

"He has always written with complete clarity," wrote Granville Hicks, *"but here, without forsaking clarity and correctness, he achieves great eloquence and even poetic power."* On the contrary, malphony exfoliates, as our author might put it. As:

The succusive, earthquake-like throwing-over of a counted-on years-old stable state of things had opened fissures. Through one of them, Arthur Winner stared a giddying, horrifying moment down unplumbed, nameless abysses in himself. He might later deny the cognition, put thoughts of the undiscovered country away, seek to lose the memory; yet the heart's mute halt at every occasional, accidental recollection of those gulfs admitted their existence, confessed his fearful close shave.

"Succussive" is cake-walking, since it means "violently shaking . . . as of earthquakes" and so merely duplicates the next word; a good writer wouldn't use four hyphenated expressions in a row; he would also avoid the "occasional, accidental" rhyme, and the reference to unplumbed abysses; he would ask himself what a mute halt is (as versus a noisy halt?); and he would sense that "close shave" is stylistically an anticlimax to so elevated a passage. It's all very puzzling. Here's Richard Ellmann of Northwestern University, who has been perceptive about Joyce's prose, finding *By Love*

Possessed "so pleasant to read," while I find almost every sentence grates.*

"Its author has become the most technically accomplished American novelist alive," wrote Whitney Balliett. Let us say rather: the least technically accomplished. To list a few defects of style:

(1) *Melodramatics.* "Deaf as yesterday to all representations of right, he purposed further perfidy, once more pawning his honor to obtain his lust. Deaf as yesterday to all remonstrances of reason, he purposed to sell himself over again to buy venery's disappearing dross." (Haven't seen "dross" in print since *East Lynne.*)

(2) *Confucius Say.* A queer strangled sententiousness often seizes upon our author. "In real life, effects of such disappointment are observed to be unenduring." "The resolve to rise permitted no intermissions; ambition was never sated." Like shot in game or sand in clams, such gritty nuggets are strewn through the book.

(3) *Pointless Inversion.* "Owned and operated by Noah's father was a busy grist mill." "Behind these slowminded peerings of sullen anxiety did dumb unreasonable surges of love swell." "For that night, untied Hope still her virgin knot will keep." The last is interesting. He must mean "tied," since the "still" implies a possible later change, and a virgin knot, once untied, must ever remain so. I think the "un-" was added automatically, because Cozzens makes a dead style even deader by an obsessive use of negative constructions, often doubled, as: "unkilled," "un-

---

* As: "Thinking last night of Ralph's 'Joanie,' those Moores, all unsuspecting; whose 'shame' or 'disgrace' of the same kind (if more decent in degree) stood accomplished, waiting merely to be discovered to them, Arthur Winner had felt able to pre-figure, following the first horrified anger, the distraught recriminations, the general fury of family woe, a bitter necessary acceptance." I find such prose almost impossible to read, partly because of an inexpressive, clumsy use of words, partly because the thought is both abstract and unclear, but chiefly because the rhythms are all wrong. Instead of carrying one forward, they drop one flat, and one must begin anew with each phrase. An artist creates a world, bit added to bit; each addition of Cozens destroys what has gone before.

hasty," "not-unhelped," "not-uneducated," "not-unmoving," "a not-unsturdy frame," "a not-unhandsome profile."
May we take it the profile is handsome, the frame sturdy,
or do they exist in some limbo betwixt and between?*

(4) *Toujours le Mot Injuste*. If there's an inexpressive
word, Cozzens will find it. He specially favors: (a) five-
dollar words where five-centers would do; (b) pedantic
Latinisms, strange beasts that are usually kept behind the
zoo bars of Webster's Unabridged.

(a) Multisonous, incommutable, phantasmogenesis (having to do with the origin of dreams), stupefacients (narcot-
ics), encasement ("snug encasement of his neck" for "tight
collar"), explicative ("one of his characteristically explicative observations"), solemnization ("wedding" becomes "the
solemnization's scene"), eventuated ("acts of eventuated
guilt," a phrase undecipherable even with the Unabridged),
and condign ("condign punishment"—means "deserved
p.").

* Author's Note, as of 1962: "Virgin knot untied" is an echo of Shakespeare
who, in Act. IV, Scene 3 of *Pericles* has Marina say: "If fires be hot,
knives sharp, or waters deep / Untied I still my virgin knot will keep. /
Diana, aid my purpose!" This gloss I owe to Mr. Cozzens, to whom I
sent a copy of my review. He wrote me he had become bored by the
unanimous critical praise for *By Love Possessed* and found my "novel
pronouncements" an interesting change; however, he went on, he couldn't
take me seriously as a judge of style since I preferred Hemingway and
Faulkner to W. Somerset Maugham. The riposte on "virgin knot untied"
was the only solid point he made and I must admit it troubled me. Taking
on Cozzens was one thing, but Shakespeare? Daunted but still hopeful, I
wrote to the only Shakespearean scholar I knew, John Berryman, who
replied: "*Pericles* is not in the folio, only substantive text is the lousy
Quarto of 1609; moreover Sh only wrote the last three acts. But he did
write this line, I think, just as it stands. He sometimes got fouled up in
negatives and said the exact opposite of what he meant; I have a collection
of these passages among my papers at Princeton. . . . There are several in
Macbeth. However, he didn't mean 'tied,' he meant 'untied.' This is the
first alternative and the one I call right; it is upheld by one of the two
chief authorities on Sh's language, Alexander Schmidt, who says 'The
negative form producing an incorrectness of expression . . . i.e., not untied,
not loosed' (Sh-Lexicon 1886). Second possibility is that the line is corrupt
—'untried' immediately occurs to one." (It hadn't occurred to me, or to
Mr. Cozzens, either immediately or postmediately.) I sent this explication
on to Mr. Cozzens, apologizing for having blamed him for a slip that
was actually Shakespeare's fault but there was no reply.

(b) I must admit that reading Cozzens has enriched my vocabulary, or, more accurately, added to it. My favorite, on the whole, is "presbyopic," which of course means "long-sighted because of old age." I also like the sound of "viridity" and "mucid," though it's disappointing to learn they mean simply "greenness" and "slimy." But I see no reason for such grotesques as qualmish, scrutinous, vulnerary ("wound-healing"), pudency, revulsively, and vellications, which is Latin for twitchings.

Cozzens' style is a throwback to the palmiest days of nineteenth-century rhetoric, when a big Latin-root was considered more elegant than a small Anglo-Saxon word. The long, patient struggle of the last fifty years to bring the diction and rhythms of prose closer to those of the spoken language might never have existed so far as Cozzens is concerned. He doesn't even revert to the *central* tradition (Scott, Cooper, Bulwer-Lytton) but rather to the eccentric mode of the half-rebels against it (Carlyle, Meredith), who broke up the orderly platoons of gold-laced Latinisms into whimsically arranged awkward squads, uniformed with equal artificiality but marching every which way as the author's wayward spirit moved them. Carlyle and Meredith are even less readable today than Scott and Cooper, whose prose at least inherited from the eighteenth century some structural backbone.

That a contemporary writer should spend eight years fabricating a pastiche in the manner of George Meredith could only happen in America, where isolation produces oddity. The American novelist is sustained and disciplined by neither a literary tradition nor an intellectual community. He doesn't see other writers much; he probably doesn't live in New York, which like Paris and London unfortunately has almost a monopoly of the national cultural life, because the pace is too fast, the daily life too ugly, the interruptions too great; and even if he does, there are no cafés or pubs where he can foregather with his colleagues; he doesn't read the literary press, which anyway is much less developed than in London or Paris; he normally thinks of himself as a nonintellectual, even an anti-intellectual (Faulkner, Hemingway, Fitzgerald, Lewis, Anderson). It is a pattern of cultural isolation that brings out a writer's eccentric, even his grotesque side.

IN THE case of Cozzens, things have gone about as far as they can. At his country place in Lambertville, New Jersey, he leads a life compared to which Thoreau's on Walden Pond was gregarious. "I am a hermit and I have no friends," he understates. According to *Time,* "Years elapse between dinner guests" and he hasn't been to a play, a concert, or an art gallery in twenty years. (He did go to a movie in 1940). To those who wonder how he can write novels when he has so little contact with people, he says: "The thing you have to know about is yourself; you are people." But he seems signally lacking in self-knowledge. He fancies himself as a stylist, for instance. "My own literary preferences are for writers who write well," he says, pleasantly adding: "This necessarily excludes most of my contemporaries." The level of his taste may be inferred from the fact that he sneers at Faulkner ("falsifies life for dramatic effect"), Hemingway ("under the rough exterior, he's just a great big bleeding heart"), and Lewis ("a crypto-sentimentalist"), but admires—W. Somerset Maugham.

He is similarly deceived about himself. He thinks he is a true-blue conservative of the old school: "I am more or less illiberal and strongly antipathetic to all political and social movements. I was brought up an Episcopalian, and where I live, the landed gentry are Republicans." He is proud of his Tory ancestors, who had to flee to Canada during the Revolution: "To tell the truth, I feel I'm better than other people." But this statement itself seems to me not that of an aristocrat, who would take it for granted, but rather of an uneasy *arriviste.* Nor does illiberalism make a conservative, as we learned in the days of McCarthy.

Cozzens, like some of his sympathetically intended heroes—
Dr. Bull in *The Last Adam* is an example—goes in for
Plain Speaking, but it comes out somehow a little bump-
tious and unpleasant: "I like anybody if he's a nice guy,
but I've never met many Negroes who were nice guys." His
notion of a nice-guy Negro is Alfred Revere in *By Love
Possessed*, the colored verger of the local Episcopalian
church, which is otherwise Whites Only. Tactfully, Mr.
Revere always takes Communion last: "The good, the just
man had consideration for others. By delaying he took care
that members of the congregation need never hesitate to
receive the blood of our Lord Jesus Christ because a cup
from which a Negro had drunk contained it." This is not
ironical, it is perfectly serious, and is followed by a page of
contorted dialectic about God's love.

Perhaps the slick, pushing, crafty Jewish lawyer, Mr.
Woolf—he has even had the nerve to turn Episcopalian,
to Winner's contemptuous amusement—is not meant to
stand for Jews in general, any more than the odious Mrs.
Pratt is meant to stand for all Catholics. One only wishes
that Cozzens' mouthpiece weren't quite so explicit:
"Glimpsing Mr. Woolf's face in the mirror again, Arthur
Winner could see his lips form a smile, deprecatory, inten-
tionally ingratiating. Was something there of the patient
shrug, something of the bated breath and whispering hum-
bleness? . . . Did you forget at your peril the ancient grudge
that might be fed if Mr. Woolf could catch you once upon
the hip?"

HOW did it happen? Why did such a book impress the
reviewers? We know whodunit, but what was the motive?
Like other crimes, this one was a product of Conditions.
The failure of literary judgment and of simple common
sense shown in *l'affaire Cozzens* indicates a general lower-
ing of standards. If this were all, if our reviewers just didn't
know any better, then one would have to conclude we
had quite lost our bearings. But there were other factors.

The two most important, I think, were related: a general feeling that Cozzens had hitherto been neglected and that he "had it coming to him." And consequently a willingness, indeed an eagerness to take at face value his novel's pretensions. It is difficult for American reviewers to resist a long, ambitious novel; they are betrayed by the American admiration of size and scope, also by the American sense of good fellowship; they find it hard to say to the author, after all his work: "Sorry, but it's terrible." In Cozzens' case, it would have been especially hard because he had been writing serious novels for thirty years without ever having had a major success, either popular or *d'estime*. It was now or never. The second alternative would have meant that a lifetime of hard work in a good cause had ended in failure, which would have been un-American. So it had to be now.

The other factor in the book's success is historical. It is the latest episode in The Middlebrow Counter-Revolution. In the 'twenties and 'thirties the avant-garde intellectuals had it pretty much their way. In 1940, the counter-revolution was launched with Archibald MacLeish's essay, "The Irresponsibles," and Van Wyck Brooks's Hunter College talk, "On Literature Today," followed a year later by his "Primary Literature and Coterie Literature." The Brooks-MacLeish thesis was that the avant-garde had lost contact with the normal life of humanity and had become frozen in an attitude of destructive superiority; the moral consequences were perversity and snobbishness, the cultural consequences were negativism, eccentricity, and solipsism.*

* Brooks and MacLeish assumed it was good for writers to identify themselves with their society, which in turn assumed the society was good. If it wasn't, then the avant-garde was justified in isolating itself. Empirically, this would seem to be the case—at least most of the memorable art in every field produced between about 1890 and 1930 was done by artists like Joyce, Eliot, Picasso, Stravinsky, and others who had rejected bourgeois society. But there's no space to argue the question here. Those interested might look at my "Kulturbolshewismus—the Brooks-MacLeish Thesis" in *Partisan Review*, November-December 1941, reprinted in *Memoirs of a Revolutionist* (1957).

The thesis was launched at the right moment. By 1940 the avant-garde had run out of gas—unfortunately no rear-guard filling stations have been opened up, either—while the country had become engaged in a world struggle for survival that made any radically dissident, skeptical atti-tude a luxury. Both conditions still persist, and so the coun-ter-revolution has been on ever since.

Perhaps the first to see Cozzens as a rallying point was the late Bernard DeVoto, who had a wonderfully acute instinct in these matters. DeVoto was Cozzens' Ezra Pound. "He is not a literary man, he is a writer," he observed, a little obscurely but I see what he means. "There are a hand-ful like him in every age. Later on it turns out they were the ones who wrote that age's literature." The wheel has comically come full circle: it used to be those odd, isolated, brilliant writers who were *in advance* of their times—the Stendhals, the Melvilles, the Joyces, and Rimbauds—who later on were discovered to be "the ones who wrote that age's literature"; but now it is the sober, conscientious plodders, who have a hard time just keeping up with the procession, whose true worth is temporarily obscured by their modish avant-garde competitors. This note is struck by the reviewers of *By Love Possessed*. "Critics and the kind of readers who start fashionable cults have been mark-edly cool toward him," writes Gill, while John Fischer complains that Cozzens, unlike "some other novelists of stature," has hitherto been denied "the reverence—indeed the adulation—of the magisterial critics whose encyclicals appear in the literary quarterlies and academic journals. Aside from a Pulitzer Prize in 1949, no such laurels have lighted on Cozzens' head, and the fashionable critics have passed him by in contemptuous silence."

A highbrow conspiracy of paranoiac dimensions, it seems, is behind it all. Cozzens just won't play our game. "It may be that his refusal to become a public figure— no TV or P.E.N. appearances, no commencement addresses at Sarah Lawrence, no night-club pronouncements recorded by Leonard Lyons—has put them [us] off. By devoting himself to writing, he has made himself invisible to the world of letters." So, Mr. Gill.

And Mr. Fischer: "Even his private life is, for a writer, unconventional. He attends no cocktail parties, makes no speeches, signs no manifestoes, writes no reviews, appears on no television shows, scratches no backs, shuns women's clubs. . . . Few people in the so-called literary world have ever set eyes on him." But doesn't all this precisely describe Faulkner and Hemingway when they were making their reputations? Is the P.E.N. Club—have I ever met a member?—so powerful? Did Fitzgerald sign any manifestoes? Are we highbrows really so impressed by TV appearances, talks before women's clubs, mention in gossip columns? Could it be simply that Cozzens really isn't very good?

Another hypothesis was advanced by *Time:* "The interior decorators of U.S. letters—the little-magazine critics whose favorite furniture is the pigeonhole—find that Cozzens fits no recent fictional compartments, and usually pretends that he does not exist." But there is, in fact, a recent pigeonhole for Cozzens: the Novel of Resignation. *By Love Possessed* is, philosophically, an inversion, almost a parody of a kind of story Tolstoy and other nineteenth-century Russian novelists used to tell: of a successful, self-satisfied hero who is led by experiences in "extreme situations" to see how artificial his life has been and who then rejects the conventional world and either dies or begins a new, more meaningful life. In the Novel of Resignation, the highest reach of enlightenment is to realize how awful the System is and yet to accept it *on its own terms.* Because otherwise there wouldn't be any System. Marquand invented the genre, Sloan Wilson carried it on in *The Man in the Gray Flannel Suit,* and Herman Wouk formulated it most unmistakaby in *The Caine Mutiny.* Wouk's moral is that it is better to obey a lunatic, cowardly Captain Queeg, even if the result is disaster, than to follow the sensible advice of an officer of lower grade (who is pictured as a smooth-talking, destructive, cynical, irresponsible conniver —in short, an intellectual) and save the ship. Because otherwise there wouldn't be any U.S. navy. (If there were many Captain Queegs, there wouldn't be a Navy either, a complication Mr. Wouk seems not aware of.) In short, the conventional world, the System, is confused with Life. And since Life is Like That, it is childish if not worse to insist on something better. This is typically American: either juvenile revolt or the immature acceptance of everything; there is no modulation, no development, merely the blank confrontation of untenable extremes; "maturity" means simply to replace wholesale revolt with wholesale acceptance.

IT IS as if Tolstoy's *The Death of Ivan Ilyich* ended with the hero, after his atrocious sufferings, concluding that, as a high official of the Court of Justice, it was in the nature of things that he should die horribly of cancer, and that he must therefore bear his torment like a man for the good of the service. In the actual story, however, he is driven by his "extreme situation" to reject his whole past way of life. Only when he is finally able to give up "the claim that his life had been good" can he experience anything significant: love—the young servant's gentle care of him—and then death.

The ending of *By Loved Possessed* strikes rather a different note. From Winner's climactic six-page interior monologue that ends the book we can take three formulations that sum it up: (1) "Freedom is the knowledge of necessity." (2) "We are not children. In this life we cannot have everything for ourselves we might like to have." (3) "Victory is not in reaching certainties or solving mysteries; victory is in making do with uncertainties, in supporting mysteries."

What is the reality behind these unexceptionable bits of philosophy? It is that Winner, for complicated pragmatic-sentimental reasons, decides to cover up an embezzlement he has just discovered, an embezzlement of trust funds by his venerable law partner, Noah Tuttle, and that he has been eased of his guilt toward his other partner, Julius Penrose, about his old affair with Marjorie, Penrose's wife. In both cases, it is Penrose who gives him the line: exposing Tuttle would not only ruin Winner—who would be equally responsible for his partner's defalcations —but would also mean the disgrace of Tuttle, who is after all paying the money back slowly. As for Winner's liaison with Marjorie, Penrose has known about it all along and has never blamed Winner, considering that "indefeasible urge of the flesh." In fact, Penrose is actually obliged to Winner for *not* telling him: " 'I've always thanked you for . . . trying in every way to keep it from me.' "

In short, Ivan Ilyich feels free because he is compelled to reject his past as "not the right thing," Arthur Winner because he is allowed to accept his past, is even thanked by his best friend for having concealed from him that fact that he had cuckolded him. The last words of the book are Winner's, as he returns home: "I'm here." It's all right, nothing has to be changed: "I have the strength, the strength to, to—to endure more miseries," thinks Winner, gratefully.

Inside *The Outsider*

Two MYSTERIES intrigued the London public in the summer of 1956—the Widows of Eastbourne and the success of *The Outsider*. The question in the first case was whether the deaths, at the seashore resort of Eastbourne in the last generation, of some rich elderly ladies were facilitated by a local doctor whom many of them remembered in their wills. The second mystery, whose public is admittedly smaller, is how and why a badly written work of amateur philosophy by a hitherto unknown young author has become the most-discussed best seller in several years. I have no theories on the first mystery, which had best be left to Scotland Yard, but I have talked about the second with a number of Londoners, almost all of whom at least agree that there *is* a mystery, and I have slogged my way through the book. And I think there are some interesting answers.

The author of *The Outsider* is an earnest, humorless, and self-confident young man named Colin Wilson. As readers of *Time* and *Life* already know—the Lucepapers took him up in a big way, perhaps because his message is both positive and religious—he is the son of a factory worker, left school when he was sixteen, lived and read in a Left Bank garret in Paris, and completed his self-education with daytime reading in the British Museum and nighttime camping out in a sleeping bag on Hampstead Heath. Such are the outlines of the Wilson Myth (his sleeping bag is now as famous as the one into which Hemingway bundled Jordan and

Rabbit), on which the subject has co-operated by climbing back into his sleeping bag for *Life* photographers and submitting to the whole routine of celebrity. Some of his fellow intellectuals see a certain irony in the speed with which the author of *The Outsider* has become an insider, but such nuances don't bother Mr. Wilson, an ambitious and energetic go-getter who is convinced that he has a mission and that he can carry it through. Unlike Hamlet, he considers it a blessing, not a spite, that he was born to set right a world satisfactorily out of joint.

It is said that when Victor Gollancz, who has had much experience with intellectual books, published *The Outsider* in London in May, 1956, he had only modest expectations. Although the theme was a major one—his jacket describes it, without too much exaggeration, as "an inquiry into the nature of the sickness of mankind in mid-twentieth century"—this was not necessarily a passport to popularity; every year many weighty books fall from the presses with no more than a dignified thud. Nor did the treatment, which is heavy-footed and even academic, seem auspicious. Therefore, Mr. Gollancz printed a first edition of fifteen hundred and hoped that a second might be required. Three months later, almost twenty-five thousand copies had been sold, and the book was still selling at a great rate.

The Outsider presents an approach to life that the author feels is the only possible one for a serious and intelligent person today. His method is, essentially, to describe the problems of a large number of individuals, fictional and real, who have felt themselves to be Outsiders and to explain wherein they succeeded in solving or not solving their problems, and why. Among these individuals are T. E. Lawrence; Van Gogh; Nijinsky; Nietzsche; Blake; Tolstoy; George Fox, the seventeenth-century Quaker evangelist; Ramakrishna, the Indian mystic; and Gurdjieff, an ambiguous Balkan prophet. They also include the protagonists of Barbusse's *L'Enfer*, Sartre's *Nausea*, Camus' *The Stranger*, Granville-Barker's *The Secret Life*, Hermann Hesse's *Steppenwolf*, and several of Dostoevsky's novels. There are, in addition, extracts from and comments on works by Joyce, Kafka, Kierkegaard, T. E. Hulme, Rilke, Hemingway, Eliot, Yeats, Shaw, Wells, and many, many others. (Scope is what the book has most of.) The common denominator of this motley gathering is, or is alleged to be, their Outsiderness, a quality Mr. Wilson defines quite simply in a recent interview: "The ordinary person, the Insider, is cogged to the social current. The Outsider is cogged to the current of life itself." Less simply, the book builds up the picture with innumerable and partly contradictory definitions, such as:

The Outsider is a man who cannot live in the comfortable, insulated world of the bourgeoisie, accepting what he sees and touches as reality. "He sees too deep and too much," and what he sees is essentially *chaos*. . . . The Outsider is a man who is awakened to chaos . . . the only man who knows he is sick in a civilization that doesn't know it is sick.

From the Outsider's viewpoint, the world justifies complete pessimism. . . . The Outsider does not make light work of living; at the best it is hard going.

The Outsider's problem is the problem of denial of self-expression. . . . It is a living problem—the problem of *pattern or purpose* in life. . . . His problem is [that] . . . nothing is worth doing.

The Outsider's chief desire is *to cease to be an Outsider.*

The Outsider's problem *is* the problem of freedom. . . . A man becomes an Outsider when he begins to chafe under the recognition that he is not free.

The Outsider would seem to be a basically religious man . . . who refuses to develop those qualities of practical-mindedness and eye-to-business that seem to be the requisites for survival in our complex civilization. . . . By "religion" I am not trying to indicate any specific religious system. Religious categories . . . are such simple ideas as "Original Sin," "salvation," "damnation," which come naturally to the Outsider's way of thinking.

THIS thesis has a certain dash, and it is quite up-to-date in replacing the antiquated rationalistic-materialistic rebel, Marxian or Freudian, with a new mystical model. The author develops his argument with vigorous, bold strokes, like a man painting a barn in a hurry, and though one may find his notion of any thinker with whom one is familiar both superficial and vulgar, his line of thought is at least clearly marked. That a twenty-four-year-old should have the determination to carry out so ambitious a scheme, however crudely and with whatever outpourings of clotted journalese, must induce a legitimate pride in his parents, his teachers, and (in this case) his pastor. But these virtues, which are outweighed by far greater defects, hardly explain the almost unanimous acclaim with which the English reviewers greeted *The Outsider*—especially since none of them, so far as I know, were relatives.

A good sale for the book—though by no means the remarkable sale it has had—was practically guaranteed when the two London journals whose opinions count most heavily with book buyers, the *Sunday Times* and the *Observer*, came out with enthusiastic reviews. "This extraordinary book. . . . He has a quick, dry intelligence . . . has read prodigiously and digested what he has read, and he loves what is best," Cyril Connolly wrote in the *Sunday Times*. Philip Toynbee, of the *Observer*, found the book "an exhaustive and luminously intelligent study . . . of a kind which is too rare in England." These big guns were merely part of a barrage—"most remarkable book on which the reviewer has ever had to pass judgment" (*The Listener*); "an astonishing book" (Liverpool *Daily Post*); "thunderstruck by the amount he has read" (Elizabeth

Bowen in the *Tatler*); "an astonishing book; I think Colin Wilson will be a truly great writer" (Edith Sitwell); "brilliant, original, provocative . . . a subtle, patient writer, full of eagerness and ideas. . . . This remarkable book" (V. S. Pritchett, broadcasting on B.B.C.); "astonishing book . . . I admire his high seriousness, intelligence, and sensibility, and I feel he is a most welcome and valuable recruit to English literary criticism" (Maurice Cranston, also on B.B.C.).

Even when *The Outsider* was unfavorably reviewed—notably in the *Times Literary Supplement,* whose anonymous critic did a thorough and scholarly job; in the *Spectator,* whose Kingsley Amis, an infant prodigy of slightly earlier vintage, expectably attacked it as highbrow, a charge that is, alas, unfounded; and in *Encounter,* whose Dr. A. J. Ayer mangled it on the Procrustean bed of logical positivism—little was said about what seems to me the book's major defect, its barbarous style. This is odd, because English reviewers usually are more sensitive to style than their American colleagues; the aberration could be related to the English diffidence in the face of abstract ideas—a philosopher may seem to them a strange bird, to be exempted from stylistic requirements, just as foreigners aren't expected to speak correctly. Even that literary dandy Cyril Connolly passed over Mr. Wilson's baggy prose with a mild complaint about "a general gracelessness and a hurried pontificating manner inclined to repetitions." The consensus was that the book is important because of what it says, apart from how it says it. I think this is a false distinction. An idea doesn't exist apart from the words that express it. Style is not an envelope enclosing a message; the envelope *is* the message.

THE form of *The Outsider* is a series of summaries—of novels, of philosophical works, of lives—with interpretations by the author as connective tissue. The summaries are summary indeed:

After reading the treatise, he hits rockbottom of despair; he is exhausted and frustrated, and the treatise warns him that this is all as it should be; he decides that this is the last time he allows himself to sink so low; next time he will commit suicide before he reaches that point. The thought cheers him up and he lies down to sleep.

The author's glosses are equally crude. Like an unarmed man confronted by a burglar, Mr. Wilson picks up the first banality that comes to hand and brings it crashing down on the subject: "white heat of feeling," "plain sailing," "hair-splitting," "can be counted on the fingers on one hand," "cock a snook," "can't write for toffee" are some of the blunt instruments he uses. There are a good many sentences like "This, of course, is the hurdle on which hundreds of Nietzsche-critics have broken their shins"; "With these lines, [T. S.] Eliot was over his stile, out of the Outsider's position"; "There is no point in the novel at which Stavrogin gets on a soapbox to explain himself"; "No, Axel is on the right path, even if killing himself is a poor way out." I don't think a style as debased as this can convey any serious meaning.

Not that Mr. Wilson doesn't realize that there are many stiles, and styles, on which he might break his shins. Of self-awareness, one of the many chief problems of the Outsider, he writes, "It calls for . . . exactitude of language. . . . It is a subject which is full of pitfalls for the understanding. And writing about it drives home the fact that our language has become a tired and inefficient thing in the hands of journalists and writers who have nothing to say." It is confusing to find a writer using tired and inexact phrases to demand vigor and exactitude. His next sentence gives a clue: "Language is the natural medium for self-analysis." There is perhaps a connection between his

literary aphasia and that lack of self-awareness that causes
him to expound Blake, Nietzsche, and Kierkegaard in the
language (and spirit) of a rather unimaginative grocer:

> The visionary is inevitably an Outsider. And this is not be-
> cause visionaries are a relatively small minority in proportion
> to the rest of the community; in that case, rat-catchers and
> steeple-jacks would be Outsiders too. It is for the very different
> reason that he starts from a point that everybody can under-
> stand, and very soon soars beyond the general understanding.
> He starts from the "appetite for fruitful activity and a high
> quality of life" [this phrase, taken from Shaw, is perhaps that
> author's one broken-backed formulation in seventy years of
> writing; it took literary tactlessness of a high order to dig it
> out and resurrect it].

Many English reviewers have praised *The Outsider* for
its "direct," "fresh," and "vigorous" writing, which seems
to indicate that the English have become habituated to
the forensic-expository style of the law courts, the Oxford
Union, parliamentary debate, and letters to the editor.
This style has great merits, and in the hands of a Shaw
it is remarkably effective, but it is not suited to the discussion of the profound and subtle problems Mr. Wilson is
dealing with. Furthermore, Mr. Wilson is no Shaw. "It
is unfortunate that lack of space prevents a longer examination of Blake's work," he writes (meaning he'd rather
use the space for something else, a point that could have
been made simply by using the space for something else).
"The sentence I have italicized is the important one."
(Thanks.) "At this point, we can pass the threads of the
argument into the hands of another Russian writer, and
leave him to unravel them further for us." (Just pass the
argument, please.) Every curve in the line of discourse is
announced in advance ("as we shall see") and then re-
called ("I have tried to show"), lest the most modestly endowed citizen fall off the train. This scaffolding sometimes
achieves a really monumental effect:

In going on to speak of Eliot's development in "Ash Wednesday," I have made a point which is not especially relevant in this chapter; I have done this for the convenience of not having to split up the story of Eliot's development. Still, readers who feel dubious about the connection of the last two paragraphs with what has gone before can dismiss them as unproved; we shall have to return to the subject later from a completely different angle, and for the moment it is not important.

Thrown into the cement mixer of Mr. Wilson's mind, Dostoevsky's Stavrogin comes out:

Conceive him as a Russian combination of Evan Strowde and Oliver Gauntlett [characters in a long-forgotten play by Granville-Barker that Mr. Wilson revives because it fits his argument], add a touch of Pushkin's Eugene Onyegin, and you have a reasonably accurate picture. His story unfolds as a series of romantically paradoxical acts: he kisses some one's wife in the middle of a respectable social gathering; he pulls the nose of a retired general. . . . In short, he plays the Rimbaud-roaring-boy in the drawing room atmosphere of the town.

Or there is Mr. Wilson's evaluation of Hermann Hesse, a minor German novelist to whose work he devotes many pages: "Considered as a whole, Hesse's achievement can hardly be matched in modern literature. . . . Hesse has little imagination in the sense that Shakespeare or Tolstoy can be said to have imagination, but his ideas have a vitality that more than makes up for it." In a novelist, nothing makes up for imagination (nothing "makes up for" anything anyway), and certainly not "ideas." But "ideas" that can be botched into the jerry-built structure of his argument are all that Mr. Wilson wants from the poets, novelists, mystics, and philosophers he exploits; he reduces their work to fragments with his rough-and-ready summaries and erects his thesis with the rubble. At times, one has the impression that the masters of modern literature were Mr. Wilson's research assistants. *"The Brothers Karamazov* is Dostoevsky's biggest attack on the Outsider theme," he writes. And: "To facilitate his [William Blake's] analysis of Outsider problems, he divided man into the same three divisions that we arrived at in Chapter IV. . . . His system . . . provides a skeleton key to every Outsider in this book." Many hands make light work.

THE reasons for the success of *The Outsider* are of two varieties. One is related to the special situation of the younger generation in England, the other to a more general phenomenon of our time—the development of a sizable reading public whose cultural aspirations exceed its knowledge and sensibility. Since the war, there has been a lot of worrying about the younger generation. Like a parent with a backward child, the elders have applauded, almost desperately, any sign of talent. For an ambitious younger writer, London is now utopia: Important journalistic jobs are open to him, his critical views are printed in influential magazines and newspapers, his plays or novels are received appreciatively. The counterpart of *The Outsider* in the theatre, in both popularity and merit, is *Look Back in Anger,* a play by John Osborne, also in his twenties; it consists largely of complaining monologues by the pretentious and disagreeable young hero, which middle-aged audiences listen to respectfully as an authentic expression of the Youth Problem. And there was the success, two or three years ago, of Kingsley Amis' novel *Lucky Jim,* a very funny book but one whose spectacular reviews and sales can be explained only by the youth of both author and hero. Thus one may account for the reviews that launched the *Outsider* boom—these by Cyril Connolly and Philip Toynbee, both of whom are normally (that is, when confronted by the work of their coevals) critics of discernment. The boom may also have been helped because Mr. Wilson is socially and culturally underprivileged, for insiders in a class-conscious country like

England can be lenient in judging outsiders (the very title of the book arouses snobbish guilt).

The Outsider seems, furthermore, to have attracted many readers from the younger generation itself—the pony-tailed or sideburned patrons of the *caffè espresso* joints that have sprung up all over London in recent years. They identify themselves with the Outsider as an earlier generation romantically become Werthers; some of them imitated Goethe's hero to the extent of killing themselves. I anticipate no such results, though, in the case of Mr. Wilson, or, in fact, any results at all. Both young and old, finally, are fascinated by the idealistic nature of his message, as well as by his parade of culture. Up to now, the mood of the younger generation has been materialistic, even cynical, with an overtone of rebellion not only against bourgeois culture (this has been, after all, de rigueur since the 'nineties) but against culture in general. Kingsley Amis, as both critic and novelist, is typical of that generation. That a young man should have read so many books and have taken their ideas with such grim seriousness, that he should have advocated a religious solution—all this is novel and encouraging. The earnest, Kierkegaard-quoting Mr. Wilson is a kind of young man very different from Mr. Amis, who in his review of *The Outsider* claimed that he had never heard of Kierkegaard. (I suspect he really had, and that his disclaimer of knowledge was just vulgar boasting.)

Or is Mr. Wilson really so different? This leads me, as he would write, to my next, and last, point, which I have put at the end because it seems to me to have a quality of finality.

THE success of *The Outsider* is one more indication of the growth, since the First World War, of a public that habitually lives beyond its cultural means. These people are not the humble millions who read Will Durant's *The*

Story of Philosophy or Wells's *Outline of History*. Nor
are they exactly intellectuals. They might be called camp
followers of the avant-garde. They want to keep up, and
they are attracted by large, new theories that seem to
crystallize what is "in the air." There was James Burnham's *The Managerial Revolution,* in 1941, which resembled *The Outsider* in presenting a timely thesis in
bold, poster-like outlines (yet conveniently fuzzy ones) and
under a label that was sheer advertising genius. Mr.
Burnham's now almost forgotten theory of Managerialism
was discussed around innumerable academic campfires. In
the same way, telling the Outsiders from the Insiders
speedily became a London parlor game; a year earlier, the
game was to discriminate, following Nancy Mitford's lead,
between U (or Upper-class) and Non-U word usage.

The Outsider has a special gimmick of its own. It combines two approaches to life that are not often combined—
of the artist, the intellectual, and the mystic on the one
hand, and of the Philistine "practical man" on the other.
More accurately, it presents the second approach in terms
of the first—not, I think, as a tactic but simply because
basically the author's own values are unconsciously Philistine. Had the Reverend Norman Vincent Peale not been
there first, *The Outsider* could have been called *The
Power of Positive Serious Thinking.* It is, for all its highbrow décor, an inspirational how-to treatise—be glad
you're an outsider; face up to life; achieve peace of mind;
develop your hidden asset, will power! There is the same
reduction of everything to the common-sense level. ("The
later Tolstoy had an obsession about sexual impurity that
Kierkegaard or Nietzsche would have found funny." What
a choice of witnesses, by the way.) The same nice-Nellie
reaction to the "unpleasant"—in comic contrast to his line
of argument, but the argument is contrived and the reaction is felt. ("The subject is unpleasant to dwell on," he
writes primly, apropos the "life-denying nihilism" in Con-

rad's *Heart of Darkness.* "Further enumeration of treatments of the theme," he adds, "will serve no purpose." Dostoevsky's *Notes from Underground* he finds "so unnecessarily unpleasant as to be barely readable.") The same accent on the positive. ("Well, we can see that Fox made a better show . . . tracking his 'inner powers' to the roots and harnessing them to action. . . . He was better off than Van Gogh or [T. E.] Lawrence, for his attempt [to gain control] led to more success than theirs. . . . He showed that there is no point in getting neurotic and defeatist about it, and deciding, like Schopenhauer, that the world and the spirit are at eternal, perpetual, unresolvable loggerheads.") The same Philistine distinction between art and philosophy on the one hand and "real life" on the other: "The Outsider problem is essentially a living problem; to write about it in terms of literature is to falsify it. . . . The writer has an instinct that makes him select the material that will make the best show on paper . . . [but] the Outsider's problems will not submit to mere thought; *they must be lived.*" (I do like that "mere.") There is, above all, the same elephantiasis of "will power," whatever that term means in this post-Freudian era. ("The will's power is immense when backed by moral purpose. Reason's only role is to establish moral purpose by self-analysis. [Then] the will can operate, and the limit of its power over the body is only the limit of moral purpose to back it.")

As one trudges on through Mr. Wilson's cultural wasteland, it slowly becomes clear that this serious young man is a Philistine, a Babbitt, a backwoods revivalist of blood-chilling consistency. The gospel he preaches is as hostile to art, letters, philosophy, and other aspects of humanistic culture as was that of Savonarola, whom the Florentines burned, and John Knox, whom the Scotch didn't, thereby letting themselves in for cultural ravages they felt for centuries. "Knowledge is merely an instrument for living,"

Mr. Wilson writes. "There is no such thing as abstract knowledge; there is only useful knowledge and unprofitable blatherskite." How true this is depends on how broad one's notion of usefulness is. The remarks just quoted follow this sentence: "The Socratic conception of history (propagated in our time by Professor Whitehead) is that civilization advances in proportion as its thinkers are interested in abstractions, in knowledge for its own sake." One who can see Socrates and Whitehead as primarily "interested in abstractions" has a very narrow idea of the usefulness of philosophy. Toward the end of the book, it becomes evident that Mr. Wilson values culture only insofar as it helps him toward religious belief; "I will serve nothing but my God and my own soul," he has his final hero, the "religious man," say. "Perish all such conceptions as knowledge and civilization."

Perish also, apparently, sanity. In his last chapter, Mr. Wilson thoroughly expounds the ideas of Gurdjieff, that dubious mystagogue, so thoroughly as to suggest that in Mr. Wilson, as in other Philistine types, an excess of common sense vis-à-vis mere human affairs like art is oddly accompanied by a serious deficiency of the same commodity when it comes to arcane matters. Viz.:

In *All and Everything* Gurdjieff explains man's bondage [i.e., Original Sin] in a slightly more complex way. . . . Some cosmic catastrophe knocked two pieces off the earth, which became two satellites, the moon and another smaller moon which men have forgotten (although it still exists). These two moons, as part of the parent body, had to be sustained by "food" sent from earth (I have mentioned that Gurdjieff considers the heavenly bodies to be alive), and this "food" is a sort of cosmic ray manufactured by human beings. In other words, the only purpose of human beings is to manufacture "food" for the moon.

But human beings were, not unnaturally, irritated by this completely subject-role they were expected to play in the solar system. As they began to develop "objective reason" (Gurdjieff's fourth state of consciousness), their chafing became a danger to the existence of the moon. A special commission of archangels decided to put a stop to the development of objective reason. So they implanted in man an organ, called *Kundabuffer,* whose special function was to make men perceive fantasy as actuality. And from that day onward men have been enmeshed in their own dreams, and admirably serve their function of providing food for the moon.

There might be two opinions as to just who is the dupe of *Kundabuffer.*

The result of all the Outsider's suffering, thinking, writing, painting, and creating is, if all goes well, that he graduates into becoming a prophet, one who has got beyond "mere thought," as Gurdjieff clearly has. "The Outsider's miseries are the prophet's teething pains. . . . Gradually the message emerges." The message attracts the camp followers for the same reason Marxism attracted them in the thirties (I don't mean otherwise to equate Marxism and Outsiderism)—because it realistically recognizes the depressing state of the here and now but points to a future in which all will be well. That the key to this future is religion instead of social revolution doesn't at all, nowadays, lessen its appeal—especially since Mr. Wilson's notion of religion is broad enough to include Bernard Shaw as "a major religious teacher" because of his "mystical recognition of the possibilities of pure Will." Nor have the book's sales been hurt by its Philistinism. The camp followers feel that culture is something to be possessed rather than something to be experienced. When an author explains difficult thinkers like Blake and Kierkegaard in down-to-earth terms, when he treats the great ones of art and thought with the slightly patronizing familiarity they would use themselves if they dared, and when he does this with proper "seriousness" and under the exciting banner of the avant-garde, they naturally feel that he is their man. I think they are right.

HANDS ACROSS THE SEA

IT WILL NOT have escaped the vigilant reader that the case of *The Outsider* parallels that of *By Love Possessed,* as (see below) the 1961 *New English Bible* echoes the 1952 American *Revised Standard Version.* Those of us who have a tendency toward Anglophilia, as I do, should take warning from these parallels; the effects of masscult and midcult are by no means limited to this side of the Atlantic.

The Outsider and *By Love Possessed* were bad books which became best sellers because they were extravagantly praised by critics and journals that normally (or so one thought) were discriminating. They were so praised because both were obviously serious efforts, and the reviewers took the intent for the deed. It was their seriousness, indeed their portentousness, that disoriented the critics. Max Beerbohm, for example, a far more original and vigorous thinker than either Mr. Wilson or Mr. Cozzens (not to dwell on his considerably greater talent as a writer) never had the kind of sales they have been enjoying. The reviewers have become so disoriented through constant exposure to potboilers that they assume almost automatically that any book which is clearly *not* written for the market is to be taken seriously. This, of course, is not the case. It is the critic's job to discriminate between the true-good and the false-good, since the humbler practitioners of bestsellerdom are so easily distinguished that they don't threaten our standards. It is when you have a sincere and ambitious attempt (to create a new philosophy or to write a "big" novel) that the temptation to be a good fellow and applaud is strongest—and most dangerous. The critics and the mob find a common ground: both feel they are doing their duty by Culture.

"Mob" is perhaps too strong. The ordinary reader, precisely because he is less involved in the cultural mechanism, often reacts with more sense and sensibility than the critics. I don't know how many purchasers of *The Outsider,* after a struggle, sadly put it aside unread, but I do have some data on *By Love Possessed.* The almost universal note of the seventy-odd letters I have received and of the perhaps twice that many verbal comments is: I couldn't read the book, and so I thought I must be a terrible Philistine because all the reviewers praised it; thanks for reassuring me. Meanwhile, every week, new legions, shepherded by their literary fuglemen (O.E.D.: "soldiers placed in front of regiment while drilling to show the motions and time"), march bravely into the valley of death.

Looking Backward

In 1959 Raymond Williams published *Culture and Society, 1780-1950,* a survey which was interesting and valuable as long as it was specific, which it was most of the time, but whose concluding chapter aroused some doubts as to the author's competence as a theoretician. In 1961 he put out a sequel, *The Long Revolution,* in which theory is dominant. I found Part One, which deals with such vague topics as "The Creative Mind" and "Individuals and Societies," impenetrable; it may have something to do with the rest, but since I couldn't keep my mind on it, I'm not sure. It is followed by a slightly longer Part Two (167 pages) which deals with such concrete topics as "The Growth of the Reading Public" and "The Social History of English Writers" and contains much information and many fresh and valuable observations. Part Three (62 pages) is entitled "Britain in the 1960s;" it is more readable than Part One but no more satisfactory as an attempt at general thinking.

In *The Long Revolution,* Mr. Williams examines the incursion of the masses into the cultural scene in the last two centuries and finds it good; in fact, he argues that the best hope for culture in the future will be to democratize it still further. I think the opposite—that our aim should be to restore the cultural distinctions that have become increasingly blurred since the industrial revolution, and that out of such attempts to do this as the 1890-1930 avant-garde

movement of Joyce-Eliot-Picasso-Stravinsky has come whatever is alive in our culture today. My position is, sociologically, as "reactionary" as his is "progressive." Like
Marx, he sees history as an escalator. I should love to
agree with him; all my conditioned reflexes are for
Progress; but reality keeps creeping in. If history is in fact
an escalator, which I doubt, then I think the interests of
culture, and of human values generally, demand that we
step off it. And I see Mr. Williams' point of view, for all
its Progressivism, as a nostalgic one. I think he is living
in the past, before 1914, when a belief in simple democracy
was still intellectually possible.

Thus I agree wholeheartedly, and perhaps softheadedly,
with his political values, which are those of Guild Socialism, an admirable and obsolete British doctrine which
resembled the anarchism of Kropotkin: a vision of a communal style of life in which groups of producers—Soviets,
really, before Lenin and Stalin got to work—freely co-
operate without any coercive central authority. Thus both
classless collectivism and individual freedom would be
achieved. It is a noble and imaginative concept, more likely
to produce a decent society than the Marxian formula
of using State power as the instrument of social change, a
formula as dangerous as it has been successful, leading to
the horrors of totalitarianism or the sapless compromise
of the Weimar Republic and the British Labour Party.
The difference is that Mr. Williams thinks this vision is
the logical result of the democratization and industrialization of the last two centuries and that it can be realized
without catastrophe or revolution if the majority had the
will and the consciousness (commodities with which he
is ready to supply them in abundance), while I see Marxian
Statism as the program which best meets the needs of mass
industry. To deflect the course of history toward the Guild-
Socialist-anarchist vision will require a severe break with

the kind of society we now have, that is, will require catastrophe and revolution, in that order.

WHY doesn't Mr. Williams see this? I think because he is a preacher rather than a thinker, one more interested in exhorting than in analyzing. He conceals this hortatory bias—perhaps even from himself—by constant allusions to the complex nature of reality. He is of the "There-is-no-simple-answer" school of thought, or rather of rhetoric. True, there *is* no simple answer. But as the artist must simplify in order to produce a work that will be a coherent statement and not merely a reflection of the chaos of reality, so the thinker must generalize. Marx and Freud were good at it, for all the complexity and subtlety of their thought, which is why their ideas have proved effective. I don't think Mr. Williams' ideas are effective. In fact I don't think they are ideas at all. They are, rather, prejudices—prejudices on the right side, generous and sincere and democratic prejudices, but still *idées reçues,* unexamined assumptions. He isn't good at generalizing and this is shown by his appalling prose style—for one cannot conceive of an idea apart from the words in which it is expressed; at least I can't. Mr. Williams' prose is that of a propagandist; it is fuzzy on principle, swathed in circumlocutions, emitting multisyllabic words as the cuttlefish does clouds of ink, and for very much the same purpose. A good style comes to grips with things as soon as possible, but Mr. Williams' style puts the maximum distance between the reader and the subject. He is addicted to such opening sentences as:

The extension of culture has to be considered within the real social context of our economic and political life.

Which is shortly followed by:

In a rapidly changing and therefore confused society, in which cultural forms will in any case change but in which little is done by way of education to deepen and refine the capacity for significant response, the problems that confront us are inevitably difficult.

This sort of writing is like marking time in military drill —but the company never seems to get on the march. The style is an end in itself, a magical device for charming away, by heartwarming liblab formulations, the threatening reality. Mr. Williams is fond of that great liblab word, "challenge" (he also likes "creative") and is always talking about meeting challenges. I suspect this is because he so rarely does meet them in fact.

The sermon is his literary form. In true preacher fashion, he is forever contrasting the dismal present with the bright future which can easily come into being if only we will hearken, and in true preacher fashion he never seems to suspect that the present, which is merely the tiny tip of the long thick tail of the past, may be the product of historical forces which will continue to affect the future. He constantly insists on the gloom of the present and as constantly extrapolates from it a misty Utopia, throwing across the horrible gulf a gossamer bridge of good intentions. If this sounds like *The Poverty of Philosophy,* so be it; writers like Mr. Williams rouse the old Marx in one.

The systole and diastole of his way of thinking—more accurately, of feeling—may be anatomized on pages 301-302. He begins by deploring "the visible decline of the labour movement," of which "large sections" have gone over to "ways of thinking which they still formally oppose." This indictment he spells out:

The main challenge to capitalism was socialism, but this has almost wholly lost any contemporary meaning, and it is not surprising that many people now see in the Labour Party merely an alternative power-group, and in the trade-union movement merely a set of men playing the market in very much the terms of the employers they oppose.

Whether the author is one of those "many people" is not clear, but the implication is that this is at least a tenable viewpoint. Now comes the diastole:

I remember that I surprised many people, in *Culture and Society,* by claiming that the institutions of the labour movement . . . were a great creative achievement of the working people and also *the right basis for the whole organisation of any good society of the future.* [My italics—D.M.] Am I now withdrawing this claim? The point is, as I see it, that my claim rested on the new social patterns these institutions offered . . . this steady offering of ways of living that could be extended to the whole society . . . collective democratic institutions . . . substitution of cooperative equality for competition. . . .

Granted the potentialities of the labor movement for these "new social patterns," but if potentialities were horses then preachers might ride. First, one could make the same argument—and it is still made in ideologically backward countries like the United States—for Adam Smith's free-market capitalism, which also offered "new social patterns" which might have resulted in another kind of anarchic Utopia had it not been for the actual capitalists, who played the same role that the actual British trade-union leaders have played in sabotaging Mr. Williams' Utopia. And second, the task is not to wake us up by exhortation —we are all too painfully awake already—but to explain why these potentialities in the labor movement have not been realized, why the whole massive drift has been for five or six generations—in Germany, in England, in the United States—away from the communal-democratic pattern that Mr. Williams rightly advocates. To this task he has not addressed himself, perhaps because he takes it for granted—as we did in the Trotskyist movement in the 'thirties—that the workers are okay, it's just those treacherous (or shortsighted; or corrupt) leaders. We never wondered why such splendid fellows invariably followed such unsplendid leaders, for we were, as I think Mr. Williams is, suckers for what Alfred Braunthal once described as "the mystic cult of The Masses, who always feel the right way and always act the wrong way."

BUT, as Mr. Williams will be the first to insist, far from believing in the mystic cult of the masses, he rejects the whole concept, feeling about this six-letter word as Mr. Griffith-Jones, of the prosecution in the *Lady Chatterley* trial, did about the four-letter words in Lawrence's novel. In the last chapter of *Culture and Society*, he has a lot to say about this word, and he repeats the essence in Part Three of *The Long Revolution*. It evidently makes him uneasy. Ignoring the long use of "the masses" as a favorable term in Marxist polemics—is this perhaps a bit of Freudian socio-suppression?—he takes it as a term of abuse used by culture-snobs as a synonym for "the mob" and as a condescending formulation which press lords and movie tycoons use to describe their audiences: "We give the masses what they want."

Mr. Williams points out that no one thinks of himself as part of "the masses," which is true, but he then goes too far: "Masses are other people. There are in fact no masses; there are only ways of seeing people as masses." But of course the fact that one is not conscious of being such-and-such does not mean that one is not such-and-such; a leopard is a leopard whether he thinks he is or not, and Hitler was a mass-man whether he thought he was Siegfried or Napoleon or just Adolf Schickelgruber. However, Mr. Williams objects to the whole concept of "masses," arguing that it is false (because it implies that human beings are automata) and reactionary (because it is "a way of seeing other people which has . . . been capitalized for the purpose of political or cultural exploitation"). But, while I agree that human beings are not automata, I think they behave like such in certain situations which have been brought about by our mass-industrial society, as when they are polarized by parties like the Nazi or the Communist ones or by cultural media like American television or the big British daily newspapers. Why it is reactionary to recognize this obvious fact of modern life I do not see, especially since Mr. Williams constantly does it himself (though eschewing the actual six-letter word), deploring the flood of "bad art, bad entertainment, bad journalism," noting that "the new institutions [of culture] were not produced by the working people themselves" and denouncing the "cheapjacks" who exploit popular ignorance to make money. The question, it seems to me, is not whether "masses" is a dirty word but whether it is an accurate one.

The difference between our positions, of course, is that Mr. Williams blames it all on the cheapjacks and exploiters, while I see it as a reciprocal process, in which the ignorance and vulgarity of the mass public meshes in an endless cat's-cradle with the same qualities—plus rapacity—in the Lords of *Kitsch*. The cheapjacks do indeed sell adulterated cultural goods, but the awkward question (shall we say the challenge?) is why the masses prefer adulteration to the real thing, why the vast majority of the British people read *News of the World* instead of the *Observer* and go to see *Carry On, Nurse!* instead of *L'Avventura*. Mr. Williams says it is because they are ill educated and socially disadvantaged. This is part of the answer but far from the whole. The difficulty is that most people, of whatever education or social position, don't care very much about culture. This is not a class matter and is not even unique to our age. Some Renaissance nobles patronized the arts but most of them were more interested in hunting and fighting. Very few of my classmates in Yale '28, a notably un-disadvantaged social group, spent more time than they were forced to in that institution's excellent library—a fifth would be a generous, a tenth a realistic estimate. If between 80 and 90 per cent of the population just don't care about such matters, then standards can be maintained only by thinking in terms of two cultures, a diluted, adulterated one for the majority, rich or poor, and the real thing for the minority that wants it. The middle-brow compromise that is now being evolved in the United States is just the wrong way to attack the problem.

This is an undemocratic proposition and Mr. Williams will have none of it. He thinks that to reverse the trend of mass culture requires only a little goodwill and social discipline. "The ways of controlling such activities [*i.e.*, those of the cheapjack Lords of *Kitsch*] are well known," he writes. "We lack only the will." But the question is precisely why the will *is* lacking. (It's like hysterical paralysis —the family said, "You just have to make an effort," but Freud said: "You can't make an effort. Strange. Why not?") Also, I deny that the ways of control *are* well known. Certainly his own proposals arouse little confidence. Thus, for example, he admits that in a sizable area of mass culture—radio, television, newspapers, theatre, and cinema— "simple co-operative ownership is impossible." He proposes, therefore, that "these must be owned by the community in trust for the producers, and an administration set up which is capable of maintaining this trust." But I remember that the factories of Soviet Russia are owned by the community in trust for the producers, and I am not enthralled. I don't at all like the sound of that trustworthy administration, nor am I reassured a few pages later on when it becomes "a public authority" which actors must satisfy as to their "competence" and publishers as to their "responsibility." I've been too often charged with "irresponsibility," especially when I chance to get a new idea. On the whole, I'd rather take my chances in the capitalist jungle.

A FEW words must be said, finally, about the extraordinary reception *The Long Revolution* has had from the London critics. The only downright rude review I've seen was in the *Times Literary Supplement;* the reviewer was at once majestically rebuked in the letter columns by assorted dons, who felt he was incompetent, irresponsible, and slightly frivolous; the last charge was made because he admitted he couldn't understand Part One, but since I'm in the same boat, I prefer to think it was Mr. Williams' style and not the reviewer's acumen that was defective. All the other notices were either respectful or positively admiring. Not since Colin Wilson's *The Outsider* has a big "think book" had such notices. *The Long Revolution* is of course a much better book than *The Outsider,* mainly because of the interesting cultural history in Part Two. But they do have something in common.

There is a kind of book which is almost sure to impress the critics. It must deal with some big central issue, it must take itself very seriously (humor is fatal—Mr. Williams need worry about this problem no more than Mr. Wilson had to), and it must have the air of boldly stating some positive solution. James Burnham's *The Managerial Revolution* was an early example of the species. Others have been *The Lonely Crowd* and *The Organization Man*— titles are important, like packaging. A recent American instance is Paul Goodman's *Growing Up Absurd,* which is almost as badly written as Mr. Williams' book and which, except for a perceptive review by Dan Jacobson in the *Spectator,* has been given the usual kid-glove treatment in the London press. I don't mean to imply that all these books are on the same level or even that the genre is in itself a bad one; Mr. Goodman has many wise things to say, as did Mr. Riesman and Mr. Whyte in their books. But I think the automatic friendliness of the reviewers has less to do with merit than with the fact that the reviewers want very much to believe that the books are good. We *need* this kind of book, *someone* must tackle these perplexing and distressing problems, so all credit to *X, Y,* or *Z* for a jolly good try.

This psychology emerges with embarrassing clarity in a curious review of *The Long Revolution* by Richard Crossman in the *Guardian*. "I have often pointed out that one malady from which the Labour Party has suffered since 1945 has been its booklessness," he begins. (One might think of more dangerous maladies, but let it pass.) He then goes on to praise Mr. Williams for his intentions— "the first theoretical exposition of this new socialism," that is, the new-old socialism of the L.P. left wing, which is really the primitive pre-1914 doctrine with unilateralist trimmings, as against the old-new Gaitskellian heresies of John Strachey and C. A. R. Crosland. Mr. Crossman is definitely an Old Believer. Yet he is also a shrewd man and throughout the bulk of his review the encomiums for Mr. Williams' ideas barely win out over the criticisms of the ineptness with which they are formulated: "the author whose new thoughts are struggling to emerge through old methods of expression cannot be expected to show the easy elegancies of more traditional writers." (But a sensible man doesn't put new wine in old bottles, and the real point is why Mr. Williams has been unable to make any new bottles, why his style is so bureaucratic and academic; perhaps his ideas aren't so new after all.) After two columns of such uneasy rationalizations—at one point he excuses the author's "inconsistencies and failures" on the grounds that he has "burst the thought barrier," though one might think a brain capable of such a feat could have also avoided inconsistency—Mr. Crossman concludes with a megaton effort:

If I have expressed my disappointment with some passages so frankly, it is because *The Long Revolution* is the book I have been waiting for since 1945. . . . I cannot recommend it to those who like their ideas kept on ice and served up on silver spoons. Reading *The Long Revolution* I had the feeling that I was in at the birth, anxiously watching what was once an embryo now suddenly emerging, messily but triumphantly, as a new-born babe.

Reading Mr. Crossman's review, I had the feeling that ice and silver spoons aren't such bad props for thinking clearly about these matters, and also that metaphors about birth aren't the best way to write criticism. Newborn babies are messy, but a good book is triumphant; it is precisely the author's job to clean up the mess before he publishes; and if it can't be cleaned up, then one concludes the thinking is messy and that one is in at the still-birth of just another ideological embryo.

PART IV

Betrayals

The Book-of-the-Millennium
Club

For $249.50, which is (for all practical purposes) $250, one could buy, in 1952, a hundred pounds of Great Books: four hundred and forty-three works by seventy-six authors, ranging chronologically and in other ways from Homer to Dr. Mortimer J. Adler, the whole forming a mass amounting to thirty-two thousand pages, mostly double-column, containing twenty-five million words squeezed into fifty-four volumes. The publisher of this behemoth, which cost almost two million dollars to produce, is the Encyclopædia Britannica, which is jointly owned by Senator William Benton of Connecticut and the University of Chicago. The books were selected by a board headed by Dr. Robert Hutchins, formerly chancellor of the University of Chicago and now an associate director of the Ford Foundation, and Dr. Adler, who used to teach the philosophy of law at the University of Chicago and who now runs the Institute for Philosophical Research, an enterprise largely financed by the Ford Foundation. The novelty of the set and to a large extent its *raison d'être* is the Syntopicon, a two-volume index to the Great Ideas in the Great Books. The Syntopicon ("collection of topics") was constructed by a task force commanded by Dr. Adler, who also contributes 1,150 pages of extremely dry essays on the Great Ideas, of which, according to his census, there are exactly a hundred and two. It also contains 163,000 page references to the Great Books plus an Inventory of Terms (which includes 1,690 ideas found to be respectable but not Great), plus a Bibliography of Additional Readings (2,603 books that didn't make the grade), plus an eighty-page essay by Dr. Adler on "The Principles and Methods of Syntopical Construction," and it cost the Encyclopædia just under a million dollars. If these facts and figures have an oppressive, leaden ring, so does this enterprise.

"This set of books," says Dr. Hutchins in "The Great Conversation," a sort of after-dinner speech that has somehow become Volume I of Great Books, "is the result of an attempt to reappraise and re-embody the tradition of the West for our generation." For some, this might take a bit of doing, but Dr. Hutchins makes it sound as easy as falling off a log (with Mark Hopkins on the other end): "The discussions of the Board revealed few differences of opinion about the overwhelming majority of the books in the list. The set is almost self-selected, in the sense that one book leads to another, amplifying, modifying, or contradicting it." But if the criterion of selection really was whether a book amplifies, modifies, or contradicts another book, one wonders how any books at all were eliminated. Actually, the Board seems to have shifted about between three criteria that must have conflicted as often as they coincided: which books were most influential in the past, which are now, which ought to be now. Cicero and Seneca were more important in the past than Plato and Aeschylus but are less important today; in excluding the former and including the latter, the Board honored the second criterion over the first. On the other hand, devoting two volumes apiece to Aristotle and Aquinas could be justified only by their historical, not their contemporary, interest. The third criterion was involved here, too; these philosophers are important to the Adler-Hutchins school of thought, and the Board doubtless felt that if they are not important in modern thought, they damned well should be. My objection is not to this method of selection—jockeying back and forth between conflicting criteria is the essence of the anthologist's craft—but to the bland unawareness of it shown by the impresarios, Dr. Hutchins and Dr. Adler, who write as if the Truth were an easy thing to come by. This doctrinaire smugness blinds them to the real problems of their enterprise by giving them mechanical, ready-made solutions that often don't fill the bill.

THE wisdom of the method varies with the obviousness of the choice, being greatest where there is practically no choice; that is, with the half of the authors—by no means "the overwhelming majority"—on which agreement may be presumed to be universal: Homer, the Greek dramatists, Plato, Aristotle, Thucydides, Virgil, Plutarch, Augustine, Dante, Chaucer, Machiavelli, Rabelais, Montaigne, Shakespeare, Cervantes, Bacon, Descartes, Spinoza, Milton, Pascal, Rousseau, Adam Smith, Gibbon, Hegel, Kant, Goethe, and Darwin. A large second category seems sound and fairly obvious, though offering plenty of room for discussion: Herodotus, Lucretius, Epictetus, Marcus Aurelius, Tacitus, Aquinas, Hobbes, Locke, Berkeley, Hume, Swift, Montesquieu, Boswell, Mill, Marx, Tolstoy, Dostoevsky, and Freud. The rest of the list depended entirely upon the Board, and in this case the choice seems to be mostly foolish. Only two selections are both daring and sound: *Moby Dick* and William James' *Psychology*. The former is, of course, well known but could easily have been passed over; the latter is an extraordinarily rich and imaginative work that has been overshadowed by the Freudian vogue. The Freud volume, with no less than eighteen books and papers in it, gives an excellent conspectus of Freud's work; the Marx volume, on the other hand, contains only the Communist Manifesto and Volume I of *Capital* (mislead-

ingly titled, so that it suggests it is the whole work), which
is barely the ABC of Marx's political thought. This un-
evenness of editing is prevalent. There is a provincial
overemphasis on English literature at the expense of
French; we get Boswell, *Gulliver, Tristram Shandy,* and
Tom Jones but no Molière, Corneille, or Racine, and no
Stendhal, Balzac, or Flaubert. This is what might be called
an accidental eccentricity, the kind of error any board of
fallible mortals might make. But most of the eccentricities
are systematic rather than accidental, springing from
dogma rather than oversight.

A fifth of the volumes are all but impenetrable to the
lay reader, or at least to this lay reader—the four devoted
to Aristotle and Aquinas and the six of scientific treatises,
ranging from Hippocrates to Faraday. "There is a sense
in which every great book is always over the head of the
reader," airily writes Dr. Hutchins. "He can never fully
comprehend it. That is why the books in this set are infinitely rereadable." I found these ten volumes infinitely
unreadable. There is a difference between not fully com-
prehending Homer and Shakespeare (in that one is always
discovering something new on rereading them) and not
even getting to first base with either a writer's terminology
or what he is driving at. Aristotle and Aquinas should
have been included, I would say, but four volumes is excessive. Furthermore, no expository apparatus is provided,
no introduction relating their *Weltanschauung* to our
own, no notes on their very special use of terms and their
concepts. Lacking such help, how can one be expected to
take an interest in such problems, vivid enough to
Aquinas, as "Whether an Inferior Angel Speaks to a Superior Angel?," "Whether We Should Distinguish Irascible
and Concupiscible Parts in the Superior Appetite?,"
"Whether Heavenly Bodies Can Act on Demons?," and
"Whether by Virtue of Its Subtlety a Glorified Body Will
No Longer Need to Be in a Place Equal to Itself?" In

fact, even *with* help, one's interest might remain moderate. In the case of a philosopher like Plato, essentially a literary man and so speaking a universal human language, the difficulty is far less acute, but Aquinas and Aristotle were engineers and technicians of philosophy, essentially system builders whose concepts and terminology are no longer familiar.

The difficulty is much more urgent in the six volumes of scientific work, so urgent that almost no expository apparatus would suffice. A scientific work differs from a literary, historical, or philosophical work (the three other categories into which the editors sort the Great Books) partly because it is written in a language comprehensible only to the specialist (equations, diagrams, and so on) and partly because its importance is not in itself but in its place in the development of science, since it has often been revised, edited, and even superseded by the work of later scientists. Milton, on the other hand, does not supersede Homer; Gibbon represents no advance over Thucydides. All this is pretty obvious, but in this one instance, the editors of the Great Books exhibit a remarkable capacity for overlooking the obvious. Their dogma states that all major cultural achievements are of timeless, absolute value, and that this value is accessible to the lay reader without expository aids if he will but apply himself diligently. Because science is clearly part of our culture, they have therefore included these six useless volumes without asking themselves what benefit the reader will get from a hundred and sixty double-column pages of Hippocrates ("We must avoid wetting all sorts of ulcers except with wine, unless the ulcer be situated in a joint." "In women, blood collected in the breasts indicates madness." "You should put persons on a course of hellebore who are troubled with a defluction from the head." "Acute disease come [*sic*] to a crisis in fourteen days") or how he can profit from or even understand Fourier's *Analytical*

Theory of Heat and Huygens' *Treatise on Light* without a special knowledge of earlier and later work in these fields.

Another drawback is the fetish for Great Writers and complete texts, which results in a lot of the same thing by a few hands instead of a more representative collection. Minor works by major writers are consistently preferred to major works by minor writers. Thus nearly all Shakespeare is here, including even *The Two Gentlemen of Verona,* but not Marlowe's *Dr. Faustus* or Webster's *Duchess of Malfi* or Jonson's *Volpone.* Nearly all Milton's poetry is here, but no Donne, no Herrick, no Marvell, or, for that matter, any other English poetry except Chaucer and Shakespeare. We get Gibbon in two huge volumes but no Vico, Michelet, or Burckhardt; six hundred pages of Kant but no Nietzsche or Kierkegaard; two volumes of Aquinas but no Calvin or Luther; three hundred pages of Montesquieu's *Spirit of Laws,* but no Voltaire or Diderot. Even if in every case the one right author had been elected to the Great Writers' Club, which is not the situation, this principle of selection would give a distorted view of our culture, since it omits so much of the context in which each great writer existed.

SO much for the selection, which, for all its scholastic whimsicality, is the most successful aspect of the enterprise.* Having caught your goose, you must cook it. But

---

* It is certainly much sounder than the selection offered by its long-established and still active competitor, Dr. Eliot's celebrated Five-Foot Shelf, the Harvard Classics. Half the authors on Dr. Adler's shelf (which also measures, by chance or ineluctable destiny, five feet) appear on Dr. Eliot's, but only eight are represented by the same works; the rest appear in extracts or in shorter works, for if Dr. Adler overdoes the complete text, Dr. Eliot goes to the opposite extreme. Among the Great Books authors whose work doesn't appear in the Classics at all (if one ignores a few snippets) are Aristotle, Thucydides, Aquinas, Rabelais, Spinoza, Gibbon, Hegel, Marx, Tolstoy, Dostoevsky, and Freud. On the other hand, since Dr. Eliot went in for variety above all, he did include, though often in unsatisfactory snippets, many writers omitted by Dr. Adler. No less than ten of his fifty volumes are anthologies, and while this is overdoing it, surely the Great Books would have been enriched by a few, such as one

the editors are indifferent cooks. They have failed to overcome the two greatest barriers to a modern reader's understanding and enjoyment of the Great Books—that their authors were largely foreigners in both place and time.

Only a third of them wrote in English; almost all of them were citizens of strange countries fifty to three thousand years away. Except for a few scientific works, apparently no translations were commissioned for this undertaking. The existing translations of prose writers are probably adequate, and some are classic. But just two of the verse translations seem good to me: Rogers' Aristophanes and Priest's *Faust*. (I speak of reading pleasure, not of their fidelity. But I assume, first, that a work of art is intended to give pleasure, and that if it does not, the fault lies either with the writer, a thought too unsettling to be entertained in the case of the Great Books, or with the translator; and, second, that if any writer, Great or not, wrote verse he must have had in mind the effect of verse, in which the unit of form is the rhythmical line rather than the sentence or the paragraph, and that a prose rendering which runs the lines together produces something that is to poetry as marmalade is to oranges.) Rhoades' Virgil and Cookson's Aeschylus are in verse, but they are dull and mediocre, the former smoothly so and the latter clumsily so. Charles Eliot Norton's prose Dante

---

of English poetry and one of political writing since the French Revolution. Some of Dr. Eliot's choices are as eccentric as some of Dr. Adler's (though Eliot produced nothing as fantastic as the six volumes of scientific treatises): Robert Burns gets a whole volume, Manzoni's *I Promessi Sposi* another, and Dana's *Two Years Before the Mast* a third. But in some ways the Classics are a better buy. For one thing, they cost only half as much. And for another, there is an amateurish, crotchety, comfortable atmosphere about them that is more inviting than the ponderous professionalism of the Great Books. Moreover, while Dr. Eliot is overfond of the brief sample, the chief practical use of such collections may well be as a grab bag of miscellaneous specimens, some of which may catch the reader's fancy and lead him to further explorations on his own. When I was a boy, I enjoyed browsing in the family set of the Classics, but browsing in the Great Books would be like browsing in Macy's book department.

is unbelievably graceless ("In my imagination appeared the vestige of the pitilessness of her who . . ." "While I was going on, my eyes were encountered by one, and I said straightway thus . . ."). Jebb's Sophocles and E. P. Coleridge's Euripides are in that fantastic nineteenth-century translator's prose ("Yon man . . ." "Ay me! And once again, Ay me!" "Why weepest thou?" "Thus stands the matter, be well assured." "In fear of what woe foreshown?"). Homer is in Samuel Butler's translation, the best prose version extant, except for T. E. Lawrence's *Odyssey*, and far better than the Wardour Street English of Butcher-Lang-Leaf-Myers, but it is still prose, and Homer was a poet. In prose, he reads like a long-winded novel. It is not as if there were no excellent modern verse renderings of the Greeks: Richmond Lattimore's *Iliad*, published by Dr. Hutchins' own University of Chicago, and the eleven plays by various hands in Dudley Fitts' *Greek Plays in Modern Translation*, put out by Dial in 1947. At modest expenditure, the editors could have used these translations and commissioned others that would have for the first time made all the Greeks, Virgil, and Dante readable in English. However, since to the editors the classics are not works of art but simply quarries to be worked for Ideas, they chose instead to spend a million dollars in compiling that two-volume index, or Syntopicon.

On principle, they have ignored the other barrier, time. "The Advisory Board," Hutchins writes, "recommended that no scholarly apparatus be included in the set. No 'introductions' giving the editors' views of the authors should appear. The books should speak for themselves, and the reader should decide for himself. Great books contain their own aids to reading; that is one reason why they are great. Since we hold that these works are intelligible to the ordinary man, we see no reason to interpose ourselves or anybody else between the author and the reader." (The Doctor doesn't explain why scholarly introductions represent an editorial interposition between author and reader while a two-volume Syntopicon does not.) It is true that our age tends to read about the classics instead of reading them, to give such emphasis to the historical background that the actual text is slighted, and the Adler-Hutchins school is quite right in combatting this tendency. But surely, without distracting the reader from the text, a "scholarly apparatus" could have given the essential information about the historical and cultural context in which each work appeared and have translated terms and concepts whose meaning has changed with time. For example, while some of the theories advanced in James's *Psychology* are still fruitful, others are not—a fact that the modest and admirably pragmatic James would have been the first to accept—and the general reader would profit from such an expert discussion of the point as is provided in Margaret Knight's introduction to a recent Pelican anthology of James's writings on psychology. By presenting the complete text with no comment or exposition, the Board of Editors implies it is a "classic," timeless and forever authoritative, which of course is just what they want to suggest. This is not my concept of a classic. Nor do I agree with Dr. Hutchins when he implies that indoctrination ("giving the editors' views") is the only function of an introduction. There is a difference between informing the reader and telling him what to think that seems to escape Dr. Hutchins, possibly because in his case there isn't any difference.

WE now come to the question: Why a set at all? Even if the selection and the presentation were ideal, should the publishers have spent two million dollars to bring out the Great Books, and should the consumer spend $249.50 to own them? Some of the more enthusiastic Great Book-manites seem to think The Books have been preserved for us only through the vigilance of their leaders. Clifton

Fadiman, in the expansive atmosphere of a Waldorf banquet for the founding subscribers, saluted those present as "you who are taking upon yourselves . . . the burden of preserving, as did the monks of early Christendom, through another darkening . . . age the visions, the laughter, the ideas, the deep cries of anguish, the great eurekas of revelation that make up our patent to the title of civilized man" (applause). But with or without the present enterprise, the eurekas and the deep cries of anguish would continue to resound. The publishers themselves state that all but twenty-one of the four hundred and forty-three works are "generally available in bookstores and libraries." Most of the Great Books can be had in inexpensive reprints, and almost all the rest can be bought for less than the five dollars a volume they cost in this set. This presents a dilemma: Those who are truly interested in books probably already have most of these, while those who don't may be presumed not to be ardent readers, and not in a mood to spend two hundred and fifty dollars. Even when need and desire coincide, as in the case of young bookworms (if such there still are), it is more fun—and cheaper—to buy the books separately. Not only that, but sets, especially of different authors, are monotonous and depressing; books, like people, look better out of uniform. It bothers me to see *Tristram Shandy* dressed like the *Summa Theologica*. Milton should be tall and dignified, with wide margins; Montaigne smaller, graceful, intimate; Adam Smith clear and prosaic; and so on. Mr. Rudolph Ruzicka has done his best, by varying the type faces and the title pages, to give variety and distinction to the set. In this respect, and in the binding, he has made a vast advance over the Harvard Classics (no great feat). But he has put nearly everything into double columns, which I find textbookish and uninviting. (Even the Classics are not double-column.) This was doubtless necessary for the lengthier books, but such slim volumes as Homer, Dante, Hegel,

Bacon, and Rabelais get the same treatment. Rabelais looks particularly grotesque in this textbook format. There is, however, one work in the set to which double columns are admirably suited: Dr. Adler's Syntopicon.

WITH this formidable production I shall now grapple. I have already pointed out that insofar as the set has a *raison d'être*, the Syntopicon is it. It is, however, a poor substitute for an introductory apparatus. According to Dr. Adler, "this gargantuan enterprise" represents "about 400,000 man-hours of reading . . . over seventy years of continuous reading, day and night, seven days a week, week in and week out from birth on." Since he did not start reading at birth and is not seventy, he had to call in some help; the Syntopicon is "the product of more than one hundred scholars working for seven years," which is to say that a hundred scholars worked on it at one time or another during the seven years of preparation. (The staff fluctuated between twenty and fifty people.)

The first step was to select not some Great Ideas but The Great Ideas. A list of seven hundred was whittled down to a hundred and two, extending from Angel to World and including Art, Beauty, Being, Democracy, Good and Evil, Justice, Logic, Man, Medicine, Prudence, Same and Other, Theology, and Wisdom.* These were broken down into 2,987 "topics," the top sergeants in this ideological army, the link between the company commanders (the hundred and two Great Ideas) and the privates (the 163,000 page references to the Great Books).

---

* Inevitably, the choice was more than a little arbitrary: to the naked eye, such rejected ideas as Fact, Faith, Sex, Thought, Value, and Woman seem as "great" as some of those included. However, the Doctor has appended to his Syntopicon those sixteen hundred small ideas, running from A Priori to Zoology via such way stations as Gluttony (see Sin), Elasticity, Distinctness, Circumcision (see God), and Daydreaming (see Desire). This Inventory relates each of these small ideas to the Great Ideas (or Great Idea) under which references pertinent to the small ideas can be found, and all one needs to find one's way around in the Syntopicon is some sort of idea, Great or small (plus, naturally, plenty of time and determination).

Thus the references under "Art" are arranged under twelve topics, such as "3. Art as imitation," "7a. Art as a source of pleasure or delight," "8. Art and emotion: expression, purgation, sublimation." With Dr. Adler as field marshal, coach, and supreme arbiter, the "scholars" (bright young graduate students who needed to pick up a little dough on the side and latched on to this latter-day W.P.A.) dissected the Great Ideas out of the Great Books and, like mail clerks, distributed the fragments among the topical pigeonholes, the upshot being that, in theory, every passage on "Art as a source of pleasure or delight" in the Great Books from Homer to Freud ended up in "Art 7a." Finally, Dr. Adler has prefaced the references under each Great Idea with a syntopical essay that summarizes the Great Conversation of the Great Writers about it and that reads like the Minutes of the Preceding Meeting as recorded by a remarkably matter-of-fact secretary.

The Syntopicon, writes Dr. Adler, is " a unified reference library in the realm of thought and opinion," and he compares it to a dictionary or an encyclopedia. Words and facts, however, can be so ordered because they are definite, concrete, distinguishable entities, and because each one means more or less the same thing to everyone. Looking them up in the dictionary or encyclopedia is not a major problem. But an idea is a misty, vague object that takes on protean shapes, never the same for any two people. There is a strong family resemblance between the dictionaries of Dr. Johnson, Mr. Webster, and Messrs. Funk & Wagnalls, but every man makes his own Syntopicon, God forbid, and this one is Dr. Adler's, not mine or yours. To him, of course, ideas seem to be as objective and distinct as marbles, which can be arranged in definite, logical patterns. He has the classifying mind, which is invaluable for writing a natural history or collecting stamps. Assuming that an index of ideas should be attempted at all, it should have been brief and simple, without pretensions to either completeness or logical structure—a mere convenience for the reader who wants to compare, say, Plato, Pascal, Dr. Johnson, and Freud on love. Instead, we have a fantastically elaborate index whose fatal defect is just what Dr. Adler thinks is its chief virtue: its systematic all-inclusiveness. (He apologizes because it is not inclusive *enough:* "It is certainly not claimed for the references under the 3,000 topics that they constitute a *full* collection of the relevant passages in the great books. But the effort to check errors of omission was diligent enough to permit the claim that the references under each topic constitute an adequate representation of what the great books say on that subject.") This approach is wrong theoretically because the only one of the authors who wrote with Dr. Adler's 2,987 topics in mind was Dr. Adler. And it is wrong practically because the reader's mental compartmentation doesn't correspond to Dr. Adler's, either. Furthermore, one needs the patience of Job and the leisure of Sardanapalus to plow through the plethora of references. Those under Science, which take up twelve and a half pages, begin with four lines of references to Plato, which took me an hour to look up and read. Sometimes, as when one finds sixty-two references to one author (Aquinas) under one subdivision of one topic under one idea (God), one has the feeling of being caught in a Rube Goldberg contraption. Again, under "Justice 2. The precepts of justice: doing good, harming no one, rendering to each his own, treating equals equally," one is referred to "Chaucer, 225a-232a, esp. 231b-232a," which turns out to be the entire "Reeve's Tale," a bit of low comedy that one of the mail clerks threw into this pigeonhole apparently because Chaucer stuck on a five-line moral at the end ("esp. 231b-232a"). The one method of classification that would have been useful was not employed; there is no attempt to distinguish between major and minor references. An important discussion of Justice in Plato has no more weight than an aside by Uncle Toby in "Tristram Shandy," although it is common practice to make such a distinction by using different type faces or by putting the major references first.

"What the Corpus Juris does for the legal profession," Dr. Adler has said, "the Syntopicon will do for everyone." That is, as lawyers follow a single point of law through a series of cases, the reader can follow one topic through the Great Books. The Doctor is simply carrying on his mistaken analogy with the dictionary. The structure of law, although intricate, is a rigid framework within which concepts are so classified and defined that they mean exactly the same thing to everybody. Yet Dr. Adler actually suggests that the best way for the beginning reader, wholly unfamiliar with the Great Books, to get acquainted with them is to follow chosen topics through a series of works whose context he knows nothing about.

It is natural for Dr. Adler to compare his Syntopicon with the Corpus Juris, since he has been a teacher of the philosophy of law and a writer about it, and his mind is essentially a legalistic one. He aspires to be the great codifier and systematizer of Western culture, to write its Code Napoléon. The Syntopicon is merely the first step toward this goal. At his Institute for Philosophical Research, another group of scholars is working with him, using the Syntopicon, to produce "a dialectical summation of Western thought, a synthesis for the twentieth century."* The most celebrated attempt at such a summation was, of course, the *Summa Theologica* of Thomas Aquinas, Dr.

---

* By 1955, three years after this was written, Dr. Adler's Institute had spent $640,000 of the Ford Foundation's money and had grappled with exactly one aspect of Western Thought, namely Freedom. Their musings were embodied in a two-volume work (one was a bibliography) titled *Research on Freedom: Report of Dialectical Discoveries and Constructions.* "The production," I wrote in my book on the Ford Foundation, "lives up to its title. It is a jungle of jargon, a Luna Park of 'nuclear agreements,' 'taxonomic questions,' 'explicative issues,' etc. . . . . 'Problems of style are most vexatious,' the authors confess." Verily there is no end to the foolishness of this world.

Adler's guide and inspirer. Aquinas had certain historical advantages over his disciple—leaving aside the personal ones: the culture he summarized was homogeneous, systematically articulated, and clearly outlined because of the universal acceptance of the Roman Catholic faith as expressed in the Bible and by the Church Fathers. Dr. Adler cannot bring these qualities to and make them a part of twentieth-century thought, but he proceeds as if he could, and he has run up his own homemade substitutes for the sacred writings. Thus the true reason for his set of Great Books becomes apparent. Its aim is hieratic rather than practical—not to make the books accessible to the public (which they mostly already were) but to fix the canon of the Sacred Texts by printing them in a special edition. Simply issuing a list would have been enough if practicality were the only consideration, but a list can easily be revised, and it lacks the totemistic force of a five-foot, hundred-pound array of books. The Syntopicon is partly a concordance to the Sacred Texts, partly the sort of commentary and interpretation of them the Church Fathers made for the Bible.

In its massiveness, its technological elaboration, its fetish of The Great, and its attempt to treat systematically and with scientific precision materials for which the method is inappropriate, Dr. Adler's set of books is a typical expression of the religion of culture that appeals to the American academic mentality. And the claims its creators make are a typical expression of the American advertising psyche. The way to put over a two-million-dollar cultural project is, it seems, to make it appear as pompous as possible. At the Great Bookmanite banquet at the Waldorf, Dr. Hutchins said, "This is more than a set of books. It is a liberal education. . . . The fate of our country, and hence of the world, depends on the degree to which the American people achieve liberal education. [It is] a process . . . of placing in the hands of the American people the means of continuing and revitalizing Western civilization, for the sake of the West and for the sake of all mankind." This is Madison Avenue cant—Lucky Strike Green Has Gone to War, The Great Books Have Enlisted for the Duration. It is also poppycock. The problem is not placing these already available books in people's hands (at five dollars a volume) but getting people to read them, and the hundred pounds of densely printed, poorly edited reading matter assembled by Drs. Adler and Hutchins is scarcely likely to do that.

Appendix:

THE HARD SELL

In their first year, 1952, Adler & Hutchins (and Benton, of the Encyclopaedia Britannica, which put up the original $2,000,000) sold 1,863 sets of their densely printed, poorly edited, over-priced and over-syntopiconized collection. In 1953, they made some kind of record by selling just 138, no zeros omitted, sets. (I like to think the above review was partly responsible.) Three years later, they got in a new sales manager who went to work on what might humorously be called the reading public. The results were sensational. By 1960 sales had risen to over 35,000 sets *a year* and last year 51,083 sets were sold for a gross return of $22,000,000. The Great Books of the Western World are at this writing most definitely in business.

The story is told in an article entitled "Cashing in on Culture" that appeared in *Time* of April 20th last. It runs, in part:

The turning point came in 1956 when Benton brought into Great Books the salesman—stocky, bespectacled Kenneth M. Harden, a veteran of thirty-seven years of encyclopedia selling. [The accompanying photograph shows Mr. Harden and Mr.

Adler smiling behind three stacks of Great Books; The Salesman looks about like the Savant except he is several inches
higher; stocky is as stocky does, after all.] At the time he took
over as national sales manager, recalls Harden, Great Books
executives "felt there was a 2% cream on top of our society who
were Great Books prospects—the eggheads." Countered Harden: "Let's go after the mass market—the butcher, the baker,
the candlestick maker."

Harden set about building an indefatigable door-to-door
sales force. Operating out of Los Angeles, Harden set up a
course at which new salesmen learned how to use the Syntopti-
con [*sic* throughout the *Time* report; it seems impossible to
get that word right] and to pronounce the names of the authors (reading them is not required).

In the field, Harden's salesmen offered the Great Books (sold
in sets costing from $298 to $1,175 depending on binding) for as
little as $10 down and $10 a month, and threw in a bookcase
and a Bible or dictionary to boot. In chart-studded sales broad-
sides, they talked earnestly of the importance of a liberal education for children, and displayed Great Books reading lists for
youngsters. To help spread the Great Books idea, more than
50,000 adults were signed up in Great Books discussion groups
(run by the nonprofit Great Books Foundation).

With this kind of hard sell, Harden increased Great Books
sales 400% . . . in the first three years of his regime. Today his
salesmen average an annual salary of $9,000, make as much as
$30,000, and managers take home much more. Harden insists:
"They are not just making money. They are carrying the
banner."

Some of Mr. Harden's regional sales managers make
$100,000 a year, which is a very pleasant banner to carry.
They may not "just" be making money but they are cer-
tainly doing so. And one wonders what golden effulgence
radiates from the banner Mr. Harden himself bears aloft?
Who fished the murex up? What porridge had John
Keats?

That the public bought less than 2,000 sets of the Great

Books in 1952 and 1953 while last year they bought twenty-five times as many—this shows that Culture, like any other commodity, must now be "sold" to Americans. The difference was made by Mr. Harden's high-pressure door-to-door sales campaign, which was "backstopped," as we say on Madison Avenue, by lavish magazine advertising with full-color photographs of Men of Distinction—including Mr. Adlai Stevenson, alas—who praised The Product as unrestrainedly as so many debutantes endorsing the virtues of Pond's facial cream: He's famous, he's intelligent, he uses the Syntopicon. The operation was designed to work off on the public a massive back inventory of a slow-selling item. It reminds one of those traveling book-agents of the last century who badgered and flattered hundreds of thousands of householders, as ignorant as they were innocent, into investing in the Complete Works of William Ellery Channing. Their sales pitch was the same: Respect for Culture, Keeping up with the Adler-Joneses, and, above all, the Obligation to the Children, who would be forever disadvantaged if their parents failed to Act Now on this Opportunity for a mere $10 down, $10 a month—which means over two years of paying for the set and puts the Great Books of the Western World in the same class of goods as TV sets and washing machines. "Sorry, lady," says the man from the finance agency as he and his helper stagger out to the truck with one hundred pounds of Western Culture, "we just work here." It is a false position for Drs. Adler and Hutchins to have gotten themselves into, though of course there was that $2,000,000 investment, half of it for the Syntopicon, one of the most expensive toy railroads any philosopher ever was given to play with. Still, I wonder what they really think of stocky, bespectacled Kenneth M. Harden and the effects of the hard sell as applied to Thuycidides and Rabelais? That is, Thoosiddidees and Rabbelay: "new salesmen [learn how] to pronounce the names of the authors; reading them is not required." This last is sensible, since if the salesmen did read the works some of them have been plugging for six years, things might be even more balled up than they are now. And they are all instructed in what is after all the main point, the use of that Syntopicon—"Please, gentlemen, *not* Syntopticon"—in which the Great Writers have at last achieved systematic fulfillment, from Aeschylus (Esskuluss) to Zeno (Zeenoh). I also wonder how many of the over 100,000 customers who have by now caved in under the pressure of Mr. Harden and his banner-bearing colleagues are doing much browsing in these upland pastures? Those nineteenth-century book-agents were persuasive fellows, too, but few of the deckled-edged sets they wedged into the family book case ever emerged again, and the limp-leather Emersons and Carlyles they placed on the sitting-room tables tended to remain there. I don't expect answers to these rhetorical questions from the Doctors, since they didn't reply to my 1952 critique—unless their employing Mr. Harden was a kind of answer. But I do wonder.

Updating the Bible

On SEPTEMBER 30th of 1952, two million people in over three thousand communities in the United States and Canada attended meetings celebrating the appearance of the Revised Standard Version of the Bible. Within eight weeks, over 1,600,000 copies were sold; the total a year later was 2,300,000, and it was still on the best-seller lists. The publishers, Thomas Nelson & Sons, have spent a million dollars on a promotional campaign. The Revised Standard Version is "authorized"; that is, the National Council of the Churches of Christ, which includes all the major Protestant denominations, was in charge of the committee of Biblical scholars that prepared it, and most of the denominations have authorized its use in their churches. The committee, headed by Dean Luther A. Weigle of the Yale Divinity School, spent fifteen years on the task. They encountered many and great problems of scholarship, of interpretation, of archaeology, theology, philology, and English usage, but the greatest problem was a competitor that has been in the field for over three centuries and has been fatal to the ambitions of all contenders up to now. This was, of course, the King James Version. Although Dean Weigle's committee was instructed to revise not the King James but a revision of it made in 1901, the American Standard Version, they well understood which was the champion they had to beat. For the King James Version has long occupied a unique place in both the culture and the religion of English-speaking peoples.

In January, 1604, King James I summoned the leading divines of the Church of England to a conference at Hampton Court Palace to settle matters in dispute between the High Church and the Puritan factions. The dispute was not resolved, and James's successor was to lose his head in consequence, but the conference bore rich and unexpected fruit. One of the Puritans' grievances was that the authorized English Bible was not true to the original; Dr. John Reynolds, a leading Puritan and the president of Corpus Christi College, proposed a new translation. An ardent scholar and theologian, James accepted the proposal with enthusiasm and appointed fifty-four scholars, from Oxford, Cambridge, and Westminster. The work was begun in 1607 and completed in the incredibly short space of four years. In 1611, the result, *The Holy Bible, Conteyning the Old Testament and the New: Newly translated out of the Originall tongues & with the former translations diligently compared and reuised by his Maiesties speciall Commandement. Appointed to be read in Churches,* came off the press. The King James Version is probably the greatest translation ever made. It is certainly "The Noblest Monument of English Prose," as the late John Livingston Lowes called his essay on the subject. "Its phraseology," he wrote, "has become part and parcel of our common tongue. . . . Its rhythms and cadences, its turns of speech, its familiar imagery, its very words are woven into the texture of our literature. . . . The English of the Bible . . . is characterized not merely by a homely vigor and pithiness of phrase but also a singular nobility of diction and by a rhythmic quality which is, I think, unrivalled in its beauty."

The King James Bible came at the end of the Elizabethan age, between Shakespeare and Milton, when Englishmen were using words more passionately, richly, vigorously, wittily, and sublimely than ever before or since. Although none of the divines and scholars who made it were literary men, their language was touched with genius —the genius of a period when style was the common property of educated men rather than an individual achievement. It also came at a time when Englishmen were intensely concerned with religion. "Theology rules there," Grotius wrote of England in 1613. In the King James Bible, the artistic flowering of the Renaissance and the religious fervor of the Reformation united to produce a masterpiece. Like the Gothic cathedrals, it was a collective expression of a culture and, like them, it was not built all at once but grew slowly over a considerable period of time. The speed with which it was accomplished was possible only because it was not so much a new translation as a synthesis of earlier efforts, the final form given to a continuous process of creation, the climax to the great century of English Bible translation. "Truly, good Christian reader," wrote Dr. Miles Smith in the preface, "we never thought from the beginning that we should neede to make a new Translation nor yet to make of a bad one a good one . . . but to make a good one better, or out of many good ones one principall good one. That hath bene our indeavour, that our marke. . . . So if we, building upon their foundation that went before us, and being holpen by their labours, doe endeavour to make that better which they left so good, no man, we are sure, hath cause to mislike us, and, they, we perswade our selves, if they were alive, would thanke us." No man, surely, has cause to mislike the King James translators, and many men have cause to thank them.

THE Englishing of the Bible—except for some earlier fragments—probably began with the Venerable Bede, who is thought to have completed a translation of the four Gospels just before he died, in 735. The first translation of

the whole Bible into English was done under the super-
vision of John Wycliffe, "the morning star of the Reformation," and appeared in 1382. The Lollards, or poor preachers, who walked through England teaching his doctrines,
used his Bible, in which, for the first time, the common
people could hear the complete word of God in their own
language. Bede and Wycliffe translated not from the
original Greek and Hebrew but from the Latin Vulgate.
The first translation from an original tongue was William
Tyndale's New Testament, put out in 1525. The fall of
Constantinople to the Turks in 1453 and the expulsion of
the Jews from Spain and Portugal toward the end of that
century sent many Greek and Hebrew scholars into exile
all over Europe, thus giving a tremendous impetus to the
study of their languages. This providentially coincided
with the beginning of the Reformation—providentially,
because translating the Bible into living languages was one
of the reformers' chief ways of bringing the word of God
directly to the people. Luther, whose German translation
of the Bible has a quality and importance comparable to
the King James Version, befriended Tyndale, whose New
Testament was printed in the Lutheran stronghold of
Worms. "If God spare my lyfe," Tyndale defiantly wrote
to a Catholic cleric, "ere many yeares I wyl cause a boye
that dryveth the plough shall know more of the scripture
than thou doest." His life was spared just long enough; in
1536 he was burned at the stake in Belguim for heresy, but
while he was in prison, in the last year of his life, he continued to work on his translation of the Old Testament,
and managed to complete the bulk of it. Tyndale's Bible
was the first and by all odds the greatest of a spate of translations that poured forth during the century, and it was
drawn on far more heavily by the King James translators
than any other version. The other important translations
were Miles Coverdale's (1535); the Matthews Bible (1537),
a combination of Coverdale and Tyndale done by a disciple

of Tyndale, John Rogers, who was later martyred under Bloody Mary; the Great Bible (1539), the first Authorized Version, prepared by Coverdale at the request of Henry VIII. The Genevan Bible, also known as the Breeches Bible because Adam's fig leaf was rendered "breeches," was issued in 1560 in Calvinist Geneva by a group of English Protestant refugees from Bloody Mary's persecution and went through a hundred and forty editions (being popular partly because of its literary quality and partly because of its legible Roman type and its handy quarto size, as against the cumbersome black-letter folios of previous Bibles); it was the Bible of the Pilgrims and of Cromwell's Ironsides. Finally, the Bishops' Bible (1568), an authorized revision of the Great Bible, was to the High Church party what the Genevan Bible was to the Puritans. The King James Version was officially a revision of the Bishops' Bible, but those who made the revision paid very little attention to it, relying mostly on Tyndale, Coverdale, and the Genevan Bible, in that order. Thus the Puritans, though they got no satisfaction out of the Hampton Court conference, had their way with the new Bible.

For the next two and a half centuries, the King James Version (K.J.V. for short) was *the* Bible to English-speaking people. Close to a hundred complete or partial translations were made during this time, but none was either authorized or widely used. Toward the end of the nineteenth century, however, archaeology and Biblical scholarship had made such progress that the Church of England appointed an interdenominational committee of scholars to revise K.J.V. The heaviest changes were made in the New Testament, for the K.J.V. translators had used a Greek text established by Beza, Stephanus, and Erasmus and based on late and inaccurate medieval manuscripts; much older manuscripts, some going back to the third century, were now available, and the Victorian scholars Hort and Westcott had established from them a text that differed in 5,788 instances from the Beza-Stephanus-Erasmus text. The Hebrew text of the Old Testament was essentially the tenth-century "Masoretic" text used by the K.J.V. translators, but since 1611 a number of important Greek versions, some from the fourth century, had come to light.

Thus when the nineteenth-century revisionists began their fifteen-year task, in 1870, they had an enormous advantage in scholarly knowledge over their speedier predecessors. This, it turned out, was not enough. When they brought out their New Testament, it was the publishing sensation of the century; despite an advance sale of a million, long lines formed in front of English bookstores on that day of publication; two Chicago newspapers got the full text by cable and ran it as a serial; three million copies were sold the first year. K.J.V. had won acceptance slowly, but the 1885 revision went up like a rocket—and came down like one. The men who made K.J.V. were both scholars and stylists; their Victorian successors, living in a more specialized age, were only scholars. Literal accuracy, rather than beauty or even sense, was their aim, to achieve which they adopted such absurd translating rules as always using the same English word for a given Greek or Hebrew word regardless of context, and sticking to the word order of the original. The result often read like an interlinear "trot." After the excitement had died down, the public returned to K.J.V. In 1901, the American Standard Version, an authorized adaptation of the 1885 English version, appeared. Although more successful, this also failed to replace K.J.V.

The Revised Standard Version (R.S.V.) was undertaken partly because Biblical scholarship has made enormous progress since 1900. Since then, a vast number of Greek papyri have been unearthed in Egypt. Some, among them the Chester Beatty papyri, are fragments of very early Biblical manuscripts. Most of them are business documents, private letters, wills, and other records of everyday life that, according to the R.S.V. scholars, "prove that 'Biblical Greek' was really the spoken vernacular of the first century A.D.—not the classical Greek which the King James translators assumed it to be." Even more important was the discovery of some Old Testament Hebrew and Aramaic manuscripts believed to date back to the time of Christ, or a full thousand years before the earliest hitherto known examples. A Bedouin shepherd looking for a lost goat in a cave on the shores of the Dead Sea came on some parchment scrolls that turned out to contain the complete text of Isaiah and a commentary on Habakkuk. Hundreds of other fragments of ancient scrolls were later found in the same cave. On April 1, 1953, G. Lankester Harding, Director of Antiquities for the government of Jordan, announced that Arab shepherds had made an even richer find among the caves of the Dead Sea—seventy Hebrew, Aramaic, and Greek scrolls of around the time of Christ, which contain no less than nineteen books of the Old Testament, including Genesis, Exodus, Psalms, Ecclesiastes, and Daniel. Terming this "perhaps the most sensational archaeological event of our time," Mr. Harding predicted it would keep Biblical scholars busy "for the next generation at least."

THE chief motive behind R.S.V., however, was stylistic rather than scholarly. The Revisers felt, correctly, that the 1885 English revision and the 1901 American version were "literal, word-for-word translations" that "sacrificed much of the beauty and power of the earlier version." They therefore set out to produce a version that would, on the one hand, "combine accuracy with the simplicity, directness, and spiritual power of K.J.V." and, on the other, be more readable for the American public of today. In pursuing this aim, they have made numerous departures from K.J.V. in ways that seem to me legitimate, and many,

many more in ways that do not. Let us begin with the former.

There are, first, the changes in translation. Being no specialist on the subject, I can only assume that where R.S.V. differs in meaning from K.J.V., the translation has been improved. (Considering the immense advances in archeology, philology, and other sciences since 1611, this is a reasonable assumption.) I am also willing to accept the Revisers' assurance that no changes have been made for doctrinal reasons. Two changes are of special importance. The Roman Catholic Church has long used John 10:16, as rendered in K.J.V., to support its claim to being the only true church: "Other sheep I have, which are not of this fold . . . and there shall be one fold, and one shepherd." R.S.V. alters this to "And I have other sheep, that are not of this fold. . . . So there shall be one flock, one shepherd." The K.J.V. version was influenced by the Catholic Vulgate, which translates two different Greek words as "fold." According to the R.S.V. translators, however, the true meaning is that, while there is more than one fold (or church), there is only one flock (the Christians in general). The revision that has raised the greatest doctrinal ruckus is the change in Isaiah 7:14 from "Behold, a virgin shall conceive" to "Behold, a young woman shall conceive." The verse is important as a prophecy of Christ's birth. The publishers of R.S.V. have pointed out that scholars now agree that the Hebrew word *almah*, used in Isaiah 7:14, means simply "young woman," while the Greek word *parthenos*, used in the New Testament account of Christ's birth, means "virgin," by no means a synonym.

The great majority of the translating changes, while often important, are of little or no doctrinal significance. When K.J.V. has Pilate say of Jesus, "Nothing worthy of death is done unto Him," the sense clearly demands R.S.V.'s "has been done *by* Him." The "unto" may well have been a misprint, just as the "at" in K.J.V.'s "strain at a gnat" is undoubtedly a misprint for "out." (The early editions of K.J.V. were full of printer's errors. One was known as "the Wicked Bible" because the printer dropped the "not" out of the Seventh Commandment, producing "Thou shalt commit adultery." In another, the 119th Psalm's "Princes have persecuted me without a cause" became, appositely, "Printers have, etc.") Another famous K.J.V. phrase, "Thou madst him [man] a little lower than the angels," (Hebrews 2:7) is now revised to "Thou didst make him for a little while lower than the angels." In I John 4:19, K.J.V. has "We love Him [God] because He first loved us," but the Revisers, finding no "Him" in the Greek, render it "We love, because He first loved us." Often the old meanings are painful to give up, but accuracy, of course, must come first. In "For what shall it profit a man if he shall gain the whole world and lose his own soul," the last word is now rendered as "life," while the Kingdom of God is no longer "within you" but "in the midst of you," a comedown from the mystical to the sociological. Some important words were mistranslated in K.J.V. Thus the Greek *doulos* is always given as "servant," though it actually means "slave," an error that gave the false impression that Jesus and Paul were not concerned with the greatest social evil of their day. The Hebrew *Sheol* often appears in K.J.V. as "hell," though it is really a general term for the afterlife, like Hades, and not a place of punishment. Tyndale correctly translated the Greek *agape* as "love," but K.J.V., influenced by the Vulgate, in which the word is translated by the Latin *caritas*, changed it to "charity." R.S.V. returns to Tyndale's rendering, which gives more sense to such phrases as "faith, hope, and love." It also uses "steadfast love" as an attribute of God in place of K.J.V.'s "mercy," another example of a gain in accuracy producing a literary loss, as happens in "His steadfast love endures forever." Very occasionally, when the Revisers feel that an inaccurate phrase is too hallowed to monkey with, they allow it to stand, as when they leave "the valley of the shadow of death" in the Twenty-third Psalm, though everywhere else they change "shadow of death" to the more literal "deep darkness" or "gloom."

The other kind of legitimate change in R.S.V. is made to clear up obscurities. The Revisers state that K.J.V. contains over three hundred words whose meanings have changed so much that they are now misleading. In the K.J.V., "suffer" is used for "let," "let" for "prevent," and "prevent" for "precede" ("I prevented the dawning of the morning" in the 119th Psalm means merely "I rose before dawn"). Other examples are "careless" for "in security," "cleanness of teeth" for "famine," "communicate" for "share," "leasing" for "lies," "feebleminded" for "faint-hearted," "reins" for "kidneys," and "virtue" for "power." Some words have become obsolete, among them "days-man" (umpire), "chapmen" (traders), "publicans" (tax collectors), "ouches" (jewel settings), and "neesings" (sneezings). Certain stylistic improvements, too, lead toward clarity. The startling advice, in I Corinthians 10:24, to "Let no man seek his own, but every man another's wealth" turns out to mean "Let no one seek his own good, but the good of his neighbor." In Job 40:8, R.S.V.'s "Will you even put me in the wrong?" is clearer than K.J.V.'s "Wilt thou also disannul my judgment?" And in Proverbs 28:21, R.S.V. is clearer with "To show partiality is not good" than K.J.V. with "To have respect of persons is not good." One is baffled by K.J.V.'s rendering of Genesis 29:17—"Leah was tender-eyed, but Rachel was beautiful"—but not by R.S.V.'s "Leah's eyes were weak." I had always thought Paul's "It is better to marry than burn" meant "burn in hellfire," but R.S.V. makes it "aflame with passion." In addition to such improvements in detail here and there, some parts of the New Testament are better rendered in R.S.V. than in K.J.V., notably the Acts of the Apostles and much of the Pauline epistles. This is because the Acts and the Epistles are largely narrative or argumentative prose, written in a rather flat, workmanlike Greek, and clearness is what is needed and what R.S.V. can supply.

HAD the Revisers limited themselves to these changes, surely no man would have cause to mislike them. But they have gone beyond legitimate and useful revision to produce a work whose literary texture is quite different from K.J.V., and they have mutilated or completely destroyed many of the phrases made precious by centuries of religious feeling and cultural tradition. Their intention was to revise the 1901 American Standard Version "in the direction of the . . . classic English style of the King James Version," but though they apparently think they have done so, they have actually shown little respect for K.J.V. For they also had a more important aim: to produce a Bible "written in language direct and clear and meaningful to people today," a Bible as close as possible to "the life and language of the common man in our day." In this they have succeeded all too well, but they don't seem to realize that this success conflicts with the first aim. The closer the Bible is brought to the "direct and clear and meaningful" sort of journalistic writing the American masses are now accustomed to, the farther it must depart from the language of Shakespeare and Milton. This is an age of prose, not of poetry, and R.S.V. is a prose Bible, while K.J.V. is a poetic one.

True, the morning stars still sing together, man is still born unto trouble as the sparks fly upward, the lilies of the field still eclipse Solomon in all his glory, Ecclesiastes still preaches "vanity of vanities," and David still laments over Saul and Jonathan, "How are the mighty fallen! Tell it not in Gath, publish it not in the streets of Ashkelon." So, too, our bombers tried to spare the more celebrated monuments of Europe, though "military necessity" often compelled their destruction. The Revisers' military necessity is the language of the Common Man. Reading their work is like walking through an old city that has just been given, if not a saturation bombing, a thorough going-over. One looks about anxiously. Is this gone? Does that still survive? Surely they might have spared *that!* And even though many of the big landmarks are left—their fabric weakened by the Revisers' policy of modernizing the grammatical usage —so many of the lesser structures have been razed that the whole feel of the place is different. In Cologne, in 1950, the cathedral still stood, alone and strange, in the midst of miles of rubble.

If the Revisers had changed K.J.V. only where modern scholarship found its translation defective, one would hardly notice the alterations. But what they are really translating is not the original Greek and Hebrew but the English of the King James Version, and the language they have put it into is modern expository prose, direct and clear, and also flat, insipid, and mediocre. To accomplish this alchemy in reverse, they have had to do a number of things. They have, first of all, modernized the usage. "Thou," "ye," "thy," and "thine" are replaced by "you" and "your;" the obsolete verb endings "-est" and "-eth" are dropped; inverted word order is generally avoided; "unto" becomes "to," "whither" "where," "whatsoever" "whatever," and so on. This was done not for comprehensibility, since any literate person knows what the old forms mean, but as part of the policy of making the Bible more "accessible" to the modern reader or listener. And, indeed, R.S.V. does slip more smoothly into the modern ear, but it also slides out more easily; the very strangeness and antique ceremony of the old forms make them linger in the mind. The 1901 American Standard Version kept the old usage, and I think rightly. For there are other considerations, too. One is the loss of familiarity. It is extraordinary what a difference modernization makes; even passages otherwise undisturbed have a blurred, slightly off-register effect. The Hebrew Old Testament is an archaic document, far more primitive even than Homer, and the old usage seems more appropriate. "Thus saith the Lord" is more Lordly than "Thus says the Lord," Praise ye the Lord!" is more exalted than "Praise the Lord!" The Ten Commandments lose when the awesome "Thou shalt not" is stepped down to the querulous "You shall not"; the prophet Nathan's terrible denunciation to King David, "Thou art the man!," collapses in the police-report "You are the man!," and God's solemn words to Adam, "Dust thou art, and unto dust shalt thou return," are flattened in the conversational "You are dust, and to dust you shall return." A better case can be made for modernizing the New Testament's usage, since it was written in the everyday Greek of the common people. But the Common Man of the first century A.D. was a considerably more poetic and (if he was a Christian) devout creature than his similar of the twentieth century, and the religious passion of Jesus and Paul, transcending modern experience, needs an exalted idiom to be adequately conveyed. "Verily, verily I say unto you" gets it better than "Truly, truly I say to you"; Jesus's "Suffer the little children to come unto me" (Mark 10:14) is more moving than R.S.V.'s "Let the children come to me," which sounds like a mother at a picnic.

The Revisers state that the old usage has been preserved in "language addressed to God or in exalted poetic apostrophe." The first exemption has been respected—why God's own language should not also be permitted some antique elevation I cannot see—but the second often has not. Surely the Psalms are "exalted poetic apostrophe," yet in the Nineteenth Psalm, "Day unto day uttereth speech, and night unto night showeth knowledge" is diminished to "Day to day pours forth speech, and night to night declares knowledge." Even the sacred (one would think) Twenty-third Psalm comes out a bit fuzzy: "He makes me lie down" for the rhythmic "He maketh me to lie down," and instead of the triumphant "Yea, though I walk through the valley of the shadow of death" the tamer "Even though I walk." The most damaging effect of modernizing the usage is the alteration of rhythm, which is all-important in a book so often read aloud; quite aside from literary grace, the ceremonial effect of the Bible is enhanced by the interesting, varied, and suitable rhythms of K.J.V. But to (partially) avoid inversion, the Revisers render "Male and female created He them" (Genesis 1:27) "Male and female He created them," breaking the rhythm's back simply by changing the position of two words. In the K.J.V., Ecclesiastes moves to a slow, mourning music:

What profit hath a man of all his labor which he taketh under the sun? One generation passeth and another generation cometh, but the earth abideth forever. . . . For there is no remembrance of the wise more than of the fool for ever, seeing that which now is in the days to come shall all be forgotten. And how dieth the wise man? As the fool.

This now steps along to a brisker, less complex, and also less authoritative measure:

What does a man gain by all the toil at which he toils under the sun? A generation goes and a generation comes, but the earth remains forever. . . . For of the wise man as of the fool there is no enduring remembrance, seeing that in the days to come all will have been long forgotten. How the wise man dies just like the fool!

Ruth's familiar and moving "Whither thou goest, I will go" loses its cadenced charm when it is transmuted into "Where you go, I will go." So, too, Philippians 4:8 ("Finally, brethren, whatsoever things are true, whatsoever things are honest, whatsoever things are just") is robbed of its earnest gravity when it is speeded up by replacing "whatsoever" with "whatever," just as Matthew 11:28 ("Come unto me, all ye that labor and are heavy laden") becomes inappropriately brisk when it is modernized to "Come to me, all who labor."

IN this modernization there is an understandable, if misguided, principle at work. But many changes seem to derive not from principle but merely from officiousness, from the restlessness that causes people to pluck imaginary or microscopic bits of fluff off coat lapels. Too frequently some great and familiar phrase is marred or obliterated for the sake of a trivial change in the sense, or none at all. "Den of thieves" is now "den of robbers," "let the dead bury their dead" is now "leave the dead to bury their own dead," "maid" becomes "maiden" in "the way of a man with a maid," hypocrites are "whitewashed tombs" instead of the familiar "whited sepulchres," "O death where is thy sting, O grave where is thy victory?" yields to the just-out-of-focus "O death where is thy victory, O death where is thy sting?," and Jesus' "Can the blind lead the blind? Shall they not both fall into the ditch?" is capriciously rephrased into "Can a blind man lead a blind man? Will they not both fall into a pit?"

More numerous are the changes that involve a slight change in sense. But granting that Joseph really wore not "a coat of many colors" but "a long robe with sleeves," that the Gaderene swine were really the Gerasene swine and Calvary was more properly called The Skull, that "the children of Israel" is less accurate than "the people of Israel" and that these children, or people, refrained from putting their new wine into old wineskins and not old bottles, that the Old Testament desert actually blossomed not like a rose but like a crocus, that Job really put the price of wisdom above pearls and not above rubies, that the silver cord was "snapped" rather than "loosed," that the widow gave not her "mites" but "two copper coins," that the writing on Belshazzar's wall was not "Mene mene tekel upharsin" but "Mene mene tekel and parsin," that the Psalmist saw the wicked man "towering like a cedar" instead of "spreading himself like a green bay tree," that Adam was not "of the earth, earthy" but "from the earth, a man of dust," and that "my cup overflows" and "by the mouth of babes and infants" are more up-to-date locutions than "my cup runneth over" and "out of the mouth of babes and sucklings"—granting all this, it is still doubtful that such trivial gains in accuracy are not outweighed by the loss of such long-cherished beauty of phrasing. Might not the Revisers have left well enough, and indeed a good deal better than well enough, alone?

Other doubts swarm. I can't understand why "The spirit of God moved upon the face of the waters" had to be changed to "was moving over the face of the waters" or why the Nineteenth Psalm had to be altered from "The heavens declare the glory of God" to "The heavens are telling the glory of God." I don't know why "there shall be weeping and gnashing of teeth" (Matthew 22:13) had to become "there men will weep and gnash their teeth" or why Paul's magnificent eloquence (in K.J.V., at least) has to be hamstrung by pettifogging and needless alterations. For example, in I Corinthians 13:1, "Though I speak with the tongues of men and of angels, and have not charity, I am become as sounding brass or a tinkling cymbal" is mutilated to "a noisy gong or a clanging cymbal," and in Ephesians 6:12, the familiar grandeur of "For we wrestle not against flesh and blood but against principalities, against powers, against the rulers of the darkness of this world, against spiritual wickedness in high places" is revised to "For we are not contending against flesh and blood but against the principalities, against the powers, against the world rulers of this present darkness, against the spiritual hosts of wickedness in the heavenly places." Substituting "noisy gong" for "sounding brass" and the weak, abstract "contending" for the vivid "wrestle" seems to me malicious mischief, if not assault and battery.

They have even rewritten the Lord's Prayer. "As we forgive our debtors" is changed to "as we also have forgiven our debtors," a bit of lint-picking that might have been forgone in the interest of tradition—and euphony. "For Thine is the kingdom, and the power, and the glory, forever. Amen" is omitted (though given in a footnote) because they believe it a corruption of the original text. But, after all, the fact that Bernini's colonnades were not part of the original plan of St. Peter's is hardly a reason for doing away with them. Some of the manuscripts discovered in that Dead Sea cave may turn out to differ importantly from what has been known for the last thousand years as "The Bible." Maybe the Ten Commandments are a late interpolation. But if they are, I should think that even the Revisers would hesitate to omit them.

THE *raison d'être* of R.S.V., however, is not scholarly but stylistic; to produce a more "readable" Bible. This being an age much more matter-of-fact than the seventeenth century—or the first century, for that matter—an age more used to skimming rapidly over a large quantity of journalistic prose than to dwelling intensively on a few poetic works, to make the Bible "readable" means to have it "make sense" to a reader who wants to know simply What's It All About. Poetic intensity or prophetic exhaltation interferes with this easy, rapid assimilation partly because such language is idiosyncratic and partly because it strikes down to depths of response which it takes time and effort for the reader to reach. Literature, and especially religious literature, is not primarily concerned with being clear and reasonable; it is connotative rather than direct, suggestive rather than explicit, decorative and incantatory rather than functional. To make the Bible readable in the modern sense means to flatten out, tone down, and convert into tepid expository prose what in K.J.V. is wild, full of awe, poetic, and passionate. It means stepping down the voltage of K.J.V. so it won't blow any fuses. Babes and sucklings (or infants) can play with R.S.V. without the slightest danger of electrocution.

In K.J.V., God describes the battle horse to Job: "Hast thou given the horse strength? Hast thou clothed his neck with thunder? . . . The glory of his nostrils is terrible. . . . He saith among the trumpets, Ha, Ha." R.S.V. steps it down to "Do you give the horse his might? Do you clothe his neck with strength? . . . His majestic snorting is terrible. . . . When the trumpet sounds, he says, 'Aha!' " The trick is turned by replacing the metaphorical "thunder" with the literal "strength," by converting the thrilling "glory of his nostrils" into the prosaic "majestic snorting" (a snort can be many things, but never majestic), and toning down the wild "Ha, Ha" into the conversational "Aha!" A like fate has overtaken the Sermon on the Mount. Comparing this as rendered in K.J.V and in R.S.V. is like hearing a poet read his verses while someone stands by and paraphrases. The exalted has become flat, the pungent bland, the rhythm crippled, phrases dear for centuries to English-speaking people have disappeared or are maimed. For example:

> But let your communication be "Yea, Yea," "Nay, Nay."
> Let what you say be simply, "Yes," or "No."

> Behold the fowls of the air.
> Look at the birds of the air.

> And why take ye thought for raiment? Consider the lilies of the field, how they grow; they toil not, neither do they spin; and yet I say unto you that even Solomon in all his glory was not arrayed like one of these.

> And why are you anxious about clothing? Consider the lilies of the field, how they grow; they neither toil nor spin; yet I tell you, even Solomon, etc. . . .

> Wherefore by their fruits ye shall know them.
> Thus you will know them by their fruits.

The Song of Solomon is now slightly off key. "Our vines have tender grapes" has become "Our vineyards are in blossom"—the Revisers have a weakness for Spelling It Out. Instead of "Thy navel is like a round goblet, which wanteth not liquor" we get "Your navel is a rounded bowl that never lacks mixed wine," which disturbingly suggests a cocktail party; the lyrical "How fair and how pleasant art thou, O love, for delights!" is changed into the mawkish "How fair and pleasant you are, O loved one, delectable maiden!" Repetition, another poetic (and hieratic) device, is generally avoided, perhaps because it is felt to be of no expository value. The K.J.V. Lord cries out, "I have seen, I have seen the affliction of my people" (Acts 7:34), but the R.S.V. Lord merely states, "I have surely seen the ill-treatment of my people." The ominous and brooding effect, in the description of hell in Mark 9, of repeating in verses 44, 46, and 48, the great line "Where their worm dieth not and the fire is not quenched" is escaped by omitting verses 44 and 46.

There *is* an attempt at poetry; a fancy "literary" word is often used in place of a homely one. Now, as Wordsworth observed, a simple word is always more poetic than a "poetic" one. A stylistic virtue of K.J.V. is the tact with which it uses stately, sonorous Latin-root abstract words *and* humble, concrete Anglo-Saxon words, each in its appropriate place. If the Revisers pull to earth K.J.V.'s swelling Latin passages, they also give a bogus elevation, a false refinement to its direct, homely passages; if they tone down some strings, they tone up others, adjusting them all to produce a dead monotone. Thus "dirt" becomes "mire" (Psalms 18:42), "clothes" "mantle" (Matthew 24:18), "I brake the jaws of the wicked" "I broke the fangs of the unrighteous" (Job 29:17), in each case a more archaic word being put in place of a modern (but homely) one. In K.J.V. sin "lieth" at the door, but it is "couching" in R.S.V.; the blind "see" and the hungry "are filled" in K.J.V., but in

R.S.V. they "receive their sight" and "are satisfied;" K.J.V. renders I Samuel 4:22: "The glory is departed from Israel, for the ark of God is taken," but this is too stark for R.S.V., which changes it to "the ark of God has been captured." Often the Revisers inflate the simplicity and understatement of K.J.V. into prose resembling cotton candy. The lovely phrase in Ecclesiastes 12:5, "Man goeth to his long home," with its somber, long-drawn-out "o"s, is Spelled Out into "Man goes to his eternal home," which sounds like a mortician's ad. K.J.V. often uses concrete action words to metaphorically suggest an abstract meaning, but R.S.V. prefers less vivid abstractions. In her perceptive article in the *Ladies' Home Journal* on the two versions, Dorothy Thompson gave a perfect example of this. Psalms 42:1 reads, in K.J.V., "As the hart panteth after the water brooks, so panteth my soul after Thee, O God." R.S.V. makes it "As a hart longs for flowing streams, so longs my soul for Thee, O God!" As Miss Thompson remarked, a hart pants but does not long, or if he does, he can, being inarticulate, express his emotions only in some action like panting. The passionate vigor of K.J.V. depends on the hart's being an animal, not a sentimental human being in a deerskin. If, however, there is a chance for a good, safe cliché—another method of making the Bible more "readable"—R.S.V. reverses this process; "When he thought thereon, he wept" becomes "He broke down and wept," "All things have I seen in the days of my vanity" becomes "In my vain life I have seen everything," and "They were pricked in their heart" becomes "They were cut to the heart."

R.S.V. has also departed from simplicity in certain matters of "taste," mostly involving sex. If only to avoid adolescent giggles in church, some Elizabethan terms must be avoided in this degenerate and refined age—as in I Samuel 25:22, in which the expression "any that pisseth against the wall" is discreetly omitted—but Nice Nellie is altogether too prominent. Thus "whore" is rendered "harlot," although the former term is still current while the latter is archaic (but, for that very reason, Nicer). Thus the wise and the foolish virgins have become "maidens"—which is more archaic and less sexy—costing us, incidentally, still another familiar expression. "My bowels boiled" is now, "My heart is in turmoil," "sore boils" are "loathsome sores," "dung hill" is "ash heap." The Revisers even fear "belly." "Fill his belly with the east wind" becomes "fill himself" and Psalms 22:10 is changed from "I was cast upon Thee from the womb; Thou art my God from my mother's belly" to "Upon Thee was I cast from my birth, and since my mother bore me Thou hast been my God," which is also a good example of Spelling It Out. " 'Belly,' " says H. W. Fowler in *Modern English Usage,* "is a good word now almost done to death by genteelism."

"THE King James Bible," write the Revisers, apropos the failure of the 1885 and the 1901 revisions to replace it, "has still continued to hold its place upon the lecterns of the majority of churches. . . . Congregations have gone on loving it best because it seemed to them incomparably beautiful." One wonders how they could think their version preserves this beauty. K.J.V.'s "dignity and profundity," they go on, "are the result of the utmost clarity, directness, and simplicity. These qualities have been earnestly sought in R.S.V." But K.J.V. also has very different qualities—strange, wild, romantic, complex turns of style, since Elizabethan English was as much in the rococo as in the classic mode. This is especially true of the Old Testament. Clarity, directness, and simplicity are hardly an adequate definition of the qualities of poetry. Milton's "simple, sensuous, and passionate" is more adequate; R.S.V. usually achieves the first, rarely the second (rhythm being the chief sensuous element in poetry), and almost never the third. "Poetry differs from prose in the concrete colors of its diction. It is not enough for it to furnish a meaning to philosophers. It must also appeal to emotions with the charm of direct impression, flashing through regions where the intellect can only grope. Poetry must render what is said, not what is merely meant." So writes the prince of modern translators, Ezra Pound, who might have made a much better job of the new Bible than the Dean of the Yale Divinity School and his learned but unliterate colleagues.

"Our conversation [compared to that of the Elizabethans] is direct and tense; our narrative . . . swift and unadorned," the Revisers state. "Our words are likely to be shorter and our sentences, too. . . . Therefore in this translation, it has been a constant purpose to make every word and sentence clear, to avoid involved constructions, and to make the current of the central thought flow in such a straight sure channel that the minds of the listeners will be carried forward unmistakably and not dropped into verbal whirlpools by the way. . . . The style is, as nearly as possible, such as the rank and file of Bible readers today will understand with as little difficulty as possible . . . so as to permit the attention of the hearer or reader to center on the message and not be diverted by the language." But style is not mere decoration, and it is precisely the function of language to "divert" the reader; form, in a work of art like K.J.V., cannot be separated from content, nor can the central current be separated from "verbal whirlpools." It is true that today K.J.V. is harder to read than R.S.V. This difficulty, though, is not a defect but the inevitable accompaniment of virtues that R.S.V. has had to remove in order to remove the difficulty. The difficulty in reading K.J.V. is simply that it is high art, which will always demand more from the reader, for it makes its appeal on so many planes. *Ulysses* and *The Waste Land,* while modern works, are more difficult in this sense than an eighteenth-century newspaper. It is the price of artistic quality, and the Revisers are unwilling to pay it. Probably the main obstacle in K.J.V. today is its archaic style—the obsolete grammatical usage, the inversions, and all the other devices of Elizabethan English. But our culture is lucky—or was until R.S.V. came along—in having in K.J.V. a great literary monument to which, because it also happens to have a religious function, practically everybody, no matter how unliterary or meagerly educated, was at some time exposed, in church or Sunday school or at home.

And why this itch for modernizing anyway? Why is it not a good thing to have variety in our language, to have a work whose old-fashioned phrases exist in the living language, to preserve in one area of modern life the old forms of speech, so much more imaginative and moving than our own nervous, pragmatic style? As it enriches us to leave beautiful old buildings standing when they are no longer functional or to perform Shakespeare without watering his poetry down into prose, so with the Bible. The noblest ancient fane must be trussed and propped and renovated now and then, but why do it in the slashing style of the notorious Gothic "restorations" of Viollet-le-Duc? In any event, I think the Revisers exaggerate the difficulty of K.J.V. Almost all of it is perfectly understandable to anyone who will give a little thought and effort to it, plus some of that overvalued modern commodity, time. Those who won't can hardly claim a serious interest in the Bible as either literature or religion.

Writing of the 1885 revised version, Allen Wikgren observes, in *The Interpreter's Bible*, "Purchasers found themselves in possession of a text in which the number of changes far exceed all previous estimates. Of some 180,000 words in the New Testament, alterations amounted to an estimated 30,000, or an average of 4½ per verse. . . . It was not long, however, before the number and character of the changes provoked a strong reaction. . . . Charges of unnecessary departure from the familiar phraseology, undue literalism, elaborate overcorrection, destruction of beauty and rhythm, impoverishment of the English language and the like flew thick and fast." All but the second of these charges can be sustained against R.S.V., even though it has not gone so far as such other modern versions as those of Moffatt, Rieu, and Smith-Goodspeed. Whether it will be any more successful in replacing K.J.V. than the 1885 version was remains to be seen. If it is, what is now simply a blunder—a clerical error, so to speak—will become a catastrophe. Bland, flavorless mediocrity will have replaced the pungency of genius. And if the salt have lost his savor, wherewith shall it be salted? That is to say (R.S.V.): if salt has lost its taste, how shall its saltness be restored?

Appendix:

THE CAMFORD BIBLE

AUTHOR'S NOTE: *Since the King James Version is both poetic and religious, the* Zeitgeist *is not easy with it. "The Bible comes from a pre-scientific age," an English bishop sadly observed recently. The latest in the long series of attempts since 1870 to replace K.J.V. with something more in harmony with the spirit of the times—that is something prosaic, nonreligious, and rational—was the publication in 1961 of the New Testament section of* The New English Bible. *This was published jointly by the university presses of Oxford and Cambridge— and so is sometimes called the Camford, or the Oxbridge, Bible —and was the first fruits of the labors of a scholarly committee headed by the Rev. Dr. C. H. Dodd and appointed by a joint conference of all the non-Catholic churches of the British Isles. The London* Observer *asked me to have a look at the Camford Bible, which had sold a million copies in advance. The following review is the result.*

THE miracle of the King James Version is that its range extends from the ornate to the simple, from the most grandiose Latinism to the most direct Anglo-Saxon. The

miracle in reverse that the Rev. Dr. C. H. Dodd, the fore-
man on the demolition job, and his wrecking crew have
performed is to extirpate, with unerring taste, both elevation and vigor. On the one hand, "Sufficient unto the day
is the evil thereof" is banalized into "Each day has trouble
enough of its own." On the other, "the brightness of His
Glory" is Wardourized into "the effulgence of God's splendor."

"Ideally, we aim at a 'timely' English version," Professor Dodd has stated, "avoiding equally both archaicisms
and transient modernisms." They have avoided neither.
Their "tax-gatherer" is less archaic than "publican" but
"tax-collector" is modern usage; the K.J.V. "Woe unto you"
is antiquated but so is their "Alas for you"; "anoint," "at-
tire," "burnished," and "perdition" are not current locutions; and it is a regression to replace "thief" by "bandit."
As for "transient modernisms," one hardly knows where
to begin—"came down on the rioters on the double," "out
of my depth in such discussions," "prominent citizens,"
"merchant princes," "my good man."

I expected that the Jacobean grand style would be taken
down more than a few pegs—that "hearken to my words"
would become "give me a hearing"; that Jesus would say
to the woman taken in adultery not "Go and sin no more"
but "You may go; do not sin again" (even more "timely"
would have been, "Don't let it happen again"); that the
subtle rhythm of "I cannot dig; to beg I am ashamed"
would be hamstrung into: "I am not strong enough to dig,
and too proud to beg."* I knew all the great passages
would be bulldozed flat, but still it was a shock to go from:
"When I was a child, I spake as a child, I understood as a
child, I thought as a child. But when I became a man, I

---

* This is barely grammatical. The American R.S.V. also destroys the
rhythm of Luke 16:3—"I am not strong enough to dig, and I am ashamed
to beg"—but it is slightly preferable to the Oxbridge version. I should
have thought it impossible to produce a worse version than R.S.V., but
they have done it in England.

put away childish things. For now we see through a glass darkly. . . ." to: "When I was a child, my speech, my outlook, and my thoughts were all childish. When I grew up, I had finished with childish things. Now we see only puzzling reflections in a mirror." Like finding a parking lot where a great church once stood.

But what I was not prepared for was the opposite—the inflation of simple Anglo-Saxon into academese. "In doing our work," the translators state in their preface, "we have constantly striven . . . to render the Greek into the English of the present day . . . the natural vocabulary, constructions, and rhythms of contemporary speech." On the contrary, despite a panel of literary advisers, they have taken the New Testament farther away from natural speech than it was in 1611. They are addicted to officialese: "this proposal proved acceptable," "these facts are beyond dispute." "A just man" is inflated into a "man of principle," "in all goodness and honesty" into "in full observance of religion and the highest standards of morality," "the proud" into "the arrogant of heart and mind," "blameless" into "of unimpeachable character." They write that they "have sought to avoid jargon" but I wonder whether "his heart sank" is less jargonish than K.J.V.'s "sorrowful," or "we are placing the law on a firmer footing" than "we establish the law," or "rescued me from Herod's clutches" than "delivered me out of the hand of Herod." I also wonder whether this allegedly simpler version is not actually longer than K.J.V. And where those literary advisers were when "stomach" was substituted for "belly"—nice girls have stomachs—or when Jesus' "O fools!" was stepped down into a Noel Coward line: "How dull you are [my dear Cedric]!" True, they did preserve "Jesus wept." But I'm sure there was strong support for "Jesus burst into tears."

THE Camford-style Sermon on the Mount might be pastiched, using only phrases that appear in this translation:

When he realized how things stood, Jesus held a meeting to look into the matter. It was no hole in the corner business. He went up the hill and began:

"And now, not to take up too much of your time, I crave indulgence for a brief statement of our case. How blest are those that know that they are poor. You are light for all the world. If a man wants to sue you for your shirt, let him have your coat as well. I also might make bold to say that you cannot serve God and Money. Do not feed your pearls to pigs, and be ready for action, with belts fastened and lamps alight. Thank you for giving me a hearing."

He then went to lunch with some distinguished persons.

We may expect even greater wonders when the Camford Old Testament appears. (The excuse given for modernizing the New Testament—that it was written in a colloquial Hellenistic idiom and not in the classical Greek that the K.J.V. translators assumed it was—won't serve for the Old Testament, whose Hebrew is uncompromisingly archaic and elevated.) I suggest the following for the opening verses of Genesis:

In the first place, God made the sky and the earth. The latter was empty and shapeless. It was quite dark on the ocean, where God's spirit was reconnoitering. Then God ordered some light, which he rather liked. He thought Day would be a good name for it.

To conclude on a personal note—the Oxbridge style is catching—I was told, by an official of the Cambridge University Press, that a dozen copies of my R.S.V. review were distributed among the panel of literary advisers on the present project. It's discouraging.*

---

* Stop Press, as of March 21, 1962: The A.P. reports that world sales of the New English Bible have reached four million copies since its publication a year ago, which is 750,000 more than the second-place British best-seller of the past year, *Lady Chatterley's Lover.* . . . ADD, Sept. 15, 1962: The R. S. V. Bible is still selling one million copies a year, ten years after publication. Over 16,000 churches have installed it in their pulpits. What hath God wrought!

The String Untuned

THE THIRD EDITION of Webster's New International Dictionary (Unabridged), published in 1961, tells us a good deal about the changes in our cultural climate since the second edition appeared, in 1934. The most important difference between Webster's Second (hereafter called 2) and Webster's Third (or 3) is that 3 has accepted as standard English a great many words and expressions to which 2 attached warning labels: *slang, colloquial, erroneous, incorrect, illiterate.* My impression is that most of the words so labeled in the 1934 edition are accepted in the 1961 edition as perfectly normal, honest, respectable citizens. Between these dates in this country a revolution has taken place in the study of English grammar and usage, a revolution that probably represents an advance in scientific method but that certainly has had an unfortunate effect on such nonscientific activities as the teaching of English and the making of dictionaries—at least on the making of this particular dictionary. This scientific revolution has meshed gears with a trend toward permissiveness, in the name of democracy, that is debasing our language by rendering it less precise and thus less effective as literature and less efficient as communication. It is felt that it is snobbish to insist on making discriminations—the very word has acquired a Jim Crow flavor—about usage. And it is assumed that true democracy means that the majority is right. This feeling seems to me sentimental and this assumption unfounded.

There have been other recent dictionaries calling themselves "unabridged," but they are to Webster's 3 as a welterweight is to a heavyweight. 3 is a massive folio volume that weighs thirteen and a half pounds, contains 450,000 entries—an "entry" is a word plus its definition—in 2,662 pages, cost three and a half million dollars to produce, and sells for $47.50 up, according to binding. The only English dictionary now in print that is comparable to 3 is the great Oxford English Dictionary, a unique masterpiece of historical research that is as important in the study of the language as the King James Bible has been in the use of the language. The O.E.D. is much bigger than 3, containing 16,400 pages in thirteen folio volumes. It is bigger because its purpose is historical as well as definitive; it traces the evolution of each word through the centuries, illustrating the changes in meaning with dated quotations. The latest revision of the O.E.D. appeared in 1933, a year before Webster's 2 appeared. For the language as it has developed in the last quarter of a century, there is no dictionary comparable in scope to 3.

THE editor of 2, Dr. William A. Neilson, president of Smith College, followed lexical practice that had obtained since Dr. Johnson's day and assumed there was such a thing as correct English and that it was his job to decide what it was. When he felt he had to include a substandard word because of its common use, he put it in, but with a warning label: *Slang, Dial.,* or even bluntly *Illit.* His approach was normative and his dictionary was an authority that pronounced on which words were standard English and which were not. Bets were decided by "looking it up in the dictionary." It would be hard to decide bets by appealing to 3, whose editor of fifteen years' standing, Dr. Philip Gove, while as dedicated a scholar as Dr. Neilson, has a quite different approach. A dictionary, he writes, "should have no traffic with . . . artificial notions of correctness or superiority. It must be descriptive and not prescriptive." Dr. Gove and the other makers of 3 are sympathetic to the school of language study that has become dominant since 1934. It is sometimes called Structural Linguistics and sometimes, rather magnificently, just Modern Linguistic Science.

While one must sympathize with the counterattack the Structural Linguists have led against the tryanny of the schoolmarms, who have caused unnecessary suffering to generations of schoolchildren over such matters as *shall* v. *will* and the *who-whom* syndrome— someone has observed that the chief result of the long crusade against "It's me" is that most Americans now say "Between you and I"—it is remarkable what strange effects have been produced in 3 by Dr. Gove's adherence to Structural Linguistics. Dr. Gove conceives of his dictionary as a recording instrument rather than as an authority; in fact, the whole idea of authority or correctness is repulsive to him as a lexical scientist. The question is, however, whether a purely scientific approach to dictionary-making may not result in greater evils than those it seeks to cure.

IN seeking out and including all the commonly used words, especially slang ones, the compilers of 3 have been admirably diligent. Their definitions, in the case of meanings that have arisen since 1900 or so, are usually superior (though, because of the tiny amount of a dictionary it is possible to read before vertigo sets in, all generalizations must be understood to be strictly impressionistic). They have also provided many more quotations (this is connected with the linguistic revolution), perhaps, indeed, too many more. It is quite true, as the promotional material for 3 claims, that this edition goes far beyond what is generally understood by the term "revision" and may honestly be termed a new dictionary. But I should advise the possessors of the 1934 edition to think carefully before they turn it in for the new model. Although the publishers have not yet destroyed the plates of 2, they do not plan to keep it in print, which is a pity. There are reasons, which will presently appear, that buyers should be given a choice between 2 and 3, and that, in the case of libraries and schools, 3 should be regarded as an up-to-date supplement to 2 rather than a replacement of it.

QUANTITATIVE comparison between 2 and 3 must be approached cautiously. On the surface, it is considerably in 2's favor: 3,194 pages v. 2,662. But although 2 has six hundred thousand entries to 3's four hundred and fifty thousand, its entries are shorter; and because 3's typography is more compact and its type page larger, it gets in almost as much text as 2. The actual number of entries dropped since 2 is not a hundred and fifty thousand but two hundred and fifty thousand, since a hundred thousand new ones have been added. This incredible massacre—almost half the words in the English language seem to have disappeared between 1934 and 1961—is in fact incredible. For the most part, the dropped entries fall into very special categories that have less to do with the language than with methods of lexicography. They are: variants; "nonce words," like *Shakespearolatry* ("excessive reverence or devotion to Shakespeare"), which seemed a good idea at the time, or for the nonce, but haven't caught on; a vast number of proper names, including nearly every one in both the King James and the Douay Bibles; foreign terms; and obsolete or archaic words. This last category is a large one, since 2 includes "all the literary and most of the technical and scientific words and meanings in the period of Modern English beginning with the year 1500," plus all the words in Chaucer, while 3, in line with its modernization program, has advanced the cut-off date to 1755. A great many, perhaps most, of the entries dropped from 2 were in a section of small type at the foot of each page, a sort of linguistic ghetto, in which the editors simply listed "fringe words"—the definitions being limited to a synonym or often merely a symbol—which they thought not important enough to put into the main text. 3 has either promoted them to the text or, more frequently, junked them.

THE most important new aspect of 3 is the hundred thousand illustrative quotations—known professionally as "citations" or "cites"—drawn from fourteen thousand writers and publications. (Another hundred thousand "usage examples" were made up by the compilers.) Most of the cites are from living writers or speakers, ranging from Winston Churchill, Edith Sitwell and Albert Schweitzer to Billy Rose, Ethel Merman and Ted Williams. The hundred thousand cites were chosen from a collection of over six million, of which a million and a half were already in the Merriam-Webster files; four and a half million were garnered by Dr. Gove and his staff. The O.E.D. had about the same number of cites in its files—drawn mostly from English literary classics—but used a much larger proportion of them, almost two million, which is why it is five or six times as long as 3.

The cites in 2 are almost all from standard authors. Its cite on *jocund* is from Shakespeare; 3's is from Elinor Wylie. Under *ghastly* 2 has cites from Gray (two), Milton (three), Poe, Wordsworth, Shakespeare, Shelley, Hawthorne, and—as a slight concession to modernity—Maurice Hewlett. 3 illustrates *ghastly* with cites from Louis Bromfield, Macaulay, Thackeray, Thomas Herbert, Aldous Huxley, H. J. Laski, D. B. Chidsey, and J. C. Powys. For *debonair,* 2 has Milton's "buxom, blithe and debonair," while 3 has H. M. Reynolds' "gay, brisk and debonair." One may think, as I do, that 3 has dropped far too many of the old writers, that it has overemphasized its duty of recording the current state of the language and skimped its duty of recording the past that is still alive (Mr. Reynolds would hardly have arrived at his threesome had not Mr. Milton been there before). A decent compromise would have been to include both, but the editors of 3 don't go in for compromises. They seem imperfectly aware of the fact that the past of a language is part of its present, that tradition is as much a fact as the violation of tradition.

THE editors of 3 have labored heroically on pronunciation, since one of the basic principles of the new linguistic doctrine is that Language is Speech. Too heroically, indeed. For here, as in other aspects of their labors, the editors have displayed more valor than discretion. Sometimes they appear to be lacking in common sense. The editors of 2 found it necessary to give only two pronunciations for *berserk* and two for *lingerie,* but 3 seems to give twenty-five for the first and twenty-six for the second. (This is a rough estimate; the system of notation is very complex. Dr. Gove's pronunciation editor thinks there are approximately that number but writes that he is unable to take the time to be entirely certain.) Granted that 2 may have shirked its duty, one may still find something compulsive in the amplitude with which 3 has fulfilled its obligations. Does anybody except a Structural Linguist need to know that much? And what use is such plethora to a reader who wants to know how to pronounce a word? The new list of pronunciation symbols in 3 is slightly shorter than the one in 2 but also— perhaps for that reason—harder to understand. 2 uses only those nice old familiar letters of the alphabet, with signs over them to indicate long and short and so on. (It also repeats its pronunciation guide at the foot of each page, which is handy; 3 does not, to save space and dollars.) 3 also uses the alphabet, but there is one catastrophic exception. This is an upside-down "e," known in the trade as a "schwa," which stands for a faint, indistinct sound, like the "e" in *quiet,* that is unnervingly common and that can

be either "a," "e," "i," "o," or "u," according to circumstance. Things get quite lively when you trip over a schwa.
Bird is given straight as *bûrd* in 2, but in 3 it is *bərd, bɜ̄d,*
and *bəid*. This last may be *boid,* but I'm not sure. Schwa
trouble. ("Double, double schwa and trouble."—*Shakespeare.*)

I NOTICE no important omissions in 3. *Namby-pamby*
is in. However, it was coined—to describe the eighteenth-
century Ambrose Philips' insipid verses—not "by some
satirists of his time" but by just one of them, Henry Carey,
whose celebrated parody of Philips is entitled "Namby-
Pamby." *Bromide* is in ("a conventional and commonplace
or tiresome person"), but not the fact that Gelett Burgess
invented it. Still, he gets credit for *blurb* and *goop. Abstract
expressionism* is in, but *Tachism* and *action painting* are
not. The entries on Marxist and Freudian terms are
skimpy. *Id* is in, but without citations and with too brief a
definition. *Ego* is defined more as Fichte, Kant, and Hume
used it than as Freud did. The distinction between *unconscious* and *subconscious* is muffed; the first is adequately
defined and the reader is referred to the latter; looking that
up, he finds "The mental activities just below the threshold
of consciousness; *also*: the aspect of the mind concerned
with such activities that is an entity or a part of the mental
apparatus overlapping, equivalent to, or distinct from the
unconscious." I can't grasp the nature of something that is
overlapping, equivalent to, *or* distinct from something else.
While *dialectical materialism* and *charisma* (which 2 treats
only as a theological term, although Max Weber had made
the word common sociological currency long before 1934)
are in, there is no *mass culture,* and the full entry for the
noun *masses* is "pl. of mass." There is no reference to Marx
or even to Hegel under *reify,* and under *alienation* the
closest 3 comes to this important concept of Marxist theory
is "the state of being alienated or diverted from normal

function," which is illustrated by "alienation of muscle." Marx is not mentioned in the very brief definition of *class struggle*.

THE definitions seem admirably objective. I detected only one major lapse:

> McCarthyism—a political attitude of the mid-twentieth century closely allied to know-nothingism and characterized chiefly by opposition to elements held to be subversive and by the use of tactics involving personal attacks on individuals by means of widely publicized indiscriminate allegations esp. on the basis of unsubstantiated charges.

I fancy the formulator of this permitted himself a small, dry smile as he leaned back from his typewriter before trudging on to *McClellan saddle* and *McCoy* (the real). I'm not complaining, but I can't help remembering that the eponymous hero of *McCarthyism* wrote a little book with that title in which he gave a rather different definition. The tendentious treatment of *McCarthyism* contrasts with the objectivity of the definition of *Stalinism,* which some of us consider an even more reprehensible *ism*: "The political, economic and social principles and policies associated with Stalin; *esp*: the theory and practice of communism developed by Stalin from Marxism-Leninism." The first part seems to me inadequate and the second absurd, since Stalin never had a theory in his life. The definitions of *Democratic* and *Republican* seem fair: "policies of broad social reform and internationalism in foreign affairs" v. "usu. associated with business, financial, and some agricultural interests and with favoring a restricted governmental role in social and economic life." Though I wonder what the Republican National Committee thinks.

ONE of the most painful decisions unabridgers face is what to do about those obscene words that used to be wholly confined to informal discourse but that of late, after a series of favorable court decisions, have been cropping up in respectable print. The editors of 2, being gentlemen and scholars, simply omitted them. The editors of 3, being scientists, were more conscientious. All the chief four- and five-letter words are here, with the exception of the most important one. They defend this omission not on lexical grounds but on the practical and, I think, reasonable ground that the word is so charged with horror—there is no question which one it is—that its inclusion would have stimulated denunciations and boycotts. There are, after all, almost half a million other words in their dictionary—not to mention an investment of three and a half million dollars—and they reluctantly decided not to imperil the whole enterprise by insisting on That Word.

TWO useful features of 2 were omitted from 3: the gazetteer of place names and the biographical dictionary. They were left out partly to save money—they took up 176 pages, and the biographical dictionary had to be brought up to date with each new printing—and partly because Dr. Gove and his colleagues, more severe than the easygoing editors of 2, considered such items "encyclopedic material" and so not pertinent to a dictionary. The force of this second excuse is weakened because although they did omit such encyclopedic features of 2 as the two pages on *grasses,* they put in a page-and-a-half table of currencies under *money* and three and a half pages of *dyes.* It is also worth noting that Merriam-Webster added a new item to its line in 1943—the Webster's Biographical Dictionary. While I quite understand the publishers' reluctance to give away what their customers would otherwise have to buy separately, I do think the biographical dictionary should have been included—from the consumer's point of view, at any rate.

However, the editors have sneaked in many proper names

by the back door; that is, by entering their adjectival forms. *Walpolian* means "1: of, relating to, or having the characteristics of Horace Walpole or his writings," and "2: of, relating to, or having the characteristics of Robert Walpole or his political policies," and we get the death dates of both men (but not the birth dates), plus the information that Horace was "Eng. man of letters" and Robert "Eng. statesman" (though it is not noted that Horace was Robert's son). This method of introducing proper names produces odd results. Raphael is in (*Raphaelesque, Raphaelism, Raphaelite*), as are Veronese (*Veronese green*) and Giotto and Giorgione and Michelangelo, but not Tintoretto and Piero della Francesca, because they had the wrong kind of names. Caravaggio had the right kind, but the editors missed him, though *Caravaggesque* is as frequently used in art criticism as *Giottesque*. All the great modern painters, from Cézanne on, are omitted, since none have appropriate adjectives. Yeats is in (*Yeatsian*) but not Eliot, Pound, or Frost (why not *Frosty?*). Sometimes one senses a certain desperation, as when *Smithian* is used to wedge in Adam Smith. *Menckenian* and *Menckenese* get an inch each, but there is no *Hawthornean*, no *Melvillesque*, no *Twainite*. All the twentieth-century presidents are in—Eisenhower by the skin of *Eisenhower jacket*—except Taft and Truman and Kennedy. Hoover has the most entries, all dispiriting: *Hoover apron* and *Hooverize*, because he was food administrator in the First World War; *Hooverville*, for the depression shanty towns; *Hoovercrat*, for a Southern Democrat who voted for him in 1928; and *Hooverism*.

This brings up the matter of capitalization. 2 capitalized proper names; 3 does not, with one exception. There may have been some esoteric reason of typographical consistency. Whatever their reasons, the result is that they must cumbersomely and forever add *usu. cap.* (Why *usu.* when it is *alw.?*) The exception is *God,* which even these cautious linguisticians couldn't quite bring themselves to label *usu. cap. Jesus* is out because of adjectival deficiency, except for *Jesus bug*, a splendid slang term, new to me, for the waterbug ("fr. the allusion to his walking on water," the "his" being firmly lower case). He does get in via His second name, which, luckily, has given us a rather important adjective, *usu. cap.*

AT first glance, 3's typography is cleaner and more harmonious. Dr. Gove estimates that the editors eliminated two million commas and periods (as after adj., n., and v.), or eighty pages' worth. A second glance shows a major and, from a utilitarian point of view, very nearly a fatal defect. Words that have more than one meaning—and many have dozens—are much easier to follow in 2, which gives a new paragraph to each meaning, than in 3, which runs the whole entry as one superparagraph. ("What! Will the line stretch out to the crack of doom?"—*Shakespeare*.) Thus 2 not only starts each new meaning of *cut* with a paragraph but also puts in an italicized heading: *Games & Sports, Bookbinding, Card Playing, Motion Pictures*. In 3 one has to look through a solid paragraph of nine inches, and there are no headings. The most extreme example I found was 3's entry on the transitive verb *take*, which runs on for a single paragraph two feet eight inches long, in which the twenty-one main meanings are divided only by boldfaced numerals; there follow, still in the same paragraph, four inches of the intransitive *take*, the only sign of this gear-shifting being a tiny printer's squiggle. *Take* is, admittedly, quite a verb. The Oxford English Dictionary gives sixty-three meanings in nine feet, but they are spaced out in separate paragraphs, as is the mere foot and a half that 2 devotes to *take*.

A second glance also suggests second thoughts about the richness of citations in 3. Often it seems *plethoric*, even *otiose* ("lacking use or effect"). The chief reason 3's entries on multiple-meaning words are so much longer than 2's is that it has so many more citations. The promotional material for 3 mentions the treatment of *freeze* as an improvement, but does anybody really need such illustrative richness as:

> 6a: to make (as the face) expressionless [with instructions to recognize no one; and in fact he did *freeze* his face up when an old acquaintance hailed him—Fletcher Pratt] [a look of incredulity *froze* his face . . . and his eyes went blank with surprise—Hamilton Basso] b. to preserve rigidly a particular expression on [he still sat, his face *frozen* in shame and misery —Agnes S. Turnbull]

The question is rhetorical.

ONE of the problems of an unabridger is where completeness ends and madness begins. The compilers of 2 had a weakness for such fabrications as *philomuse, philomythia* ("devotion to legends . . . sometimes, loquaciousness"), *philonoist* ("a seeker of knowledge"), *philophilosophos* ("partial to philosophers"), *philopolemic, philopornist* "a lover of harlots"), and *philosopheress* (which means not only a woman philosopher, like Hannah Arendt, but a philosopher's wife, like Xantippe). These are omitted by the compilers of 3, though they could not resist *philosophastering* ("philosophizing in a shallow or pretentious manner"). But why do we need *nooky* ("full of nooks") or *name-caller* ("one that habitually engages in name-calling") or all those "night" words, from *night clothes*—"garments worn in bed"—through *nightdress, nightgear, nightgown, nightrobe, nightshirt,* and *nightwear*? What need of *sea boat* ("a boat adapted to the open sea") or *sea captain* or *swimming pool* ("a pool suitable for swimming," lest we imagine it is a pool that swims) or *sunbath* ("exposure to sunlight"—"or to a sun lamp," they add cautiously) or *sunbather* ("one that takes sunbaths")? Why *kittenless* ("having no kitten")? Why need we be told that *white-faced* is "having the face white in whole or in part"? Or that *whitehanded* is "having white hands"? (They missed *whitelipped*.)

Then there are those terrible negative prefixes, which the unwary unabridger gets started on and slides down with sickening momentum. 3 has left out many of 2's absurdities: *nonborrower, nonnervous, non-Mohammedan, non-Welsh, non-walking*. But it adds some of its own: *nonscientist, nonphilatelic, non-inbred, nondrying* (why no *nonwetting*?), *nonbank* ("not being or done by a bank"), and many other nonuseful and nonsensical entries. It has thirty-four pages of words beginning with *un-*, and while it may seem carping to object to this abundance, since the O.E.D. has 380 such pages, I think, given the difference in purpose, that many may be challenged. A reasonably bright child of ten will not have to run to Daddy's Unabridged to find the meaning of *unreelable* ("incapable of being wound on a reel"), *unlustrous* ("lacking luster"), or *unpowdered* ("not powdered"). And if it's for unreasonably dumb children, why omit *unspinnable, unshinning,* and *unsanded?*

For a minor example of gnostomania, or scholar's knee, see the treatment of numbers. Every number from *one* to *ninety-nine* is entered and defined, also every numerical adjective. Thus when the reader hits *sixty* he goes into a skid fifteen inches long. *Sixty* ("being one more than 59 in number") is followed by the pronoun ("60 countable persons or things not specified but under consideration and being enumerated") and the noun ("six tens: twice 30: 12 fives," etc.). Then comes *sixty-eight* ("being one more than 67 in number") and *sixty-eighth* ("being number 68 in a countable series"), followed by *sixty-fifth, sixty-first,* and so on. The compilers of 2 dealt with the *sixty* problem in a mere two entries totalling an inch and a half. But the art of lexicography has mutated into a "science" since then. ("*Quotation mark* . . . sometimes used to enclose . . . words . . . in an . . . ironical . . . sense . . . or words for which a writer offers a slight apology.") In reading 3 one sometimes feels like a subscriber who gets 238 copies of the May issue because the addressing machine got stuck, and it doesn't make it any better to know that the operators jammed it on purpose.

My complaint is not that 3 is all-inclusive—that is, un-abridged—but that *pedantry* is not a synonym of *scholar-ship*. I have no objection to the inclusion of such pomposities, mostly direct translations from the Latin, as *viridity* (greenness), *presbyopic* (farsighted because of old age), *vellication* (twitching), *pudency* (modesty), and *vulnerary* (wound-healing). These are necessary if only so that one can read James Gould Cozzens' *By Love Pos-sessed*, in which they all occur, along with many siblings. And in my rambles through these 2,662 pages I have come across many a splendid word that has not enjoyed the popularity it deserves. I think my favorites are *pilpul,* from the Hebrew *to search,* which means "critical analysis and hairsplitting; casuistic argumentation"; *dysphemism,* which is the antonym of *euphemism* as, *axle grease* for *butter* or *old woman* for *wife; subfusc,* from the Latin *subfuscus,* meaning brownish, which is illustrated with a beautiful citation from Osbert Sitwell ("the moment when the word Austerity was to take to itself a new subfusc and squalid twist of meaning")—cf., the more familiar *subacid,* also well illustrated with "a little subacid kind of . . . im-patience," from Laurence Sterne; *nanism,* which is the antonym of *gigantism; mesocracy,* which is the form of government we increasingly have in this country; and *lib-lab,* which means a Liberal who sympathizes with Labor— I wish the lexicographers had not restored the hyphen I deleted when I imported it from England twenty years ago. One might say, and in fact I will say, that H. L. Mencken, whose prose was dysphemistic but never subfusc, eschewed pilpul in expressing his nanitic esteem for lib-lab mesocracy. Unfortunately, 3 omits 2's *thob* ("to think according to one's wishes"), which someone made up from *think-opinion-believe,* or else I could also have noted Mencken's distaste for thobbery.*

DR. GOVE met the problem of *ain't* head on in the best traditions of Structural Linguistics, labeling it—reluctantly, one imagines—*substandard* for *have not* and *has not,* but giving it, unlabeled, as a contraction of *am not, are not,* and *is not,* adding "though disapproved by many and more common in less educated speech, used orally in most parts of the U.S. by many cultivated speakers esp. in the phrase ain't I." Once the matter of education and culture is raised, we are right back at the nonscientific business of deciding what is correct—*standard* is the modern euphemism—and this is more a matter of a feeling for language (what the trade calls *Sprachgefühl*) than of the statistics on which Dr. Gove and his colleagues seem to have chiefly relied. For what Geiger counter will decide who is in fact educated or cultivated? And what adding machine will discriminate between *ain't* used because the speaker thinks it is standard English and *ain't* used because he wants to get a special effect? "Survival must have quality, or it ain't worth a bean," Thornton Wilder recently observed. It doesn't take much *Sprachgefühl* to recognize that Mr. Wilder is here being a mite folksy and that his effect would be lost if *ain't* were indeed "used orally in most parts of the U.S. by many cultivated speakers." Though I regret that the nineteenth-century schoolteachers without justification deprived us of *ain't* for *am not,* the deed was done, and I think the *Dial. or Illit.* with which 2 labels all uses of the word comes closer to linguistic fact today.

* "You may have imported the word *lib-lab,*" writes John K. Jessup of Wilton, Conn., "but you were anticipated in Waldo R. Browne's dictionary of labor terminology (Huebsch, 1921, p. 299). *Thob* was created by a rhetoric master at Taft School named Henshaw ("Pimp") Ward, who retired from teaching as soon as he began to get royalties from his book." Miriam Allen deFord, writing from San Francisco, gives the title of the book as *Builders of Delusion* and notes that *thobbing* occurs in Chapter XI.

The pejorative labels in 2 are forthright: *colloquial, erroneous, incorrect, illiterate.* 3 replaces these self-explanatory terms with two that are both fuzzier and more scientific-sounding: *substandard* and *nonstandard.* The first "indicates status conforming to a pattern of linguistic usage that exists throughout the American language community but differs in choice of word or form from that of the prestige group in that community," which is academese for "Not used by educated people." *Hisself* and *drownded* are labeled *substand.,* which sounds better than *erron.*—more democratic. *Nonstandard* "is used for a very small number of words that can hardly stand without some status label but are too widely current in reputable context to be labeled *substand.*" *Irregardless* is given as an example, which for me raises doubts about the compilers' notion of a reputable context. I think 2's label for the word, *erron. or humorous,* more accurate.

The argument has now shifted from whether a dictionary should be an authority as against a reporter (in Dr. Gove's terms, prescriptive v. descriptive) to the validity of the prescriptive guidance that 3 does in fact give. For Dr. Gove and his colleagues have not ventured to omit all qualitative discriminations; they have cut them down drastically from 2, but they have felt obliged to include many. Perhaps by 1988, if the Structural Linguists remain dominant, there will be a fourth edition, which will simply record, without labels or warnings, all words and non-words that are used widely in "the American language community," including such favorites of a recent President as *nucular* (warfare), *inviduous,* and *mischievious.* But it is still 1962, and 3 often does discriminate. The trouble is that its willingness to do so has been weakened by its scientific conscience, so that it palters and equivocates; this is often more misleading than would be the omission of all discriminations.

One drawback to the permissive approach of the

Structural Linguists is that it impoverishes the language by not objecting to errors if they are common enough. ("And how should I presume?"—*T. S. Eliot.*) There is a natural tendency to confuse similar-sounding words. Up to now, dictionaries have distinguished *nauseous* (causing nausea) from *nauseated* (experiencing nausea); but 3 gives as its first definition of *nauseous,* without label, "affected with or inclining to nausea." So the language is *balled up* and *nauseous* is telescoped into *nauseated* and nobody knows who means which exactly. The magisterial Fowler —magisterial, that is, until the Structural Linguists got to work—has an entry on Pairs & Snares that makes sad reading now. He calls *deprecate* and *depreciate* "one of the altogether false pairs," but 3 gives the latter as a synonym of the first. It similarly blurs the distinction between Fowler's *forcible* ("effected by force") and *forceful* ("full of force"), *unexceptional* ("constituting no exception to the general rule") and *unexceptionable* ("not open or liable to objection," which is quite a different thing). A Pair & Snare Fowler doesn't give is *disinterested* (impartial) and *uninterested* (not interested); 3 gives *disinterested* as a synonym of *uninterested.**

Each such confusion makes the language less efficient, and it is a dictionary's job to *define* words, which means, literally, to set limits to them. 3 still distinguishes *capital*

* The logical lunacy to which this nose-counting approach to usage can be carried is illustrated by a possibly apocryphal anecdote. There is an outfit in New York which uses vocabulary tests to determine aptitude. Several years ago the compilers of 3 asked them if they would mind listing the words which were most commonly confused. They did so, with some trouble, and sent the results to Springfield, Massachusetts, the home of 3. They then discovered that Dr. Gove and his colleagues had wanted the list not in order to warn readers against these confusions but so they could enter the words as synonyms. When they protested, they were told that when an error is common enough, it is no longer an error. The language has changed. It is curious, by the way, that it doesn't seem to have occurred to the not very perspicacious Goveites that to decide that an error has become so firmly entrenched as to be standard is just as much an exercise of authority, or at least of discrimination, as to decide the other way.

from *capitol* and *principle* from *principal,* but how many more language-community members must join the present sizable band that habitually confuses these words before they go down the drain with the others? Perhaps nothing much is lost if almost everybody calls Frankenstein the monster rather than the man who made the monster, even though Mrs. Shelley wrote it the other way, but how is one to deal with the *bimonthly* problem? 2 defines it as "once in two months," which is correct. 3 gives this as the first meaning and then adds, gritting its teeth, *"sometimes:* twice a month." (It defines *biweekly* as "every two weeks" and adds "2: twice a week.") It does seem a little awkward to have a word that can mean every two weeks *or* every eight weeks, and it would have been convenient if 3 had compromised with scientific integrity enough to replace its perfectly accurate *sometimes* with a firm *erroneous.* But this would have implied authority, and authority is the last thing 3's modest recorders want. ("Let this cup pass from me."—*New Testament.*)

The objection is not to recording the facts of actual usage. It is to failing to give the information that would enable the reader to decide which usage he wants to adopt. If he prefers to use *deprecate* and *depreciate* interchangeably, no dictionary can prevent him, but at least he should be warned. Thus 3 has under *transpire*—"4: to come to pass; happen, occur." 2 has the same entry, but it is followed by a monitory pointing hand: *"transpire* in this sense has been disapproved by most authorities on usage, although the meaning occurs in the writings of many authors of good standing." Fair enough.* I also prefer 2's handling of the

---

* I am indebted to Ralph T. Catterall, of the Virginia State Corporation Commission, for the following quotation from J. S. Mill's *Logic* (Book IV, Chapter 5):

> So many persons without anything deserving the name of education have become writers by profession, that written language may almost be said to be wielded by persons ignorant of the proper use of the instrument, and who are spoiling it more and more for those who understand it. Vulgarisms, which creep in nobody knows how, are

common misuse of *infer* to mean *imply*—"5: loosely and erroneously, to imply." 3 sounds no warning, and twice under *infer* it advises "compare imply." Similarly, 2 labels the conjunctive *like* "illiterate" and "incorrect," which it is, adding that "in the works of careful writers [it] is replaced by *as*." 3 accepts it as standard, giving such unprepossessing citations as "impromptu programs where they ask questions much like I do on the air—Art Linkletter" and "wore his clothes like he was . . . afraid of getting dirt on them—*St. Petersburg (Fla.) Independent.*" *Enthuse* is labeled *colloq.* in 2 but not in 3. It still sounds *colloq.* if not *godawf.* to me, nor am I impressed by 3's citations, from writers named L. G. Pine and Lawrence Constable and from a trade paper called *Fashion Accessories.* Or consider the common misuse of *too* when *very* is meant, as "I was not too interested in the lecture." 2 gives this use but labels it *colloq.* 3 gives it straight and cites Irving Kolodin: "an episodic work without too consistent a texture;" Mr. Kolodin probably means "without a very consistent texture," but how does one know he doesn't mean "without an excessively consistent [or monotonous] texture"? In music criticism such ambiguities are not too helpful.

IN dealing with words that might be considered slang, 2 uses the label wherever there is doubt, while 3 leans the other way. The first procedure seems to me more sensible, since no great harm is done if a word is labeled slang until its pretensions to being standard have been thoroughly tested (as long as it is admitted into the dictionary), while damage may be done if it is prematurely accepted as

---

daily depriving the English language of valuable modes of expressing thought. To take a present instance: the verb *transpire* . . . But of late a practice has commenced of employing this word, for the sake of finery, as a mere synonym of *to happen* . . . This vile specimen of bad English is already seen in the despatches of noblemen and viceroys: and the time is apparently not far distant when nobody will understand the word if used in its proper sense.

standard. Thus both 2 and 3 list such women's-magazine locutions as *galore, scads, scrumptious,* and *too-too,* but only 2 labels them slang. (Fowler's note on *galore* applies to them all: "Chiefly resorted to by those who are reduced to relieving the dullness of matter by oddity of expression.") Thus *rummy, spang* (in the middle of), and *nobby* are in both, but only 2 calls them slang.

Admittedly, the question is most difficult. Many words begin as slang and then rise in the world. Some slang words have survived for centuries without bettering themselves, like the Jukes and the Kallikaks. *Dukes* (fists) and *duds* (clothes) are still slang, although they go back to the eighteenth and the sixteenth century, respectively.

The definition of *slang* in 3 is "characterized primarily by connotations of extreme informality . . . coinages or arbitrarily changed words, clipped or shortened forms, extravagant, forced, or facetious figures of speech or verbal novelties *usu.* experiencing quick popularity and relatively rapid decline into disuse." A good definition (Dr. Gove has added that slang is "linguistically self-conscious"), but it seems to have been forgotten in making up 3, most of whose discriminations about slang strike me as arbitrary. According to 3, *scram* is not slang, but *vamoose* is. *"Goof* 1" ("to make a mistake or blunder") is not slang, but *"goof* 2" ("to spend time idly or foolishly") is. *"Floozy* 1" ("an attractive young woman of loose morals") is standard, but *"floozy* 2" ("a dissolute and sometimes slovenly woman") is slang. Can even a Structural Linguist make such fine distinctions about such a word? The many synonyms for *drunk* raise the same question Why are *oiled, pickled,* and *boiled* labelled slang if *soused* and *spiflicated* are not? Perhaps cooking terms for *drunk* are automatically slang, but why?

I don't mean to *imply* (see *infer*) that the compilers of 3 didn't give much thought to the problem. When they came to a doubtful word, they took a staff poll, asking everybody to check it, after reviewing the accumulated cites, as either slang or standard. This resulted in *cornball*'s being entered as slang and *corny*'s being entered as standard. Such scientific, or quantitative, efforts to separate the goats from the sheep produced the absurdities noted above. Professor Austin C. Dobbins raised this point in *College English* for October, 1956:

> But what of such words as *boondoggle, corny, frisk, liquidate, pinched, bonehead, carpetbagger, pleb, slush fund,* and *snide?* Which of these words ordinarily would be considered appropriate in themes written by cultivated people? According to the editors of the ACD [the American College Dictionary, the 1953 edition, published by Random House] the first five of these words are slang; the second five are established usage. To the editors of WNCD [Webster's New Collegiate Dictionary, published by Merriam-Webster in the same year] the first five of these words represent established usage; the second five are slang. Which authority is the student to follow?

Mr. Dobbins is by no means hostile to Structural Linguistics, and his essay appears in a recent anthology edited by Dr. Harold B. Allen, of the University of Minnesota, an energetic proponent of the new school. "Perhaps the answer," Mr. Dobbins concludes, "is to advise students to study only one handbook, consult one dictionary, listen to one instructor. An alternate suggestion, of course, is for our textbooks more accurately to base their labels upon studies of usage." Assuming the first alternative is ironical, I would say the second is impractical unless the resources of a dozen Ford Foundations are devoted to trying to decide the matter scientifically—that is, statistically.

Short of this Land of Cockaigne, where partridges appear in the fields ready-roasted, I see only two logical alternatives: to label all doubtful words slang, as 2 does, or to drop the label entirely, as I suspect Dr. Gove would have liked to do. Using the label sparingly, if it is not to produce bizarre effects, takes a lot more *Sprachgefühl* than the editors of 3 seem to have possessed. Thus *horse* as a verb ("to engage in horseplay") they accept as standard. The citations are from Norman Mailer ("I never horse around much with the women") and J. D. Salinger ("I horse around quite a lot, just to keep from getting bored"). I doubt whether either Mr. Mailer or Mr. Salinger would use *horse* straight; in these cites, I venture, it is either put in the mouth of a first-person narrator or used deliberately to get a colloquial effect. Slang is concise and vivid—*jalopy* has advantages over *dilapidated automobile*— and a few slang terms salted in a formal paragraph bring out the flavor. But the user must know he *is* using slang, he must be aware of having introduced a slight discord into his harmonics, or else he coarsens and blurs his expression. This information he will not, for the most part, get from 3. I hate to think what monstrosites of prose foreigners and high-school students will produce if they take 3 seriously as a guide to what is and what is not standard English.

Whenever the compilers of 3 come up against a locution that some (me, or I) might consider simply wrong, they do their best, as Modern Linguists and democrats, to be good fellows. The softening-up process begins with substituting the euphemistic *substandard* for 2's blunt *erroneous* and *illiterate*. From there it expands into several forms. *Complected* (for *complexioned*) is *dialect* in 2, *not often in formal use* in 3. *Learn* (for teach) is *now a vulgarism* in 2, *now chiefly substand.* in 3. (*Chiefly* is the thin end of the wedge, implying that users of standard English on occasion exclaim, "I'll learn you to use bad English!") *Knowed* is listed as the past of *know,* though *broke* is labeled substandard for *broken*—another of those odd discriminations. Doubtless they counted noses, or citation slips, and concluded that "Had I but knowed!" is standard while "My heart is broke" is substandard.

(To be entirely fair, perhaps compulsively so: If one reads carefully the five closely printed pages of Explanatory Notes and especially paragraphs 16.0 through 16.6 (twelve inches of impenetrable lexical jargon), one finds that light-face small capitals mean a cross-reference, and if one looks up KNOW—which is given after *knowed* in light-face small capitals—one does find that *knowed* is dialect. This is not a very practical or sensible dictionary, one concludes after such scholarly labors, and one wonders why Dr. Gove and his editors did not think of labeling *knowed* as substandard right where it occurs, and one suspects that they wanted to slightly conceal the fact or at any rate to put off its exposure as long as decently possible.)

The systematic softening or omitting of pejorative labels in 3 could mean: (1) we have come to use English more loosely, to say the least, than we did in 1934; or (2) usage hasn't changed, but 3 has simply recorded The Facts more accurately; or (3) the notion of what is a relevant Fact has changed between 2 and 3. I suspect it is mostly (3), but in any case I cannot see *complected* as anything but *dialected*.

IN 1947 the G. & C. Merriam Co. published a little book entitled *Noah's Ark*—in reference to Noah Webster, who began it all—celebrating its first hundred years as the publisher of Webster dictionaries. Toward the end, the author, Robert Keith Leavitt, rises to heights of eloquence which have a tinny sound now that "Webster" means not 2 but 3. In one paragraph, which the G. & C. Merriam Co., for some peculiar reason, has refused to let me quote, Mr. Leavitt paints a glowing picture of Webster's Unabridged as the arbiter of bets, the authority on which courts and legislatures rely, the last resource of businessmen when contracts need defining, and the great wellspring of accurate knowledge for thousands on thousands of "young-sters lying sprawled under the table" happily absorbing information that teachers had vainly tried to impart.

While this picture is a bit idyllic—Clarence Barnhart's American College Dictionary, put out by Random House, is considered by many to be at least as good as the Webster Collegiate—it had some reality up to 1961. But as of today, courts that Look It Up In Webster will often find themselves little the wiser, since 3 claims no authority and merely records, mostly deadpan, what in fact every Tom, Dick, and Harry is now doing—in all innocence—to the language. That freedom or imprisonment should depend on 3 is an alarming idea. The secretary correcting her boss, if he is a magazine publisher, will collide with the unresolved *bimonthly* and *biweekly* problem, and the youngsters sprawled under the table will happily absorb from 3 the information that *jerk* is standard for "a stupid, foolish, naïve, or unconventional person." One imagines the themes: "Dr. Johnson admired Goldsmith's literary talent although he considered him a jerk." The editors of the New Webster's Vest Pocket Dictionary, thirty-nine cents at any cigar store, label *jerk* as *coll.* But then they aren't Structural Linguists.

THE reviews of 3 in the lay press have not been enthusiastic. *Life* and the *Times* have both attacked it editorially as a "say-as-you-go" dictionary that reflects "the permissive school" in language study. The usually solemn editorialists of the *Times* were goaded to unprecedented wit:

A passel of double-domes at the G. & C. Merriam Company joint in Springfield, Mass. [the editorial began], have been confabbing and yakking for twenty-seven years—which is not intended to infer that they have not been doing plenty work—and now they have finalized Webster's Third New International Dictionary, Unabridged, a new edition of that swell and esteemed word book.

Those who regard the foregoing paragraph as acceptable English prose will find that the new Webster's is just the dictionary for them.

But the lay press doesn't always prevail. The irreverent may call 3 "Gove's Goof," but Dr. Gove and his editors are part of the dominant movement in the professional study of language—one that has in the last few years established strong beachheads in the National Council of Teachers of English and the College English Association. One may grant that for the scientific study of language the Structural Linguistic approach is superior to that of the old grammarians, who overestimated the importance of logic and Latin, but one may still object to its transfer directly to the teaching of English and the making of dictionaries. As a scientific discipline, Structural Linguistics can have no truck with values or standards. Its job is to deal only with The Facts. But in matters of usage, the evaluation of The Facts is important, too, and this requires a certain amount of general culture, not to mention common sense—commodities that many scientists have done brilliantly without but that teachers and lexicographers need in their work.

The kind of thinking responsible for 3 is illustrated by Dr. Gove's riposte to the many unfavorable reviews of his dictionary: "The criticisms involve less than one per cent of the words in the dictionary." This quantitative approach might be useful to novelists who get bad reviews. It is foolproof here; a reviewer who tried to meet Dr. Gove's criterion and deal with a sizable proportion of 3's words— say, ten per cent—would need 45,000 words just to list them, and if his own comments averaged ten words apiece he would have to publish his five-hundred-thousand-word review in two large volumes. Some odd thinking gets done up at the old Merriam-Webster place in Springfield.

Dr. Gove's letter to the *Times* objecting to its editorial was also interesting. "The editors of *Webster's Third New International Dictionary* are not amused by the ingenuity of the first paragraph of your editorial," it began loftily, and continued, "Your paragraph obscures, or attempts to obscure, the fact that there are so many different degrees of standard usage that dictionary definitions cannot hope to distinguish one from another by status labeling." (But the

Times' point was precisely that the editors did make such distinctions by status labeling, only they were the wrong distinctions; i.e., by omitting pejorative labels they accepted as standard words that, in the opinion of the *Times,* are not standard.) There followed several pages of citations in which Dr. Gove showed that the *Times* itself had often used the very words it objected to 3's including as standard language. "If we are ever inclined to the linguistic pedantry that easily fails to distinguish moribund traditions from genuine living usage [the adjectives here are perhaps more revealing than Dr. Gove intended] we have only to turn to the columns of the *Times,*" Dr. Gove concluded. The *Times* is the best newspaper in the world in the gathering and printing of news, but it has never been noted for stylistic distinction. And even if it were, the exigencies of printing a small book every day might be expected to drive the writers and editors of a newspaper into usages as convenient as they are sloppy—usages that people with more time on their hands, such as the editors of an unabridged dictionary, might distinguish from standard English.

THERE are several reasons that it is important to maintain standards in the use of a language. English, like other languages, is beautiful when properly used, and beauty can be achieved only by attention to form, which means setting limits, or de-fining, or dis-criminating. Language expresses the special, dis-tinctive* quality of a people, and a people, like an individual, is to a large extent defined by its past— its traditions—whether it is conscious of this or not. If the

---

* Meyer Schapiro, of Columbia University, has pointed out to me that the division of this word, etymologically, should be "di-stinctive" since it comes from the Latin verb *stinguere* (to prick) plus the prefix *dis* (apart). It should logically be spelled "disstinctive"—in which case it could be divided to make the sense I'm after here—but language, as we know, is not logical. He also suggests that consulting a dictionary is like consulting a doctor in that what one wants to know is what is wrong (or right) and that it is the function of a dictionary, as of a doctor, to decide this for the patient-consulter.

language is allowed to shift too rapidly, without challenge from teachers and lexicographers, then the special character of the American people is blurred, since it tends to lose its past. In the same way a city loses its character if too much of it is torn down and rebuilt too quickly. "Languages are the pedigrees of nations," said Dr. Johnson.

The effect on the individual is also unfortunate. The kind of permissiveness that permeates 3 (the kind that a decade or two ago was more common in progressive schools than it is now) results, oddly, in less rather than more individuality, since the only way an individual can "express himself" is in relation to a social norm—in the case of language, to standard usage. James Joyce's creative distortions of words were possible only because he had a perfect ear for orthodox English. But if the very idea of form, or standards, is lacking, then how can one violate it? It's no fun to use *knowed* for *known* if everybody thinks you're just trying to be standard.

Counting cite slips is simply not the way to go about the delicate business of deciding these matters. If nine-tenths of the citizens of the United States were to use *inviduous*, the one-tenth who clung to *invidious* would still be right, and they would be doing a favor to the majority if they continued to maintain the point. It is perhaps not democratic, according to some recent users, or abusers, of the word, to insist on this, and the question comes up of who is to decide at what point change—for language does indeed change, as the Structural Linguists insist—has evolved from *slang, dial., erron.,* or *substand.* to *standard.* The decision, I think, must be left to the teachers, the professional writers, and the lexicographers, and they might look up Ulysses' famous defense of conservatism in Shakespeare's *Troilus and Cressida:*

> *The heavens themselves, the planets and this centre*
> *Observe degree, priority and place,*
> *Insisture, course, proportion, season, form,*

Office and custom in all line of order. . . .
Take but degree away, untune that string,
And, hark, what discord follows! Each thing meets
In mere oppugnancy. The bounded waters
Should lift their bosoms higher than the shores
And make a sop of all this solid globe.
Strength should be lord of imbecility
And the rude son should strike his father dead.
Force should be right, or rather right and wrong
(Between whose endless jar justice resides)
Should lose their names, and so should justice too.
Then every thing includes itself in power,
Power into will, will into appetite
And appetite, a universal wolf,
So doubly seconded with will and power,
Must make perforce a universal prey
And, last, eat up himself. . . .

Dr. Johnson, a dictionary-maker of the old school, defined *lexicographer* as "a harmless drudge." Things have changed. Lexicographers may still be drudges, but they are certainly not harmless. They have untuned the string, made a sop of the solid structure of English, and encouraged the language to eat up himself.

The Decline and Fall of
English

Now that english has become the most widely used common language in the world, the great lingua franca of our time, it is ironical that signs of disintegration are appearing in its chief home, the U.S.A. It is as though Alexander the Great, encamped on the Indus, had received news of an insurrection back in Macedon.

In *Words and Idioms* (1925) the late Logan Pearsall Smith wrote:

> More and more, too, this standard speech, and the respect for its usages, is being extended, and there is not the slightest danger at the present day that its authority or dominance will be questioned or disregarded. The danger lies rather in the other direction—that in our scrupulous and almost superstitious respect for correct English we may forget that other and freer forms of spoken English have also their value. . . . The duty of [the educated classes] is, under normal conditions, one of conservatism, of opposition to the popular tendencies. But when the forces of conservatism become too strong, they may do well to relax their rigour and lean more to the democratic side.

Mr. Smith, an American living in England, was a connoisseur of English whose *Trivia* is still readable because of its style. But he was a bad prophet. In 1957 another authority, Sir Ernest Gowers, addressing the English Association in London, felt obliged to strike rather a different note:

Strange things are happening in the English language. The revolt against the old grammarians seems to be producing a school of thought who hold that grammar is obsolete and it does not matter how we write so long as we can make ourselves understood. It cannot be denied that if we had to choose between the two, it would be better to be ungrammatical than unintelligible. But we do not have to choose between the two. We can rid ourselves of those grammarians' fetishes which make it more difficult to be intelligible without throwing the baby away with the bath water.

The democratic ignoramus (who may have a Ph.D.) is now to be feared more than the authoritarian pedant. For the forces of tradition and conservation in the use of English have been weakened, and the forces of disintegration strengthened, to a degree which Logan Pearsall Smith could not have anticipated a mere thirty-five years ago.

It is not a question of the language changing. All languages change and often for the better—as the de-sexualization of English nouns and the de-inflection of English verbs and adjectives. I don't know which "grammarians' fetishes" Sir Ernest had in mind, but my own list would include: "It's me" (the man who says "It's I" is a prig); the split infinitive (often much neater, as "to thoroughly examine"); prepositions at the end of sentences (which H. W. Fowler in *Modern English Usage* sees as "an important element in the flexibility of the language"); the who-whom bother (I have my own opinion of the receptionist who says "Whom do you wish to see?"); and all the nonsense about "shall" v. "will" and "can" v. "may."

Such finicky "refinements," analogous to the extended little finger in drinking tea, have nothing to do with the problem of good English. What is to the point is that the language is being massacred, particularly by us Americans. When the comedian Phil Silvers says "I feel nauseous" when he means "nauseated," or the television commentator David Susskind speaks of "a peripatetic rush" when he means "precipitate," or the Consumers Commercial Corporation begins a sales letter: "As a good customer of ours, we want to be sure you know that . . .", or models in ads request each other to "Scotch me lightly" or to "cigarette me" (not to mention "to host" and "to gift")— when these little contretemps occur, one shrugs and lights a Winston, which tastes good like a cigarette should. But then one reads the opening of a feature article in the respected New York *Herald Tribune:* "Bernard Goldfine's troubles keep multiplying. Aside from the prospect of spending more time in prison, his family already is fighting . . . over the estate." Or, in a recent issue of *Dissent,* a highbrow quarterly, such locutions as "Mr. Jadhav's angry retort to my remarks about Rommanohar Lohia and his Socialist party are regrettable . . ." Or, in a *New York Times* review: "Oddly enough, of all the great plays that the great Eugene O'Neill wrote, only nine talking films (according to our reckoning) have been made of them."

The *Times* is especially disturbing because of its justified prestige as a newspaper. Its critical departments tirelessly chip away at the structure of English prose. The *Times Book Review,* the most influential critical organ in America as far as sales go, is a veritable lead mine of bad English. As, recently:

> Though random samplings disclose the daily Buchwald column to be considerably less of a gastronomic delight than his year-end ragouts, still . . . the pay-dirt to raw-ore ratio runs high, and his humor remains a green isle in the rising tide of dullness.

AND the rot extends much higher than journalism. Those who should be the guardians of the language, namely the members of our learned professions, have developed a new vocabulary which is as barbarously specialized as the beatniks' lingo and which has had as disastrous an effect on English. "The concept of sociocultural levels is a heuristic means of analyzing developmental sequences and internal structures. The approach seeks hierarchies both of organization and of sequence—the autonomous nuclear family, extended families of various types superimposed upon the nuclear family, or a multicommunity state unifying hitherto independent settlements." So a recent article in *Daedalus,* the official organ of the American Academy of Arts and Sciences, a prestigious review which any aspiring academic would be proud to be printed in. American universities are factories of bad prose. On a single page of the February 4, 1962, *New York Times Book Review* two college presidents masquerading as critics commit grammatical howlers that should not be forgiven a fifth-grader. "The worst effect of this composite approach," writes Dr. Edward D. Eddy Jr., president of Chatham College, "is to instill in the college graduate the notion that somehow he or she must be different than others because a degree was granted." Dr. Eddy's degree hasn't made him different "than" others. Dr. Francis H. Horn, president of the University of Rhode Island, swings into action lower down the same page: "An eminent mathematician with more than thirty years experience as teacher and administrator, his voice must be heard and his observations receive serious consideration. . . ." Now, class . . .

Even when the writer is professionally engaged in the study of English, the result, while grammatical, is often deplorable. Thus Professor Albert H. Marckwardt, a scholar of repute, can find no better words to end his recent work on *American English* than:

It is our responsibility to realize whither the language is tending, and the duty of our schools and teachers to promulgate healthy linguistic attitudes. If this is done, we may be certain that some individuals can and will attain greatness in the use of the language, which in turn will make of it a more flexible and sensitive medium for the rest of us. In this sense, a new era lies before all the English-speaking people.

Physician, heal thyself.

As for Dr. Marckwardt's coming "new era" to be promoted by "healthy linguistic attitudes," these concepts strike a chill into anyone who has been following what some of our learned men have been doing to English of late. The revisions of the King James Bible are a case in point, as is the third edition of the unabridged Merriam-Webster dictionary. This last, as I have noted earlier, is one of the many unfortunate effects of that new method of language study called Structural Linguistics.*

THE origins of Structural Linguistics go back to the end of the last century when the Danish scholar Otto Jespersen put forward a theory that change in language is not only natural but good, and when the Oxford English Dictionary began publishing its thirteen volumes. Up to then the prevailing view of English was that it was a logical structure based on Latin and that any departure from the rules deduced from this assumption meant deterioration and vulgarization. The difficulty was that English, like all living languages, was in fact in a constant state of change, and that the changes were usually away from the grammarians' and purists' notions of what English really *was*. By the end of the nineteenth century, there seemed to be two languages: English as she was spoke and English as the grammarians insisted she should be spoke (and wrote) —a real language versus a Platonic archetype that was as mystical and hard to grasp as the Holy Ghost. The im-

---

* A distinction is sometimes made between Structural Linguistics and Descriptive Linguistics, the former term being used for the purely scientific methods developed by such scholars as Chomsky, Lees, and Harris, and the latter for the application of these methods to teaching and lexicography. It is useful (and fair) to distinguish the scholars from the vulgarizers, but this terminology is not common, so I have followed the usual practice and used Structural Linguistics to cover both the doctrine and its practical application.

portance of the Oxford English Dictionary, which began to appear in 1884 and published its last volume in 1928, was that it followed the changes in the meaning of each word by giving examples of usage from the Anglo-Saxon period on. There was no doubt about it, the language had constantly changed.

Structural Linguistics is an American invention and its impact has been felt mostly in America. I am incompetent to judge its technical claims but my impression is that it is—scientifically—greatly superior to the approach of the old grammarians. The trouble is that, like some other scientific advances—one thinks of Freud—it has been applied to areas which, because they involve qualitative judgments, simply cannot be reduced to the objective, quantitative terms of science. Such areas are the teaching of English and the making of dictionaries.

The basic principles of Structural Linguistics are defined as follows in *The English Language Arts*, a book published in 1952 by the Commission on the English Curriculum of the National Council of Teachers of English:

1. Language changes constantly.
2. Change is normal.
3. Spoken language is the language.
4. Correctness rests upon usage.
5. All usage is relative.

At first glance, these principles seem unexceptionable, indeed almost truisms. But a closer look reveals that the last three are half-truths, the most dangerous of formulations; half a truth is *not* better than no truth at all.

It may be natural for the Structural Linguists, who have devoted most of their attention to primitive languages, to assume that the "real" language is the spoken one and not the written one, but this has not always been true: many of the words coined from Latin and Greek in the Elizabethan period, words we still use, were introduced by scholars or poets in their writings. Today, what with far greater literacy and the proliferation of printed matter, the written word would seem to be even more important than in the past.

"Correctness rests upon usage" is more nearly true, but the Structural Linguists underestimate the influence of purists, grammarians and schoolmarms. It is true that Swift, an arch-conservative, objected to such eighteenth century neologisms as *mob, bully, sham, bubble* and *banter,* all of which have since become standard English. But he also objected, and successfully, to contractions like *disturb'd,* to *phiz* for *face, hyp* for *hypochondriac,* and *pozz* for *positive.* The purists have won at least two major victories: they have made the double negative, often used by Shakespeare and a perfectly legitimate means of emphasis, a stigma of illiteracy, and they have crusaded so effectively against *ain't* that, though Webster's Third alleges differently, it can't be used any more even as a contraction of *am not* without danger of cultural excommunication. One may deplore these victories, as I do, but we cannot deny they have taken place, as the Structural Linguists sometimes seem to do.

"All usage is relative" is either a truism (different classes and localities speak differently) or else misleading. "The contemporary linguist does not employ the terms 'good English' and 'bad English' except in a purely relative sense," *The English Language Arts* explains. "He recognizes the fact that language is governed by the situation in which it occurs." But this principle leads to an undemocratic freezing of status, since "irregardless" and "he knowed" are standard usage in certain circles, and those not the richest or best educated. So the Horatio Alger of today, bemused by teachers well grounded in Structural Linguistics, will keep on massacring the king's English because his fellow newsboys do ("language is governed by the situation in which it occurs") and the philanthropic merchant will be so appalled by Horatio's double negatives that he will not give him The Job. In their *Modern American Grammar and Usage* (1956) J. N. Hook and E. G. Mathews, writing in the orthodox canon, observe apropos of what they delicately call "substandard English"; "We must re-emphasize that this language is not wrong; it is merely not in harmony with the usages generally found in books . . . or heard in the conversations of those persons with a strong consciousness of language." They then give an example of substandard English: "Bein's he uz a'ready late, he done decide not to pay her no mind." If this is not wrong, it seems hardly worth the bother to teach English at all.

One of the far-out books in the canon is a 1960 paperback called *Linguistics and Your Language,* by Robert A. Hall, Jr., professor of linguistics at Cornell. Browsing through Professor Hall's book is an unsettling experience. "A dictionary or grammar is not as good an authority for your own speech as the way you yourself speak," he observes. Thus: *"Hisn, hern* and so forth are often heard from illiterate people, perhaps more often than from people who know how to read and write; but there is no necessary connection." (I do like "perhaps more often" and "no necessary connection.") Then Dr. Hall goes all the way: " 'Correct' spelling, that is, obedience to the rules of English spelling as grammarians and dictionary-makers set them up, has come to be a major shibboleth in our society. . . . Consequently, anyone who goes through our schooling system has to waste years of his life in acquiring a wasteful and, in the long run, damaging set of spelling habits, thus ultimately unfitting himself to understand the nature of language." English spelling is indeed maddeningly illogical, but we're stuck with it. For one thing, if spelling is to be "relativized" according to "the situation in which it occurs," it would be impossible to look up a word in the dictionary, which would be all right with Dr.

Hall who believes that the free, democratic and linguistically structured citizen should not bow to authority. Logically, Dr. Gove should agree with him, but in fact Dr. Gove edited Webster's Third. And logically, Dr. Hall should not submit to shibboleths of "correct" spelling imposed on us by authoritarian grammarians, but in fact he does; every word in his book is "correctly" spelled.

One of Dr. Hall's special fields is pidgin English and one gets the impression he thinks it just about as good as any other kind—after all, it *communicates,* doesn't it? Me writem big fella book along say teacher man no savvy more nobody other fella.

DR. HALL is a member of the academic establishment, which brings up the question of how effectively Americans are being taught to use their language. Last year the National Council of Teachers of English published a disturbing report: *The National Interest and the Teaching of English.* Its main findings were: some four million U.S. school children have "reading disabilities"; 150,000 students failed college entrance tests in English in 1960; two-thirds of America's colleges have to provide remedial work in English. The same note was sounded in another recent report, by the Council for Basic Education. This report estimates that 35 per cent of all U.S. students are seriously retarded in reading. It blames mostly the "whole-word" or "look-say" method of reading instruction which has become standard in American public schools, by which the child is taught to recognize only whole words instead of to build up words by learning his alphabet and its sounds (the "phonic" system which was traditional until the 'thirties). The child learns not his ABC's but his AT-BAT-CAT's. This device enables the successful pupils to recognize 1,342 words by the end of the third grade. The report claims that the old-fashioned phonic method would produce twice as big a vocabulary by the end of the *first* grade.

There is also the comparison of Soviet and American school programs recently made by Dr. Arther S. Trace: *What Ivan Knows That Johnny Doesn't.* Dr. Trace confined himself to demonstrating the inferiority of our textbooks and curricula in reading, history, literature, foreign languages and geography—we already know how superior Soviet schools are in physics and mathematics. His findings about reading are to the point here. Ivan in the *first* grade uses a primer that has 2,000 words, which is just 500 more than Johnny gets in his *fourth*-grade readers. Ivan reads Tolstoy in the first grade; Johnny reads Mary Louise Friebele, whose works include *A Good, Big Fire, The Blue and Yellow Boats,* and *A Funny Sled.* By the fourth grade, Ivan is coping with a vocabulary of 10,000 words, which is more than five times as many as Johnny has learned in school (though, of course, he is at liberty to pick up as many extracurricular words as he likes; our educationists have not so far discovered a way to prevent children getting wised up outside the classroom, such as supplementing Mary Louise Friebele with a little Dickens read by flashlight under the bedclothes). This result is achieved, according to Dr. Trace, by another Rube Goldbergian device called "vocabulary control" which actually is designed to *reduce* the number of new words that a school child will encounter. The theory is that too many new words may have a traumatic effect.

As might be expected, the illiteracy of the young is even worse when it comes to writing. The University of Pittsburgh recently tested 450,000 high-school students and found that only one out of a hundred was able to produce a five-minute theme without faults in English. In my own slight experience teaching English—three months at Northwestern University several years ago—I was struck by the contrast between the fluency of my students when they spoke in class and the difficulty most of them had in producing a grammatical and correctly spelled composition. The only explanation I could think of was that they had learned to speak outside the classroom—and to write inside it.

The jeremiads of the National Council of Teachers of English seem to be written from the moon. They offer no criticism of the things outside observers think are responsible for student illiteracy: the "look-say" method of teaching reading, infantile textbooks, and "vocabulary control." For these are part of official doctrine and it would be unthinkable that the illiteracy the Council deplores might be caused by the educational techniques the Council approves. The Council has quite a lot to say about Structural Linguistics, and all favorable. If only, one gathers, more teachers were indoctrinated with this approach, what wonders would follow.

The English scholar I. A. Richards, who, with C. K. Ogden, wrote *The Meaning of Meaning* and later invented Basic English, delivered himself of some thoughts and emotions on this topic in 1955:

There are vast areas of so-called "purely descriptive" linguistics which are a grim danger at present to the conduct of language, to education, to standards of intelligence. . . . The appeal to mere *usage* . . . is a case in point. Every useful feature of language was *not in use* once upon a time. Every degradation of language too starts somewhere. Behind usage is the question of efficiency. Inefficient language features are not OK, however widespread their use. Of course, to the linguistic botanist it is important to preserve all varieties until they have been collected and described. But that is not the point of view of the over-all study of language, its services and its powers. That over-all view is, I am insisting, inescapably NORMATIVE. It is concerned . . . with the maintenance and improvement of the use of language.

The word "normative," which implies there is a norm or standard, produces the same reactions in a Structural Linguist as "integration" does in a Southern White Supremacist. Dr. Richards instanced as an example of the degradation of English the growing interchangeability of *disinterested* and *uninterested,* which Webster's Third gives as synonyms. The Structural Linguist position on these words was explained in a recent article in *College Composition and Communication* by Dr. Robert J. Geist. Dr. Geist could see no reason for making a fuss: "I think it can safely be stated that a word means what a speaker intends it to mean and what a hearer interprets it to mean." That there might be some discrepancy between what a speaker intends and what a hearer interprets, and that language is efficient only insofar as it reduces this discrepancy—these truisms didn't occur to Dr. Geist at the moment of writing the foregoing sentence. But he seems to have vaguely sensed later on that something was wrong; at least he does add a parenthesis: "(I use *disinterested* to mean *impartial* only.)" Like other permissive linguists, he doesn't dare to practice what he preaches.

THE whole matter of the development of English is more complicated than it is thought to be by either the old-school grammarians or the Structural Linguists. In the early period of the language, when it was in a state of chronic (and creative) flux, nobody bothered much about correctness. Even spelling was not taken seriously—our greatest writer spelled his name Shakespeare, Shakspere, or Shakspeare as the spirit moved him. It was not until 1721 that the first real dictionary appeared, when Nathaniel Bailey had the novel idea of trying to include *all* the words. Up to then, there had only been lists of "hard words." Such lists were welcomed because of the enormous accretion of new words, mostly invented from Greek or Latin roots, in the Elizabethan and Jacobean periods.

Conservatives denounced these as "inkhorn terms"—i.e., used only in writing to show one's learning—and so many of them were. But most have survived. A contemporary rhetorician composed a parody "inkhorn" letter; while many have perished (*revolute, obtestate, fatigate, splendidious*), most are still current (*affability, ingenious, fertile, contemplate, clemency, verbosity*). By 1650, the language was settling down, the new words were largely accepted, and even spelling was beginning to be standardized. "Some people if they but spy a hard word are as much amazed as if they met with a hobgoblin," Edward Phillips wrote contemptuously in his *New World of Words* (1658).

But usage was not really fixed until the eighteenth century when the literate public expanded suddenly—between 1700 and 1800 the publication of new books quadrupled—because of the rise of the bourgeoisie and the beginning of the industrial revolution. The new-rich classes wanted to show they were cultured gentlemen and so offered a market for dictionaries and grammars, which played the same social role as the books of etiquette which first became popular then. (In Soviet Russia a similar sudden rise in literacy similarly connected with industrialization has produced similar effects—*kulturny* is a potent word there, applied to everything from diction to using a handkerchief to blow one's nose.) In the eighteenth century the literary atmosphere was favorable to the language's becoming standardized. The creative surge of 1550-1650 had ebbed and now, from Pope to Johnson, there followed an Augustan age of classic consolidation. Swift was an impassioned conservative who hoped to "fix the language." But he was not alone in fearing that, if change went on unchecked, in a few generations his own works "shall hardly be understood without an interpreter." He tried to revive Dryden's proposal for an English Academy—on the model of the French Academy founded by Cardinal Richelieu in the preceding century—which would have for its object, in the words of the French Academy's statute: "to give definite rules to our language, and to render it pure, eloquent and capable of treating the arts and sciences [and] to establish a certain usage of words." Nothing came of this project, despite impressive intellectual backing. Even Dr. Johnson, hardly a permissive type, opposed it in the preface to his dictionary (1755) as hostile to "the spirit of English liberty." Johnson also advanced a more pragmatic criticism: "Those who have been persuaded to think well of my design require that it should fix our language and put a stop to those alterations which time and chance have hitherto been suffered to make in it without opposition. With this consequence I will confess that I flattered myself for a while; but now begin to fear that I have indulged expectations which neither reason nor experience can justify." He pointed out that there is "no example of a nation that has preserved their words and phrases from mutability"—later purists must have shuddered at the confusion of plural and singular—and noted that "the French language has visibly changed under the inspection of the academy." The grammarians of the eighteenth and nineteenth centuries, lacking Johnson's common sense, objected to change per se because their model of a proper language, Latin, had not changed for 1,500 years. But it had not changed because it was a dead language for precisely that period; the Latin that continued to live, monks' Latin, changed until it became a patois related to Latin as pidgin English is related to English.

ON the other hand, while no permanent deep freeze is possible in a language, the fact is that English has been to some extent "fixed" in the last two centuries. (Johnson's dictionary was an important factor in the fixing.) The forces that tended this way in the eighteenth century became much stronger in the nineteenth when there was

more literacy, more social mobility, and more industrialization—there seems to be some relation between the requirements of a rationalized industrial society and the
standardization of language. More and more people came
into the cultural market place—ambitious workingmen
who wanted to "better" themselves, *nouveaux riches* who
wanted to be considered gentlemen. The upper classes
hitherto had used English with the easy negligence of
proprietors who can do as they like with their own, but
now the rich were not so secure in their ownership. Now
began the long dominance of the grammarians and the
schoolmarms. The economic base was exposed by Bernard
Shaw: "People know very well that certain sorts of speech
cut off a person forever from getting more than three or
four pounds a week all their life long—sorts of speech
which make them entirely impossible to certain professions." The ambitious workingman who uses Webster's
Third as a guide will be in for some rude shocks when
he says "I ain't" to the personnel director.

Or he may not be. The personnel manager may say
"ain't" to *him*. Perhaps the most ominous sign of the decay
of English in the United States, the vanishing of the very
notion of standards under the pressure of the vulgarians
and the academicians, is the recent decision of the Sherwin
Cody School of English to drop its traditional advertising
punch line: "DO *you* MAKE THESE MISTAKES IN ENGLISH?"
For forty years this has been a classic of correspondence-
school advertising, on a par with "THEY LAUGHED WHEN I
SAT DOWN AT THE PIANO." Now it is obsolete. "The key
fact is," an executive of the school has explained, "people
don't want to speak good English any more. The correspondence course used to be popular among people who
wanted to advance themselves and speak better. Now no
one cares about grammatical errors." And indeed the horrible examples that the school's ads used to cite—"Leave

them lay," "Between you and I"—would be swallowed without a wink by any good Structural Linguist.

ENGLISH is not just a convenient means of communicating, as the Structural Linguists seem to think. The language of a people, like its art and literature and music and architecture, is a record of its past that has much to say to the present. If this connection is broken, then a people gets into the condition of a psychotic who has lost contact with his past. Superseding the King James Version of the Bible with a translation in the modern idiom is like updating Shakespeare—"The problem of existence or nonexistence confronts us." Language is a specially important part of a people's past, or culture, because everybody is exposed to it and has to learn to use it. The evolution of words is a capsule history of the race, as one can verify by reading a few pages of the Oxford English Dictionary. There is always a struggle between tradition and novelty. If the society is too permissive, novelty has it too easy and the result is language that has lost contact with its past and that is, usually, ineffective as communication because it is vague and formless—in beatnik slang "man" and "like" have degenerated to mere interruptions, more stammer than grammar.

Language does indeed change, but there must be some brakes and it is the function of teachers, writers and lexicographers to apply them.* It is their job to make it

---

* Everybody, including myself, now sneers at the "schoolmarms," and they do have some ghastly mistakes on their conscience. But at least they accepted responsibility and at least they understood their pupils needed prescription as well as description. And the worst mistake they made, as my friend Dean Moody Prior, of Northwestern University, has recently pointed out to me, was to humbly transmit to their students the theories about language that were dominant in the scholarly circles of their day. I can see the linguists of the year 2,000 (who will by then have developed some vast new theory, perhaps based on the Jungian racial unconscious) sneering at the "schoolmarms" of the sixties with their myopic and dogmatic adherence to outworn notions, i.e., Structural Linguistics. And I can see the schoolmarms again taking the rap (slang) rather than the eminent

tough for new words and usages to get into circulation so that the ones that survive will be the fittest. *Mob* made it despite Swift, but *pozz* didn't; the point is not that Swift was right or wrong but that he had a sense of the language, which he used as well as any writer has, and that he cared enough about it to raise the question. Today the best English is written and spoken in London—the contrast is painful between the letters-to-the-editor departments of the London *Times* and the *New York Times*—because there an educated class still values the tradition of the language. For English, like other languages, is an aesthetic as well as a practical means of communication. It is compounded of tradition and beauty and style and experience and not simply of what happens when two individuals meet in a barroom, or a classroom. "We must write for the people in the language of kings," Bertolt Brecht once said. Americans seem to be reversing his maxim.

---

scholars whose theories they accepted with a faith as incautious as it was touchingly modest. When does a teacher become a schoolmarm? When the Authorities he or she relies on are considered outdated by the new Authorities. Up to then, he or she is a member in good standing of the National Council of Teachers of English and a useful member of society.

PART V

Examinations

Amateur Journalism

THE AMERICAN IN LONDON is impressed and depressed by many things—the beauty of the parks; the dome of St. Paul's; the splendor of Hampton Court and the squalor of cheap restaurants; the comfort of the Underground, the taxis, the theatres; the discomfort of the climate, the money, the pubs. But he is at once impressed by, and continues to marvel at, the fact that there are seven weekly publications which are worth reading regularly; and not only worth reading (in the sense one feels one ought to) but interesting to read. These notes are mostly about the *Economist,* the *Listener,* the *New Statesman and Nation,* the *Observer,* the *Spectator,* the *Sunday Times* and the *Times Literary Supplement*—plus three dailies on the same level, the *Times,* the *Telegraph* and the *Guardian.* The dailies are less surprising to an American, since we have a number of comparable papers (except for their coverage of art, music, theatre and books), such as the *Times* and *Herald Tribune* of New York, the *Washington Post,* the *St. Louis Post-Dispatch,* and the *Christian Science Monitor.*

But there is nothing like these weeklies in America. In the thirties, the *Nation* and the *New Republic* were written for and read by "everybody" interested in ideas, politics, and art. But their bemusement by the Soviet myth isolated them from an increasingly large section of their readers and contributors—the Moscow Trials and similar issues split the American intelligentsia much more deeply than the British—and their clinging to the platitudes of liberal orthodoxy in the forties and fifties has not repaired the damage. They are now shrunken, drearily predictable, and of little interest to most American intellectuals.* There are other comparable magazines, of course— *Harper's,* the *Atlantic,* the *Reporter,* the *Saturday Review,* to name the most widely read—but these are all more or less vitiated by the "middlebrow" approach, that is, they are edited with a wary eye on an amorphous public whose tastes and interests fluctuate somewhere between lowbrow and highbrow. This means at best a compromise between quality and "what the readers will take" and at worst a genteel slickness that is more trying than the simple vulgarity of the lowbrow press.

The English weeklies are not exactly highbrow—their circulations are too large, their writing too relaxed, their spirit too clearly that of a confident and sizable social group rather than of an embattled minority—but they are not in the least middlebrow, either. I think they may best be described as "amateur." The word has acquired a pejorative overtone, in this businesslike, science-minded civilization. No one is insulted if he is called a professional or an expert, but nobody likes to be brushed off as an amateur, usually with "mere" in front. But the amateur is not necessarily inferior in skill to the professional; the difference between them is simply that the former does because he wants to what the latter does for pay. In journalism, this means that the amateur is less vulnerable to the pressure of the market, and so to what I regard as the most corrupting influence on art and letters today, that of the cheap cultural goods sold in bulk to the mass public. The amateur may not know as much about any particular subject as the expert does, but what he does know (which

---

* Note as of 1962: These strictures no longer apply to The *New Republic,* which has become a sophisticated political magazine with very good critical sections on books, theatre, art, music and films.

may be rather impressive) he knows as part of his own life and of our culture in general, instead of in the narrow way the specialist knows it. Even those who fling "amateur" about as a term of abuse complain of the increasing tendency for knowledge to be subdivided into a myriad of special fields that are each worked intensively without much relation to the whole. The amateur, even the dilettante, would seem a necessary figure if our culture is not to dry up into academicism. The London weekly press is delightfully amateurish in spirit. (I am aware that, in literal fact, its editors and writers are paid, but the pay seems much less the central motive than is the case in America. This, I think, is what gives it its special distinction.

THE brutal snobbery of "Gentlemen v. Players," the Victorian way of discriminating between athletes, is, of course, intolerable, and it is hard today to imagine a society in which half the players in a game would concede such an invidious distinction to the other half. But it did express something attractive about the British cult of the amateur: that certain activities should be pursued "for the sake of the game" only, not for profit and not even for success. In writing, the cult of the amateur has much to recommend it. Americans write as professionals, either as scholars concerned with academic advancement (whence the barbarous jargon, the cramped, cautious specialization of the academic quarterlies) or as professional journalists—and, more important, editors—concerned with attracting as wide and profitable an audience as possible (whence the hard, sleek superficiality of the nonacademic press). But the book reviews, the drama and art criticism, and the articles in the London weeklies seem to me to be written with that pleasurable spontaneity, that recklessness (oddly combined, for an American, with a most impressive expertise) which comes when the writer is not trying to educate his readers or to overawe them or to appease them or to flatter them, but is treating them as equals, fellow members of a clearly defined group of people who share certain common interests and certain common knowledge. Since he is not writing to impress his academic colleagues, he can write simply, informally, personally, sticking his neck as far out as he likes. Since he is not writing for a mixed audience whose lowest common denominator he must always keep in mind, he doesn't have to go in for elaborate explanations of the obvious, nor does he have to capture the reader's attention with a startling journalistic "lead" and try to keep it with debased rhetorical devices and constant appeals to the l.c.d.

Oddly enough, considering the informality of American manners, our writing is much stiffer than English writing, more artificial, removed to a greater distance from the reader, since an easy, personal style is risky with an amorphous audience. English reviewers speak in their own individual voices—the headlong rush of Pritchett, the neat, balanced style of Connolly—and yet are clear and to the point, like good conversationalists. Sometimes this personal manner goes over the edge and we get the facile bravura of Kingsley Amis, or passages like the following:

Though her most discerning admirers rave about "Claudine à l'École," I must admit that it is my least favourite of her novels—so little charm and *joie de vivre,* so much lechery and sharpness! The lanky Anais, the stupid Marie Belhomme, the Lesbian headmistress and her flirtatious doxy, the bottom-pinching, ear-tweaking Superintendent . . . what a ruttish lot they all are! The peaches and cats and nectarines and crowded summer nights of the later books have been contracted to a crowd of simian little girls, ogling, simpering, whining, nibbling at blue lead pencils and cigarette papers. *Zero de Conduite* for Colette!

This is not very convincing, yet even this kind of teddy-boyishness is better than the cautious impersonality so common in American reviewing. English critics actually criticize; they are much more severe on shoddy work than their American colleagues, who go in mostly for summarizing the contents (even of novels) and showing they know where to pigeonhole the work, and often forget to mention what they thought of it. Judgments like the following are rare in the American press:

But there is, about most of this book, such a dilettante air, such evidence of sheer ignorance of recent critical trends, such consistent avoidance of anything alive and growing that one's tolerance is admittedly strained to the limit.

This book is sad stuff—obtuse, dull, ill-made. It is a relief to turn to Major Shepphard's book, so neatly written and constructed.

It is impossible to say at the end of the book what Dr. Meissner believes about almost any of the various aspects of education he has written about, while his expeditions into theology and moral philosophy are, to put it gently, obscured by a thick haze of verbal confusion.

Nor is it that American critics, though cautious, are more scholarly; on the contrary, the knowledge of his subject shown by the average English reviewer is far greater; reading the articles on art and music in the London *Times* and the *Manchester Guardian* after years of having to put up with the thin gruel provided in these departments by the *New York Times* and the *New York Herald Tribune* is like turning from *Reader's Digest* to the *Encyclopædia Britannica* (that is, the old eleventh edition, before we Americans got hold of it).

THE amateur's interests, by definition, are wide-ranging since they include whatever he cares for (*amo*), and one can care for more aspects of life than one can know as an expert. When it is also considered that, as will be shown later, there are roughly only two publics in Britain—the classes and the masses—as against a great many in America, one can understand why American magazines are more specialized than their British equivalents.* Thus the American businessman reads *Barron's Weekly* and the *Wall Street Journal* for current business news, *Fortune* for longer-range stuff, *Time* for a systematic review of the news in general, and, if he is odd enough to be interested in books, some literary magazine for that. But the City man gets it all in the *Economist,* which also, unlike our business magazines, is read by many nonbusinessmen because it covers and comments on the week's events more thoroughly than any other weekly does; its overseas news is remarkably full; and its book section is excellent and covers not only economic books but also biographies, literary criticism, philosophy, etc. The oneness of the London reading public is shown not only by a business magazine's having so broad a range but also by the existence of weekly departments on business in the *Spectator* and the *New Statesman;* it is quite impossible to imagine such a thing in the *Nation* and the *New Republic.*

Similarly, in America the contact between scholars and nonscholars is slight; there are two worlds in literature, for instance, the academic, with its professional journals, and the lay, which reads the *Saturday Review,* the "little" magazines, and the Sunday book sections of the *Times* and *Herald Tribune.* But in England learning is not the province of specialists but the common possession of the whole educated class. So one gets that remarkable institution, the *Times Literary Supplement,* which every week publishes general articles and reviews of a quality and

---

* An exception is *Punch,* which prints only humorous material, in contrast to the *New Yorker,* which also, and indeed chiefly, prints fiction, poetry and reportage. This seems to me a more workable formula: the funny bone begins to ache when it is struck too consistently, the humorous note to become a little thin and forced; while the *New Yorker's* serious material is a relief from the cartoons and jokes (and, of course, vice versa).

authority achieved in America only occasionally in some "little" magazine or academic quarterly, and also covers such specialized works as *Historie de la Boîte à Musique et de la Musique Mécanique,* a Swiss work priced at £7 10s., *Historia de la Literatura Chilena* (Santiago), and *Bibliografia di Bernard Berenson* (Milan), this last being treated in the front-page lead article.

One special aspect of what might be called amateur expertise is the amount of highly informed comment on events in other parts of the world that appears in the British press. Our own coverage is comparatively thin and the interpretation comparatively provincial, with the important exception of the *New York Times.* Reading the London weeklies, and the *Times* and *Guardian,* is to be constantly reminded that one is at the center of what was until recently a world empire. It is taken for granted that readers know what, and where, the Trucial States are, what is the difference between an emir and an emu, and that what was Benares in Kipling's day is now called Banaras. These reports combine great knowingness with off-hand comments from an *echt*-British point of view, revealing that combination of insularity (as to evaluation) and cosmopolitanism (as to knowledge) which has long made the Englishman abroad a confusing figure to the *indigènes:*

> The Protectorate states produce almost nothing, and often seem quite incorrigibly addicted to the pleasures of violence and deceit. The conscientious Englishman, having discovered Upper Aulaki on his map, may well go on to wonder why on earth a harassed British government wants to have anything to do with this disagreeable backwater.

This freedom with off-the-cuff value judgments is another characteristic of amateur journalism, and is not common practice in the American press, which has a sober, professional abhorrence of what it calls "editorializing."

Our papers report the sessions of Congress, for example, in cold factual details; interpretation is left to the editorial columns. But a British newspaper treats Parliamentary debates as if they were sporting events, noting who was in good form and "editorializing" all over the place with the jaunty expertise that in America is permitted only in a report on the latest Giant v. Dodgers game. Thus a front-page story in the *Daily Telegraph* leads off with what to the American eye is a shocking, if fascinating, slug of pure opinion:

> Foreign affairs plodded along at a humdrum jogtrot in the House of Commons tonight. The debate was cosy and un-distinguished.
>
> The Prime Minister's opening statement was slightly marred by a throat affliction, for which he apologized to the House. This may also have accounted for a notable lack of vigour in his arguments.
>
> It is often possible for accomplished orators to disguise the unoriginality of their subject-matter by the resounding force of their delivery. This resource was not at Sir Anthony's command today.

THE London mass-circulation newspapers come as something of a shock to an American, accustomed to the relatively high standards in typography, layout, and content of the New York *Daily News* (a remarkably competent, clever job, given the standards of mass journalism—which, of course, should not be given, or accepted), the Chicago *Tribune,* and even the Hearst papers. (The *Telegraph* is an exception; although its circulation is large, it is on a level comparable to the *Times* and the *Guardian*—and most American papers.) A glance at one of these "news-papers," with myriads of tiny trivial items swarming confusedly over the front page, with heads in a jumble of sizes and styles that recall an old-fashioned patent-medicine throwaway or the most amateurish efforts of one of our schools of journalism, with dingy blots of news photos and ads and cartoons and maps and weather reports and Late News Bulletins all smothering each other like plants in a South American rain forest (sometimes desperately fenced off with boxes), a glance at this welter of civilization is enough to make one want to do a Lawrence, T.E. or D.H. A front page of the *Daily Express* contained twenty-nine different items, including "Six New Admirals Named" (with tiny figures of six admirals under the head, to give it more punch); a small map of the Levant with an arrow pointing to Jerusalem labeled "ISRAEL SAID TO BE MASSING TROOPS," this in connection with a major item, "From Our Diplomatic Correspondent," all of five inches long, that began "King Hussein's Arab Legion looked to its guns last night as threats of new trouble flashed across the Middle East and caused a diplomatic flurry in London" (nothing happened); and a one-inch item, "LET THE QUEEN STAY WITH US," which revealed that a Canadian M.P. had "suggested" that the Queen should live in Canada "three to five months every four years." A front page of the *News Chronicle,* which I gather is considered rather a highbrow paper of its kind, had twenty-five items in almost as many sizes and faces of type, while the *Evening News* hit the jackpot with fifty different front-page stories, including such enigmatic bulletins as "THEY STOLE SHIRTS. . . . Shirts were stolen during the night from E. and K. Thomas, drapers in Blyth-road, West Kensington. The thieves made two other break-in attempts in the same block." With the mass periodicals put out frankly for entertainment—the above papers are, in theory, engaged in giving the news— the comparison is the same. *Life* is in every way—technically, aesthetically, and in the cultural level of its articles—far above *Picture Post.* And there is nothing but nothing in America to compare with that malformed colossus of the British press, the *News of the World.*

The excellence of some of the press in London is con-

nected, I think, with the degradation of the rest. The gap
reflects, and in fact is only made possible by, the gulf between the classes.* In England there is hardly any middlebrow press. But in America, where class distinctions are
fuzzier, highbrow culture competes with mass culture,
merges into it in a subtle and bewildering and demoral-
izing way. Except for the scholarly journals and a few
"little" magazines like *Partisan Review,* there is no dis-
tinctively highbrow press and each periodical finds its
place in the infinitely graduated spectrum between low-
middlebrow and high-middlebrow.

LIBERAL intellectuals in England and in America are
worried because the circulation of serious journals is in
the tens of thousands while that of mass magazines is in
the millions. While it would admittedly be cheering if the
figures were reversed, I think this anxiety overdone for
several reasons: (1) an audience of fifty or even five thousand is large enough for all practical purposes (that is,
for the communication of art and ideas to a public large
enough not to be monolithic and ingrown); (2) a smaller
audience on a higher level will be more affected by what
it reads than a larger audience on a lower level, partly because the material itself will be more significant, more able
to "make a difference" to them, and partly because they
will be intelligent enough to let it make more of a difference; (3) the smaller group will be in general more articulate, energetic, intelligent, and powerful (that is, with
higher status and more important jobs) than the masses
who drowse over the *News of the World* or the American

* In America, one's accent "places" one as to—place. The Southern drawl,
the Midwestern nasal tone, the clipped New England twang, the brisk,
brutal New York delivery, all are social equals. But in England the
"right" accent is one and indivisible. A most unsnobbish father confessed
to me that he had to send his children to "good" schools, at no matter
what scraping and scrimping economies, simply because he couldn't bear
to hear them talking with the accent they would pick up in the free
State schools.

tabloids, and so it will make more of a difference what they read. This line of thought is obnoxious to conventional liberals because it is "undemocratic" (they really mean inegalitarian, not the same thing at all, since, as the Nazis and Communists have demonstrated, leveling can produce a most undemocratic mass society), but it may nonetheless have some validity.

What seems to me alarming is not the contrast between the circulations of the highbrow and the lowbrow periodicals, but rather the influence of the latter on the former, the gravitational pull that is exerted by a large body (of money, or readers) on a much smaller one. This pull is greater in America than in England because of the blurring of class lines and consequently of cultural traditions—defining a tradition as a code held to not out of conviction (as a principle is held) but for the much deeper, more stubbornly resistant reason that it is simply the way one is. A journal like the *Times Literary Supplement* seems to be edited and read by people who know who they are and what interests them. That the vast majority of their fellow citizens do not share their interest in the development of English prose, the bibliography of Belorussia, André Gide's treatment of his wife, the precise relation of folksong and plainsong, and "the large blot" in a letter of Dr. Johnson's which has given much trouble to several of his editors, to cite some matters gone into quite thoroughly in the issue of September 14, 1956—this seems not in any way to trouble them. But the editors and readers of the *T.L.S.*'s opposite number in America, the *Saturday Review,* have no such clear notion of their cultural identities and interests. The editors feel the pressure of competition with *Time,* the *Saturday Evening Post,* and the other great middlebrow commercial magazines—it is hard just to get on the newsstands, the commercial slicks being so much more numerous than is the case in England. Nor do their readers have a very clear idea of their cultural identity, so that a graduate student will drop *Look* to pick up the *Kenyon Review* (or, more likely, the other way around). It is felt, also, that there is something snobbish, perhaps even un-American about ignoring the popular press, as indeed there is. The effect of the gravitational pull of mass media on the highbrow press in America is illustrated by the evolution of *Harper's* and the *Atlantic*. In the nineteenth century these magazines were the organs of an elite,* printing Emerson, James, Henry Adams, Howells, and Lowell and maintaining a dignified level of taste and thought (if it was also rather stuffy, this was because it was a somewhat provincial elite). They both have now slicked themselves up to become the competitors of the commercial magazines. A modern Adams or James would not find sympathetic reception in these streamlined journals, nor in any other American magazines of sizable circulation—until he became famous, of course, as in the case of Hemingway and Faulkner.

If one wants to publish a serious article in America—that is, something one takes seriously as an expression of one's own special way of looking at things—there are three possibilities. One is the academic quarterlies, which range from purely professional journals like *Psychiatry*, the *Review of Politics*, and the *Journal of the History of Ideas* to more general organs like *Yale Review, Virginia Quarterly*, and *Foreign Affairs*. Another possibility is the "little" magazines, which are subsidized by individuals (*Partisan, Hudson*) or organizations (as *Commentary*, which is published by the American Jewish Committee) or which come

---

* "Elite" and "tradition" are used here in a cultural as well as a social sense. The relation of the two meanings is complicated, since the social is by no means synonymous with the cultural aristocracy, but I think it can be said that class lines make it easier for a cultural elite to survive. Certainly the two countries where "mass culture" has most corrupted and stifled the real article are the two in which traditional class lines have been almost wholly wiped out, the USA and the USSR.

out of some campus (*Kenyon, Sewanee, Accent, Chicago.*)*
The third is the *New Yorker,* which, although it is one of
the most profitable of the commercial magazines, is edited
with less worry about the reactions of its readers (more
accurately, of a hypothetical reader who exists only in the
editor's mind and who always seems to be less intelligent
than any actual reader one meets) than are middlebrow
magazines like *Harper's* or the *Reporter.* It therefore per-
mits the writer to express himself without regard for the
conventions of American journalism, taking the space he
needs, using long sentences, interesting syntax, and difficult
words, and going into all kinds of recondite by-ways simply
because the subject seems to lead there. At least, such has
been my experience. I think this is because the *New
Yorker's* audience, though large—its circulation is around
400,000—is, like the audience of the *Economist* or the
Spectator, clearly defined as to tastes and interests. The
definition was made by the late Harold Ross, who founded
the magazine and edited it until his death a few years ago,
and expresses a peculiar kind of snobbishness, neither intellectual nor social, in fact directed against both, and yet
partaking of both. It is a "we happy few who know the
good things in life" affair that is expressed perfectly in the
first cover (which is repeated once a year) showing the
magazine's incarnation, "Eustace Tilley," an old-fashioned
dandy in a top hat and high collar, lifting his monocle to

* Both these types flourish far more abundantly in America than in
England, in curious contrast to the feebleness of our weekly press. (I can't
think why this should be so.) The American thus has at least one advantage over the English writer—he has many more places in which to
publish long, ambitious articles. The almost complete absence of such
articles is the chief weakness of the London weeklies; 2,000 words is their
usual top and, for some kinds of writers and themes, this is not enough
room to turn around in. There is an exaggerated fear of being "heavy" or
"boring," but some ideas, and writers, are "heavy" by nature, often the
greatest—would Marx, Freud or Kierkegaard have been able to make the
New Statesman, one wonders—and an unrelieved diet of short, graceful
articles has its own kind of monotony. It seems odd that an important
literary critic like F. R. Leavis, because he writes long, weighty articles,
appears in *Commentary* but not in the British weeklies.

inspect a hovering butterfly. Within this plot of artificial grass, fenced off from American mass culture as the more natural English enclosure is fenced off, some freedom of expression is possible. There are serpents in this Eden: the magazine's own "formula" is often monotonous and over-restrictive, and the editorial pencils sometimes fly too busily. But the thoroughness with which the *New Yorker* violates the canons of professional middlebrow journalism is always inspiriting. Timeliness is disregarded in a regal way: books are reviewed long after they have appeared; topical articles are held for months; comment rather than news is the aim. The make-up is wildly unprofessional: nothing is "featured," on the cover or inside; the contributions run on consecutively, with the author's names at the end in small type; there is not even a table of contents. The *New Yorker* is, in effect and in its editors' minds, a weekly letter to its readers, whose tastes are disregarded simply because they are assumed to be those of the editors and writers who compose the letter.

THE special quality of British literary journalism is related to the existence in London of a close-knit intellectual community. "What has astonished me, and what astonishes any American," Irving Kristol wrote in *Encounter* after he had been a while in London, "is the extent to which al-most *all* British intellectuals are cousins. . . . In America it is otherwise, to put it mildly. . . . It is by no means impossible that the senior editors of the *New Yorker* should never have met the senior editors of *Time*." As an alumnus of both these magazines, I can testify this is ac-curate; intellectual circles in New York are neither con-centric nor interlocking, and one knows "personally" (the very expression suggests the American lack of contact) only a small proportion of the authors whose books and articles one reads. The London intellectual community is much broader, including businessmen, lawyers, and even publishers, even Members of Parliament; most literary parties of any size produce an M.P. or two, but in New York one could write about politics for years without seeing a Congressman except in the newsreels.

Indeed, "community" is too mild; it is more like a family, a large, variegated family, serious-minded but with a strong sense of play. They know the family jokes (what is "Butskellism"?), the eccentric uncles (G.B.S.), the ancestors (several weeklies have discussed at length whether a seventeenth-century man of science named Robert Hooke was a nice man or not). They are very much concerned with preserving the old home and with the proper appreciation of its charms; John Betjeman and Geoffrey Grigson are in constant communication with their cousins on the matter, sounding alarms about proposals to alter the landscape or to tear down some interesting structure, describing some nook in the great old pile, some country village or city vista that they feel has not been enough appreciated. They love to play intellectual games together; each week the *New Statesman* sets its readers a task and prints the winning entries; these are almost always witty and ingenious; it appears that every Englishman is born with a silver pen in his mouth.

The two most striking examples of family journalism are the *Listener* and the *Times*. The former is, of course, notable because it consists entirely (except for an excellent book section, whose reviews, like those of the *T.L.S.*, are unsigned*) of broadcast programs of the B.B.C.; a magazine on such a level as the *Listener*, and drawn only from

---

* This sort of anonymity is interestingly different from that of *Time* magazine. *Time* writers don't sign their work because it isn't theirs; they are the middle workers on an assembly line that begins with their researchers and ends with a corps of editors who blue-pencil and rewrite until the final product has the glossy, brash, dynamic *Time* style. English anonymity doesn't imply collective fabrication; it is just that the family is so closely knit that "everybody" knows who wrote last week's *T.L.S.* lead articles, just as "everybody" knows who writes the London Diary in the *New Statesman*.

this source, would in America have to appear not weekly but annually. The *Listener* is family talk around the tea table. The elders reminisce; the learned uncles discuss Kant or Josephus, without either pedantry or condescension; the cousins in Parliament or on the press analyze current events; those with a taste for exploring or gardening or book-collecting talk about their hobbies; someone who has picked up some curious information on Scottish architecture or the migration of herring passes its along; there is talk about books and art and cooking.

As for the *Times*, it is the quintessence of family journalism, devoting its first page entirely to classified ads (the petty concerns of the individual take precedence over wars and revolutions), and presenting the news in a remarkably confusing and illogical form simply because that is the way it has always been done and the members of the family know their way around in it as well as they know the way the furniture is placed in the living-room. Topicality is not a fetish; special articles may be on the Algerian situation or on the battle of Poitiers; the latter type I find the more interesting, and so, I suspect, do the readers. A topic has to have some "news peg" from which to hang, in the professional American press, but in England it is merely a question of whether it interests a reading public whose tastes the editors know intimately because they share them. The readers of the *Times*, as might be expected in this kind of journalism, supply much of the paper's interest. There is, of course, the famous letters column, which the leader of Her Majesty's Opposition may use to pose awkward questions to the party in power or which a sportsman may use to protest against some local regulation prohibiting trout-tickling or chubb-fuddling. Even more typical is the custom of writing letters to the *Times* about distinguished friends who have recently died. These letters appear in the Obituary column and are not, as one might expect, the usual conventional pieties, but are thoughtful, moving, and full of interest (the English knack for the concrete detail and the English concern for truth at all costs come out in this unlikely context) even though they may end "He will leave an irreplaceable gap" or "Truly, as one of his biographers remarked, we shall never look upon his like again." This custom, unknown in America, where writing is a matter for the professionals (though, to adapt Clemenceau, it is really too important a matter to be left to writers), implies that the readers of the *Times,* as well as the friends who take the trouble to compose the letters, feel close enough to the dead to want to keep their memory alive a little. It is a family affair.

"WE shall be obliged to explain away the ugly fact that nearly all English writers and editors are on speaking terms," V. S. Prichett once wrote, apropos a P.E.N. congress in London and the questions that would be asked about English intellectual life. In the 'thirties, the friendly personal relations between pro- and anti-Stalinists in London used to bewilder us New York radicals. Even anarchists, with us a wretched little sect looked on by all the Marxist groups—when they thought about such oddities— as contemptuously as if they were Holy Rollers or Seventh Day Adventists, even they seemed to have their accepted place in the English political zoo. Our tone was quite different; New York was more of a jungle than a zoo. To us it was inconceivable that the Communist lion could lie down, even for a tactical moment, with the Trotskyist cat, or that issues like the Moscow Trials and the role of the Communists in the Spanish Civil War could be discussed in an amicable spirit. The Communists formally prohibited their people from "fraternizing with the class enemy"—a Party member who was detected talking with a Trotskyist in a Fourteenth Street cafeteria in anything but an exasperated shout was liable to expulsion. We Trotskyists had no such rule and in fact deplored such "bureaucratic monolithism"—we were, in a way, more in the English style—but words like "betrayal," "frame-up," "sell-out," "counterrevolution," and "GPU falsification" leaped to our tongues and pens. We regarded our English colleagues with a mixture of envy, contempt and amusement. Either they were not serious, or we were too much so.*

Things don't seem to have changed much. One finds John Strachey and Clement Attlee writing in the neo-conservative *Spectator,* which criticizes the Tory government quite as freely as the liberal-progressive *New Statesman*. The continuing success of the latter, in contrast to the desiccated state of our own liberal press, is due not to any greater perspicacity on the Stalinist issue but rather to the typically British way it has avoided going to extremes. Guided by the skillful journalistic touch of Kingsley Martin (a cool operator, very different from such an American counterpart as the all-too-ardent Freda Kirchwey) it has trimmed its sails to the moderate winds of English political feeling. After the Moscow Trials, the American Left intellectuals split into two sharply opposed camps, with the balance steadily swinging toward the anti-Communists as time went on; the liberal weeklies, less supple than the *New Statesman* and also confronted with a less easily bridged gap, became increasingly the prisoners of the anti-anti-Communists. But the *New Statesman* is read by "everybody"; its soft-headedness on Russia is offset by strong and varied cultural departments, and it has never become as shrill and one-sided as its American counterparts.

* I think, on the whole, it was they who were not serious enough. Not because the English spirit was not as sensitive as ours to the inhumanities and injustices of Stalinism, but because it seems to be hard for an English intellectual to take abstract ideas seriously. Unhappily much of the appeal of Stalin's (or Khrushchev's) Russia to the rest of the world, which doesn't share the British phlegm about abstract ideas, has been the philosophical-moral system created by Marx and the socialists and illegitimately usurped by the Soviet Communists. One thing one does miss in London is a keen interest in general ideas such as one finds in the Continental intellectual press and to some extent, though less than formerly, in our own.

This is not to say the *New Statesman* isn't the sister-under-the-smooth-British-skin of its American poor relations. Like them, it suffers from the pernicious anemia of modern liberalism, a point of view that combines the worst features of tradition (as, stereotyped reactions) and utopian rebellion (as, lack of realism, moral smugness). The term should really be liberalistic, implying a vulgarization and distortion of the original article. "Liberal" is a proud adjective, historically (Herzen, Emerson, John Stuart Mill) and etymologically ("open to the reception of new ideas," says the Shorter Oxford Dictionary). But it has been devaluated in our time, confused with "progressive" (toward the MVD labor camps?) and "democratic" (the plebiscitary dictatorships? the mediocrity of "public opinion"?). Comparing the *New Statesman* with the *Spectator,* I find the latter both more interesting and more admirable. It is more interesting because its "line" is less predictable than the *New Statesman*'s, its writers often reacting to the actual situation, which never quite fits into any preconceived ideas, instead of to formulae by the Fabians out of Marx. It is more admirable because it faces up to events instead of evading them.* When Nasser moved in on Suez, the *Spectator* thought this was a matter of some importance to

---

* Or, as in the case of the reportage by John Freeman on the satellite countries in the July 21, 1956, *Statesman,* distorting them to fit the formula. Under the interesting title, "A Profile of the People's Democracies"—interesting because "people's democracy" is the cant phrase devised by the Moscow Office of Public Relations (to translate freely) for certain political operations that sound better that way—Mr. Freeman wrote a kind of inter-office memo to the Communist gauleiters of Eastern Europe. He gave them full credit, and perhaps a bit more, for the post-Stalin "thaw" and advised them, for prudential reasons, to liberalize their policies still more. One had the general impression that it was all an experiment in socialism, conducted in the spirit of the Webbs, and that if only outside critics would pipe down, the people of Eastern Europe could stride into the Dawn of a New Era arm in arm with their Fabian shepherds. Mr. Freeman was quite definite as to who are the saboteurs of progress—Radio Free Europe, the Voice of America, and "even some of the BBC programmes," plus the *émigrés*. In short, almost everybody outside the satellites who is concerned with their problems. His advice to the *émigrés* is blunt: Shut Up or Go Home. "All those who now choose to remain abroad should

England and devoted a forthright (and, it must be admitted, rather indignant) first-page editorial to the subject. The *New Statesman,* reacting in routine fashion as the professional friend of the colonial underdog, felt that the obvious first-page editorial for the issue after Suez was a denunciation of British misdeeds in the Seychelles Islands. "A STRONG SMELL FROM THE SEYCHELLES" it boldly headlined. Suez was discreetly embalmed on page four in a turgid editorial which got around to mentioning the unpleasantness in its forty-first line, and then went on to blame it all on the U.S. State Department, "which has effectively provoked the crisis" by refusing to finance Colonel Nasser's dam.

Similarly, the *Statesman* gave the Poznan uprising in Poland its page-four treatment, while the *Spectator,* again reacting to actuality and unhampered by previous ideological commitments—the liberals have their own tradition by now, an ever lengthening burden of mistakes, disasters, and betrayals that drags after them like Marley's iron chain of ledgers and cash boxes—hailed the workers of Poznan on page one. The most characteristic passages, both in style and content, were: (1) "These events must pose once again for the rulers of Eastern Europe the revolutionary dilemma stated in its most lapidary form by Saint-Just: '*Un gouvernement a la vertu pour la principe; sinon la terreur. Que veulent ceux qui ne veulent ni la vertu ni la*

---

understand that, by doing so, they are losing any influence they may once have enjoyed among their compatriots. It is, after all, difficult for Poles or Czechs who have to sweat it out at home to feel respect for those who, from the shelter of a hostile country, promote activities which are at best aimed at sabotaging the system and which can easily lead to bloodshed and reprisals." One wonders what Herzen or Lenin, who promoted activities from the shelter of a hostile country aimed at sabotaging an earlier—and how much milder!—Russian despotism, would have said to such advice. Indeed, one knows. But of course they were opposed to the despots and were not taken in by cant about Holy Russia, the Czarist equivalent of People's Democracy. [Note, as of 1962: A month after this article appeared, the Hungarian people made their superb revolution. I might also add that Mr. Freeman is now the editor of the *New Statesman.*]

terreur?' If relaxation of the terrible pressure exercised by Communist States on their citizens is followed by blind outbursts of protests, how can the necessary evolution of society proceed except in convulsions?" (2) " 'The time has come,' a very representative group of Labour M.P.s has written to the Polish president, 'when all citizens of our great continent should enjoy liberty . . . and an adequate standard of life.' The Polish government should realise that Socialists everywhere will endorse this appeal for 'generous restraint' and understand that any 'cooperation for peace and reconstruction' depends on its answer." Readers are invited to guess which passage appeared in which journal, also to distinguish which is an "insider" and which an "outsider" reaction; there will be no prizes.

AS COMMON law is the quintessence of British justice and boiled vegetable marrow that of British cooking, so the peculiar, and great, contribution of the English to journalism is the letter-to-the-editor. It fits into my thesis in several ways: it is strictly amateur, being produced free, gratis, and without cost; it is a cozy, family-circle kind of communication; and it affords full scope for the sort of informal writing at which the English excel. In each of the weeklies and dailies I am considering here the letters section is given a prominent place—usually the individual letters are listed in the table of contents—and I find myself turning to it first. Its contents are varied, exciting, amusing, instructive, or just simply odd.

There seems to be something especially congenial to the English temperament about the act of writing a letter-to-the-editor. The form has been developed to a high pitch through the generations, and is now capable of great flexibility, ranging from one-sentence grace notes ("Sir,—England needs quality, not equality. Yours faithfully. . . .") to such lengthy and complex fugues as the many-voiced discussion, lasting weeks in the *Spectator*, of the place of the Virgin Mary in Catholic theology. There are letters by everybody from Marie Stopes to Lord Astor about everything from the Suez crisis to the reason circus rings are forty-two feet in diameter. There are letters from politicians whose bills have been criticized ("Sir,—You have honoured me by commenting on the Bill I have introduced, so I hope you will afford me a little space. . . .") and from authors whose books have been criticized—who, being authors, employ a wide variety of styles from Ironic Elaborate ("Sir,—I have always admired the creative imagination of many of your book reviewers, but never more so than in Paul Johnson's review of my book, *Time and Place*, in your columns last week. . . .") to Bar-Room Blunt ("Sir,—How bitchy can a reviewer get?"). Letters from Indignant Readers: "Sir,—I do not understand why the *Spectator*, which is supposed to be an independent weekly, employs Mr. Charles Curran as its chief political commentator. He is about as independent of the Tory central office as a tortoise is of its shell." Letters from contributors who have been misunderstood: "Sir,—May I say that when I described Professor Oakeshott's inaugural lecture as 'a wily defence of the shabby against the new' I meant by 'shabby' 'time-worn' and not, as one reader supposed, 'underhand'?" Letters from writers of previous letters who feel they have been maltreated by writers of previous letters: "Sir,—I am sorry that Lord Esher has introduced a personal and offensive note into a correspondence that has hitherto been conducted on the level of principle. . . ." And, finally, letters which, in prose as in provenance, epitomize the art form, as the following contribution to a discussion in the *Times* on the decline of the walking-stick (Am.: cane):

Sir,—Have your correspondents forgotten the solemn judgment of a Chinese sage upon the English, that even the best of them take a stick with them when they go for a walk? "For what purpose except to beat the innocent?"

Yours, &c.,

GILBERT MURRAY

Yatscombe, Boar's Hill, Oxford.

Howtoism

THE WAY to deal with eelworm in phlox is to spray with Murphos, a paraltrion curb. The way to avoid being slighted by bus drivers, waiters and salesgirls is to be unselfish, self-confident, thoughtful, enthusiastic and happy. The way to stop a long-winded speaker is for the chairman to rise, thank him for his splendid contribution, and lead the audience in thunderous applause. The way to resist a male seducer is for the lady to sit in an armless straight chair and pop a piece of salt-water taffy into her mouth every time he is about to kiss her. The way to saw curves on a bevel with a band saw is to make a layout on the top side of the workpiece and then tilt the table to the angle required. The way to get out of a cocktail party is to write, "Gosh, I'm sorry, but I had already made plans to go to the country, and I'd be leaving three ardent golfers in the lurch if I fouled out now." The way to keep matches dry in a rowboat is to put them in a fruit jar whose lid has been fastened to the underside of the seat; to get at them, unscrew the jar from the lid. The way to hem a circular flounce on a slipcover is too complicated to go into here. The way to make a "Stradivarius" violin is to do what it tells you to do in *You Can Make a "Stradivarius" Violin,* a publication of Popular Mechanics Press. The way to raise the Devil is as follows: draw a circle with consecrated coal and chalk and write around it, "I forbid you, Lucifer, in the name of the Blessed Trinity, to enter this circle"; then take a stand inside the circle and recite: "I conjure thee, Lucifer, by the ineffable names ON, ALPHA, YA, REY, SOL, MESSIAS,

INGODUM that thou comest to do, without harming me" [you then tell him what you want]. *Nota bene:* this works only on Mondays; on Tuesdays, for instance, Lucifer must be addressed as "NAMBROTH," on Saturdays as "NABAM" (Note to printer: no typos please, matter of life and death) and on Sundays he will answer only to "AQUIEL" and will ask for a hair of your head which on no account should be given him—he can be fooled with a hair from a fox.

The above useful information is a dipperful from the great American reservoir of know-how. The howto book professes to tell, and often does tell, the reader how to do, be, become, make, or cope with something. How to eat, talk, breathe, sleep, cook with sour cream, play canasta, give a church supper, raise parakeets, bet on the horses. How to be healthy, wealthy, wise, and happily married. How to become popular, articulate, refined, charming, virile, cultured, and couth. How to cope with children, sex, religion, old age, Christmas, in-laws, and other common problems of life.

The R. R. Bowker Company publishes *How-to-Do-It Books: A Selected Guide,* two hundred pages of descriptive bibliography compiled by Robert E. Kingery, of the New York Public Library. Mr. Kingery has cut a few paths through the jungle of howtoism, culling out a mere 3,500 titles, which he has arranged under nine hundred heads, from Abacus to Yoghurt, but traversing even these well-blazed trails is fatiguing. Alcoholics, Allergy, and Alligators; Candle-Making and Candy-Making; Chiggers and Children; Diving Boards and Divorce; Embroidery, Emotions, Enameling, Encyclopedias, Entertaining, and Etching; Mental Illness cheek by jowl with Metalwork; Money (Counterfeiting) cozying up to Money-Making Ideas; Survival (Atomic Bombs) modulating into Swans. There are books on how to succeed as a motel operator, a woman, a baby sitter, a committee member, a guest, a parent, a child, a lover, a Chevrolet owner, and a baton twirler.

(*The Baton: Twirling Made Easy!*) There are howtos on
encouraging bees and earthworms (Thomas J. Barrett's
Harnessing the Earthworm) and on discouraging ants,
budbugs, cockroaches, moths, silverfish, and termites.
There are howtos on pigeons and pigs and poker; on
poultry, pregnancy, printing, and poison ivy; on sleuthing
(*The Art of Detection, or, How to Be a Sleuth*) and sleeping (*How to Sleep Successfully*); on standing (*Your Carriage Madam!*, by Janet Lane) and sitting (*Sitting Pretty*,
by, needless to say, the same author); on rabbits, rheuma-
tism, riddles, rifles, and rugs; on lace and lizards, lacrosse,
and lampshades; on wood carving, meat carving, soap
carving, and ice carving; on how to make mobiles, be a
widow (three titles, including Donald I. Rogers' *Teach
Your Wife to Be a Widow*), and get tall (Paul O'Neil's
Why Be Short?); on how to collect books, bottles, buttons,
and butterflies; on how to buy things (almost a full page
of titles) and even one book on how to throw things away
—Morgan Towne's *Treasures in Truck & Trash*, which
tells "how to pick out the treasures from the junk in the
cellar and attic, how much they are worth, and where to
sell them," and which is by no means the only entry among
Mr. Kingery's 3,500 that sounds as though it might really
be quite useful in dealing with one of the many special
problems that bother people in this intricate age. After
all, it is not the fault of the howto author that modern
life gets more and more complicated, calling on him to
settle problems that are more and more arcane. One sometimes wonders, however, whether a feedback is not at work
here and whether a number of these problems would perhaps never have arisen to bother us if books had not been
written telling us how to solve them.

Howtos build on each other the way coral reefs are
formed—the new generations flourishing on the bones of
the dead, the mass steadily rising. Howto authors make a
living by taking in each other's washing, or even their own

—quoting from each other or from their own earlier works to add authority (and padding)—and they may go so far as to marry each other, like the Overstreets. Harry A. wrote *The Mature Mind, A Declaration of Interdependence, About Ourselves,* et al.; Bonaro W. wrote *Understanding Fear, How to Think About Ourselves,* et al.; as man and wife they have jointly produced *The Mind Alive.* Howto writers are to other writers as frogs are to mammals; their books are not born, they are spawned. A howtoer with only three or four books to his credit is looked upon as sterile—or, more likely, is just beginning his career. Some howtoers, like the utility man on a ball team, can play any position; a typical example is Raymond F. Yates, whose forty-odd books include *The Antique Collector's Manual, Atomic Experiments for Boys, Weather for a Hobby, Model Gasoline Engines, The Hobby Book of Stenciling and Brush-Stroke Painting, Fun with Your Microscope,* and *How to Make Beautiful Gifts at Home.* More commonly, however, the howtoer turns out the old, reliable model year after year, merely varying the emphasis and the title. Norman Lewis, for instance, has written *Word Power Made Easy, How to Speak Better English, The Lewis English Refresher and Vocabulary Builder, How to Read Better and Faster, Power with Words, Thirty Days to a More Powerful Vocabulary* and two word-power books for kids. Howtoers have, in fact, discovered a method of reproduction unknown to frogs—simple variation of a title. Thus, Betty Cornell followed up her *Betty Cornell's Glamour Guide for Teens* with *Betty Cornell's Teen-Age Popularity Guide,* and Peter Steincrohn simply republished his *You and Your Fears* under the more fashionable title of *How to Master Your Fears.* The importance of the title in howto writing cannot be exaggerated. Sometimes a howto seems to be nothing *but* a title. There are various kinds. Cute: *Your Health, Sir!* (a medical howto). Finger-Jabbing, or Now Hear This: *Sex and You.* Dignified: *The*

Techniques of Creative Thinking. Encyclopedic: *How to Clean Everything.* And, above all, Optimistic: *How to Make Your Daydreams Come True, Be Glad You're Neurotic, You Can Start All Over* (for widows and divorcées), *Love Without Fear, Forever Young, Forever Healthy.* In the bright lexicon of howtoism, there is no such word as failure. "Why should not Failure have its Plutarch as well as Success?" asks Samuel Smiles, the Victorian inspirationalist; his answer was because failure makes "depressing as well as uninstructive reading." Howtoism recognizes failure only as a spur to success, limitations only as something to be overcome, tragedy as merely an error that can be rectified with proper know-how.

IT may have struck the attentive reader that some of the above works are, to say the least, supererogatory. Granted that there's a right way and a wrong way to do everything and that most people want to do things right, one may still wonder whether it is needful, or even possible in a single lifetime, to read up on the technique of *every* activity one engages in. Do we really need, for instance, Dorothy Biddle's and Dorothea Blom's *Christmas Idea Book*—221 pages about Christmas decorations, indexed from "Angels" to "Wreath Theme"? Or Dorothea F. Sullivan's *How to Attend a Conference?* Or Philip Francis's *How to Serve on a Jury?* Or Jeremy Martin's *How to Prepare for Your Draft Test?* (No one has yet written *How to Do Time: A Handbook for Prospective Convicts.**) Can one imagine even the most devoted vestryman studying the New York Protestant Council's *Principles of Church Ushering?* Or the most conscientious housewife sending for the Depart-

---

* Incorrect. "Practically the first thing you are handed when entering a Federal penitentiary," Mr. Leon Wilson of New York City wrote me after the article appeared, "is a blue pamphlet filled with pointers on how to do your time in a 'constructive' manner—choice of companions, dangers of becoming involved in arguments about sentences, personal cleanliness, desirability of careful attention to religious 'duties,' as they are officially called."

ment of Agriculture's *Tools for Food Preparation and Dish-washing?* The answer to the last question is yes; General Eisenhower denounced the dishwashing guide during the 1952 Presidential campaign as "a symbol of the shameful wasting of tax funds," with the result that after he got elected, the Department had to print fifteen thousand more copies of it to meet the demand from alerted housewives.

The fact is the country is in the grip of a howto mania comparable to the dancing mania that swept over Europe in the fourteenth century. There has always been something in the American soul that responds to the howto book. We are an active, ingenious, pragmatic race, concerned with production rather than enjoyment, with practicality rather than contemplation, with efficiency rather than understanding, and with information rather than wisdom. Our frontier past and our industrialized present both incline us toward a preoccupation with technique, with know-how rather than know-why. This fascination with technique has been building up since the war, stimulating, and being stimulated by, a growing spate of howto books on every conceivable department of life and a few inconceivable ones. This may be because as world issues appear increasingly hopeless of solution, people console themselves with efforts in spheres where solutions are more manageable—the practical and the personal. As this trend continues, the man in the American street is increasingly on his happy way toward losing his amateur standing. "Amateur," from the Latin *"amare,"* "to love," is defined by the Oxford English Dictionary as "1. One who loves or is fond of; one who has a taste for anything. 2. One who cultivates anything as a pastime, as distinguished from one who prosecutes it professionally, hence sometimes used disparagingly, as dabbler, or superficial student or worker." "Professional" also has its disparaging side in the Oxford—"one who 'makes a trade' of anything that is properly pursued from higher motives, as a *professional politician."* This disparaging connotation has just about died out over here, however, as the example itself shows— is Truman, or was Taft, looked down on for being a professional politician? Some old fogies may view the rising tide of howtoism with alarm because it professionalizies activities they think should be pursued for love, or for fun, or just for the hell of it. But that man in the American street is insulted if he is called "amateur" or "dilettante," flattered if he is rated "professional" or "expert" or "specialist," and not at all convinced that there is any higher motive for activity than success.

It is—or, at any rate, used to be—different in England, where the cult of the amateur once flourished to such an extent that it was considered a bit ungentlemanly, if not downright shady, to do anything too well. Undue preparation and study of techniques, whether for playing games or running an empire, were thought unsporting; old-style British athletes never went to indecorous lengths in their training, and in consequence they got some nasty jolts from upstart Australians and Americans who took a more professional attitude toward sports and played to win rather than for fun. Similarly, the Athenians looked down on the Spartans for training so intensively for war. The Spartans won the war but the Athenians built the Parthenon.

A completely professionalized life, which is what would result if one tapped the full resources of howto literature, would be monstrous. Albert A. Ostrow's *How to Enjoy Yourself!*, gives detailed instructions on how to enjoy family life, how to have fun on a vacation, and how to get the most out of laughter. Although Mr. Ostrow, who is also the author of *Pastimes for Two* and *Time Fillers,* is an expert enjoyment man, his book is depressing, and still more so is the fact that it was published at all. Besides being intolerably dull, the professionalized life is likely to be complicated. For example, *Esquire Etiquette,* which the editors of *Esquire* got out as "a guide to business, sports, and social conduct," deals thus with the problem of leaving things behind after a weekend visit: "If you're a chronic forgetter, try this: before you leave home, paste a little list inside your suitcase, itemizing all its contents, then check and double-check the list as you pack up to go home." This solution is obviously unworkable, since a chronic forgetter would forget to check the list as he packed up, or if he remembered, it would turn out to be an old list and he would drive his host crazy trying to find things he hadn't brought. Even if it did work, the solution would be more complex than the problem, which is rarely a recommendation. Or take baby sitting, not usually considered a skilled trade, but on which Mr. Kingery lists three technical manuals. The latest of these is Mary Furlong Moore's *The Baby Sitter's Guide,* comprising 120 pages of know-how—all very intelligent, reasonable, practical, and sure to produce a baby sitter of awesome competence, but still 120 pages. Is life long enough, even at sixteen, to master all this? It takes more than a page just to chart the contents of "the baby sitter's kit"—a small suitcase containing, among other things, "bright rubber balls (in different sizes for different ages). A small flashlight. . . . Large-size crayons for small children (ages 2 to 5). Regular-size crayons for children (ages 6 to 10). A dozen or so strips of bright-colored cloth. . . . A pair of blunt-end scissors. . . . Plenty of Scotch Tape. . . . A shiny tin pie pan and big spoon (for very small children)." *Ars longa est* indeed in the howto world.

It is amazing, when one explores this world, to find how many crafts one has been practicing without being aware they *are* crafts. Driving a car, for instance. I have been driving for some forty years without accidents and also without benefit of Paul W. Kearney's *How to Drive Better and Avoid Accidents* or Truman S. Smith's *Driving Can Be Safe.* Or picnicking, which I've been doing even longer without help from John E. Shallcross' *Complete Picnic Book*. Or reading, on which I haven't been wised up since the third grade but on which there is a whole shelf of howtos, including general treatises, like Norman Lewis' *How to Read Better and Faster*, and specialized ones, like I. A. Richards' *How to Read a Page*, which presumably prepares one for Mortimer J. Adler's *How to Read a Book*. (I have looked in vain for *How to Read a How-to-Read Book*.) An impressive newcomer in this category is a large volume called *How to Become a Better Reader*, which Dr. Paul Witty, director of Northwestern University's reading clinic, has written "after twenty years in the reading-improvement field." Dr. Witty estimates that the average person (me?) reads at only two-thirds his potential speed and at half his potential rate of comprehension. To improve, the average person is supposed to read a series of rather mediocre articles and stories Dr. Witty offers, and score for each his reading time and his remembrance of the content. It all sounds practical enough but much too elaborate—a common fault of howtos, whose authors often tell the reader both more than he cares to know (for instance, Dr. Witty presents a seven-page bibliography of nothing more specific than "books you may want to read") and a lot that he knows already ("If you do not learn to appreciate poetry, you will miss a reading experience that can enrich your life," the Doctor observes).

Or bringing up children. Mr. Kingery lists over seventy books on the subject, including *Complete Book of Mothercraft*. Middle-class America has developed the professional parent, who I am not. All Mr. Kingery's listings seem to me dispensable save two—Spock and Gesell, the twin household gods who watch over the American nursery and playroom. Dr. Gesell's painstaking studies, in *Child Development*, of what kind of behavior may be expected from the child at each age level are not only authoritative but reassuring, in the same way the Kinsey Reports are: lots of others do it, too. And Dr. Spock's *Baby and Child Care,* which contains five hundred pages of sensible, definite advice, is, in the Pocket Books edition, the biggest buy in the whole howto field. I have used Spock and Gesell, but to qualify as a professional parent I should have subscribed to *Parent's Magazine* and I should have consulted the following works, each of which covers some problem I solved, or failed to solve, in a hopelessly amateurish way: *Naming Your Baby, Your Child and Other People; At Home, at School, at Play, So Your Child Won't Eat!* (nope), *Better Home Discipline* (uh-huh), *Jealousy in Children, Happy Journey; Preparing Your Child for School, Your Child Can Be Happy in Bed* (m-m-m), *Money Management—Children's Spending,* and *Children's Rainy-Day Play* (by June Birdsong).

Although there are many howtos outlining the duties of adults toward children, I have come across none that reverse the field. It was different in the old days, when etiquette books were as often aimed at children as at their elders. *"De Civilitate Morum Puerilium"* appeared in London in 1532, subtitled "A lytell booke of good maners for chyldren nowe lately compyled and put forth by Erasmus Roterodam in latyne tonge with interpretacion of the same in to the vulgare englyshe tonge by Robert Whytyngton laureate poete." (Howto authors were considerably more eminent then.) The contemporary parallel runs in the opposite direction, as Dorothy Baruch shows with her *How to Live with Your Teen-Ager.* We have come a long way from William Fitzhugh, of Virginia, who observed in 1687 that children would "better be never born than ill-bred."

If howtoism makes life complicated, it also makes it much too simple. To the howto author, and to a commercially important part of the American public, literally every aspect of human existence presents itself as a technical problem that can be solved if one has the know-how.

Everything that was once a matter for meditation and retreat into the wilderness has been reduced to the level of technique. I don't know whether anybody has yet written *How to Be a Mystic* (Simon & Schuster, $3.75), but one E. Stanley Jones *has* written *How to Be a Transformed Person*. Mr. Jones, who is billed by his publishers, the solid and reputable religious-book house of Abingdon-Cokesbury, as "America's Best-Loved Author of Devotional Books," is also the author of, *inter alia, Victorious Living* and *Growing Spiritually,* the second of which promises to "show how to become a spiritually mature person . . . how to cast off anxiety, fear, and worry . . . how to fill the daily life with love, peace, and joy," a claim that ought to be looked into by the Federal Trade Commission. America's B.-L.A.O.D.B. has rung up total sales of more than a million and a half copies. The teachings of Christ are howtoized in Ernest Trice Thompson's *The Sermon on the Mount and Its Meaning for Today,* which the John Knox Press advertises as "not idle idealism but a practical way of life for the atomic age." The problem of belief, which used to bother people in the old-fashioned days, has been tackled by the prolific Dr. Ralph W. Sockman in his current *How to Believe.* Dr. Sockman, pastor of Christ Church here since 1917, and director of New York University's Hall of Fame on the side, writes out of twenty-five-years experience as a broadcaster, during which, he says, he has received "two million and more letters"—or an average of 220 every day, including, as is only fitting, Sunday. Dr. Sockman is nothing if not conscientious. His 224 pages raise and, after a fashion, dispose of every hard question imaginable, from "Is not religious faith pretty largely wishful thinking?" (No, for then "what accounts for the fear of hell?") to "Is the universe honest?" (Yes, because God would not permit man's yearning for immortality to exist if it were not to be satisfied, and a dishonest universe would not satisfy it). Dr. Sockman even grapples with my own particular problem: "If a person has no interest in religion, what can be done about it?" His reply is: (1) "The responsibilities involved in rearing children" may cause one to look to God for guidance; (2) "It often takes emergency or disaster to crack the shell of life and let the gleams of God break through;" (3) "Is it smart to go through life without looking into the force called religion, which has inspired the world's finest art, its greatest music, its noblest living?" Smart or not, and despite some personal experience with children and emergencies, though not with disasters, I failed to get the essential know-how from "How to Believe," maybe because I couldn't read very much of it. (This is a too little recognized drawback to many howto books. The first, and often insoluble, problem is how to get through the book that tells you how to solve the problem.)

THERE is nothing new under the sun, including howtoism. Ovid's "Art of Love," still in print after two thousand years, is a more practical handbook on sex and seduction than many of its modern competitors, although—or perhaps because—it was written without benefit of Freud. As Judaic-Christian morality began to shadow the pagan world, the howto began to yield to the moral treatise, or oughtto. Sometimes the two genres were combined, as in the Book of Proverbs. "Go to the ant, thou sluggard," "A soft answer turneth away wrath," and "Look not thou upon the wine when it is red" are both moral precepts and practical advice. Existing in a general atmosphere of piety, the straight howto tended to have a defiantly cynical and worldly air. Machiavelli advised his prince that he "should make it a rule, above all things, never to utter anything which does not breathe of kindness, justice, good faith, and piety: this last quality it is most important for him to appear to possess, as men in general judge more from appearances than from reality," while the morality of Lord

Chesterfield's famous "Letters to His Son" can be summed up as Save the surface and you save all. Or as Dr. Johnson put it: "They teach the morals of a whore and the manners of a dancing-master." Such works aimed at success rather than virtue, to put it mildly. With the rise of the bourgeoisie and its science, the choice between the howto and the oughtto became—or at least appeared to more and more people to become—unnecessary. The cake could both be had and eaten as the notion spread that if something "worked" it was good and—the other way around—that the virtuous were intended by the Lord to be prosperous as well. The stage was now set for the grand entrance of howtoism.

Our own Benjamin Franklin, that smug Philadelphian paragon of benevolent practicality, was typical of the new dispensation. Bourgeois, industrious, competent, and rationalistic to an almost lunatic degree, Franklin often wrote in the howto vein, as in *The Art of Making Money Plenty, in Every Man's Pocket; Way to Wealth;* and *To a Young Man—on How to Choose a Mistress.* His *Autobiography* and his *Poor Richard's Almanack* also are full of know-how. But the genre by no means began in this country with Franklin. There were several howto-oughttos among our seventeenth-century best sellers—notably Samuel Hardy's *Guide to Heaven* (not a travel book but a book containing "Good Counsel How to Close Savingly with Christ") and Bishop Bayly's *The Practice of Piety.* The trend became secular in the eighteenth century, as etiquette and self-help books multiplied. Lord Chesterfield's *Letters* went through thirty-one American editions between 1775 and 1800. George Washington at fifteen wrote down his own rules of conduct ("In Speaking to men of Quality do not lean nor Look them full in the Face. . . . Cleanse not your teeth with the Table Cloth Napkin Fork or Knife"), and when the celebrated Parson Weems, who later became the first President's myth-making biographer, put out *The Immortal Mentor; or, Man's Unerring Guide to a Healthy, Wealthy, and Happy Life,* Washington gave it a handsome blurb: "Invaluable . . . perused it with singular satisfaction." Eleazar Moody's *The School of Good Manners* ("If thy superior be relating a story, say not, 'I have heard it before.' . . . If he tell it not right, snigger not") sold well throughout the century. Things got even more so in the nineteenth century. Generations of ambitious apprentices on both sides of the Atlantic pored over Samuel Smiles' *Self-Help; with Illustrations of Character, Conduct and Perseverance.* A Philadelphia publisher—the city seems to have been the center for such works, perhaps because of the heritage of Franklin —in 1851 came up with *It Is Never Too Late to Learn: Facts for the People: or Things Worth Knowing. A Book of Receipts in Which Everything Is of Practical Use to Everybody;* and in 1876, Thomas L. Haines and Levi W. Yaggy put out *The Royal Path of Life; or, Aims and Aids to Success and Happiness,* which sold almost a million copies.

The self-help howto has reached its peak in our century, as evidenced by the productions of a number of well-publicized members of the Catholic, Protestant, and Jewish clergy; of late years, these books, reflecting the tolerance produced by a complete lack of cultural standards, have democratically shared the top reaches of the nonfiction best-seller lists. They are "inspirational" self-helps, as against the "success" kind, in which the bead is drawn directly on the $$$ bull's-eye. The "inspirational" writer has no worries at all about repeating himself, since he never says anything definite; any up-to-date cleric can bat out a dozen howtos with his left hand. Earlier "inspirationals" include Arnold Bennett's *How to Live,* Douglas Fairbanks' *Making Life Worth While,* Bruce Barton's *More Power to You* and *The Man Nobody Knows,* and Elbert Hubbard's *Love, Life and Work . . . How to Attain the Highest Happiness for One's Self with the Least Possible Harm to Others,* and the works of those poor-man's philosophers who used to fascinate Mencken and Nathan: Dr. Frank Crane and Ralph Waldo Trine. Among earlier "success" books were Frank C. Haddock's *Power of Will,* which sold 750,000 copies between 1907 and 1927. Nor should two other Menckenian favorites be forgotten— Napoleon Hill, who, still in business at the old stand in 1954, got out a book bearing the almost perfect title, *How to Raise Your Own Salary!,* and the late Orison Swett Marden, author of *Heading for Victory, Pushing to the Front, Getting On,* and other works. A closely related group, no longer so popular as it was several generations ago, when Pushing to the Front looked easier than it does now, is the "success story," or like-me howto, such as P. T. Barnum's *How I Made Millions; or, The Secret of Success* (1884) and *The Americanization of Edward Bok* (1920). The title of the latter, though certainly not its mood, was perhaps suggested by that of a best seller that had appeared some years earlier—*The Education of Henry Adams,* which might be called a not-like-me, how-not-to failure story.

HOW TO books may be divided into the practical-technical and the theoretical-philosophical. The first kind tells how to make something definite, like a boat, or how to engage in some specific activity requiring skill, like playing poker or raising dahlias, while the second kind tells how to make something indefinite, like love, or how to engage in some vague and general activity, like raising children or growing old. The practical howto is legitimate because it deals with activities in which know-how is what is chiefly required for success, because there is some agreement on what success *is,* and because technique is something that can be taught by a book. Although the word "success" crops up constantly in the philosophical howtos, especially in the marriage manuals, this is sheer bravado. Experts are in general agreement on the right way to step a mast or countersink a bolt, but when it comes to methods of achieving happiness, there is little agreement; in fact, the term "expert" is absurd in a field where the problems concern values rather than information.

The most ancient, and still the most important, of the practical howtos are those devoted to what the Britannica calls "the art of . . . converting . . . raw materials, by the application of heat or otherwise, into a digestible and pleasing condition." The Chinese and the Egyptians had cookbooks several millennia before this continent had any recorded cooks; Archestratus of Gela, a great traveler in the time of Pericles, made a collection of exotic recipes that was versified by the indefatigable Ennius; Apicius wrote a famous Roman cookbook; and our own Mr. Kingery's list of books on cooking runs to thirteen pages, his biggest category. There are books on cooking indoors, outdoors, and on shipboard; cooking in ovens, casseroles, chafing dishes, and pressure cookers; cooking to please men and children (but not women); cooking wholesale (*Fish Cookery for 100*) and cooking retail (*Cooking for One,* by Elinor Parker—for two, double the recipe or get Janet Hill's *Cooking for Two*); dietary cooking (*Good Food for Bad Stomachs*), religious cooking (*Cooking for Christ: The Liturgical Year in the Kitchen*), expensive cooking (*Escoffier Cook Book*), and cheap cooking (*500 Delicious Dishes from Leftovers*). In Mr. Kingery's list there are French cookbooks, German cookbooks, Greek, Polish, Hungarian, Japanese, Texan, and even Scotch cookbooks, but, naturally, no English ones; cookbooks whose titles charm the ear (*Continental Dessert Delicacies*) and cookbooks with a leaden, dyspeptic ring to them (*One Hundred and One Quickies* and *The Can-Opener Cookbook*); cookbooks dealing with interesting topics like

376 AGAINST THE AMERICAN GRAIN

mushrooms, oysters, curries, and beefsteaks, and with dull
subjects like wholegrain cereals, salads, and vegetables.

Gardening howtos run a close second in Mr. Kingery's
bibliography, with twelve pages. Photography is third, with
nine pages, but it is hard pressed by works on how to kill
or how to raise various kinds of fish, birds, and mammals—
*How to Tempt a Fish, Crow Shooting, How to Live with
a Cat, Simplified Dog Behavior for Home, Car, and Street,
All About Parrakeets,* and so on. The hottest theme in
practical howtos today is, however, the care and treatment
of the home. In 1940, 44 per cent of all houses were occupied by owners; in 1950, for the first time since Colonial
days, over half the houses of America were occupied by
owners. A former president of the National Association
of Real Estate Boards estimates, by methods not revealed,
that some twenty million Americans are now "earnest
students of houses." And the first thing an earnest American does is buy a howto book.

Etiquette books are a transitional form between the
practical and the philosophical genres. They have been
with us a long time. In stable societies such as existed before the rise of capitalism and exist still among primitive
peoples, etiquette, like many other topics now dealt with
by howto books, was taught by parents to the young and
was also absorbed naturally by imitation. But in our fluid
society, where social classes are ill defined and where
people rise from a lower status and are unsure of themselves, there has for many years been a demand for etiquette books. The dominant ones today are by Emily
Post, Amy Vanderbilt, and the editors of *Vogue,* and all
are addressed to women, the culture bearers in this field,
as in so many other fields of American life. Miss Post's
Etiquette, first published in 1922, and the oldest of the
three, goes in for definite rules, on the lines of a home-
carpentry guide; the two later ones show a tendency to
widen out. *Amy Vanderbilt's Complete Book of Etiquette,*

for instance, is subtitled *A Guide to Gracious Living* and discourses on such matters as the tone of voice one uses in conversing with children, how to behave in taxis and airplanes, the problem raised "when a parent requires [financial] support," and how to cope with celebrities and gossip columnists (grin and bear it). *Esquire Etiquette* is the first full-scale etiquette book for men, which may or may not be a fact of sociological significance, and it, too, covers a much broader area than was ever dreamed of in Emily Post's philosophy, including instruction on "the rush," "the brush," and other aspects of intersexual conduct. Since the Post era, in short, the etiquette book, like etiquette, has melted. An extreme example is Jennifer Colton's *What to Do When,* which has chapters on dealing with gossip, *faux pas,* divorce, and "What to Do When You Want to Get Rid of People." As social forms have grown less rigid, good manners have more and more come to mean a combination of tact and common sense, which is one of the few indisputable advances in American culture in our time. The new-style etiquette book draws heavily on psychology, the ruling science of howtoism, and begins to compete with the problem-solving, and even the inspirational, kind of howto.

THE "philosophical" howtos may be divided into those that tell the reader how to cope with life and those that tell him how to cope with himself—the "problem" books and the "self-helps." The problem most often solved is sex. The exigencies of intersexual conduct have produced a whole howto library, ranging from "charm" books to clinical Baedekers, complete with diagrams. Since a howto is at once a symptom of deficient know-how and a cure for it, the size of this library may be interpreted in contradictory ways. On the one hand, it might appear that Americans are remarkably ignorant and inept in sexual matters. On the other hand, it is hard to see how any American could long remain unenlightened. However, inasmuch as no one reads a howto unless he thinks it can teach him something, and inasmuch as it is quite possible to read one and learn practically nothing, the first hypothesis would seem to have a distinct edge.

Adolescents were the main target of the earlier sexual howtos. Even in the pre-Freudian era, though adults might affect to be above sex, no such fiction could be maintained about adolescents. One celebrated attempt to answer the customary questions—or, more accurately, to give the impression of answering them—was *What a Young Boy Ought to Know,* by Sylvanus Stall, D.D., originally published in 1897 and reissued periodically up to 1936.* This is a book "for boys who naturally ask questions about the origins of their birth and for parents who desire to answer them cleanly and truthfully." The author dwells extensively, though gingerly, on masturbation, backing into the subject with a long discourse on Hands, which are rated as ingenious devices ("Man is the only animal to whom God has given a perfect hand") but also dangerous ones ("We are sorry to say boys use their hands so as to debase themselves below the level of the most degraded brutes"). The tone is extremely pious: Part I is entitled "God's Purpose in Endowing Plants, Animals, and Man with Reproductive Organs." A modern counterpart of Dr. Stall's tract is Evelyn Mills Duval's *Facts of Love and Life for Teen-Agers,* published by the Y.W.C.A. Despite its quasi-religious provenance, this gives only two pages to Dr. Stall's pet subject and even these are mostly debunking the myth of its horrible consequences. There is a great deal on dating and petting and such, and there is a reasonably explicit discussion of physiological matters. (The aptly-

---

* By no means the only instance of longevity in sex how-to books. Dr. Marie Stopes' *Married Love,* which first appeared in 1917, is still on the pocket-book racks in the drugstores, as are Exner's *The Sexual Side of Marriage* (1932) and Fielding's *Sex and Love Life* (1927). There has been, after all, no technological change in the field.

named Dr. Stall ventures no closer to the point in this respect than to quote "And they twain shall be one flesh," though he does come clean about fish and oysters in Chapter IV, which he summarizes, "The Papa and Mama Natures United in the European Oyster . . . The Female Fish Lays the Eggs: the Male Fish Fertilizes Them with a Fluid While Swimming Over the Eggs . . . The Fishes Are Hatched by the Action of the Water and the Warmth of the Sun . . . Baby Oysters and Fishes Are Orphans.") Dr. Stall's rhetoric is unctuous ("my dear young friend"), Mrs. Duvall's brisk and businesslike. The two books, however, share a characteristic common to all howtos, ancient and modern; namely, considerable tolerance for the obvious. "If God had created each person separately, a full-sized man or woman, without parents and without a childhood, all the conditions of our lives would be different from what they now are," speculates Dr. Stall. Mrs. Duvall is terser but no less tolerant. "There are all kinds of grandparents, just as there are all kinds of people," she writes. Somewhere in between Dr. Stall and Mrs. Duvall comes *Face Your Life with Confidence: Counsels for Youth,* by William E. Hulme, Ph.D., chaplain of Wartburg College, in Waverly, Iowa. A match for Dr. Stall in piety and intelligence, Dr. Hulme nevertheless follows Mrs. Duvall in concentrating on boy-girl relationships. His rhetoric is breezy to the point of tornado force. "No one was more death on the phony than Jesus Christ," he states on the dust jacket of his book. In Chapter 33, which bears the heading "God, Sex and You," he advises, "Make your date a threesome with the Lord. Take Him along . . . and He will show you a grand time." Dr. Stall's "my dear young friend" approach is modernized into the real-life, case-history dialogue: " 'How's this for a rare one?' said a tall rangy young man as he pulled up a chair. 'I got a mother-girl friend problem.' 'That's not as rare as you think, Benny,' I said. . . ." In amount of solids per cubic foot of gas, Dr. Stall rates a little higher, mostly for his chapter on the sex life of the European oyster.

After adolescence, for some reason, sex howtos are very largely addressed to women. Maybe it's harder to be a woman. Lawrence K. and Mary Frank have just published *How to Be a Woman,* but I do not find its male counterpart; it seems to be assumed that a man can manage to be a man without special guidance. It is reasonable there should be a whole shelf on motherhood, including Leontine Young's *Out of Wedlock,* which McGraw-Hill advertises as "the first book-length study of the problems of the unmarried mother," but only a couple on fatherhood—and those with condescending titles like *Babies Need Fathers Too* and *Stork Bites Man: What the Expectant Father May Expect.* But why are there two titles listed by Mr. Kingery on how to be a divorcée and none on how to be a divorcé? Why is there a book on wisdom for widows but nothing for widowers? And why, from her teens on, is a woman deluged with works on how to get and keep men, while the male would-be seducer finds little in print later than Ovid?

Betty Cornell leads the way—at least for the recent crop —with *Betty Cornell's Teen-Age Popularity Guide,* which starts, *"Hi!* I'm Betty Cornell," and, like many of these how-to-be-a-woman books, is common sense chromium-plated with charm. In a resolutely bright and chatty way, it covers topics like skin problems, money, and personality ("First of all, let me say that every girl can be attractive"). Whether following Miss Cornell's precepts would make an adolescent girl popular, I don't know, but I suspect that she would become a terrible prig (an up-to-date prig, of course), all glamorized and personalized and adjusted, gay (but not frivolous), serious (but not too), intelligent (but not "intellectual"), and with a pasteurized smile that would curdle your blood as Miss Cornell's on the jacket of her book curdles mine. Lelord Kordel's *Lady, Be*

Loved!, which is blurbed as "What men want in women—candidly revealed by an enlightened male," is realistic and down-to-earth—often a few feet underground, indeed—and is written with the real howto afflatus, earnest and encouraging. "I hope that this carefully planned volume will prove a happy combination of the idealistic and the practical," the author says in the introduction, and the hope is at least half fulfilled. A compendium by Jill Edwards called *Personality Pointers* is now available—overpriced at thirty-five cents—and it seems to have everything, including "Pointers to the Light Touch," which begins, "The third field in which we desire to develop a daily rhythm of habits pertains to those qualities which make us different from everyone else." It also contains a four-page list of "Important Paintings Worthy of Study," and "The Self-Searcher," a twenty-three-page list of questions to ask oneself, which, with some omissions, runs like this: "Do I know what *my* colors are? Do I make my vowels sing? Am I direct, sincere, and simple? Do I know the proper way to sit in and rise from a chair? And I lovable? Am I original? Am I valiant? Have I made a legal will? Do I know where it is? Do I hang up my clothes as soon as I take them off? Do I sew a snap-fastener onto each end of a piece of tape about an inch and a half long, and sew these tapes in the center of all shoulder seams? Am I so poised, so on my center, so innately joyous that life cannot sway me this way and that? Do I always keep my feet close together?"

That so many howtos are written to instruct women in the art of pleasing men and so few the other way around could be taken as evidence of male dominance in American life. It could also be taken as evidence of the contrary, just as the fact that there are manuals for men on how to hunt deer but none for deer on how to hunt men does not indicate the dominance of deer. Crude observation inclines me toward the second theory. In the past, there was the professional lover, always male—the Don Juan or Casanova who made a career out of seduction—and this may well explain why Ovid and other early writers of sexual howtos wrote primarily for men. But in this country today, marriage and not seduction is the career, and the professional lover is replaced by the professional married man and the professional parent. Since women have always been greater partisans of marriage than men, it would seem they have won.

There is no space to do justice to the great army of marriage howtos. Some are serious and useful, like Theodoor van de Velde's pioneering and scholarly *Ideal Marriage*. Some are cheap and worthless, like Eustace Chesser's *How to Make a Success of Your Marriage* and Edwin W. Hirsch's *Modern Sex Life*. Almost all deal with marriage in terms of "success" (a typical title is *Building a Successful Marriage*), and to such an extent that sometimes one feels that one is reading about how to open a profitable stationery store and wouldn't be surprised to see a big horseshoe emblazoned "success" among the flowers at the marriage altar. "Sexual inadequacy will vanish when the husband or wife has achieved the proper mood which 'Pattern of Life Adjustment' affords those who once were victims of bad emotional habits," writes Dr. Hirsch. "By adjusting one's pattern of life so that one finds oneself efficient, one also acquires a philosophy of life. Wastage of emotional energy is generally due to lack of experience in addition to an inadequate cultural background." Dr. Hirsch concludes the success story of one of his adjusted patients: "A charming lady is now his wife and graces a pretentious home in which they entertain in style." One of the less attractive-sounding of the new marriage books is Dr. Abraham Franzblau's *Maturity in Marriage*, which the publishers aver "shows the way to achieve a mature marriage," adding ominously, "and how to raise children so that they may be prepared for it." The industrious Dr.

Franzblau has brought in God to back up Freud: "In his synthesis of religion and psychiatry, Dr. Franzblau makes a convincing brief for monogamy," his publishers say. This exclusive concern of sexual howtos with the married state is a bit confusing. One would think a person had to get married to have sexual problems.

THE aging have never lacked for good advice. Cicero wrote *De Senectute,* and wiseacres like Bacon and Montaigne were not exactly mute on the subject. Such early efforts were not real howtos, being reflective instead of practical, and having on the whole a rather somber approach. Their aim was to reconcile the aging to their lot through the consolations of philosophy, and not to show them how to beat the rap. Their modern descendants are doggedly cheerful, like *Life Begins at Forty,* the perfectly titled best seller with which Walter B. Pitkin got in on the ground floor, way back in 1932; *You Are Younger Than You Think,* by Martin Gumpert, a pioneer in the lately discovered science of geriatrics; and Charles H. Lerrigo's *The Better Half of Your Life: How to Live in Health and Happiness from Forty to Ninety.* More and more Americans are apparently in need of this sort of cheering up, in view of the fact that the national age level has moved steadily upward in recent decades; the average American male, who died at forty-nine in 1900, makes sixty-six or more today, and our women live even longer. Such vital statistics have caused a great burgeoning of howtos. Ray Giles' *Live Better After Fifty* is one of those general vade mecums, covering everything from hobbies and "pension fright" to the art of making friends though elderly. Mr. Giles is a veteran howto writer (one of his earlier works is *How to Retire—and Enjoy It!,* which should be carefully distinguished from Raymond P. Kaighn's *How to Retire and Like It*) and, consequently, a master of jaunty prose. Stylistically, at least, his chapters live up to their titles, some of which are "Star Wagons," "Shake Off Your Handcuffs!," "For Wider Horizons, Keep Learning!," and "There's Always Collecting!" Jerome Kaplan's *A Social Program for Older People,* a manual on organizing social activities for what are delicately termed "senior citizens," sounds practical and authoritative. Having aged enjoyably, senior citizens face one last problem. So far, nothing has come out bluntly titled *How to Die,* but this gap will doubtless soon be filled, as others have been.* Meanwhile, we must make do with the Westminster Press's *And Peace at the Last,* described as "the new Pastoral Aid Book to help the minister and the parishioner come to an understanding and acceptance of death," and Philosophical Library's *The Disposal of the Dead,* a British work which covers "The Law of Burial," "A Short History of Cremation," "The Law and Practice of Exhumation," and other topics, and which, because of the usual English gift for antiquarian anecdote, often makes lively reading.

From one point of view, Dr. Anna K. Daniels' *The Mature Woman: Her Richest Years* is geriatrics, from another it is one more how to for women, and from still a third it is an "inspirational" work. But though the book is hard to classify, it is not hard to evaluate. It is terrible. And it is terrible in a way that is typical of a large, blowzy, sleazy class of psychological howtos, all of which have the kind of chapter headings Dr. Daniels goes in for—headings such as "Women, like Wine, Improve with Years," "Life Is Love, Love Is Life," and "It's Never Too Late to Love." Such books ramble from one psychological cliché to another, stringing these Técla pearls of "scientific" wisdom

---

* Mr. Alan M. Fern of Chicago has since informed me that the gap was filled five centuries ago with *Ars Moriendi,* or *The Art of Dying,* which ran through some eight editions in the fifteenth century.

on a thread of common-sense advice that any grandmother would be glad to supply gratis.

THE most general problem of all is how to be a good person—in Americanese, a happy and successful person—and here the howto reaches its nadir. The quality of howtos fluctuates with their material, the best ones dealing with the most specific and most practical subjects. Many people can write intelligently and usefully about the tricks of their own trade, but to say something new and sound about life as a whole takes an exceedingly uncommon kind of mind, and one that is unlikely to be interested in writing a howto. For instruction in these matters, the wise reader will turn to Plato, Montaigne, Freud or Whitehead, whose work is to howto literature as theoretical physics is to plumbing. But evidently few readers are wise, whence the fact that the late Rabbi Joshua Loth Liebman's *Peace of Mind* and the Reverend Norman Vincent Peale's *The Power of Positive Thinking* were for years on the best-seller lists, and Monsignor Fulton J. Sheen has successfully perpetrated some forty best sellers with titles like *Lift Up Your Heart, Peace of Soul,* and his current *Life Is Worth Living.*

These best-selling philosophizers and their less eminent colleagues in the self-help industry approach the subject from various points of view, but the broad idea has been the same for centuries. It was expressed in the full title of a best seller published here in 1751: *The Family Companion; or, The Oeconomy of Human Life, on the Perusal of which, and following the Instructions laid down therein, all Persons may be Healthy, Wealthy, and Wise, Even from the Crowned Head to the Meanest Subject. Every Man will be here Instructed in the True Methods of Attaining Happiness and Wisdom in whatever Situation in Human Life the Almighty has been Pleased to Place him.*

Of late years there has been an interesting shift from the

"success" book to the "inspirational." The former persists but is read only by the most consecrated salesmen, the most ambitious young tycoons. The general public—its economic worries and competitive zeal relaxed by a generation of prosperity, while in the same interval its anxieties in other directions have been sharpened by the permanent world crisis—is interested less in success than in peace of mind. The secular Dale Carnegie has been succeeded by a rout of rabbis, reverends, and monsignors. Mr. Carnegie offered not a regenerated psyche but merely the key to riches and popularity, and so, illustrating the rule that the more modest the aim the better the howto, he wrote a relatively useful work. This very modesty of aim, however, makes the Carnegie approach obsolete for the present-day reader, worried by even more disturbing problems than how to please the boss. There is, indeed, something alarming in the craving of contemporary Americans for reassuring, soothing messages. Are we as jittery as all that? Certainly one would be justified in thinking so from such as *The Conquest of Fatigue and Fear, Relax and Live, How to Control Worry,* and *Freedom from Fear* (". . . this wise and helpful book shows everyone how to face his fear, understand it, and live with it").

To provide a semblance of peace of mind, the self-help writer has two powerful drugs in his pharmacopoeia: psychology and religion. The psychologists are doing all right. Neither James L. Mursell's *How to Make and Break Habits* nor Harry and Bonaro Overstreet's *The Mind Alive* nor Louis E. Bisch's *Cure Your Nerves Yourself* nor Dorothy C. Finkelor's *How to Make Your Emotions Work for You* will bankrupt their publishers. But the big sales are being rung up by the men of God, perhaps because they can mix psychology—or what passes for it in the howto world—with religion, while the lay psychologists cannot reverse the process with any show of authority. The Reverend Dr. Peale, who is pastor of the Marble Collegiate Church, in

New York City, first hit the jackpot with *A Guide to Confident Living* (1948) and now, with even more success, he has repeated the mixture as before in *The Power of Positive Thinking,* which starts out, "This is simply a practical, direct-action personal-improvement manual . . . a system of creative living based on spiritual techniques." Big medicine, that, every word of it, like the rest of the three-page introduction, which offers the diligent reader the rewards of both worlds—This and the Other—by means of the most powerful incantations: ". . . a practical method . . . successful living . . . peace of mind. . . . You will become a more popular, esteemed, and well-liked individual . . . scientific yet simple principles of achievement, health, and happiness . . . new life, new power, increased efficiency, greater happiness . . . a happy, satisfying, and worthwhile life . . . applied Christianity; a simple yet scientific system of practical techniques, of successful living that works." It works, it's simple (yet scientific), it's scientific (yet simple), it guarantees happiness & success & worthwhileness & peace & salvation, and, best of all, it has been reduced by the intellectual labors of Dr. Peale to a system, a technique (these two words, or synonyms for them, appear twenty times in the three pages), that gets both God and Freud on the job, with "scientific counseling and . . . the application of religious faith." Let the Gold Dust Twins do your work! The actual text of Dr. Peale's book turns out to be a mite disappointing—proves, in fact, to be just the usual collection of real-life stories ("In a busines office high above the city streets two men were having a serious conversation . . .") and exemplary instances ("The late Harlowe B. Andrews of Syracuse, New York, one of the best businessmen and competent spiritual experts I ever knew . . ."), interlarded with the standard commonplaces ("Most of our obstacles, as a matter of fact, are mental in character") and spiced with religiosity (Chapter 4: "Try Prayer Power"). Neither in title nor in content does Dr. Peale's book seem superior to dozens of its competitors, or even distinguishable from them. Why a hundred Americans should plunk down their two dollars and ninety-five cents for *The Power of Positive Thinking* for every two or three who purchase, say, *Peace and Power Within* or *You Can Master Life* is a mystery of mass behavior as puzzling as the periodic suicides of lemmings in the Arctic Ocean. There *might* be something in the nature of a hint if in writing *The Power of Positive Thinking* Dr. Peale had again had the services of Dr. Smiley Blanton, who collaborated with him in writing the earlier *The Art of Real Happiness* and who is blessed with a name quite unimprovable for his particular line of work.*

AN impression may have advertently been left, in the course of this examination, that howto books fall short of delivering the goods they promise. While this is true in general, fairness demands a little more accentuation of the positive than has perhaps been apparent up to now. For one thing, some useful howtos actually do exist. Many, possibly most, of the "practicals" fall into this class; among the ones I have looked into, I was especially struck by Frazier Forman Peters' *How to Buy a House . . . and Get Your Money's Worth*, a marvel of specificity, as is Haydn Pearson's *Profitable Country Living for Retired People; The Pocket Household Encyclopedia,* which offers 627 pages of useful know-how and, with the pocket Spock, covers the practical side of domesticity for seventy cents; and Charles Simmons' *Plots That Sell to Top-Pay Magazines,* which analyzes, with an objectivity bordering on the cynical, the thirty basic plots of slick-magazine fiction. Pickings are slimmer in the "philosophicals," but there are, among

---

* Similarly, *Principles of Canoeing* demanded Pierre Pulling for its author, and who better to write *How to Play the Cinema Organ* than George Tootell? On the other hand, it was surely a mistake to have *So You Think It's Love—Dating, Necking, Petting, and Going Steady* put out by the Public Affairs Committee.

those I ran across, *A Marriage Manual,* by Drs. Hannah and Abraham Stone, which is admirably terse, concrete, and clearly organized; Aaron Copland's *What to Listen for in Music,* which is now available as a pocket book; Rudolf Flesch's *How to Make Sense,* a collection of essays on usage and style that is much better than its vulgar title; and E. Pickworth Farrow's *Psychoanalyze Yourself: Enabling a Person to Remove Unreasoning Fears and Depression from His Mind,* which, also despite its title, turns out to be a serious book, with a foreword by Freud himself, who says he used it to analyze his own dreams.

For another thing, there is a surprising amount of useful information and counsel in many howtos that are not very good as a whole. Even Dale Carnegie's *How to Win Friends and Influence People,* the butt of automatic japes by every good egghead, offers much sound advice and has a perfectly sensible theme, which is that the way to influence people is to persuade them to want what you want by tact, praise, modesty, and a little hypocrisy. There are only two flaws, both typical, in the book: (1) excellent though its advice is, it has been in the public domain a long time—as the author himself points out, Benjamin Franklin said it all, copiously, two centuries ago—and (2) the ore is extremely crude, the golden nuggets of wisdom being impacted in tons of verbosity, platitude, error, and superfluous anecdotage. *Esquire Etiquette* well illustrates the amalgam. On the one hand, its pages on "cigaretiquette" tell you not to smoke in front of a "No Smoking" sign or in church, not to drop ashes on your vest ("even if you are wearing a gray suit") or on the floor, and to offer cigarettes to others when you smoke. On the other hand, there is doubtless some validity in tips like "Whatever you do, don't ever ask a woman if you may kiss her. There's only one thing she can say, but there are several things she can do. Make a move, or don't, but don't have a lot of conversation about it." I'm undecided about the gold content of a third nugget. A man can properly give a woman, it is alleged, "almost anything, so long as it is not personal, not expensive, and not 'maintenance' "—he can give her, for example, a thirty-dollar tennis racket but not a thirty-nine-cent pair of tennis socks. My indecision is due to simple ignorance. If such a rule of thumb really exists among real people, it's a fascinating one, and under certain circumstances it could be essential to know about it.

THE best howto ever published was written by a German named Ludwig Börne in 1823 and is entitled *The Art of Becoming an Original Writer in Three Days*. After so conscientious an examination of the great gray mass of howtoism, we may treat ourselves, for dessert, to the full text of this model of the genre—for among its virtues is the cardinal one of conciseness:

There are men and books that teach Latin, Greek or French in three days, and bookkeeping in only three hours. So far, however, no one has offered a course in How to Become a Good Original Writer in Three Days. And yet, it's so easy! There is nothing to learn, but plenty to *un*learn; nothing to acquire, but much to forget. The minds and books of today's writers are like those old manuscripts where you first have to scratch off the boring disputations of a church step-father or the mumblings of a monk before you get down to a Roman classic. Every human mind is born with beautiful ideas—new ideas, too, since in every human being the world is created anew. But life and education write their useless stuff over them and cover them up.

To see things as they really are, consider this: We know an animal, a fruit, a flower in their true shape; they appear to us the way they are. But would anyone understand the true nature of a chicken, an apple tree, or a rose if he knew only chicken pie, apple sauce, or rose perfume? And yet that's all we ever get in the sciences and in anything that we take in through our minds rather than our senses. It comes to us changed and made over; we never get to know it in its raw, naked form. Thinking is the kitchen where all truths are killed, plucked, cut up, fried, and pickled. What we need most today are *unthinking* books —books with *things* in them rather than thoughts.

There are very few original writers. Our best writers differ from the poorer ones far less than you might think. One writer creeps to his goal, another runs, a third hobbles, a fourth dances, a fifth drives, a sixth rides on horseback: but the goal and the road are common to all. Great new ideas are found only in solitude: but where is solitude to be found? You can get away from people—and at once you are in the noisy market-place of books; you can throw away the books too; but how do you clear the mind of all the conventional ideas that education has poured into it? The true art of self-training is the art of making yourself ignorant: the finest and most useful of the arts but one that is rarely and poorly practiced. In a million people there are only a thousand thinkers and in a thousand thinkers only one self-thinker. People today are like gruel, kept in shape only by the pot; you find hardness and firmness only in the crust, the lowest layer of the people; and gruel stays gruel—if a golden spoon scoops out a mouthful, it tears relatives apart but does not end relationships.

The true search for knowledge is not like the voyage of Columbus but like that of Ulysses. Man is born abroad, living means seeking your home, and thinking means living. But the home of ideas is the heart; if you want fresh water, you must draw from that source; the mind is but a river, on whose banks live thousands who muddy its waters by washing, bathing, flax-steeping, and other dirty business. The mind is the arm, the heart is the will. Strength can be acquired, increased and trained; but what good is strength without the courage to use it? A cowardly fear of thinking curbs us all; the censorship of public opinion is more oppressive than that of governments. Most writers are no better than they are because they have ideas but no character. Their weakness comes from vanity. They want to surpass their fellow writers; but to surpass someone you must meet him on his own ground, to overtake someone you must travel the same road. That's why good writers have so much in common with bad ones; the good one is like the bad one but a little bigger; he goes in the same direction but a little farther.

To be original you must listen to the voice of your heart

rather than the clamor of the world—and have the courage to teach publicly what you have learned. The source of all genius is sincerity; men would be wiser if they were more moral.

And now follows the application that I promised: Take several sheets of paper and for three days in succession, without any pretense or hypocrisy, write down everything that comes to your mind. Write what you think about yourself, about women, about the Turkish War, about Goethe, about the Fonk Trial, about the Last Judgment, about your boss—and after three days you will be beside yourself with surprise at all the new, unheard-of ideas you had. That's the art of becoming an original writer in three days!

So, Ludwig Börne in 1823. Among the practical results of his treatise was the basic technique of psychoanalysis— Freud has told how the idea of using free association was first suggested to him by Börne's little essay. There is no evidence that James Joyce ever read it, but its spirit is his. With *The Art of Becoming an Original Writer in Three Days,* howtoism achieved its greatest triumph a century before it was born.

The Triumph of the Fact

T HE WESTERN WORLD has paid a good deal of attention to data ever since some unrecorded genius had the original idea of finding out whether a live person weighs more, less, or the same as a dead person, not by speculating on the Vital Principle and the Intrinsic Substance of the Soul, as described in Aristotle and the Church Fathers, but by weighing a condemned criminal before and after execution. The historical moment at which this unknown (and indeed fictitious) genius made his great intellectual leap might be called, had it existed, the end of the Middle Ages. But commonplace as this aspect of the scientific method has been for centuries throughout the West, it has achieved in the United States a unique importance. Our mass culture—and a good deal of our high, or serious, culture as well—is dominated by an emphasis on data and a corresponding lack of interest in theory, by a frank admiration of the factual and an uneasy contempt for imagination, sensibility, and speculation. We are obsessed with technique, hagridden by Facts, in love with information. Our popular novelists must tell us all about the historical and professional backgrounds of their puppets; our press lords make millions by giving us this day our daily Fact; our scholars—or, more accurately, our research administrators —erect pyramids of data to cover the corpse of a stillborn idea; our way of "following" a sport is to amass an extraordinary amount of data about batting averages, past performances, yards gained, etc., so that many Americans who can't read without moving their lips have a fund of sports scholarship that would stagger Lord Acton; our politicians are mostly former lawyers, a profession where the manipulation of Facts is of first importance; we are brought up according to Spock, Gessell and the other Aristotles of child care; we make love according to the best manuals of sexual technique; and before we die we brief our wives with Donald I. Rogers' *Teach Your Wife to be a Widow* (Holt, 1953, $2).

SOON after he started sharing quarters in Baker Street with Sherlock Holmes, young Dr. Watson was shocked to find that his brainy friend was an ignoramus:

Of contemporary literature, philosophy and politics he appeared to know next to nothing. Upon my quoting Thomas Carlyle, he inquired in the naïvest way who he might be or what he had done. My surprise reached a climax, however, when I found incidentally that he was ignorant of the Copernican theory and of the composition of the solar system. That any civilized human being in this nineteenth century should not be aware that the earth travelled around the sun appeared such an extraordinary fact that I could hardly realize it.

"You appear to be astonished," he said, smiling at my expression of surprise. "Now that I do know it, I shall do my best to forget it."

Holmes then develops a rather bogus theory about the brain being like an attic with a fixed capacity. "Depend upon it," he concludes, "there comes a time when for every addition of knowledge you forget something that you knew before. It is of the highest importance, therefore, not to have useless facts elbowing out the useful ones." This is too much for the good doctor:

"But the solar system!" I protested.
"What the deuce is it to me?" he interrupted impatiently. "You say that we go around the sun. If we went around the

moon, it would not make a pennyworth of difference to me or to my work."

There is something magnificent about this carrying the principle of utility to its logical conclusion. And Holmes was right to insist that the only good reason for acquiring any knowledge, even of whether the earth goes around the sun or the moon, is its utility for the individual knower. But his idea of utility was too narrowly practical. Like Holmes, I know little about the physical sciences and am not curious to know more—*pace* Sir Charles Snow—but my lack of interest is due not just to their irrelevance to my professional needs but, more important, to my feeling that they aren't useful to me in a broader sense, one which Holmes's logic doesn't recognize—they don't appeal to my kind of mind and feelings. Others do find the physical sciences "useful" in this sense, as I myself find literature and history and philosophy "useful," and so they are rightly concerned to know that the earth goes around the sun rather than the moon. (I do happen to have picked up that particular bit of information somewhere, but in general, when the solar system is on the agenda, I feel like echoing, "What the deuce is it to me?")

One of the nicest touches in the characterization of Sherlock Holmes is that he is not entirely consistent even here. Dr. Watson's well-known inventory of the great detective's knowledge put "Nil" opposite Literature, Philosophy and Astronomy, while Politics was "Feeble," Botany "Variable—well-up in belladonna, opium, and poisons; knows nothing of practical gardening," and Sensational Literature "Immense." This is all as one might expect, but there is one incongruous item: "Plays the violin well." Doyle realized that, to be a man and not a monster, even the folk hero of applied science had to have at least one nonutilitarian interest, one skill of importance to him only because it fed his sensibilities. Cocaine was for Holmes

another method of transcending the brute, confining realm
of the Practical.

SHERLOCK HOLMES'S attitude was American—Ben
Franklin would have approved—but old-fashioned American. It is, of course, still widespread. Our colleges are still
full of what Ortega y Gasset calls "barbarians of specialization": historians who know all about medieval land tenure
but never enter an art museum; economists who manipulate
the tools of their trade with precision and refinement and
get their non-economic ideas from the *Reader's Digest;*
political "scientists"—the quotes are intentional—whose
literary tastes don't differ from their butcher's (Marx read
Aeschylus once a year); English professors who have devoted
a lifetime's study to the Elizabethan sonnet and who haven't
read Auden or Baudelaire.* Our businessmen still are notorious for their lack of interest in arts and letters—they
leave such kickshaws to their wives. Our politicians still are
men of narrow culture; compare Eisenhower and Franklin
D. Roosevelt, whose antipathy to reading is well known,
with such early presidents as Jefferson, Madison and the
two Adamses. The liberal arts are still being displaced in
our high schools and colleges by vocational courses:
Teacher's College, Columbia University, notes with satisfaction that "driver-education is the fastest-growing program in the country's high schools," four out of ten of
which now teach their pupils how to become "safer members of traffic society."

But this aspect of the Triumph of the Fact is a holdover
from the period, which ended roughly with the 1929 stock-
market crash, when our capitalism was still in the stage of
production. Here I am concerned with a kind of fact-

* The atrocious prose style of most of our academic historians, philosophers, sociologists, psychologists, and even literary scholars is a case in
point—*cf.* that three-volume *Literary History of the United States,* edited
by Spiller, Thorp, Johnson, and Canby. The late Richard Chase wrote a
memorable review of it in the winter, 1950, *Sewanee Review.*

fetishism that is characteristic of the age of consumption the economy has moved into. Compared to the straightforward old utilitarian attitude toward Facts, this new approach is decadent, even a bit perverse. Instead of being interested only in useful information, we now tend to the opposite extreme, valuing Facts in themselves, collecting them as boys collect postage stamps, treating them, in short, as objects of consumption rather than as productive tools. This attitude, of course, is not wholly new, as Dr. Watson's horror at his friend's ignorance about the solar system shows; but we have carried it much further. A newspaper review, for example, of Cassell's Encyclopaedia of World Literature has this passage:

How useful it may be to have "Who's Who" information on Arabic, Cuban, Dalmatian, Flemish, Persian, Raeto-Romanisch, Sanskrit and Slovak writers is problematical. But that the information should be available somewhere seems like a good idea and here it is.

We just like to have the little things around, like pets. Because the gathering of Facts is an important part of the scientific method, which with us has more prestige than the artistic, ethical, or philosophical modes of apprehending reality, a confused but powerful notion has arisen that the mere accumulation of Facts is a sensible activity. The Well-informed Man is our Poet, our Sage, our Prophet.*

---

* "This smooth and easy assimilation of fact, this air of over-all sophistication, is what Americans have learned more and more to admire in journalism, in business, in conversation. . . . It is our national style, *intellect-wise*. A recent article in a liberal weekly on 'The Mind of John F. Kennedy' turns out to be an entirely admiring study of Kennedy's range as an administrator. This vocational or psychological use of the word 'mind' is so typical of our time and place that it probably never occurred to the author to extend the word to cover 'beliefs.' Instead we are told that Kennedy's 'marshaling of related considerations' defines Kennedy's mind 'as political in the most all-encompassing sense. The whole of politics, in other words, is to such a mind a seamless fabric in which a handshaking session with a delegation of women is an exercise directly related to hearing a report from a task force on Laos.' And this ability to assimilate on the jump necessary quantities of fact, to get statements of

Journalists like Walter Winchell and John Gunther have made careers out of exploiting the enormous American appetite for Facts. Every year a great range of books appear to soothe our itch for information: digests of everything from anthropology to palm reading; popular encyclopedias and introductory guides to painting, music, philosophy, world history; manuals on birds, politics, economic theory, American history, baseball, polar exploration, what not. Such curiosity is not in itself bad, though often rather pointless, and the level of this kind of popularization is probably higher today than it has ever been before. What is bad is the devaluation of other modes of understanding if only because one hasn't time for everything. (The non-expandable attic isn't the brain, but rather time.) Books that are speculative rather than informative, that present their authors' own thinking and sensibility without any apparatus of scientific or journalistic research, sell badly in this country. There is a good market for the latest "Inside Russia" reportage, but when Knopf published Czeslaw Milosz' *The Captive Mind*, an original and brilliant analysis of the Communist mentality, it sold less than 3,000 copies. We want to know how, what, who, when, where, everything but why.

Henry Luce has built a journalistic empire on this national weakness for being "well informed." *Time* attributes its present two-million circulation to a steady increase, since it first appeared in 1925, in what it calls "functional

---

a problem that carry 'action consequences'—this is what we have come to value as the quality of intellectual all-roundedness or savvy."

So Alfred Kazin in a most perceptive article, "The President and Other Intellectuals," reprinted in his recent collection, *Contemporaries*. Let me add that it is precisely Kennedy's ability to treat a handshaking session on the same plane as a foreign-policy decision that bothers me most about his presidential style. The decision to invade Cuba by proxy was probably taken in the same spirit; the pragmatic failure has been copiously explored by the New Frontiersmen but I have seen no expression of awareness that there was also a moral issue involved. Morality is qualitative, after all, not quantitative, that is, not factual.

curiosity." Unlike the old-fashioned idle variety, this is "a kind of searching, hungry interest in what is happening everywhere—born not of an idle desire to be entertained or amused, but of a solid conviction that the news intimately and vitally affects the lives of everyone now. Functional curiosity grows as the number of educated people grows." The curiosity exists, but it is not functional since it doesn't help the individual function. A very small part of the mass of miscellaneous Facts offered in each week's issue of *Time* (or, for that matter, in the depressing quantity of newspapers and magazines visible on any large newsstand) is useful to the reader; they don't help him make more money, take some political or other action to advance his interests, or become a better person. About the only functional gain, (though the *New York Times*, in a recent advertising campaign, proclaimed that reading it would help one to "be more interesting") the reader gets out of them is practice in reading. And even this is a doubtful advantage. *Times*'s educated people read too many irrelevant words—irrelevant, that is, to any thoughtful idea of their personal interests, either narrow (practical) or broad (cultural). Imagine a similar person of, say the sixteenth century confronted with a copy of *Time* or the *New York Times*. He would take a whole day to master it, perhaps two, because he would be accustomed to take the time to think and even to feel about what he read; and he could take the time because there *was* time, there being comparatively little to read in that golden age. (The very name of Luce's magazine is significant: *Time*, just because we don't have it.) Feeling a duty—or perhaps simply a compulsion—at least to glance over the printed matter that inundates us daily, we have developed of necessity a rapid, purely rational, classifying habit of mind, something like the operations of a Mark IV calculating machine, making a great many small decisions every minute: read or not read? If read, then take in this, skim over that, and let the rest go by. This we do with the surface of our minds, since we "just don't have time" to bring the slow, cumbersome depths into play, to ruminate, speculate, reflect, wonder, *experience* what the eye flits over. This gives a greatly extended coverage to our minds, but also makes them, compared to the kind of minds similar people had in past centuries, coarse, shallow, passive, and unoriginal. Such reading habits have produced a similar kind of reading matter, since, except for a few stubborn old-fashioned types— the handcraftsmen who produce whatever is written today of quality, whether in poetry, fiction, scholarship or journalism—our writers produce work that is to be read quickly and then buried under the next day's spate of "news" or the next month's best seller; hastily slapped-together stuff which it would be foolish to waste much time or effort on either writing or reading. For those who, as readers or as writers, would get a little under the surface, the real problem of our day is how to *escape* being "well informed," how to resist the temptation to acquire too much information (never more seductive than when it appears in the chaste garb of duty), and how in general to elude the voracious demands on one's attention enough to think a little. The problem is as acute in the groves of Academe as in the profane world of journalism—one has only to consider the appalling mass of words available in any large college library on any topic of scholarly interest (that is, now that the "social sciences" have so proliferated, on any topic). The amount of verbal pomposity, elaboration of the obvious, repetition, trivia, low-grade statistics, tedious factification, drudging recapitulations of the half comprehended, and generally inane and laborious junk that one encounters suggests that the thinkers of earlier ages had one decisive advantage over those of today: they could draw on very little research.

If the kind of curiosity *Time* exploits is not functional, neither is it exactly "idle" (which implies a kind of leisurely enjoyment). It is, rather, a nervous habit. As smoking gives us something to do with our hands when we aren't using them, *Time* gives us something to do with our minds when we aren't thinking. This sort of mental indulgence—most of the daily papers should also be included—is considered a sensible use of time, as against "wasting" it on movies or detective stories. Only the honorific status of science can explain why the enjoyment of trivial and debased art products is looked down on while acquiring data in similarly trivial and debased forms is thought admirable.

A FRIEND of mine complained to her eight-year-old child's teacher that fairy tales, myths, and other kinds of imaginative literature had been almost eliminated from the curriculum in favor of handbooks of information. "But children want to know how things work," she was told. "They aren't really satisfied by escape books." Similarly when I asked why my fourteen-year-old son and his classmates were learning a great deal about the natural resources of Latin America but nothing about ancient history or Greek literature, I was told that Latin America is "closer to them" than Homer. I venture to doubt both these explanations. The books I read in my childhood were, with the important exception of *The Book of Knowledge* (and even that had much art and literature in it), almost all works of the imagination, from *Grimm's Fairy Tales* to the *Rover Boys*. Today the informative genre is dominant. A recent very successful series, for example, is called "First Books" and presents a fact-crammed *First Book* on practically everything: ballet and bees, chess and electricity, puppets and presidents, space travel and snakes, trains, trees, trucks—even, God save us, a *First Book of Negroes*. There are three or four extremely popular series of biographies of famous Americans—and also of less famous ones, since the demand seems inexhaustible and there is a limit to rewrites on Ben Franklin of Old Philadelphia. In one recent year, three different firms published children's biographies of a minor Indian chief named Cohees, doubtless on the theory that being (a) real and (b) American, Chief Cohees is "closer" to our children than Achilles or King Arthur.

Speaking on "Mass Information or Mass Entertainment," Dr. George Gallup, a high priest of research, expressed a point of view common among serious-minded, public-spirited Americans:

> One of the real threats to America's first place in the world is a citizenery which daily elects to be entertained and not informed . . . The present lack of interest in the information-type show is shocking. The total number of hours devoted to just two shows, *I Love Lucy* and *Show of Shows,* is greater than the hours spent on all information or educational shows put together . . . In the entire history of radio, not one serious educational show has ever reached top rating, and most programs of this type have such small audiences that they are kept on the air solely for prestige . . .*

The newspaper itself has had to make concessions. Within the last two decades, the number of comic strips printed daily and Sunday has increased by many times, and . . . more adults read the most popular comics on a given day than read the most important news story on the first page . . . In a recent study of metropolitan newspapers, it was found that the average reader spends less than four minutes a day on the important news. He spends ten times as much on sports, local gossips, and the service and entertainment features.

Although we have the highest level of formal education in the world, fewer people buy and read books in this nation than in any other modern democracy. The typical Englishman with far less education reads nearly three times as many books; if

---

* Fact-fetishism is to some extent a class phenomenon, most pronounced among our college graduates, the white-collar "intellectariat" of which the solid core is *Time's* two million readers. As Dr. Gallup's figures here show, the mass audience, though as good Americans they love, honor, and obey The Facts, choose entertainment over information when it comes to making use of their leisure.

he leaves school at fourteen, he reads as many books per year as our college graduates.

Public-spirited, serious-minded—yes—this indictment, delivered at a peculiarly American Ritual of The Fact: the ceremonies at the University of Iowa several years ago, incident to the burying of a "time capsule," a big metal container packed with typical books, newspapers, and other artifacts of our culture, so that future archaeologists will have no trouble assembling The Facts about American twentieth-century civilization. But there are subtleties to the question of Information and Entertainment that are perhaps not dreamed of in the Gallup Poll. That almost all the Entertainment on radio and TV is of poor quality is true, but is the Information much better? Are the dynamic "news commentators" superior to the hopped-up comedians? Are the interviews with senators, the panel discussions that worry some vast problem for twenty-five minutes, the once-over-lightly travelogues-cum-statistics on The Communist Problem in Asia—are these really more "serious" and "cultural" than the "Ed Sullivan Show"? Furthermore, there is, though Dr. Gallup forgets to note it, good Entertainment as well as the cheap kind. The works of Homer, Shakespeare, Bernard Shaw, and F. Scott Fitzgerald are Entertainment, in the Doctor's categorizing —they are certainly not Information. The fault would seem to lie not in the predominance of one genre over the other, but in the low level of both. Finally, may there not be a compensatory relation between Information and Entertainment as practiced in our mass culture, the former being so aridly factual, the latter so tropical, lush, unrestrained? *Kitsch* and Know-How, soap opera and quiz show —neither of these polar extremes provides the temperate climate in which mind and feelings can flourish; one extreme is the craved antidote to the other, each calls its opposite number into being. As the frontiersman escapes from the excessive factuality of his life, preoccupied with food and shelter, by occasional debauches of raw alcohol, raw sex, raw sentiment (the tear-jerking ballad about Home and Mother being a *cultural* bender), so we shuttle from extreme practicality to extreme frivolity, from the hard glare of the prosaic to the inchoate mists of daydreaming, either obsessing ourselves with Facts or compulsively escaping from them.

ONE explanation of our passion for sports, as contrasted with our apathy toward arts and letters, may be that the quality of performance in sports can be determined statistically. It was a Fact, at the moment this essay was written, that Mickey Mantle of the Yankees had a higher batting average than Ken Boyer of the Cardinals—one that could easily have been proved by turning to the figures, which were .388 and .343 respectively—but it is impossible to prove that William Faulkner has a higher batting average than, say, J. P. Marquand. An umpire, like a scientist, deals with measurable phenomena according to generally accepted rules, but the critic works with standards peculiar to himself, although they somehow correspond to standards each of his readers has individually developed. From the purely factual-scientific point of view, the wonder is not that there is so much disagreement in aesthetic matters but that there should be any agreement at all. Agreement *is* possible, however, because, while Faulkner's superiority over Marquand cannot be proved, it can be demonstrated. This is a different operation involving an appeal—by reason, analysis, illustration, and rhetoric—to cultural values which critic and reader have in common, values no more susceptible of scientific statement than are the moral values-in-common to which Jesus appealed but which, for all that, exist as vividly and definitely as do mercy, humility, and love.

In short, arguments about sports performances can be

settled *à l'Américaine* by an appeal to The Facts, since quality can be measured by quantity. This is very reassuring and explains why we take sports seriously, art not. Although, as I have already observed, any stock boy—or any vice-president-in-charge-of-production—knows the batting averages of dozens of ballplayers, half our high-school graduates and a quarter of our college graduates did not read a single book in 1955. And 39 per cent of the college graduates, asked to name the authors of twelve famous works—*Leaves of Grass, Gulliver's Travels, The Origin of Species,* etc.—could not name more than three. (*Time,* May 7, 1956, reporting a Gallup poll). For sophisticated literary criticism one must go to the "little" magazines, but for the same thing in sports one merely opens up the daily paper, or turns to the Luce weekly *Sports Illustrated,* whose savants analyze Ben Hogan's technique with the scholarship (is he in the Jones tradition? the Hagen canon? or was he influenced by the Sarazen school?) and the subtle discriminations (his backswing is perhaps excessive but his putting is classically restrained) of R. P. Blackmur on Henry Adams.* These speculations are reinforced by the *kind* of interest Americans have in sports. Not only are we, as has often been noted, spectators rather than participants, but most of the time we aren't even spectators. Every morning we "follow" sports in the newspapers, scanning the reports—and statistics—on games we have not seen with the nervous avidity of a stockbroker reading the ticker. But while the broker's interest in The Facts is personal and practical, since his living depends on them, the sports

* Luce had the idea, ten years ago, of starting a highbrow cultural magazine, but after dropping a hundred thousand or so and drawing up, via his then advisor for the arts, Mr. William S. Schlamm, a list of "candidates for possibly sustained contact" that included Mr. Blackmur as well as Auden, Eliot, Orwell and Trilling, he gave it up. Perhaps he realized the hopeless insubstantiality of the field. Or perhaps he decided to merge the unborn magazine into *Sports Illustrated,* which has printed articles by James T. Farrell on baseball and William Faulkner on ice hockey and by now may well be negotiating with Mr. Auden for a few observations on Pancho Gonzales' net style.

mania is an abstract passion, unrelated to personal interest and exercised for the most part not even as a spectator, but as a reader. My youngest son, at eleven, on some minor clash at the breakfast table, suddenly and mysteriously burst into tears; I found later that he had just read in the morning paper that the New York Rangers had lost a crucial hockey game.

IT IS their respect for The Facts that makes most Americans so touchingly willing to give information to anyone who asks them for it. We take easily to being profiled, galluped, kinseyed, luced, and otherwise made the object of journalistic or scientific curiosity. With amazing docility, we tell the voice on the phone what TV program we are looking at (so that advertisers can plan their strategy for extracting $$$ from us), answer impertinent questions from reporters (whose papers then sell the answers back to us), co-operate on elaborate and boring questionnaires administered by sociologists (so they can get their, not our, associate professorships), and voluntarily appear as stooges on broadcast shows which bare the most intimate details of our lives or—if we miss out on a Fact question—put us through stunts as if we were laboratory animals in the grip of a mad scientist. In the last instance there is, of course, "something in it" for us, but the prizes seem not worth the humiliation, and I suspect are often more of an excuse than a motive; i.e., that the participant thinks of himself objectively—as an object, a Fact—and not subjectively—in value-terms like pride, honor, or even vanity—and so either welcomes or doesn't mind the public exposure of his Factuality; but that he senses there is something monstrous in this detachment and is glad to conceal it by affecting greed, a base motive but at least a subjective one.

In the thirty years I have been asking people questions as a journalist, I have often wondered why almost no one refuses to give an interview, even though, in many cases, there is more to be lost than gained by so doing. There are some obvious reasons for this—vanity, the American illusion that publicity is always in some vague way to one's advantage, and the pleasure most people take in hearing themselves talk, especially when the listener is professionally sympathetic and informed. A less obvious reason perhaps is that the gathering of data by journalists has come to be accepted as a normal and indeed praiseworthy practice, and people seem to feel it their duty to "co-operate." If the story is about themselves, they take the line they "have nothing to hide," they "stand on the record," and insist they "just want to give you the facts and let you decide." In reality, they often have plenty to hide, but it would be a cynical and untypical American who would admit this even to himself.

These assumptions—that it is virtuous to give information and somehow disreputable to refuse to—would arise only in a highly scientized culture. Commenting on David Riesman's complaint about the difficulty of "drawing a portrait of the autonomous man in a society dependent on other-direction," Paul Goodman has acutely observed: "It does not strike Professor Riesman that his scientific difficulty might lie in the questionnaire form he employs. For why would a free self-regulating person choose to submit to the impertinent questions of a mere theorist, rather than laugh at him, or pat his head, or be Socratically ignorant and turn the questioning the other way, or maybe weep like Heraclitus? If the sociologist seriously has need, on some practical issue, of the opinions and assistance of a free man, then obviously he must come, himself committed to an active position, and argue, reason, implore; risking getting rejected, getting a black eye, or getting more involved than he bargained for." (*Resistance*, December 1949.) The great majority of Americans, of course, are "other-directed" and so give Riesman no trouble; answering questionnaires is a ritual they delight to perform.

Naturally, our government agencies go in for question-naires, and on a scale which amazes Europeans, used though they are to bureaucracy. One of the biggest post-Hitler best sellers in Germany was Ernest von Salomon's *Der Fragebogen* (The *Questionnaire*), an autobiography written in the form of answers to the stupefyingly complex set of questions by which the American authorities tried—and failed—to decide who had "really" been a Nazi. Refugees wishing to flee to the land of liberty must be able to supply an enormous mass of personal data, including every address they have had for the past twenty-five years. The inscription on the base of the Statue of Liberty should be revised: "Give me your tired, your poor, your huddled masses yearning to breathe free, provided they have satisfactorily filled out forms 3584-A through 3597-Q."

OUR popular fiction is curiously affected by our mania for information. We are fascinated by the lingo, the folkways, the techniques peculiar to a profession or a social group, and we want to get the inside dope on the way of life of a telephone linesman, a Renaissance nobleman, a professional game hunter in Africa. The charms of many a best-selling historical novel are not all to be found inside the heroine's bodice. The late Samuel Shellabarger, for example, who made a small fortune turning out this kind of merchandise, had no success until he spent three years "getting up" the background for a heavily documented piece of nonsense called *Captain from Castile*. This was followed by three more erudite best sellers entitled *Prince of Foxes* (the author's clever name for Machiavelli), *The King's Cavalier,* and *Lord Vanity*; and Dr. Shellabarger—he was, fittingly, a professor of English—was at work writing, or rather researching, a fifth when he died in 1954. An obituary noted that he "did painstaking background research for his historical swashbucklers, studying the literature, the customs, and the other externals of the period. 'I suppose I am a fool,' he once said, 'but if I have a character going from one side of the city to another, I want to know what he sees and hears.' " What he thinks and feels might also have been interesting, though probably not in this particular instance.

In the art workshops of the Renaissance, the figures in the foreground were done by the master, while the apprentices filled in the background, a sensible division of labor which has been inverted by the fiction hacks of today, who work up the background with great care and botch in a few lay figures to carry the story. The same process may be observed in the evolution of the *New Yorker* profiles, which began thirty years ago as brief studies in personality and have grown steadily more encumbered with documentation, until often the reader feels he has learned everything about the subject except what kind of a person he is. Or in the Luce magazines' obsession with factual trivia—a huge and expensive research department produces a weekly warehouseful of certified, pasteurized, 100 per cent double-checked Facts, and everything is accurate about any given article except its main points. Or in Hollywood, which gives us miracles in "authenticity" of costume and furniture, all verified by experts, but doesn't bother about the authenticity of the human beings who wear the costumes and sit on the period chairs, reversing Marianne Moore's famous description of the poet as one who creates "imaginary gardens with real toads in them." (In Hollywood, the gardens are real but the toads are synthetic and all of them are named Natalie Wood.)

A case in point is the best-selling novel, *Andersonville*, a sprawling compost heap of historical research piled up by MacKinlay Kantor, one of our most diligent and successful literary artisans. Or cf., the typical *Saturday Evening Post* story. In one specimen, two lovers converse as follows:

"Pop won't admit it," said Maggie, "but he's going to lose his shirt. He was low bidder on a job of building a con-

crete flume across Arroyo Diablo. That's on the desert, about
a hundred miles east of here."

"Pop's been low bidder on every job he's built," Dugan
said. "That's how contractors get work . . ."

"The bolts at the corners of the timber collars that locked
the forms together sheared in two," Maggie said.

"That's important," Dugan declared. "A bolt that size
wouldn't shear under a pressure of less than 1000 pounds. The
timbers would have split first." [to which Maggie, in love's
eternal duet:] "Only these bolts didn't get sheared in a mate-
rials-testing lab. The real collar bolts were removed and the
sheared ones hammered back in place top and bottom."

After seven thousand words of this, one has learned a
good deal about the contracting business and about the
tensile qualities of timber bolts but not much about
Maggie and Dugan. This is reasonable (if not sensible),
since the lovers are only stooges for the timber bolts. Another idyll, "No Room for Love," turns on the *echt*-Amer-
ican theme, should a boy marry his girl or his car, and
produces yards of dialogue like:

"What do you do when the head bolts are frozen?"

"You tap them easy with a hammer. You don't want to crack
the head. Then you put a long-handled wrench . . ."

"You got rust on your cylinder block. Face it."

"For Pete's sake, listen, will you? Krucek's got a used '41
block in there, never been rebored."

"You got a '39 car. It'll mean new pistons, and you got a
pitted camshaft."

Fairness compels me to note that this dialogue is not between the lovers, and also that the car loses out: "For once
in his life, Charlie was more interested in a girl than a
motor."

THE Triumph of the Fact in modern fiction is, of course,
by no means limited either to America or to mass culture.
It is one of the things that distinguish the nineteenth-

century novel, and is obviously connected with the industrial revolution and the rising prestige of science. Balzac
and Zola aspired to nothing less than to re-create, in all
their minute factual details, the different occupational and
class worlds of their times; the former succeeded better
than the latter precisely because he relied on inventive passion rather than scientific method—as Joyce succeeded in
Ulysses, for the same reason. Flaubert was an especially
interesting case, from this point of view, split as he was between naturalism and symbolism, science and art-for-art's-
sake. In *Madame Bovary* the conflicting drives are harmonized into a masterpiece, but the synthesis breaks down
in *Salammbô* and *Bouvard and Pécuchet.* Flaubert could
escape the prosaic nineteenth century by turning to ancient
Carthage, but the naturalistic technique, which he could
not escape, produces a dead, cold, and—in the scenes of
battle and torture—even repulsive effect. *Bouvard and
Pécuchet,* which is meant to satirize the bourgeois mania
for accumulation and for technical knowledge, becomes itself a monstrous example of the thing he is attacking, because of the author's own obsession with technique (style)
and accumulation (naturalistic detail).

The same strain runs through our own literature. It appears in Poe's fascination with solving cryptograms and
perpetrating hoaxes, his invention of the detective story—
the only literary genre whose point is the discovery, by
scientific method, of a Fact (whodunit?)—and especially
in his preoccupation with technique. His celebrated account, in "The Philosophy of Composition," of how he
wrote *The Raven* reads like a cookbook:

Holding in view that a poem should be short enough to be
read in one session as well as have that degree of excitement
which I deem not above the popular, while not below the
critical taste, I reached at once what I conceived the proper
length for my intended poem—a length of about 100 lines. It
is, in fact, 108 . . . Regarding, then, Beauty as my province

[he has given a page of reasons] my next question referred to the *tone* of its highest manifestation—and all experience has shown that this tone is one of *sadness* . . . The length, the province, and the tone being thus determined, I betook myself to ordinary induction, with the view of obtaining some artistic piquancy which might serve me as a keynote in the construction of the poem. [He decides on a refrain whose application should be continually varied, and which therefore must be brief, ideally one word.] The question now arose as to the character of the word which was to form the close of each stanza. That such a close, to have force, must be sonorous and susceptible of protracted emphasis, admitted no doubt; and these considerations inevitably led me to the long *o* as the most sonorous vowel, in connection with *r* as the most producible consonant . . . It would have been absolutely impossible to overlook the word, "Nevermore . . ." The next desideratum was a pretext for the continuous use of this one word . . . etc.

Whether Poe actually used this recipe in composing *The Raven* is doubtful—I'm inclined to agree with Marie Bonaparte that he didn't, though for common-sense rather than Freudian reasons—but only a nineteenth-century writer would have gone in for this particular kind of mystification.

In their descriptions of the techniques of whaling and of river piloting, large sections of *Moby Dick* and of *Life on the Mississippi* read like *Fortune* articles written by geniuses, if this may be conceived. (It almost happened with James Agee's *Let Us Now Praise Famous Men*.) The whole middle section of *Moby Dick* is a strange mixture of story and encyclopedia, with chapters on such topics as "The Line" (what kind is used, how it is coiled in the tubs, etc.), "The Crotch" ("a notched stick of a peculiar form, some two feet in length, which is perpendicularly inserted into the starboard gunwhale near the bow, for the purpose of furnishing a rest for the wooden extremity of the harpoon"), "The Blanket" (all about the whale's skin), "The Head," "The Tail," and "Measurement of the Whale's

Skeleton." Even in the climactic last chapters, when the quarry is at last engaged, Melville adds a typical footnote: "This motion is peculiar to the sperm whale. It receives its designation (pitchpoling) from its being likened to that preliminary up and down poise of the whale-lance. . . ." *Moby Dick* is a happy Triumph of the Fact: from an intense concern with the exact "way it is," a concentration on the minutiae of whaling that reminds one of a mystic centering his whole consciousness on one object, Melville draws a noble poetry. Whitman also draws poetry, of a less noble kind, from Facts; a good deal of *Leaves of Grass* reads like, in Emerson's phrase "an auctioneer's inventory of a warehouse":

> *The paving man leans on his two-handed rammer, the*
> *reporter's lead flies swiftly over the notebook,*
> *the sign painter is lettering with blue and gold.*

> *The housebuilder at work in the cities or anywhere,*
> *The preparatory jointing, squaring, sawing, mortising,*
> *The hoist-up of beams, the push of them in their places,*
> *laying them regular.*
> *Setting the studs by their tenons in the mortises*
> *according as they were prepared . . .*

Many of his poems, as *Salut au Monde*, try magically to swallow the world by naming everything in it; to incorporate it all in Walt, democratically embracing everything and everybody, repeatedly proclaiming that one Fact is just as good as another Fact, that it is justified by merely existing (in Walt's cosmic, omnivorous belly).

> *I do not call one greater and one smaller,*
> *That which fills its period and its place is equal to any.*

> *I am large, I contain multitudes.*

Even the corpse is on his visiting list:

> *I think you are good manure, but that does not offend me.*

Where Melville contemplated his Facts singly, turning each over in his mind until it had yielded up both its own concrete quality and its meaning as symbol, Whitman was too often the greedy child, grabbing Facts in double handfuls and dropping them quickly to pick up bright new ones:

> *Beginning my studies, the first step pleas'd me so much,*
> *The mere fact consciousness . . .*
> *I have hardly gone and hardly wish'd to go any farther,*
> *But stop and loiter all the time to sing it in ecstatic songs.*

The quality that all these celebrations of the Fact, from the *Satevepost* to *Moby Dick,* have in common is knowingness. "This is the way it is." One could add *The Red Badge of Courage,* a tour de force of the Knowing ("You think a battle is a planned, orderly affair, but it's really like this") which has been overrated; Stendhal and Tolstoy did it first —and better, raising the *knowing* to the higher plane of understanding. There is Hemingway: "This is how you go about shooting water buffalo. You take a .44 Borley-Thompson express rifle with supercharger and you . . ." Or Fitzgerald: "Let me tell you just what it is like to be very rich in the United States in 1924." Or their epigone, John O'Hara, who, lacking their passion and their sense of literary form, depends wholly on verisimilitude, which he gets by a magisterial "placing" of each character at his or her precise social level by means of carefully discriminated details, so that in O'Hara's world (though possibly not in the real one) a Yale man gets drunk in a wholly different way from a Penn State man. Knowingness was the stock-in-trade of Rudyard Kipling, the only widely popular writer since Dickens who can be called a genius (though of course a much lesser one). The note is struck in the opening sentences of most of his *Plain Tales from the Hills,* as:

Far back in the seventies, before they built any public offices at Simla and the broad road round Jakko lived in a pigeon-hole in the P.W.D. hovels, her parents made Miss Gaurey marry Colonel Schreiderling.

Or:

There are more ways of running a horse to suit your book than pulling his head off in the straight. Some men forget this. Understand clearly that all racing is rotten—as everything connected with losing money must be. In India, in addition to its inherent rottenness, it has the merit of being two-thirds sham . . . Every one knows every one else far too well for business purposes. How on earth can you rack and harry and post a man for his losings, when you are fond of his wife, and live in the same Station with him? . . . If a man wants your money he ought to ask for it . . . instead of juggling about the country with an Australian larrikin, a "brumby," with as much breed as the boy, a brace of *chumars* in gold-laced caps, three or four *ekka*-ponies with hogged manes, and a switch-tailed demirep of a mare called Arab because she has a kink in her flag. Racing lead to the *shroff* quicker than anything else.

Being *Kitsch*—though of the highest grade—Kipling's *Plain Tales* exploit the realistic method rather than use it. His is a bright, dramatic, easily assimilated kind of naturalism, so entertaining that it brings out more clearly than more serious works could one reason for our thirst for the Facts: namely, that the modern world being vast, abstract, and hard to understand, there is something reassuring about a hard, definite Fact. Because we can understand the parts—the Facts—we have the comforting illusion that we understand the whole. And Kipling enhances the appeal of his Facts by limiting them to a very small world. All the folklore, the customs, the gossip, the social color and feel of British India in the late nineteenth century are there, handled with the affection and the untroubled mastery of the village historian. He invites us right inside, and we feel at home, as we cannot in the uncomfortably complex real world. The peculiar charm of Kipling's India, like Gatsby's

Long Island or D'Artagnan's France or Dickens' London,
lies partly in the knowingness with which it is presented.

MAY not much of Senator McCarthy's puzzling success—
how did he get so far on so little?—be laid to the mingled
boredom and fear the American feels vis-à-vis world politics, the boredom being caused by inability to understand
and the fear by inability to act. Like Kipling, McCarthy
created a small, neat, understandable world—*cops and robbers, to be continued in our next headlines*—in which the
issues were reduced to personalities, the shadings eliminated in favor of melodramatic black and white. It was a
world the newspaper reader could understand and where
he could see Results. That it was also as fictional a world
as Kipling's—more so, in fact, since Kipling knew a lot
about British India while McCarthy never bothered to find
out anything about American Communism—was irrelevant. The Senator was a good enough dramaturge to persuade the public to believe in his provincial little world,
and his daily revelations had the same interest that village
gossip does. After all, since when did gossip have to be true
to be interesting?

In other ways, also, McCarthy's years of power—surely
one of the strangest episodes in our political history, which
suffers from no paucity of the cockeyed—represented a
melancholy Triumph of the Fact.

For half a century, what Theodore Roosevelt contemptuously dubbed "muckraking"—after Bunyan's Man with a
Muck-Rake—was a monopoly of the liberals. The reformers' ritual began, and often successfully ended, with
Getting The Facts. Popular magazines flourished on the
formula, notably *McClure's* with series like Lincoln Stef-
fens' "The Shame of the Cities" and Ida Tarbell's "History
of the Standard Oil Company." Brandeis invented the
"sociological brief," which substituted socio-economic data
for legal reasoning—in a ratio of 50 to 1 in his famous 1907

brief in defense of the Oregon Ten-Hour Law. "There is no logic that is properly applicable to these laws except the logic of facts," he explained, echoing Tom Paine's "Facts are more powerful than arguments." But the reformers' chief instrument was the legislative investigating committee, from the Hughes insurance investigation (1905) and the Pujo Committee's hearings on the "Money Trust" (1913) through the Nye munitions investigation (1933)* to the LaFollette civil-liberties hearings (1937) and the massive economic researches of the Senate's "Monopoly Committee" (1938-40). The assumption was that The Facts would favor civic virtue, and indeed they generally did. Malefactors trembled when Al Smith, the reform governor of New York, rasped "Let's look at the record!"

The junior Senator from Wisconsin turned Let's-Get-the-Facts in the opposite direction. He was not the first to try, of course. In the 'twenties and 'thirties, the Lusk and Fish committeess of the New York legislature, and the "Dies Committee" (on Un-American Activities) of Congress, among others, investigated Communism; but their chairmen lacked McCarthy's flair for melodrama. More important, the times were not ripe: it was not until the late 'forties, when Soviet Russia first emerged as a powerful and dangerous enemy, that the national temper grew edgy enough for the rise of a McCarthy.

The puzzling thing about McCarthy was that he had no ideology, no program, not even any prejudices. He was not anti-labor, anti-Negro, anti-Semitic, anti-Wall Street, or anti-Catholic, to name the phobias most exploited by previous demagogues. He never went in for patriotic spellbinding, or indeed for oratory at all, his style being low-keyed and legalistic. Although he was often called a fascist and compared to Hitler, the parallel applied only to his

---

* Whose "merchants of death" theme was so infectious that even *Fortune* caught it, producing a muckraking feature of its own, "Arms and the Men," 9,650 of whose 10,000 words were devoted to the infamies of foreign munition-makers, leaving just 350 for the DuPonts and other native sinners.

methods. Not only was the historical situation hopeless for a radical change like fascism, the country being unprecedentedly prosperous, but McCarthy never showed any interest in reshaping society. Half confidence man, half ward politician, he was simply out for his own power and profit, and he took advantage of the nervousness about communism to gain these modest perquisites. The same opportunism which made him dangerous in a small way prevented him from being a more serious threat, since for such large historical operations as the subversion of a social order there is required—as the examples of Lenin and Hitler showed—a fanaticism which doesn't shrink from commitment to programs which are often inopportune.

The contrast in demagogic styles between Hitler and McCarthy is related to national traits—and foibles. Hitler exploited the German weakness for theory, for vast perspectives of world history, for extremely large and excessively general ideas; McCarthy flourished on the opposite weakness in Americans, their respect for the Facts. A Hitler speech began: "The revolution of the twentieth century will purge the Jewish taint from the cultural bloodstream of Europe!" A McCarthy speech began: "I hold in my hand a letter dated . . ." He was a district attorney, not a messiah.

Each of the bold forays which put the Wisconsin *condottiere* on the front pages between 1949 and 1954 began with factual charges and collapsed when the facts did: the long guerilla campaign against the State Department; the denunciation of General Marshall as a traitor working for the Kremlin (set forth in a 60,000 word speech in the Senate, bursting with Facts, none of them relevant to the charge); the Voice of America circus; the Lattimore fiasco; and the final suicidal Pickett's charge against the Army and the President. That the letter dated such-and-such almost always turned out to have slight connection with the point he was making (on one occasion it was a blank sheet of paper), that the Facts about the Communist conspiracy he presented with such drama invariably proved to be, at best, irrelevant and, at worst, simple lies—this cramped McCarthy's style very little.* He had working for him our fact-fetishism, which means in practice that a boldly asserted lie or half-truth has the same effect on our minds as if it were true, since few of us have the knowledge, the critical faculties or even the mere time to discriminate between fact and fantasy.

Furthermore, our press, in its typical American effort to avoid "editorializing"—that is, evaluating the news, or The Facts, in terms of some general criterion—considers any dramatic statement by a prominent person to be important "news" and, by journalistic reflex, puts it on the front page. (If it later turns out that the original Fact was untrue, this new Fact is also duly recorded, but on an inside page, so that the correction never has the force of the original non-Fact. Such are the complications of "just giving the news" without any un-American generalizing or evaluating; in real life, unfortunately, almost nothing is simple, not even The Facts.) A classic instance was the front-paging, several years ago, of a series of charges against Governor Warren of California, who was up before the Senate for confirmation as Chief Justice of the U.S. Supreme Court. The charges were serious indeed, but the following day they were exposed as the fabrications of a recent inmate of a mental hospital; despite their prima facie absurdity, they had been automatically treated as major news because the notoriously irresponsible Senator Langer had given them to the press over his name.

---

* Nor did it bother Jack Lait and Lee Mortimer, two Hearst journalists who during the McCarthy Era turned out a series of sensational best sellers—*New York Confidential, Chicago Confidential, U.S.A. Confidential,* etc. These were fact-crammed guidebooks to the seamier side of American life which differed in two ways from the old exposés of the muckrakers: the Facts were marshaled *against* the underdog (Negro, radical, Jew, labor union) and—they were often not Facts.

In the case of McCarthy, the tragicomic situation prevailed for years that although the *New York Times* and most of the country's other influential newspapers were editorially opposed to him, they played his game and, in the sacred name of reporting The Facts, gave him the front-page publicity on which his power fattened. (Thus when he "investigated" the scientists at Fort Monmouth, the *Times* solemnly printed his charges day after day on page one, and then, some weeks later, printed a series of feature articles of its own, demonstrating that the charges were without substance; a little checking in the first place might have evaluated the Monmouth "investigation" more realistically and relegated it to an inside page; but this, of course, would have been "editorializing.") When McCarthy's charisma evaporated after the TV public had had a chance to see him in action during the army hearings and after the Watkins Committee had reported unfavorably on his senatorial conduct, the press began running his exposés on the inside pages and he disappeared like a comic-opera Mephisto dropping through a trap door.

SIGNIFICANTLY, the Communist issue in postwar America took the form not of a confrontation of principles or even of a propaganda battle, but rather of legalistic haggling over Facts. (McCarthy's muckraking-in-reverse was simply the demagogue's instinctive adaption to the *Zeitgeist*.) The Hiss trial, the Lattimore imbroglio, the prosecution under the Smith Act of the Communist Party leadership, all turned on questions of fact: Did Hiss turn over State Department documents to Chambers? Was Lattimore working with the comrades at the Institute of Pacific Relations? Were the Communist leaders conspiring to advocate the overthrow of the government by violence? In the simple old days, revolutionaries used the courts as forums: Trotsky's ringing indictment of capitalism at his trial for leading the 1905 revolution, Debs's similar court-

room behavior during the First World War. But Hiss
and Lattimore insisted they had always been respectable
to the point of tedium, and the Communist leaders, far
from lecturing Judge Medina on the evils of capitalism,
competed with the prosecution in avowals of devotion to
Jeffersonian democracy. The post-Stalin degeneration of
Communism into conspiratorial *real-politik* was in part
responsible; cf., the widespread use of the Fifth Amend-
ment to assert the right *not* to state one's politics (the old-
style radicals had insisted on the opposite right).* But there
was also involved the American habit of reducing large
issues to matters of Fact. What other nation would have
spent so much time, money, and newsprint to arrive at
definitive political biographies of so many of its citizens?
(Consider one aspect of the federal government's security
checks alone: the amount of expensive man-hours devoted
by earnest, clean-cut young FBI agents, all of them law-
school graduates, to interviewing many thousands of
citizens about the political and personal—sex and alcohol
—pasts of many thousands of other citizens working for the
government or aspiring to do so.) The evil effects of this
obsession have been copiously exposed in the liberal press,
and for the most part I agree, but there is also perhaps
discernible a political virtue. Granted the criteria for "pro-
Communism" were much too broad, still at least a serious
attempt was made in each individual case to establish some
kind of factual basis for judgment; whole classes of people
were not condemned en masse.

One of the most frightening aspects of the Moscow Trials
was that both defendants and accusers seemed to have lost

---

* I do not mean to imply that all, or even most, of those who "took the
Fifth" did so to avoid stating past or present Communist loyalties. Some
sincerely believed that inquiries into political allegiances are contrary to
democratic principles; more were reluctant to admit party membership
in the past lest they be forced to tell on old friends or associates. One can
sympathize with such motives and yet admire more the behavior of our
pacifists—the heirs in this respect of Debs and Trotsky—who are willing,
indeed eager to "bear witness" publicly to their dissident beliefs.

the ability to distinguish between a fact (the defendant committed this or that criminal act) and an inference (his political views were such that it was reasonable to suppose that he committed the act, or, if he didn't, it was merely because he didn't have a chance to, and so he was guilty because he was the sort of person from whose politics certain criminal acts "logically followed"). In Soviet Russia questions of fact are decided by appealing to general principles, just as it was in the Middle Ages—the wheel has come full circle again.

I prefer our own naïve, unimaginative overvaluation of the Fact. It leads us, at least in form, to think of questions as having two sides. Thus a widely distributed monthly financed by a Texas millionaire of pronouncedly illiberal views is called *Facts Forum* and goes in for features like the one in the November, 1955, issue: "Who Is Right about the Fund for the Republic?" in which Commander Collins of the American Legion and President Robert M. Hutchins of the Fund for the Republic state their antithetical views at equal length. Or there is the example of Fulton Lewis, Jr., a virulently antiliberal radio commentator who used to attack the Fund for the Republic almost nightly. When the Fund bought time on the same network to ask listeners to write in for their annual report, Mr. Lewis commented (September 15, 1955): "Now this, I think, is a really excellent idea, and I want to co-operate with Mr. Hutchins in full. So let me urge you strongly to send for the annual report of the Fund for the Republic, 60 East Forty-second Street, New York City. In that way you can have before you this report and see the pretty words and grandiose language while I am explaining to you night by night what each item means and what is really going on."

Perhaps Mr. Lewis' let's-look-at-the-record, nothing-up-my-sleeves approach was hypocritical and demagogic. But hypocrisy is preferable to unashamed evil, if only because it puts some restraints on behavior; in the old saw about

hypocrisy being the tribute that vice pays to virtue, everyone accents "vice"; but one might also emphasize "tribute."
As for demagogy, it seems to me good that we have a
tradition that makes this kind of demagogy profitable. It is
surely better to overvalue Facts than to deny their existence. There was something moving about Vice-President
Nixon's anguished cry to the Communist-led students in
Lima when they stoned him during his 1958 Latin American tour: "Don't you want to hear *facts?*" Attorney-
General Kennedy took the same tack, more successfully,
when he faced a noisy mob of Socialist students in Japan
last winter.

BEST of all, however, is to understand the nature of Facts
and to treat them accordingly, neither with Russian contempt nor American awe. "A commodity," Marx writes on
the first page of *Capital,* "is a very queer thing, abounding
in metaphysical subtleties and theological niceties." So is
and does a Fact. The word comes from the Latin factum (a
thing done, a deed) and is defined by the Oxford Dictionary
as "a particular truth known by actual observation or authentic testimony as opposed to what is merely inferred; a
datum of experience as distinguished from the conclusions
that may be based upon it." Facts are thus the raw material
from which general conclusions, or theories, may be inferred. But the process also runs the other way. The meaning of a Fact, indeed its very existence in a psychological
sense, depends on the context in which it appears—depends,
that is, on "the conclusions that may be based upon it." A
Fact by itself is useless, impotent, phantasmal, as weak and
wavering as the shades of the dead that Ulysses met in the
underworld. And as the shades became strong enough to
speak only by drinking the blood from Ulysses' sacrifices, so
a Fact can acquire reality only by drinking the blood of
theory, by becoming related to other Facts through some
kind of assumption, hypothesis, generalization. Indeed, a

Fact not thus fortified is usually too weak even to be perceived; as a rule, one pays attention only to data that fit into some general idea of things one already has.* "The facts speak for themselves," we say, but this is just what they don't do. Rather, they are like Swift's Laputans who have to be roused to practical discourse by attendants touching their lips with inflated bladders. Here, the bladders are one's assumptions.

The meaninglessness of facts *qua* facts is shown in the opening scene of Dickens' *Hard Times* where Mr. Gradgrind, the type of "hard-headed" Victorian bourgeois, tries to explain his doctrine to a classroom of children:

"Now," says Mr. Gradgrind, "what I want is Facts. Teach these boys and girls nothing but Facts. Facts alone are wanted in life. Plant nothing else, and root out everything else. You can only form the minds of reasoning animals upon Facts: nothing else will ever be of any service to them. This is the principle on which I bring up my own children, and this is the principle upon which I bring up these children. Stick to Facts, Sir!"

· · · · ·

"Bitzer," said Thomas Gradgrind, "your definition of a horse."

"Quadruped, Graminivorous. Forty teeth, namely twenty-four grinders, four eye-teeth and twelve incisors. Sheds coat in the spring; in marshy countries, sheds hoofs, too. Hoofs hard, but requiring to be shod with iron. Age known by marks in mouth." Thus (and much more) Bitzer.

· · · · ·

* Cf., the Ames experiments, at Dartmouth, in visual perception. In one of the simpler demonstrations, a playing card of usual size is placed some distance in front of one twice as big. The spectator almost always sees the more distant card as the nearer one, since what he "sees" is determined by two assumptions based on past experience: that playing cards are always the same size (hence he assumes the bigger card to be this size) and that of two objects the same size, the one that appears to be smaller will be the more distant one. Thus his already-held theory about the size of playing cards prevents him from accepting the Fact reported by his optic nerve.

"Very well," said this gentleman, briskly smiling, and folding his arms. "That's a horse. Now let me ask you girls and boys, would you paper a room with representations of horses?"

After a pause, one half the children cried in chorus, "Yes, sir."

Upon which the other half, seeing in the gentleman's face that yes was wrong, cried out in a chorus, "No, sir!"—as the custom is, in these examinations.

"I'll explain to you then," said the gentleman after another and a dismal pause, "why you wouldn't paper a room with representations of horses. Do you ever see horses walking up and down the sides of rooms in reality? in fact? Do you?"

"Yes, sir!" from one half. "No, sir!" from the other.

"Of course No," said the gentleman, with an indignant look at the wrong half. "Why, then, you are not to see anywhere what you don't see in fact; you are not to have anywhere what you don't have in fact. What is called Taste is only another name for Fact."

Before Bitzer gives his factual picture, Mr. Gradgrind has asked Sissy Jupe to define a horse. She is unable to satisfy him although her father is a horse trainer and she has ridden and worked with horses all her life. This, indeed, is precisely why she cannot conceive of a horse in the Gradgrind-Bitzer manner. If facts take on meaning only from experience, the converse is also true: experience makes it impossible to reduce the thing experienced to abstract factuality.

The above passage also suggests the difference between the practical approach to facts and the aesthetic. Half the children see nothing wrong in horses walking up and down a wall, since theirs is the innocent eye of the artist rather than the sophisticated (using the word in its older sense of corrupted) eye of the fact-fetishist.

A HUNTER looks at a wood in one way, an artist in another. The latter's eye takes in every twig, branch, trunk, shadow, color, highlight, etc. The former's eye also records all this data, but his mind rejects everything except the particular Fact (brown fur, speckled feathers) it is looking for. The hunter knows what he will see (or rather, what he hopes he will see) before he looks. Since the artist's aim is to render the wood in itself and as a whole (he may do it by three lines, as in a Chinese landscape, or by a Dutch proliferation of detail) his problem is how to be conscious of everything. The hunter's problem is just the reverse: to be conscious of only what he has decided, in advance, to see. The same distinction could be made between the way a Wordsworth looks at a field and the way a farmer looks at it.

We Americans are hunters rather than artists, a practical race, narrow in our perceptions, men of action rather than of thought or feeling. Our chief contribution to philosophy is pragmatism (*pragma* is Greek for *factum*); technique rather than theory distinguishes our science;* our homes, our cities, our landscapes are designed for profit or practicality but not generally for beauty; we think it odd that a man should devote his life to writing poems but natural that he should devote it to inducing children to breakfast on Crunchies instead of Krispies; our scholars are strong on research, weak on interpreting the masses of data they collect; we say "That's just a fact" and we mean not "That's merely a fact" but rather "Because that is a fact, there is nothing more to be said."

This tropism toward the Fact deforms our thinking and impoverishes our humanity. "Theory" (Greek *theoria*) is literally a "looking at" and thence "contemplation, reflection, speculation." Children are told: "You may look but you mustn't touch," that is, "You mustn't *change* what you look at." This would be good discipline for Americans,

---

* "In the United States," Dr. Theodore Von Karman, a leading authority on aerodynamics, recently told the press, "we concentrate on know-how. In Europe, we work on think-how."

just to look at things once in a while without touching them, using them, converting them into means to achieve power, profit, or some other practical end. The artist's vision, not the hunter's.

Other Da Capo titles of interest

AMERICANS IN PARIS. By George Wickes. New foreword by Virgil Thomson. 302 pages, 16 pages of photos (0-306-80127-2) $6.95

CONSUELO: A Romance of Venice. By George Sand. 799 pages (0-306-80102-7) $8.95

LAND OF THE FREE. By Archibald MacLeisch. Introduction by A. D. Coleman. A dramatic mating of poetry and photographs. 93 pages, 88 photos (0-306-80080-2) $7.95

MAUPRAT. By George Sand. New introduction by Diane Johnson. 324 pages (0-306-80077-2) $6.95

OSCAR WILDE. By H. Montgomery Hyde. 410 pages, 53 photos (0-306-80147-7) $8.95

THE TRUE LIFE OF SWEENEY TODD: A Novel in Collage. By Cozette de Charmoy. 94 pages, illustrated (0-306-80060-8) $5.95

TRAVEL IN VOGUE. 255 pages, 128 illustrations (0-306-80185-X) $10.95

Available at your bookstore

or Order Directly from DA CAPO PRESS
233 Spring Street, New York, New York 10013